Think Tanks in America

Think Tanks in America

THOMAS MEDVETZ

THE UNIVERSITY OF CHICAGO PRESS   CHICAGO AND LONDON

The University of Chicago Press, Chicago 60637
The University of Chicago Press, Ltd., London
© 2012 by The University of Chicago
All rights reserved. Published 2012.
Paperback edition 2014
Printed and bound by CPI Group (UK) Ltd, Croydon, CR0 4YY

21 20 19 18 17 16 15 14   2 3 4 5 6

ISBN-13: 978-0-226-51729-2 (cloth)
ISBN-13: 978-0-226-14366-8 (paper)
ISBN-13: 978-0-226-51730-8 (e-book)
10.7208/chicago/9780226517308.001.0001

Library of Congress Cataloging-in-Publication Data

Medvetz, Thomas.
    Think tanks in America / Thomas Medvetz.
        pages. cm
    Includes bibliographical references and index.
    ISBN-13: 978-0-226-51729-2 (cloth : alkaline paper)
    ISBN-13: 978-0-226-51730-8 (e-book) 1. Government consultants—United States.
2. Research institutes—United States. 3. Policy sciences—United States.
4. Political planning—United States.   I. Title.
    JK468.C7M43 2012
    320.60973—dc23

                                                    2012014464

♾ This paper meets the requirements of ANSI/NISO Z39.48-1992 (Permanence of Paper).

FOR MY PARENTS, THEODORE AND RITA MEDVETZ

Contents

Tables and Figures

Acknowledgments

This book could not have been written without the help of numerous mentors, colleagues, friends, and family members. First and foremost, I would like to thank Loïc Wacquant for his generous intellectual guidance and moral support. Both through direct instruction and by example, Loïc has enriched my understanding of the sociological craft in ways that I can hardly begin to articulate. My sincere appreciation also goes to Jerome Karabel, who supervised the thesis on which this book is based, and to Gil Eyal and George Lakoff, who offered valuable feedback as members of my dissertation committee. Gil likewise read and commented on an early draft of the book. At Berkeley, many talented teachers and peers shaped my thinking in important ways, including Emily Beller, Michael Burawoy, Ryan Centner, Anthony Chen, Malcolm Fairbrother, Claude Fischer, Neil Fligstein, Marion Fourcade, Mike Hout, Isaac Martin, Stephanie Mudge, Fareen Parvez, Eréndira Rueda, Jeff Sallaz, Ofer Sharone, Lisa Stampnitzky, Ann Swidler, Robb Willer, and Pete Younkin.

From 2007 to 2008, I spent a luxurious year as a postdoctoral fellow at Cornell University's Institute for the Social Sciences. My thanks to Ron Herring, Kenneth Roberts, Rebecca Givan, Kyoko Sato, Sarah Soule, Susan Spronk, and the other members of the Contentious Knowledge team for their collegiality and intellectual camaraderie. I wrote the final version of this book at the University of California, San Diego surrounded by a vibrant community of scholars in the Sociology Department. Among them, Amy Binder, John Evans, Isaac Martin, and John Skrentny deserve special recognition for reading portions of the text and offering useful advice. I would also like to thank Andrew Cheyne, Charlotte Goor, and Timothy Young for their superb research assistance during the project's closing phases. Finally, UCSD Geographic Information System coordinator Tracey Hughes supplied the technical prowess needed to construct figure 3.4.

Several institutions provided material support for this research, including the Social Science Research Council; the National Science Foundation; the Phi Beta Kappa Society; the University of California, Berkeley Graduate Division; the University of California, San Diego; and the Hellman Fellows fund. I owe a major debt of gratitude also to the members of the Washington, DC, and New York policy circles who gave generously of their time and effort to help with the research, especially my interviewees. Among them, I would like to thank Karlyn Bowman at the American Enterprise Institute, Steve Clemons at the New America Foundation, Grover Norquist at the Americans for Tax Reform, Bruce Stokes of the *National Journal*, and Fred Smith Jr. at the Competitive Enterprise Institute for sharing their thoughts and experiences. Several archivists also assisted in the data collection process, including Kathleen Higgs at the Carnegie Endowment for International Peace, Eric Eisinger and Sarah Chilton at the Brookings Institution, and Gene Hosey at the American Enterprise Institute.

It has been a tremendous honor to work with the University of Chicago Press, especially my editor Doug Mitchell, whose impeccable reputation preceded him but still failed to do him justice. (A compilation of Doug's witty emails would make a compelling book of its own.) Three anonymous University of Chicago Press reviewers offered constructive and encouraging feedback on the original manuscript. My thanks also to Mary Corrado for her skillful and patient editorial assistance, and to Tim McGovern, Isaac Tobin, Ben Balskus, and Jeff Waxman for seeing the book through various stages of its production.

Over the years I spent working on this project, I've been fortunate to receive advice and encouragement from many colleagues in the social sciences, including Sarah Babb, Craig Calhoun, Neil Gross, Katherine McClelland, and Richard Swedberg. I would also like to thank Emily Hoagland, Marissa Laham, Caroline Lee, Mike McQuarrie, and Peter O'Grady for their friendship and intellectual guidance. Finally, I owe my deepest gratitude to my parents, Theodore and Rita Medvetz, whose unfailing love and support made everything else possible.

T. M. M.
La Jolla, California
January 2012

Abbreviations

ADC	Aid to Dependent Children
AEA	American Enterprise Association
AEI	American Enterprise Institute for Public Policy Research
AFDC	Aid to Families with Dependent Children
AIR	American Institutes for Research
ASSA	American Social Science Association
CAP	Center for American Progress
CASBS	Center for Advanced Study in the Behavioral Sciences
CBPP	Center on Budget and Policy Priorities
CCF	Chicago Civic Federation
CEA	Council of Economic Advisers
CED	Committee for Economic Development
CEI	Competitive Enterprise Institute
CEIP	Carnegie Endowment for International Peace
CFR	Council on Foreign Relations
CNAS	Center for a New American Security
CSIS	Center for Strategic and International Studies
DLC	Democratic Leadership Council
EPI	Economic Policy Institute
FEE	Foundation for Economic Education
FPA	Foreign Policy Association
HEW	Department of Health, Education, and Welfare
HUD	Department of Housing and Urban Development
IFRI	Institut Français des Relations Internationales (French Institute for International Relations)
IGR	Institute for Government Research
IIE	Peterson Institute for International Economics

IPR	Institute of Pacific Relations
IPS	Institute for Policy Studies
JCPES	Joint Center for Political and Economic Studies
JOBS	Job Opportunity and Basic Skills Training Program
NAF	New American Foundation
NBER	National Bureau of Economic Research
NCF	National Civic Federation
NCPA	National Center for Policy Analysis
NIRA	National Institute for Research Advancement
NYBMR	New York Bureau of Municipal Research
OEO	Office of Economic Opportunity
PhRMA	Pharmaceutical Research and Manufacturers of America
PNAC	Project for the New American Century
PPI	Progressive Policy Institute
PRWORA	Personal Responsibility and Work Opportunity Reconciliation Act of 1996
RAND	Research and Development Corporation
RSC	Republican Study Committee
SDS	Students for a Democratic Society
SSI	Supplemental Security Income
UAW-CIO	United Auto Workers-Congress of Industrial Organizations

Gaining Ground

The Rise of the Policy Expert

Those who frequent the borderland between scholarly and ordinary knowledge . . . have a
vital stake in blurring the frontier and denying or eliminating what separates scientific analysis from partial objectifications. —Pierre Bourdieu

In 1982, Charles Murray was a 39-year-old independent writer with a
background in government program evaluation. "Charles, at the time,
was a not-very-well-known social scientist, but his analytical and writing
skills impressed us greatly," says Lawrence J. Mone, president of the Manhattan Institute for Policy Research, the conservative think tank that hired
Murray.[1] Eight years earlier, Murray had completed a PhD in political
science at Massachusetts Institute of Technology with a dissertation titled
"Investment and Tithing in Thai Villages: A Behavioral Study of Rural
Modernization." While the topic of the study placed Murray outside the
mainstream of his discipline, it nonetheless established a theme that he
would return to again and again in his writing: the idea that government
bureaucracies do more harm than good, even for their supposed beneficiaries. After finishing graduate school, Murray left the academic world and
worked for seven years at the American Institutes for Research (AIR),
a private research firm in Washington, DC. "You must understand, I was
never attracted to the university track," Murray says. "I'm temperamen-
tally—I find that the whole faculty world is uncongenial."[2]

The job at AIR did not suit him much better. "I would write these
research reports," Murray remembers, "and they were lovingly crafted.
And I worked . . . fifty, sixty hour weeks, routinely. But nobody ever read
the damn things. You send them in to the sponsor and they're put on the
shelf and nothing ever happens." Not only was the audience for Murray's

work small, but the job afforded him little in the way of intellectual freedom: "What you worked on were the things that the government wanted
to write contracts for," he says. Equally disenchanted with, and marginal
to, the worlds of government and academic research, Murray soon discovered an occupational niche located structurally in between the two:
the growing world of public policy "think tanks." Murray quit his job at
AIR and applied for positions at the Manhattan Institute, the Heritage
Foundation, and the American Enterprise Institute—three of the top
conservative think tanks. Each organization would eventually play a critical role in his success. Heritage vice president Burton Yale Pines received
Murray's job application and became the first sponsor of his developing
book project. As Murray recalls, "Burt Pines called me in for an interview.
I was talking about the way that social programs that I'd evaluated just
hadn't worked . . . and he gave me, I think, $2,500 to write a monograph
that I spent three months writing. It was entitled *Safety Nets and the Truly
Needy*, and that was the forerunner of . . . the book." Murray then joined
the staff of the Manhattan Institute, where he converted the monograph
into *Losing Ground*, a sweeping historical account of American social
policy that sought to show the pernicious effects of government welfare
programs.

   Losing Ground's publication in 1984 was a momentous occasion for
the Manhattan Institute, an organization still trying to establish a distinctive identity. (Until 1981, it had been called the International Center for
Economic Policy Studies.) The organization launched an aggressive pro-
motional campaign for the book.[3] In an internal memorandum, Manhattan president William Hammett wrote that, "Any discretionary funds at
our disposal for the next few months will go toward financing Murray's
outreach activities."[4] As Murray remembers, Hammett "had about 500
copies sent to the office, and I spent a day inscribing those copies . . . and
they were sent out to lots of senior senators and Supreme Court justices
and people of that sort." The organization also sent Murray on a national
speaking tour, booked him on numerous radio and television programs,
and, with funding from the conservative Scaife and Olin Foundations, convened a two-day symposium that brought together twenty leading welfare
reform scholars to discuss the book.[5] *Losing Ground* quickly became an
object of media attention. In Murray's view, the first important notice was
a September 1984 *Newsweek* column by Robert Samuelson. "Bob was
one of the ones that was sent a copy. But unlike Supreme Court justices
and senators, he actually read the damn thing," Murray says. "And Bob

Samuelson, when he writes about something, that starts things going." Samuelson called *Losing Ground* a "well-documented polemic" and concluded, "We cannot reduce poverty simply by being generous. Ultimately, only economic growth and individual effort will suffice."[6] A week later, *Washington Post* columnist William Raspberry called Murray's book "thoughtful, well-reasoned and, in many ways, deeply disturbing."[7] An echo effect began in the press. For example, in 1986, journalist Nicholas Lemann discussed Murray's arguments in a two-part *Atlantic Monthly* essay called "The Origins of the Underclass."[8] "Once that got started," Murray says, "you cannot overestimate the degree to which journalists . . . just pick up on whatever else is going on." In the ensuing years, *Losing Ground* would be profiled, reviewed, and discussed in hundreds of newspaper and magazine articles.[9]

Meanwhile, a very different conversation was developing about *Losing Ground* among academic social scientists, who found fault with the book for containing measurement errors and for using data selectively to support its claims. Economists David Ellwood and Mary Jo Bane, for example, tested and found no support for Murray's finding that welfare benefits caused an increase in single motherhood.[10] Other critics charged Murray with neglecting important macroeconomic changes in his analysis of the poverty rate, overlooking evidence demonstrating the poverty-reducing effects of welfare entitlements, and failing to engage sufficiently with previous research.[11] Some also noted that despite *Losing Ground*'s suggestions to the contrary, there had been no considerable rise in antipoverty spending over the previous decade, and that such increases, where they did exist, had gone primarily to the elderly. Summarizing the academic reception, sociologist S. M. Miller wrote in the November 1985 issue of *Contemporary Sociology* that "Murray's major theses" had been "substantially undermined, as social scientists' serious reviews have supplanted the puff pieces that first greeted the book."[12]

Even apart from the negative scholarly reviews, there were signs that *Losing Ground*'s arguments might have little impact outside of conservative intellectual circles. To some observers, the book's ambitious prescription for ending welfare entitlements to working-age able-bodied citizens—including Aid to Families with Dependent Children (AFDC), food stamps, and medical assistance programs—went entirely beyond the political pale.[13] To make matters worse, the Reagan administration had shown no interest in comprehensive welfare reform as a policy priority. As Murray himself puts it, "The people in the Reagan administration were

actually quite scared of *Losing Ground*. Because, you know, the Reagan
administration's line was that the problems were welfare queens who were
cheating and you had to stop the cheating. They didn't want to have a
radical rethinking of the whole welfare structure. There simply was, in
the Reagan administration, zero policy to back it up with." In 1987, sociologist William Julius Wilson summarized the political orthodoxy of the
day by suggesting that the "laissez-faire social philosophy represented by
Charles Murray is . . . too extreme to be seriously considered by most
policymakers."[14]

The political winds shifted dramatically over the next several years,
however, as conservatives carried on Murray's antiwelfare drumbeat.
Murray himself left the Manhattan Institute in 1990 amid controversy
surrounding his then-forthcoming book, *The Bell Curve* (cowritten with
Harvard psychologist Richard Herrnstein) and became a fellow at the
American Enterprise Institute.[15] Three years later, Murray re-entered
the welfare debate with a well-timed polemic in the *Wall Street Journal*.
The October 1993 column argued that illegitimacy was the engine of social
problems such as crime, drugs, poverty, and illiteracy, and that increasing
rates of single motherhood among poor and less educated white women
would lead to the emergence of a white "underclass."[16] The column
touched a nerve. The next month, ABC's David Brinkley devoted a portion of his Sunday morning telecast to the topic, with Murray present as
a featured guest.[17] Other media outlets continued the debate. As Murray
remembers,

> [*NBC Nightly News* anchor] Tom Brokaw was interviewing Bill Clinton the
> next week and somebody called me and said, "You've got to turn on Tom
> Brokaw . . . ," at which point Clinton said, "Well, Charles and I have had lots
> of disagreements over the years." You sort of imagine us drinking beer in the
> college dorm together or something. We had never met. "We've had a lot of
> disagreements over the years, but I think he's done the country a real service."
> I was watching the TV and I said, "Holy shit."

Murray, the pundit once considered too conservative by the Reagan administration, was now being cited approvingly by President Clinton as an
expert on welfare policy, if not a personal friend. Clinton went on to declare that "[Murray's] analysis is essentially right."[18]

The defeat of Clinton's health care plan and the Republican takeover
of Congress in 1994 further amplified the salience of welfare as a political

issue. Needing a policy achievement with which to appeal to centrist and conservative swing voters in the 1996 elections, Clinton decided to make welfare reform the new centerpiece of his first-term domestic agenda. Over the next two years, culminating in the passage of the Personal Responsibility and Work Opportunity Reconciliation Act of 1996, Murray's arguments remained a compulsory point of reference in the debate. The legislation captured both the spirit and many of the specific features of his proposals, including work requirements, the elimination of welfare as an entitlement program, and the focus on out-of-wedlock births. Following the law's passage, it became almost de rigueur for fans and critics alike to refer to Murray as having supplied the "intellectual groundwork" for welfare reform.[19] As Murray summarizes, "It took ten years for *Losing Ground* to go from being controversial to conventional wisdom. And by the way, there is very little in *Losing Ground* right now that's not conventional wisdom."

The Rise of Think Tanks in America

Charles Murray's transformation from academic journeyman to guru of welfare reform mirrors another notable success story: the rapid rise of public policy "think tanks," both in the United States and around the world. As we have already seen, three such organizations—the Heritage Foundation, the American Enterprise Institute, and the Manhattan Institute—helped catapult Murray from marginality into the mainstream despite persistent doubts from social scientists about the tenability of his claims. Apart from welfare reform, think tanks have been involved in formulating some of the marquee policy ideas of our time. An early blueprint for the Iraq War, for example, was sketched in the late 1990s by a group of neoconservative foreign policy specialists at the Project for the New American Century. The zero-tolerance policing method known as the "broken windows" approach originated in the Manhattan Institute in the early 1980s before being implemented in New York City and exported to other countries. Likewise, the antievolution theory of intelligent design was born in the Seattle-based Discovery Institute during the 1990s. In other areas as well, such as environmental, tax, and regulatory policies, think tanks have been visible participants in policy debate.[20]

At a more general level, think tanks have become fixtures of the national policy-making scene by helping to satisfy what the *Washington Post* once called the "desperate daily need for intellectual meat to feed the hearings, the speeches, [and] the unrelenting policy grinder."[21] On Capitol Hill, for example, they supply expert testimony at legislative hearings. In the 24-hour world of cable news, think tank–affiliated "quotemeisters" speak as pundits about the burning issues of the day. Think tanks have also become indispensable to the practice of "politics as a vocation." Consider, for example, some of the notable roles they have played in the careers of recent American presidents: Ronald Reagan famously distributed copies of the Heritage Foundation's policy guide *Mandate for Leadership* to his inner circle upon taking office in 1981. A decade later, a young Arkansas politician named Bill Clinton emerged from relative obscurity with substantial help from a think tank called the Progressive Policy Institute, an offshoot of his party's "New Democrat" movement.[22] And if plans for the Iraq War originated in a think tank, then perhaps it was fitting that Clinton's successor, George W. Bush, considered managing his post–White House reputation in these terms in 2006: "I would like to leave behind a legacy or a think tank, a place for people to talk about freedom and liberty and the de Tocqueville model."[23] Bush followed through on these plans by forming the George W. Bush Institute in 2011, but he was not the first ex-president to align himself with a think tank: Gerald Ford joined the American Enterprise Institute as a distinguished fellow in 1977, while Jimmy Carter created the Atlanta-based Carter Center in 1982. Finally, even the "candidate for change," Barack Obama, adhered to what has now become the conventional practice among incoming presidents. After the 2008 elections, Obama selected his transition chief from one think tank, the Center for American Progress, and several of his key staff members from another, the Center for a New American Security.[24]

This book brings the tools of sociological investigation to bear on the rise of think tanks in the United States. It poses a series of basic questions about their origins, history, and modes of influence. What caused the "veritable explosion" of think tanks in this country over the last four decades?[25] What forces shape their intellectual production? Do think tanks have an impact that matches their growing visibility, or has their influence been overstated? If they are influential, then how so? If not, then why has there been such a flurry of activity in this sphere? To put the central question in stark terms: Are think tanks the new machinery for creating policy and bounding public debate in America, or do they operate merely as "window dressing" for a political process that is actually centered elsewhere? To answer these questions, this book reports on a wide-ranging empirical study that brings together several kinds of data, including historical/archival records, in-depth interviews conducted with representatives from dozens of think tanks (from rank-and-file employees to think tank founders and presidents), firsthand observations carried out in several think tanks, and an original database of the educational and career backgrounds of more than 1,000 think tank–affiliated "policy experts." (For a detailed overview of the data, see the appendix.)

My central argument is that think tanks, the products of a long-term process of institutional growth and realignment, have become the primary instruments for linking political and intellectual practice in American life. Their proliferation over the last forty years has resulted in the formation of a new institutional subspace located at the crossroads of the academic, political, economic, and media spheres. Like a territorial buffer zone, this *space of think tanks*, as I will call it, has the paradoxical quality of being defined most readily in terms of what it is not, or in terms of its negative relationships with the more established institutions that it helps to separate and delimit. Nonetheless, through their growing interconnectedness, think tanks have collectively developed their own social forms, including their own conventions, norms, and hierarchies, built on a common need for political recognition, funding, and media attention. These needs powerfully limit the think tank's capacity to challenge the unspoken premises of policy debate, to ask original questions, and to offer policy prescriptions that run counter to the interests of financial donors, politicians, or media institutions. To grasp the importance of think tanks in American life, we must recognize another way in which they are like a buffer zone. As I will argue, the space of think tanks produces its main effects, not with its interior landscape, but with its *structure* or *boundary*. By occupying a crucial point of juncture in between the worlds of political, intellectual, economic, and media production, think tanks increasingly regulate the circulation of knowledge and personnel among these spheres. As a result, any intellectual figure who wishes to take part in American political debate must increasingly orient his or her production to the rules of this hybrid subspace. Thus, my argument in this book is that the growth of think tanks over the last forty years has ultimately undermined the value of independently produced knowledge in the United States by institutionalizing a mode of intellectual practice that relegates its producers to the margins of public and political life.

Before I can elaborate this argument, however, I will need to discuss the three main perspectives from which scholars have previously

examined think tanks. As I will explain in the next section, the first of
these approaches grasps think tanks as machinery of ruling class power
oriented to the protection of capitalism and the defense of elite interests;
the second approach classifies think tanks more open-endedly as instruments in a political setting marked by pluralistic struggle; and the third
approach locates think tanks within their wider institutional environments
while attempting to uncover their effects at various stages of the political process. I will argue that while each of these perspectives has served
as the basis for illuminating studies of think tanks, none of them allows
us to grasp what is most distinctive about the rise of think tanks in the
United States or elsewhere in the world. Moreover, the gaps and tensions
among these theories actually deepen some of the mysteries surrounding
the topic. My goal in the next section, then, will be to survey briefly the
terrain of existing knowledge about think tanks as a way of clarifying the
aims of this study.

Three Views of the Think Tank

The first perspective—derived from the elite theory tradition inaugurated
by C. Wright Mills—depicts think tanks as the intellectual machinery of a
closed network of corporate, financial, and political elites.[26] Mills' follow-
ers have argued that think tanks should be analyzed, not as neutral centers
of research and analysis, but instead as instruments deployed strategically
in the service of a ruling class political agenda. A characteristic expression
of this view comes from G. William Domhoff, who argues that, "In concert with the large banks and corporations in the corporate community,
the foundations, think tanks, and policy-discussion groups in the policy-
planning network provide the organizational basis for the exercise of
power on behalf of the owners of all large income-producing properties."[27]
On this view, while think tanks may issue reports or policy recommendations that are distinctive for their technicality and seeming rigor, their actual purpose is to assist in the business of "top down policymaking."[28] The
elite theory approach is often set against the pluralist perspective, which
builds on a longstanding tradition that grasps public policy making as the
product of a dynamic interplay among organized interest groups, each with
its own resources, strategies, and goals.[29] In the pluralist view, think tanks
should be analyzed, not as weapons of ruling class power, but as one kind
of organization among many in a wide array of societal groups that com-

pete to shape public policy—including labor unions, lobbying firms, social movement organizations, and regional and identity-based associations.

The pluralist and elite theories of think tanks developed together during the 1960s and 1970s in the context of a wider scholarly debate about the nature and distribution of political power in the United States. Having set the terms for much of the early discussion about think tanks, they remain major reference points in the academic literature. Nevertheless, recent scholarship on think tanks has been deeply critical of both perspectives. Most scholars, for example, argue that the language of pure cooptation built into the elite theory perspective is far too mechanical, too functionalist, and too seamless to characterize think tanks adequately. While elite theory may offer a compelling macrostructural view of the networks connecting think tanks to economic, military, and political elites, it is less illuminating when it comes to how these networks actually translate into political influence.[30] For example, the elite theorists exhaustively trace specific personnel connections among think tanks—how many trustees of the Council on Foreign Relations sat on various corporate boards, how many went on to serve in high government offices, and so on. And yet across many studies, these scholars have surprisingly little to say about all but the broadest contours of a think tank's activity. Nor, of course, can the elite theory perspective account for the existence of think tanks that orient themselves *against* ruling class interests, or those that lack ties to the rich and powerful. From the point of view of this theory, such organizations are merely "static" in an otherwise elite phenomenon.

The pluralists, for their part, aimed to correct these shortcomings by refusing to assign any essential character or role to think tanks. Yet the extreme openness of their theory also came at a cost, since they could make fewer general claims about think tanks, which then tended to dissolve into the wider sea of interest group struggles. However, if the pluralist approach was in this sense too "open," then in another sense it was too closed. As scholars such as Steven Lukes have shown of pluralist theory in general, the perspective focuses almost exclusively on decision-making processes carried out in the context of open, visible political struggle.[31] It pays much less attention to the hidden dimensions of power, such as agenda-setting processes and what the elite theorists called "non–decision making." When applied to the study of think tanks, this omission becomes a serious error. After all, if the guiding assumption of the pluralist approach is that the relevant target of a think tank's activity is always a specific policy outcome, then think tanks can be described as influential only to the degree that they directly shape such outcomes. The problem, as other scholars have noted, is that think tanks may have other important effects not captured in a "billiard ball" model of cause and effect. Put differently, even if it is rare to find the "smoking gun" of direct policy influence in the world of think tanks, this is no reason to conclude that they are not influential in other ways. As the elite theorists already pointed out, it may be that think tanks are influential in their ability to create cohesion among political elites or otherwise shape the relations among classes.

These are the standard critiques of the elite and pluralist perspectives, and while I agree with each of them, I would argue that scholars have overlooked what is actually the most glaring problem with the two approaches. The problem becomes apparent, however, only from a vantage point informed by the sociology of intellectuals. Put simply, if we take a step back and consider the wider relationship between the elite theorists and the pluralists themselves, then the debate begins to seem less like a straightforward argument about think tanks per se than a euphemized battle between two sets of intellectuals over their own proper social role. After all, the main thrust of the elite theory perspective was to say that think tanks, and by extension, those who aided and identified with them, were not "truly" intellectuals, but rather servants of power. It was no coincidence, then, that their opponents in the debate (not just the pluralists, but all defenders of American-style liberal democracy) tended to occupy structural positions more proximate to, and sometimes inside of, think tanks. Nelson Polsby, for example, a major pluralist scholar, was a fellow at the Brookings Institution and the Roosevelt Center for American Policy Studies and a member of the Council on Foreign Relations. Likewise, Seymour Martin Lipset, who was generally critical of both the Marxist and elite theory traditions, spent the latter part of his career at the Hoover Institution. It should come as no surprise, then, that the pluralists usually adopted a more sanguine view of think tanks, even as they charged the elite theorists with making unverifiable claims about the hidden mechanisms of power.

Of course, these observations alone do not invalidate either theory. However, they do help to underscore the main problem with both approaches. Put simply, despite their differences, both theories built their ultimate conclusions *into their definitions of a think tank*. The pluralists, for example, often used the language of cognitive autonomy to define think tanks, and to differentiate them from non–think tanks. Polsby, for example, distinguished "true" think tanks from mere "public policy research institutes" in the following terms: Whereas "a true think tank obliges its inhabitants to follow their own intellectual agendas," those at public policy research institutes "are generally not free to do what they please with their time or to follow their intellectual priorities without constraint."[32] As a definitional tenet, this distinction instantly disables any attempt a scholar might make to determine whether or not "actually existing" think tanks (by which I now mean organizations so named in public debate) truly enjoy cognitive autonomy. Put differently, Polsby's statement is tautological: either a think tank maintains a certain level of cognitive independence or else it is not "really" a think tank.

The elite theorists avoided this particular tautology, yet so focused were they on the task of revealing that policy making in the United States was not truly a pluralistic struggle that when they examined think tanks, all they could see was a menagerie of intellectual mercenaries and lobbyists-in-disguise. Their tendency, then, was to revert to the opposite view: namely, that any think tank disconnected from the elite machinery of power was therefore somehow a "lesser" think tank and should be relegated to the margins of the discussion.

The overarching point is that both the pluralists and the elite theorists tended to lock themselves into certain categorical judgments about the nature of think tanks, even prior to their empirical investigations as such. More broadly, I would argue, both perspectives became mired in what Gil Eyal and Larissa Buchholz call the "problematic of allegiance" in their approach to intellectuals.[33] By this phrase, Eyal and Buchholz mean a mode of analysis centered on the question of an intellectual's ultimate loyalties or commitments. In the classical sociology of intellectuals, for example, the prototype of the intellectual was the "engaged man of letters" marked by his allegiance to the ideals of truth and justice (as exemplified by Émile Zola of the Dreyfus Affair).[34] The main problem with thinking about intellectuals in this way, as Eyal and Buchholz show, is that it tends to draw scholars into the very struggles over intellectual authority that their work ostensibly aims to describe from an impartial point of view. Consequently, even seemingly neutral academic debates on questions of intellectual loyalty quickly become forms of *boundary work*, or strategic attempts by intellectuals to establish where the "true" dividing line is between intellectuals and nonintellectuals.[35] An argument about the so-called "demise of the intellectual," for example (a common trope in the classical sociology of intellectuals), can also be read as an attempt to undermine or discredit efforts made by other intellectuals to lay claim to the title itself. To remedy the problem, Eyal and Buchholz recommend shifting the sociology of intellectuals toward the study of "how forms of expertise can acquire value as public interventions."[36]

The purpose of this seeming digression into the sociology of intellectuals is to suggest that the "problematic of allegiance" was projected into the early scholarly debate on think tanks. Whereas the elite theorists were concerned mainly with showing that think tanks were not truly organs of intellectual production, the pluralists were inclined to defend them. Doubtless both sides would disagree with my characterization and insist that their theories managed to transcend their social moorings. Yet their best defense would be to point out that their ultimate concerns lay, not in the development of a theory of think tanks per se, but in a more general attempt to theorize American politics, for which think tanks were only empirical anchors. And yet this defense would unwittingly underscore my central point, albeit in a different sense, since it would show that neither theory was especially well suited to capturing what was distinctive about think tanks. As Abelson puts it, the pluralists typically portrayed think tanks as "one voice among many" in the political sphere, while the elite theorists sought to show that the same organizations were nodes in an elite policy-planning network.[37] On the other hand, if our aim is to understand think tanks without subsuming them into a pre-devised theory of politics, then neither approach has much to offer.

A two-pronged methodological lesson follows from this discussion. The first prong is that we should be careful not to smuggle into the analysis any essentialist conclusions about a think tank's ultimate political or intellectual proclivities. Instead, we should adopt a more flexible theoretical approach that allows us to investigate the properties and purposes of think tanks as empirical questions. The second prong, which might initially seem to be at odds with the first, is that we cannot excuse ourselves from the task of clarifying what we mean by the term *think tank*. Analytically prior to the question of what think tanks do, after all, is the question of what they *are*—and neither of the first two approaches offers a compelling answer. Here, then, is the first challenge of this book: How can we define the study's subject matter clearly without also prejudging it?

With this question in mind, let me turn now to the third, and chronologically the most recent, of the three perspectives that scholars have used to examine think tanks. I am referring to the family of approaches that fall under the heading of institutionalism, which focus on the structural environments in which think tanks are embedded, the rules and norms that shape their behavior, and the organizational arrangements and processes to which they must respond. Does institutional theory offer a set of useful tools for analyzing think tanks? More specifically, does it overcome the limitations of the pluralist and elite theory perspectives? With respect to the first problem mentioned above—that of prejudging think tanks—I believe the benefits of an institutionalist framework are obvious. The approach does not lock us into a tautological argument about what a think tank does. Nor does it force us to draw any advance conclusions about a think tank's political or intellectual propensities. Instead, the working premise of an institutionalist approach is that think tanks comprise a heterogeneous array of organizations with a wide range of possible effects. As Abelson puts it, scholars operating in this tradition attempt to describe how think tanks "shape the political agenda, contribute to policy formation, and assist in policy implementation."[38] I would also point out that, when it comes to describing the think tank–affiliated actors commonly known as "policy experts," the institutionalist framework seems to offer an escape from the problematic of allegiance that hampered the classical sociology of intellectuals.* On this point, the main contribution comes from the subset of institutionalist studies focused on *epistemic communities*, or networks of politically engaged experts and professionals who share certain basic cognitive frames and assumptions.[39] By depicting think tank–affiliated policy experts as members of an epistemic community, institutionalist scholars free themselves from having to weigh in on the futile debate over whether or not these actors are "truly" intellectuals. Instead, they can shift their focus to the structure, reach, and function of the networks in which policy experts are embedded.

Given these advantages, it might seem as if an institutionalist approach represents the perfect antidote to the shortcomings of the pluralist and elite theories. Yet I would disagree. In fact, I would argue that the solutions it offers to the problems sketched above are partial at best. Consider first the question of a think tank's potential influence. The chief merit of the institutionalist framework, as I noted, is that it widens the analytic net to capture the effects of think tanks at every stage of the policy process.

---

* For stylistic purposes, I will omit the quotation marks around the phrase "policy expert" from this point forward. However, as I will elaborate below, I use the term in an emic sense to refer to a *political folk category* whose history and meaning must be examined empirically. Moreover, my central point about the term will be that it offers a selective—indeed misleading—description of think tank–affiliated actors by highlighting only a particular dimension of their activity (namely, that which involves the use of knowledge and technical proficiency).

Yet even this expanded focus, I would argue, remains too narrow, as a simple rhetorical question illustrates: Given the tremendous uncertainty surrounding think tanks, why should we assume that their effects are focused entirely, or even *primarily*, within the sphere of official politics? One of the central arguments of this book, in fact, will be that the impact of think tanks extends well beyond the political sphere into other social settings. Situated at the crossroads of the academic, political, business, and media spheres, think tanks have generated effects in each setting.

For example, as suppliers of media sound bites, facts and figures, and opinion pieces, they have been major participants in what Ronald Jacobs and Eleanor Townsley call "the rise of organized punditry."[40] Think tanks have also exercised a degree of influence in academic circles by serving as models for university-based policy institutes and employers of public policy school graduates—the growth of which over the last half-century coincides historically with the proliferation of think tanks. Moreover, think tanks have generated effects in the world of business by supplying vehicles through which corporations and wealthy individuals can intervene in political affairs, often without the unwanted visibility that accompanies more direct forms of political intervention. In this way, think tanks have expanded the strategic repertoires of market actors in American politics, especially the members of the "business-activist" movement that has played a leading role in the promotion of promarket ideology since the 1960s.[41] To summarize these effects, I would argue that it is at the macrostructural level, or in the articulation of the spheres of politics, the media, business, and academia, that we must look for the main effects of think tanks.

I am also not convinced by the institutionalist solution to the problem of how to depict think tank–affiliated actors. While the concept *epistemic community* certainly moves beyond the problematic of allegiance as described above, it is still limiting as an analytic tool. After all, in the international relations literature from which the concept derives, the term refers to a network of policy-oriented actors whose members share a certain brand of expertise, such as legal or scientific knowledge. (In a widely cited article, Peter M. Haas defines *epistemic community* as "a network of professionals with recognized expertise and competence in a particular domain and an authoritative claim to policy-relevant knowledge within that domain or issue area."[42]) But when applied to the world of think tanks, this idea tends to conceal as much as it illuminates. In the first place, think tank–affiliated actors are not obviously engaged in a coherent professionalization project, being equipped with different resources, credentials, and forms of expertise.

An institutionalist scholar might reply that multiple epistemic communities therefore coexist within the world of think tanks. But this only pushes the operative question to a different level: Why should we assume that think tank–affiliated actors are first and foremost "experts"? As I will argue, credentialed knowledge is only one of several resources that policy experts must deploy in order to succeed, even on their own terms. Other socially valued resources circulating in the space of think tanks include network ties to political elites and journalists, media savvy, the ability to raise money, and specialized political skills. Crucially, then, it is the *relative values* of these resources that remains the central unanswered question about the role of policy experts. For example, does the ability to raise money trump academic achievement in the space of think tanks, or is being "good on television" sufficient to compensate for a lack of relevant knowledge about a given policy issue? Furthermore, what counts as "relevant" knowledge? These are not questions with simple answers, nor can they be treated as entirely settled within the world of think tanks. Instead, they are also *stakes* in an ongoing competition among policy experts, who inevitably arrive at the think tank endowed with different resources, forms of expertise, and credentials.

Together these observations point to what I believe is actually the most glaring problem with the institutionalist framework. Like its predecessors, this approach offers no analytic concept of a think tank, no adequate sense of the *distinctive social or organizational forms* denoted by the term. Whereas scholars operating in the elite theory tradition reduced think tanks to appendages of the "policy-planning network," the pluralists vacillated between the idea that think tanks were havens for freethinking intellectuals and the notion that they could be subsumed analytically into the vast sea of interest groups. The institutionalist approach usefully shifts our focus to the rules and constraints within which think tanks are embedded and the personnel networks they coordinate, albeit without clearly elucidating what a think tank is. To be sure, most scholars working in this tradition have taken care to formulate operational definitions of the term *think tank*, some of which I will discuss in the next chapter. Yet, as I will argue, these definitions are theoretically problematic because they inevitably rest on the arbitrary premise that "true" think tanks are marked by formal independence from bureaucratic, party, market, academic, and media institutions. As I will show, there are good reasons to discard this assumption altogether, since in certain ways think tanks are also highly *dependent* on these same institutions for their existence. Let me close this section, then, by noting what is undoubtedly the central irony in the study of think tanks. Despite decades of research on the topic, no one has yet offered a satisfying answer to the most basic question of all: *What is a think tank?*

Plan of the Book

Chapter 1 will address this question at length. The approach I will take is derived from the work of Pierre Bourdieu and recent extensions of his theory by scholars such as Gil Eyal and Loïc Wacquant. It rests on a seeming paradox: To clarify the status of the ambiguous creatures known as think tanks, we will need to build the *structural blurriness* of the object into our conceptualization itself. However, it is not the mere fact of blurriness that distinguishes think tanks from other organizations, since many social institutions exhibit this characteristic. Rather, it is the particular brand of blurriness exhibited by think tanks that holds the key to their identity. My argument will be that think tanks are best understood, not as a discrete class of organizations per se, but as a fuzzy network of organizations, themselves divided by the opposing logics of academic, political, economic, and media production. It is this series of oppositions that drives the interior dynamics of the space of think tanks. We can overcome any challenge posed by the fuzziness of think tanks by historicizing the organizational network in which they are embedded—that is, by documenting its formation and determining how its members have marked themselves off from more established institutions. Built into a think tank's practical repertoire, I will argue, is an elaborate symbolic balancing act that involves gathering multiple institutionalized resources from neighboring social spheres, including samplings of academic, political, economic, social, and media capital.

Chapter 2 will proceed with the task of historicizing the space of think tanks by relating the long "prehistory" of think tanks to a transformation in what Bourdieu calls the *field of power*, or the system of struggles in which holders of various institutionalized resources "vie to impose the supremacy of the particular kind of power they wield."[43] Focusing on the period from the 1890s to the early 1960s, I will argue that the forerunners of American think tanks emerged in the context of a precarious encounter

among elites, including politically moderate capitalists, aspiring bureaucrats and diplomats, and the members of an emerging intelligentsia. At
one level, this process can be read (just as the elite theorists would suggest) as a strategic collaboration among different segments of the "ruling
class." However, at another level, the same process must be understood
as part of a *struggle interior to the upper class* over the relative values of
their different resources or media of power. To their progressive capitalist
cofounders, for example, the forerunners of the think tank were useful,
both as tools for brokering compromises with organized labor and for resisting the expansion of the New Deal. More broadly, the same organizations were part of a wider effort by capitalists to "become modern" by
harnessing the tools of science and rationality for their own ends. On the
other hand, for the aspiring diplomats, foreign policy specialists, and social scientists, the forerunners of the think tank were significant mainly as
vehicles of professionalization.

The result of this ambivalent encounter among elites was the formation
of a large, segmented machinery of "technoscientific reason" that filled
the gap left by the absence of an official government technocracy in the
United States. Chapter 3 will use this claim as a point of departure for an
analysis of the formation of the space of think tanks starting in the 1960s.
To understand how a diffuse set of organizations became oriented to one
another in their judgments and practices, I will situate this process in the
context of a wider struggle among groups with different claims to politically relevant knowledge. As scholars such as Eyal have argued, the 1960s
was a decade of "intense and undecided conflict over the prototype of
intellectual work," both in the United States and in other countries around
the world.[44] In the United States, I will argue, this conflict took the form
of a series of challenges to the technocratic specialists who had become
the leading suppliers of policy advice during the first half of the twentieth
century. The main such challenge, I will argue, was issued by an emergent
group of conservative "activist-experts" who sought to undermine the
power of technocrats from a standpoint of greater intellectual openness
and public engagement in what Eyal calls the "field of expertise." As the
activist-experts gained influence, however, their struggles with the technocrats gave rise to a convergence between the two groups. The main result
of this process was the formation of a new subspace of knowledge production with its own orthodoxies, conventions, and interior dynamics. As the
technocrats and activist-experts drew closer together and became more
interconnected, they gradually settled on common norms and criteria of

intellectual judgment distinct from those of academia. It was through this process, I will argue, that think tanks collectively acquired an identity of their own.

Having traced the formation of the space of think tanks historically, I will turn to an analysis of its present day form and functioning. Chapter 4 will develop both a structuralist mapping, or a *social topology*, of the space of think tanks and a general theory of "policy research" as a loosely coordinated system of intellectual practices. The chapter will begin by examining the external forces and determinations that are brought to bear on think tanks. To succeed in their complex missions, I will argue, think tanks must carry out a delicate balancing act that involves signaling their cognitive autonomy to a general audience while at the same time signaling their *heteronomy*—or willingness to subordinate their production to the demands of clients—to a more restricted audience. To reconcile this opposition, think tanks gather a combination of resources from the "parent" fields of academia, politics, the market, and the media, and assemble these into novel packages. To function stably, think tanks depend on a set of social agents who subscribe to the ethos of policy research. Turning then from structure to agency, chapter 4 will examine what I call the "occupational psyche" of the policy expert, or the antithetical combination of drives, perceptions, habits, and reflexes needed to excel in the world of think tanks. The most successful policy experts, I will argue, are those who blend styles, skills, and sensibilities that mirror the structural oppositions among the fields on which think tanks depend for their resources and recognition.

By depicting think tanks as inhabitants of an *interstitial field*, we can arrive at a better understanding of both the considerable differences among think tanks and the unifying forces that draw them together in the practice of policy research. But how should we understand the distinctiveness of policy research as a form of intellectual practice? In one sense, it is tempting to describe the work of a think tank using a language of pure constraint—the think tank's dependence on clients being the main factor that prevents it from questioning the basic orthodoxies of policy debate or posing its studies against the interests of donors, politicians, or journalists. However, I will argue that the same conditions that undermine the cognitive freedom of think tanks also operate as curious sources of flexibility and *power*. The nature of this power must be understood largely in terms of its reconfiguring effects within the wider space of knowledge production in the United States. By claiming for themselves a central role in policy debate, think tanks effectively limit the range of options available to more autonomous American intellectuals, whose products become increasingly dispensable in political and media fields dominated by moneyed interests and political specialists. The main conclusion of chapter 4, then, is that think tanks produce their most important effects, not in spite of, but precisely through their "blurriness." It is this quality, I argue, that enables them to suspend conventional questions of identity and carry out practices not possible in any of their parent fields.

A brief thought experiment can help to illustrate these points and bring this introductory discussion full circle. How would we identify the source of Charles Murray's efficacy in the welfare reform debate of the 1990s as described in the opening vignette? In the classical sociology of intellectuals, the standard approach would have been to classify Murray using some typology of intellectual role-sets. We would be forced to decide, for example, whether Murray most closely resembled a noble "public intellectual," an aloof "ivory tower" figure, a servile "technician," or some other ideal-type. However, I believe we should be wary of this approach, not least because existing attempts to classify Murray in this way typically end up saying more about the *classifier* than about the presumed object of classification. To label Murray an "exemplary social scientist" (as American Enterprise Institute president Christopher DeMuth did while bestowing on him the Irving Kristol Award in 2009), for example, or to call him a "conservative evildoer" or a producer of "racist pseudo-science" (as progressive journalist and Center for American Progress fellow Eric Alterman did in his book *What Liberal Media?*) is to locate *oneself* in the system of political and intellectual struggles that one is attempting to analyze.[45] Murray himself, however, remains strangely untouched by these descriptions.

A better approach, I believe, is to recognize that Murray's successful intervention in the welfare debate of the 1980s and 1990s depended not on his ability to embody a particular intellectual type but rather on his ability to exist "in between" types by merging disparate skills and switching roles as the situation demanded. As the opening vignette illustrated, Murray first entered the welfare debate with all of the outward appearances of a "public intellectual," or someone who could challenge the political orthodoxy of the day from a standpoint of relative autonomy while speaking in terms that were accessible to the lay public. However, he also gained a degree of authority from the appearance of technical proficiency that came from his experience as a former government policy analyst.

Once the Republicans took control of Congress, however, Murray subtly repositioned himself as a crusader and spokesman for the antiwelfare movement by testifying on Capitol Hill and serving on an official White House–sponsored commission to move the legislation forward. We can even find a hint of "ivory tower" scholasticism in Murray's story, although the site of his privileged seclusion was not a university. As Murray himself says in an interview, "In the think tank world . . . I have—and this is not really an exaggeration—I have essentially spent the last twenty-one years doing exactly as I pleased, every day and all day."[46]

Chapter 5 will put the general theory of think tanks developed in the book into action by examining the history of struggles over poverty and welfare policy in the United States from the late 1950s to the passage of the 1996 welfare reform legislation. I will argue that the formation of the space of think tanks during this period was one of the main institutional processes leading to the discursive shift from a problematic of *deprivation*—or a policy debate centered briefly on mass poverty and its structural underpinnings—to a problematic of *dependency* that identified welfare receipt itself as a form of moral degeneracy and a source of social ills. By transforming the institutional structures of knowledge production and consumption in the United States, the growth of think tanks made possible a shift in the cognitive framework within which policy makers worked to achieve policy solutions in the last decades of the twentieth century.

In describing the history and present day role of think tanks, I would like this book to contribute to a wider discussion about the "time-honored question of the relationship between social knowledge and public action."[47] With this aim in mind, the concluding chapter will relate the study of think tanks to three ongoing debates connected to this question. The first requires us to consider think tanks in what will surely seem like a paradoxical and unfamiliar context: namely as heirs to the long and deep-seated *anti-intellectual* tradition that commentators since Alexis de Tocqueville have identified as part of the national culture. Resituating the topic within a framework centered on the relations among intellectual groups, I will argue that the charge of anti-intellectualism is best understood as a strategic stance or "position-taking" in the intellectual field—one that typically involves an attempt by a relatively autonomous intellectual group to discredit its less autonomous counterparts. Focusing our attention on the struggles among intellectual groups will point the way toward a clearer understanding of the circumstances under which think tanks are likely to be regarded as organs of intellectualism or anti-intellectualism.

The second debate I will address concerns the status of the so-called "public intellectual." At one level, the lively debate on this topic engendered by Russell Jacoby's 1987 book, *The Last Intellectuals*, might seem to offer a natural starting point for the study of think tanks. After all, in the standard narrative associated with Jacoby, the putative demise of the public intellectual takes place concurrently with the rise of think tanks, suggesting the possibility of a causal linkage. But at another level, the debate on public intellectuals only promises to hinder our understanding of think tanks. Having become predictably mired in confusion over the meaning of the central concept, the debate on public intellectuals has generated more heat than light. In keeping with the relational approach of this study, I will argue, first, that the term *public intellectual* is best understood as referring, not to a flesh-and-blood actor per se, but to a specific position in a space of relations among actors with claims to knowledge and expertise. Furthermore, while the germ of a public intellectual project may have incubated briefly in the late 1950s and early 1960s, it was quickly snuffed out. And yet the main process leading to its failure has been largely overlooked by scholars. Thus, against the prevailing wisdom, I will argue that the recent historical period has been marked neither by the demise of the public intellectual, as some writers have claimed, nor by the opposite process, that is, by a simple growth in the public role of intellectuals, as others have argued. Instead, the proliferation of think tanks has made possible a new kind of public figure in American life known as a "policy expert," whose authority is built on a claim to mediate an encounter among holders of various forms of power.

The last discussion with which I will engage in chapter 6 is the ongoing debate in academic sociology about the prospects for, and the desirability of, a civically engaged "public sociology." Initiated in 2004 by sociologist Michael Burawoy, this discussion has generated a spirited conversation about the soul and direction of the sociological discipline. However, I will argue that the debate, being framed largely in terms of the relations between sociologists and their "publics" and among sociologists themselves, has generally failed to take into account the place of sociology within the wider American intellectual field. In particular, writings on public sociology have largely overlooked what I will argue is the chief obstacle to civic-sociological engagement in the United States: namely, the rise of heteronomous knowledge producers in the space of public debate since the 1960s. Relating public sociology to the rise of think tanks will provide a useful starting point for a theory of the institutional conditions under which sociological knowledge is produced, consumed, and (most often) ignored in American public debate. By issuing policy prescriptions tailored to the preferences of sponsors and consumers (especially politicians and journalists), think tanks tend to relegate the most autonomous sociologists to the margins of policy debate and draw others toward a more technocratic style of political-intellectual engagement.

CHAPTER ONE

Indistinction

Rethinking the Think Tank

The peculiar difficulty of sociology, then, is to produce a precise science of an imprecise, fuzzy, wooly reality. For this it is better that its concepts be polymorphic, supple, and adaptable, rather than defined, calibrated, and used rigidly. —Loïc Wacquant

For the scholar who wishes to understand the think tank and its place in American society, the basic problem is that the central concept itself is fuzzy, mutable, and contentious. As Simon James noted a little more than a decade ago, "Discussion of think tanks . . . has a tendency to get bogged down in the vexed question of defining what we mean by 'think tank'—an exercise which often degenerates into futile semantics."[1] While the academic discussion on this topic has certainly deepened in the intervening years, the view I will develop in this chapter is that the so-called "dilemma of definition" to which James and other scholars have pointed has never truly been resolved.[2] The task I set for myself, then, is to render the subject matter of this book more intelligible while still preserving a sense of the fuzziness that I will insist is built into the think tank itself. As Wacquant suggests in the epigraph above, social reality itself is inevitably "wooly" and imprecise. It is for this reason that we will need to develop a conceptual approach to think tanks that remains flexible while still capturing the particular kind of wooliness they exhibit.

My argument will be that think tanks are best analyzed, not as organizations of an entirely novel or discrete "type," but as a constitutively blurry network of organizations, themselves internally divided by the opposing logics of academic, political, economic, and media production. To clarify the status of these ambiguous creatures, I will apply and extend the analytic method developed by Pierre Bourdieu, especially as it is built

into the concepts of *social space, field, capital,* and *field of power.* My starting point will be to establish what Bourdieu (quoting philosopher Gaston
Bachelard) calls an "epistemological break" from both everyday and scholastic commonsense uses of the term. As I will show, these uses typically
rest on the false presupposition that think tanks are marked by formal
independence from bureaucratic, market, academic, and media institutions. This is an arbitrary and misleading definitional assumption, I will
show, inasmuch as think tanks are also genetically *dependent* on the same
institutions for their resources, personnel, and legitimacy. Any definition
of a think tank based on the idea of independence or dependence is bound
to miss the fact that the opposition itself poses a strategic dilemma for the
think tank. To be recognized as a think tank in the first place, an organization must gather a complex mixture of institutionalized resources (or
forms of *capital,* in Bourdieu's terminology) from the academic, political,
economic, and media fields. However, the same organization must also
seek to avoid the appearance of complete dependence on any of these
institutions.

To manage this dilemma, I will argue, think tanks perform a complex
juggling act that involves using each form of association to mark their
putative separation from the other institutions. For example, the best
strategy available to a think tank for avoiding the charge that it is simply
a "lobbying firm in disguise" is to bolster its academic credibility by
aligning itself temporarily with the world of scholarly production. By the
same token, a think tank can avoid the charge that it is merely an "ivory
tower" institution—disconnected from everyday political battles—only
by boosting its political know-how and cultivating extensive ties to politicians, activists, and other political actors. Nevertheless, the danger of
having "too much" political connectedness is that of appearing subservi-
ent to a particular party or political faction—a risk that can be mitigated
through financial independence. To raise money, a think tank must orient
itself to the market for donations by tailoring its work to the interests of
potential sponsors. Finally, think tanks can bolster the image of independence by seeking publicity, which nevertheless requires establishing social
ties to journalists and media institutions. The result of this "quadruple
bind" is a precarious and never-ending balancing act, or a dynamic game
of separation and attachment vis-à-vis the fields of academic, political,
economic, and media production.

These observations push the discussion of think tanks beyond a conventional reading of Bourdieu's field theory. After all, I will argue, think

tanks seem to thrive, not as members of a particular field, but in what sociologist Gil Eyal calls the "spaces between fields."[3] The idea of a space between fields will therefore become useful for capturing a key dimension of the think tank's existence: namely, its capacity to suspend conventional questions of identity, to establish novel forms and combinations, and to claim for itself a kind of mediating role in the social structure. Yet there is a twist to my argument. The twist is that as think tanks have become ever more enmeshed in relations of "antagonistic cooperation" with one another, they have also developed certain field-like properties of their own.[4] To reconcile these two points, I will depict think tanks as members of an *interstitial field*, or a semi-structured network of organizations that traverses, links, and overlaps the more established spheres of academic, political, business, and media production. The upshot of this approach is that we must combine two separate but complementary modes of analysis: On the one side, we must pay special attention to the curious forms of freedom and flexibility that think tanks enjoy by virtue of their liminal positions in social space. On the other side, we must try to understand the specific *illusio* of policy research, or the historically unique form of interest that makes membership in a think tank compelling to a particular category of social agents. The tension between these two modes of analysis will remain a major theme in this book, one that can be resolved only through a historical approach.

A Murky Object: Think Tanks in Popular Discourse

A brief history of the term *think tank* will offer some sense of the semantic continuities and discontinuities marking its use over the last century and a half. Dating to the late nineteenth century, the phrase itself did not originally refer to an organization. Instead, it was a colloquial and often vaguely condescending expression for a person's head or brain. Playful references to "think tanks" can be found in novels, advertisements, and newspaper articles from the 1890s until about the 1960s. The first-ever mention of the phrase in the *New York Times*, for example, appeared in an 1898 crime report in which a one-armed vagrant caught trespassing in the home of a wealthy Harlem couple pled with the arresting officer: "Say, cop . . . Something's the matter with me think tank."[5] A few years earlier, a *Washington Post* sportswriter described a disappointing Brooklyn Dodgers outfielder as a good hitter who nonetheless "lacks a balance wheel in his 'think tank.'"[6] What is arguably most striking about these early uses is how often they refer to some kind of *lack* or failing of the mind, and to a suspicion of the intellect in general. Thus among the *Oxford English Dictionary*'s sample sentences is a passage from a 1964 newspaper article in which former President Harry Truman jokes about the onset of senility: "Truman . . . said he hoped to live to be 90 but only 'if the old think-tank is working.'"[7]

The *Oxford English Dictionary* lists the organizational sense of the term *think tank* as having entered the English language in 1958. One particular organization appears to have enabled this semantic shift from brain to research organization. This was the Stanford University–based Center for Advanced Study in the Behavioral Sciences (CASBS), which acquired the nickname "the Think Tank" (singular, and usually capitalized) around this time for its high concentration of "brainpower" and technical proficiency. Until 1960, nearly all published references to think tanks as organizations referred specifically to CASBS, although for reasons I will discuss below, the center today does not count itself (and is not typically counted) as a think tank. In 1958, the *New York Times* noted with seeming fascination CASBS's "formidable generating capacity in cerebral energy" and the "virtually complete freedom" its fellows enjoyed "to pursue their work as they wish . . . , [to] set up free swinging topical discussion groups or lead a semi-monastic life reading and writing."[8] Descriptions of this sort helped establish the first of two foundational ideas that now underpin the folk concept *think tank*: the idea that a think tank is a privileged sanctuary for independent reflection and analysis on matters of public importance.

Over the next decade, the semantic reach of the term grew considerably, and its center of gravity shifted accordingly. Most often, *think tank* referred to meetings of experts convened by political or market actors, sometimes in conjunction with universities, to offer "advice and ideas on national or commercial problems."[9] A *Washington Post* postmortem on the 1964 Barry Goldwater campaign, for example, alluded to "the 'think tank'—the name Republican politicians contemptuously gave to Sen. Goldwater's brain-trust at the Republican National Committee."[10] In this and other cases, the term's meaning was both informal and vague. A notable shift in usage occurred in the 1960s, however, as the term began to attach more consistently to the growing set of post–World War II military planning agencies, of which the RAND Corporation was the prototype.[11] This change was likely abetted by the double meaning of the word *tank*, as both a repository (of knowledge, technical proficiency, etc.) and a military vehicle. At the same time, several organizations that are today counted as exemplary think tanks were not typically classified as such in public discourse. I am referring to the Brookings Institution, the Council on Foreign Relations, the Carnegie Endowment for International Peace, and several other policy-oriented research centers established during the Progressive Era. During the 1960s, journalists and public figures usually referred to these organizations on a case-by-case basis using generic terms such as "research institute," "private research center," and "nonprofit research corporation." As I will elaborate in the next chapter, these organizations were not consistently associated with the military planning groups, or with other organizations later described as think tanks.

Muddying the term's meaning further in the 1960s were occasional references to think tanks that alluded, not to brains or research organizations, but to computers and other technical devices. Thus in 1962 a nonprofit organization issued a report predicting that, "Government will become a matter of whirring computers. . . . The 'think tanks' will successfully invade the managerial field to displace many at the 'middle manager' level."[12]

As many of these examples suggest, a pejorative, sometimes ominous, connotation attached to the term *think tank* and the people associated with it. Newspaper reporters of the early 1960s were especially given to the idea that think tank–affiliated researchers lived in states of gratuitous luxury, infantile dependence, or narcissistic self-absorption. A 1963 *Los Angeles Times* profile of the Huntington Hartford Foundation ("Plush Retreat is Genius Think Tank"), for example, managed to capture all three images in its sneering description of the foundation as a "154-acre establishment" that "rooms, boards and cleans up after its Fellows."[13] Surrounded by "lush eucalyptus trees . . . spectacular canyon vantage points [and] border-to-border quiet," the article noted, the Huntington Hartford Foundation fellow lives in a "modern cottage" with "none of the discomforts of home, such as bedeviled children, borrowing neighbors or braying telephones. He may have visitors, but only if he invites them. . . . He may socialize with his peers at breakfast and dinner in the main building but the world has been simplified for him so that it revolves around his private pursuit of what may be beautiful or true." The same article also mentioned a local joke that mistook the foundation for a treatment center for albinos, when in fact "any pallor or pink eyes had . . . come from the indoor non-sport of artistic effort." As I will argue later in the book, think tanks have long been sites in which the question of the social value of intellectual activity is posed most acutely. Accordingly, they have become focal points for both pro- and anti-intellectual strains of American cultural discourse.

The term *think tank* came into wider use in American public discourse during the 1970s as the number of organizations devoted expressly to public policy research and planning grew exponentially. As I will discuss in chapter 3, the so-called "advocacy explosion" of this era yielded dozens of new organizations designed to influence policy making through the application of social research. At the same time, a profusion of journalistic accounts announced the arrival of think tanks on the national political scene. Paul Dickson's 1971 book *Think Tanks* is one notable example of this pattern that also offers a snapshot of the category's shifting boundary.[14] In keeping with earlier uses of the term, Dickson focused largely on the postwar military planning groups to the relative neglect of their Progressive Era predecessors. (For example, the book contains an entire chapter on the RAND Corporation, whereas the Council on Foreign Relations, the Carnegie Endowment for International Peace, and the American Enterprise Institute garner no mention at all.) Nevertheless, Dickson's book is also noteworthy for describing the Brookings Institution as a think tank—something that was rare at the time—albeit on only 8 of the text's 363 pages.

Over the next two decades, the meaning of the term gradually became more codified in public discourse as a body of writing on the topic grew. As the next section will elaborate, the emergence of an academic literature on the subject was a key part of this process, and one that cannot be separated from the discursive creation of the think tank. During the same period, as a category of social actors began to identify themselves with the term, think tanks entered the competition to define themselves. The publication of numerous think tank directories during the 1990s and 2000s, including the National Institute for Research Advancement's (NIRA) *World Directory of Think Tanks*, gave the category further recognizability and geographic reach.[15] Also part of this pattern were numerous reports on think tanks issued by foundations, nongovernmental organizations, and other civil society organizations, which increasingly interacted with them. In 2003, for example, the United Nations Development Program published a frequently cited definition of think tanks as "organizations engaged on a regular basis in research and advocacy on any matter related to public policy."[16] Despite the term's growing codification, however, the absence of any firm legal basis for the category ensured that its boundary remained fuzzy, both in general public and specialized political discourses. In the United States, most organizations that are now described as think tanks operate as 501(c)(3)s ("charitable, non-profit, religious, and educational") under the Internal Revenue Code. However, some do not.[17] Furthermore, the vast majority of 501(c)(3)s—of which more than a million exist in the United States—are rarely or never described as think tanks. Nor does the tax category have direct counterparts in other national settings, where think tanks are also a growing part of public life.

The increasing prevalence of activist and advocacy-oriented think tanks after 1970 gave rise to the second major idea underpinning the present-day folk concept. In many writings, think tanks are depicted as stables for "hired guns" whose seeming intellectualism is only a veneer for their self-interest or servility. Because this image is virtually the opposite of the first, the semantic content of the term *think tank* now oscillates between two radically different profiles in public discourse. On the one side is the idea of the privileged haven or sanctuary for intellectuals. One finds this image, for example, in popular writings that describe think tank–affiliated actors as "public intellectuals." In 2006, the *Economist*, under the heading "Public intellectuals are thriving in the United States," cited the existence of "Grand Academies in the form of lavishly-funded think-tanks, well over 100 of them in Washington alone" to support its view that in "the world of public policy today . . . it is America that is the land of the intellectuals and Europe that is the intellect-free zone."[18] On the other side, however, is the image of the think tank as a mercenary organization—or essentially a lobbying firm in disguise. Christopher Buckley's satirical novel *Thank You for Smoking* captures this latter idea well in its sardonic portrayal of a think tank–like organization called the Academy of Tobacco Studies that operates as a shameless front group for the tobacco industry. (The novel's main character, Nick Naylor, is a charismatic but disreputable PR virtuoso who boasts of his ability to defend virtually any claim, no matter how untenable.) A similar portrait of the think tank occasionally appears in journalistic accounts, such as the four-part National Public Radio series whose title ("Under the Influence") suggested that Washington think tanks were marked by a combination of servility and mental impairment.[19]

Think Tanks in Academic Discourse

The topic of think tanks was slow to catch on among academic scholars, not least because of the liminal characteristics of the organizations themselves, which placed them seemingly in between the subject matter of traditional academic disciplines. Even well into the 1980s, for example, there was no consensus among political scientists that think tanks counted as proper objects of study, a fact that Thomas Dye and Joseph Peschek separately attribute to the tendency among political scientists to distinguish between public and private uses of power and to define the latter as outside of their purview.[20] Meanwhile, historians and sociologists, perhaps ceding the topic to political scientists, made only passing references to think tanks. The topic received its first serious consideration from scholars working in the elite theory tradition inaugurated by C. Wright Mills, especially G. William Domhoff. Even in these studies, however, think tanks appeared first at the periphery of the analysis and then gradually moved toward the center.

A notable illustration of this point can be found in the evolution of Domhoff's recurrently updated text, *Who Rules America?*[21] In the book's 1967 first edition, the term *think tank* is not mentioned at all, even though the author refers to several organizations that are now consistently included in that category. (Domhoff describes the Council on Foreign Relations and the Committee for Economic Development as "associations," the Carnegie Endowment for International Peace as a "foundation," and the RAND Corporation as "the Air Force 'think factory.'"[22]) While all of these organizations are said to constitute important links in the elite "policy planning network," it is not obvious that they are all members of the same organizational species. In the 1983 second edition of the book, however, think tanks play a more prominent role in the analysis.[23] The term appears repeatedly, and more importantly the author identifies think tanks, along with "policy groups, foundations, and university research institutes," as one of the "four main components" of the "policy-planning network."[24] In the third (1998), fourth (2002), and most recent (2006) installments of *Who Rules America?*, think tanks not only are treated as a distinct organizational breed but also merit their own section of the text.[25] In fact, in these later editions, think tanks are said to perform the "deepest and most critical thinking within the policy-planning network."[26]

The growing salience of the think tank concept in Domhoff's studies reflected a wider trend among scholars toward recognition of think tanks as distinct "things," which has led in turn to more in-depth studies of their history and functioning. As the topic became an area of explicit focus in the 1990s and 2000s, scholars grew more determined to formulate rigorous operational definitions of the concept. Yet my view is that none of these studies have dealt successfully with the *problem of demarcation*, or the absence of a clear boundary separating think tanks from similar organizations, such as university-based policy institutes, government research bureaus, and research-based advocacy groups. Let me turn now to a discussion of this problem.

Think Tanks and the Problem of Demarcation

How have scholars dealt with the problem of demarcation? For the most part, they have tried to resolve it through a kind of definitional fiat, that is, by simply stating that "true" think tanks are policy-oriented research organs marked by formal separation from government, party, and market institutions. The premise of independence has thus become a common, albeit subtle, feature of scholarly definitions, especially in studies carried out in the institutionalist tradition. Stone, for example, defines think tanks as "relatively autonomous organizations engaged in the research and analysis of contemporary issues *independently* of government, political parties, and pressure groups."[27] Rich similarly defines think tanks as "*independent*, non-interest-based, nonprofit political organizations that produce and principally rely on expertise and ideas to obtain support and to influence the policymaking process."[28] Weaver and McGann offer a compatible definition likewise informed by the notion of independence: think tanks are "non-governmental, not-for-profit research organizations with *substantial organizational autonomy* from government and from societal interests such as firms, interest groups, and political parties."[29] The tenet of independence is sometimes expressed in negative terms as well, such as when Stone decrees that organizations established by presidential hopefuls "*are not think-tanks* as [their] prime purpose is to advance the policy positions of particular candidates and ensure their electoral success rather than to engage in rigorous research."[30] And while the idea of formal independence from universities is not signaled in any of the definitions listed above, it nonetheless appears as a de facto feature of many think tank lists, which often exclude university-based research centers *eo ipso* from the category.[31]

I am not convinced by this definitional approach, or by the tenet of independence, for several reasons. The first reason is that it tends to leave out certain widely agreed-upon examples from the think tank category. Why would any definition of the term *think tank* exclude such prominent cases as the Hoover Institution (affiliated with Stanford University) or the Progressive Policy Institute (until recently, the research arm of the

Democratic Leadership Council)? Second, the premise of independence tends to privilege the experience of North American and British think tanks over their Asian, African, Latin American, and continental European counterparts. It is worth noting that in the non-Anglophone world, the term *think tank* sometimes refers to organizations affiliated directly with corporations, state agencies, universities, and even churches.[32] Third, even if we limit our focus to North American and British think tanks, the emphasis on independence is *historically* misleading in that it leaves us hard pressed to explain why the concept developed first to refer to organizations that were direct offspring of corporations, government agencies, and universities (e.g., RAND, CASBS), and then only gradually expanded to include their more independent cousins (e.g., Brookings, Council on Foreign Relations).

Finally, I would argue that the tenet of independence leads too easily to the suggestion that think tanks exhibit, not just formal, but also *cognitive* independence. Scholars often conflate the two notions, such as when Dror writes that the "ideal-typical" think tank contributes "rational" or "scientific" knowledge to the policy process, or when Stone contends that "think-tanks do not have a fixed or dependent policy position—*they are intellectually independent.*"[33] The problem with these definitional statements is that they prejudge the character of the think tank and its products. In doing so, they beg the very question we would most like to answer in a study of this kind: What sorts of intellectual practices do think tanks engage in, and what sorts of intellectual products do they create?

More broadly, what all of these critiques point to is the profound arbitrariness of independence as a definitional tenet. Indeed, I can distill the central point of this discussion into a simple query: Why not define a think tank in terms of its *dependence* on the very same institutions from which it is usually described as independent? After all, the vast majority of organizations labeled as think tanks typically rely on a patchwork of other outfits—for example, private foundations, government agencies, activist networks, and business corporations—for donations and other forms of material support, such as research contracts. They also depend on government agencies, politicians, and media organs for recognition, which in turn is usually pivotal to their fundraising efforts. More subtly, the same organizations rely on universities, bureaucratic agencies, political parties, media organs, and business corporations as informal training centers in that they commonly recruit personnel from these organizations. Finally, many think tanks exhibit a curious form of dependence on certain "non–think tanks" in their penchant for imitating their practices, copying their products, and incorporating their organizational forms. Many think tanks, for example, have endowed staff positions reminiscent of university professorships; some also adopt the characteristics of legislative aide offices or public relations firms; and most generate written materials that blend the features of legislative aide memos, scholarly articles, journalistic reports, executive summaries, "talking points" memoranda, or some combination of these.

To be sure, other scholars have made many of these same observations. In fact, I would argue that the most common stance among scholars is actually not one of wholehearted belief in the arbitrary premise of independence, but rather a kind of hedging with respect to the task of definition. It is common, in other words, for scholars to begin their discussions with a seemingly precise definition of a think tank based on the idea of formal independence—only to step backwards and acknowledge again the problem of demarcation. Stone, for example, refers to the "absence of firm boundaries between think-tanks and other organizations," and to the fact that think tanks "fade into interest groups, merge with university bodies . . . [and] seem to become extra-party political campaigning groups."[34] Rich similarly maintains that "drawing irrefutable distinctions between think tanks and other types of organizations is neither entirely possible nor desirable; rather institutional boundaries are frequently amorphous and overlapping."[35] Finally, McGann half-jokingly adapts Supreme Court Justice Potter Stewart's famous characterization of pornography to think tanks: "I know one when I see one."[36] But rarely do scholars make much of this uncertainty or consider its wider implications. Meanwhile, striking incongruities among actual *counts* of think tanks suggest that when scholars use the term, they are not necessarily referring to the same organizations. For example, in 1996 Hellebust put the number of American think tanks at more than 1,200 (up from 62 in 1945). Yet only a few years earlier, Smith referred to the "approximately one hundred policy research groups now in Washington." In 2004, Rich counted just over 300 American think tanks. Finally, McGann's estimate that there are somewhere between 115 to 1,400 think tanks in the United States only seems to confirm the futility of any such count.[37]

Toward a Relational Conception of Think Tanks

With so much uncertainty surrounding the idea of a think tank, is it even possible to conceptualize the subject matter of this book with any kind of precision? I believe it is possible, but only if we adopt, not just a different definition, but a different *mode of definition* altogether. Let me begin by stating directly what I think is the central problem with the standard approach outlined above. Put simply, its key misstep lies in the assumption that the study of think tanks must be focused on a particular object, entity, or "thing." I have already indicated two reasons why such an approach is bound to fail. In the first place, there are no substantive properties shared by all members of the think tank category as the term is currently used in political discourse. Instead, think tanks comprise a heterogeneous ensemble of groups linked by a set of "family resemblances," in Wittgenstein's sense of the term.

Second, and even more important, the very act of treating a think tank as a prefabricated object subtly *harnesses the scholar* to its mission. What do I mean by this? I will elaborate below, but for now let me simply point out that for those involved in the world of policy research and advocacy, the practice of calling one's organization a "think tank" is rarely a neutral act of self-description. It is also a strategic move in a social game, the rules of which we should try to understand in this book. For some organizations, especially those that would otherwise be labeled activist groups or lobbying firms, to become a think tank is to rise above mere interest-group struggles and claim membership in the ranks of experts. By the same token, those at the most scholarly think tanks often bristle when their "less respectable" counterparts are lumped into the same category.[38] But apart from whatever competition exists among think tanks over the discursive boundary of the category, the same organizations also share a common interest in the concept's recognizability.

The overarching point is that the boundary of the think tank category is an object of subtle but perennial contestation among social actors and groups. We might conclude from this point that it is an "essentially contested concept" in philosopher W. B. Gallie's sense of the term.[39] For the moment, however, the relevant point is a methodological one: To decree that certain organizations are the "true" think tanks while others are not "really" think tanks would be to take part in the very struggles that partially constitute the phenomenon we set out to investigate. Worse yet, it would be to lend the stamp of social scientific authority to a process that is better grasped as the creation of a *political folk category*. For methodological purposes, then, let me begin my reconstruction of the think tank concept by establishing a clear break from both ordinary and scholastic commonsense definitions of this term, which generally try to locate its meaning in a particular essence, substance, or population of organizations. Instead, I will define the subject matter of this book in relational terms—by shifting the unit of analysis to the relations of force and meaning surrounding the folk category, including the social determinations that gave rise to its emergence in social life. More to the point, I will focus on the institutional positions of the organizations that acquire this label and the forces and conditions that shape their practices.

Among the theoretical tools available for describing think tanks in these terms, I find Bourdieu's concepts of *social space* and *field of power* to be especially useful. Social space refers to the idea that the entire social structure can be depicted as a multidimensional set of positions organized by the volume and composition of authority ordering the relationships among individuals, groups, and classes. In modern societies, social space is composed partly of *fields*, or relatively autonomous domains of action in which agents and groups vie over socially valued resources and the criteria by which they are won or lost. Each field is a site for the creation of a particular species of capital, or an institutionalized resource, of which the main forms include money and other financial assets (economic capital), socially valued knowledge and credentials (cultural capital), and access to social networks (social capital). One of the main benefits of distinguishing among forms of capital is to suggest that power relations in modern societies do not unfold along purely "vertical" lines, but also contain a "horizontal" dimension. For example, Bourdieu would argue that a struggle between physicians and HMOs cannot be described simply as a hierarchical relationship between dominating and dominated groups—and even less as a relationship between exploiting and exploited groups, in the Marxist sense. Yet neither can this struggle be dismissed as somehow "false" merely because it involves two fractions of the upper class. Instead, Bourdieu's approach would be to describe struggles such as these as internecine contests within the field of power among holders of different species of capital—in this case, economic and cultural capital, the two main sources of access to positions of authority in advanced societies, according to Bourdieu.[40] At stake in the field of power, Bourdieu posits, are the relative values of the different species of capital.

What benefits does this framework offer the study of think tanks? The first advantage is to establish a break from the substantialist approach that tries in vain to define think tanks in terms of their independence from other kinds of organizations. Instead, we can shift the focus of the analysis to the social relations (of hierarchy, struggle, partnership, and so on) that surround and make possible the think tank. Even this formulation, of course, seems to raise an obvious conundrum: How do we know which agents, groups, and organizations to include within the study and which to leave out? I can answer this question with a point of clarification: the purpose of shifting to a relational mode of analysis is not to arrive at a better *theoretical* definition of a think tank, but to convert the query itself ("What is a think tank?") into an empirical question. What I have sought to show, in other words, is that a proper understanding of think tanks must begin by identifying the historical conditions under which the category itself first became meaningful, and even consequential, as a principle of classification in the social world. The same approach must also remain open to ongoing revisions in the term's meaning and consequence. Both injunctions point to the need for an arsenal of specifically sociological concepts such as those sketched above.

For the moment, then, let me provisionally link the concept *think tank* to a particular set of positions in the social structure. As the persistent efforts of scholars to differentiate think tanks from academic, political, market, and media institutions suggests, and as figure 1.1 illustrates, the position I am referring to is a privileged central location within the field of power at the crossroads of these canonical fields. Let me emphasize, however, that the thinking behind this diagram represents only a hypothesis meant to guide the empirical investigation, not a theory per se, and that the task of specifying the actual conditions of the think tank's existence remains in front of us.

Nevertheless, we have arrived at a useful starting point. The basic image to emerge from this discussion is that of a constitutively "hybrid" organization: part academic research center, part technocratic agency, part advocacy group, part PR or lobbying firm, and so on. At this point, however, the reader might sensibly ask what kind of organization is *not* in some way hybrid. After all, we would only have to look at a think tank's closest neighbors in the social structure—universities, government agencies, activist networks, political parties, and business corporations, for example—to see that there is no such thing as a purely academic, political, or economic organization. If think tanks can be understood only in terms of their relationships to these fields, then aren't we back to square one? After all, doesn't this formulation only push the problem to a higher level by implying the need for sound definitions of what it means to be "academic," "political," "economic," or "media-oriented"? This is a useful line of questioning, and one that leads to a new insight. The answer is that even after we have accounted for those aspects of a think tank's existence that

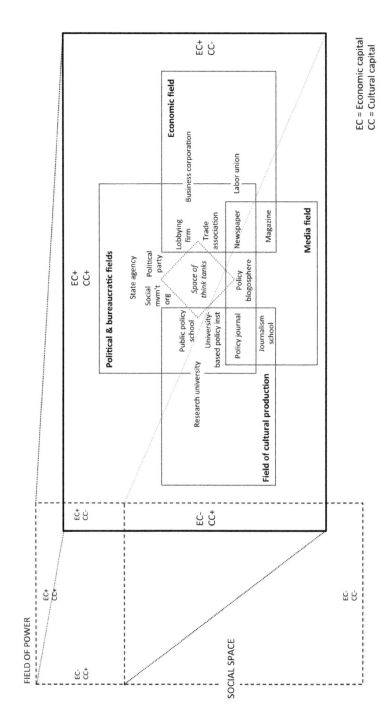

FIELD OF POWER

EC+
CC+

EC-
CC+

EC+
CC+

EC-
CC+

EC-
CC-

SOCIAL SPACE

Political & bureaucratic fields

State agency

Social   Political
mvm't   party
org

Public policy
school

University-
based policy inst

Research university

Field of cultural production

Policy journal

Journalism
school

*Space of
think tanks*

Policy
blogosphere

Lobbying
firm

Trade
association

Newspaper

Magazine

Media field

Business corporation

Labor union

Economic field

EC+
CC+

EC+
CC-

EC = Economic capital
CC = Cultural capital

FIGURE I.I Think tanks in social space.

originate in other fields, there remains an aspect of its existence that can be grasped only in terms of the *relationships among think tanks*. To understand the products and practices of a Brookings Institution or a Heritage Foundation, for example, it is not enough merely to consider how each organization expresses the interests of its audience or its sponsors. Instead, part of what is created by Brookings and Heritage is determined by the relationship between Brookings and Heritage.[41]

One of the main arguments of this book, in fact, will be that as think tanks have become oriented to one another in their judgments and practices, they have established a semidistinct social universe with its own logic, history, and interior structures, not to mention its own agents. It is in this historical process of differentiation that we must find the reality of the think tank. Put simply, think tanks exist as such only insofar as they have formed their own relatively stable institutional niche.

Figure 1.2 illustrates this point visually by depicting the space of think tanks as a layered set of forces and relationally defined positions in which principles of academic, political, economic, and media hierarchy all impose themselves to a certain degree. The key feature of this diagram is its three-dimensionality, which implies that an overarching set of oppositions (between the logics of academic, political, economic, and media production) transcends each of its individual manifestations. As the diagram's top level suggests, the identity of each organization in the space of think tanks, while thoroughly unique, can still be ascertained largely from the combination of its relationships to the field's academic, political, economic, and media poles. Think tanks such as the Hoover Institution and the Institute for International Economics, for example, are known for their close and visible ties to academia, while others are known mainly for their affiliations with political networks and institutions, such as government agencies (e.g., RAND Corporation, Urban Institute), legislative coalitions (Northeast-Midwest Institute), political parties (Progressive Policy Institute), and social movements (Worldwatch Institute). Still other think tanks exist in close proximity to business firms (Competitive Enterprise Institute) or labor unions (Economic Policy Institute), and thus to the economic field. Finally, a small number of think tanks sit nearest the field's media pole (e.g., New America Foundation), as revealed by their strategies of cultivating ties with organs of the news media and journalism. For purposes of illustration, this figure identifies the Brookings Institution as one of the most scholarly think tanks, Heritage as a consummately "political" organization, the Cato Institute as a think tank situated nearest the field's

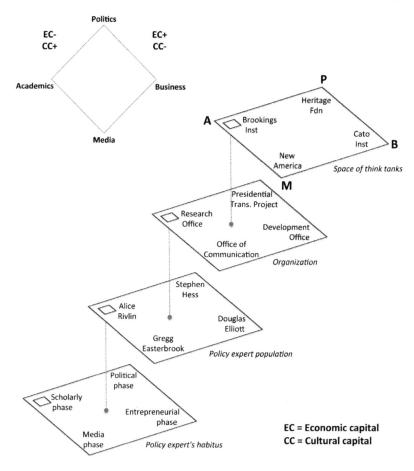

FIGURE 1.2 Three-dimensional view of the space of think tanks.

business pole, and the New America Foundation as a media-oriented think tank.

In truth, however, none of the organizations listed here is quite as monochromatic as this sketch implies. As I will show in chapter 4, all think tanks face certain pressures to move toward the most stable location in the field: the center. Accordingly, the next layer in the diagram posits that principles of academic, political, business, and media judgment are all visible *inside of each think tank*, albeit to varying degrees and in varying proportions. To illustrate this point, the diagram zooms in on one think tank, the Brookings Institution, and lists a specific office or subdivision associated with each of

its main "faces." Brookings has an academic profile, best represented by
its multiple research divisions and its quasi-scholarly publishing house, the
Brookings Institution Press. It also has a political face consisting of various routinized initiatives, such as its Presidential Transition project, which
is geared toward advising new executive officeholders. Brookings also has
a market-oriented face, best exemplified by its Development Office, and
a media-oriented profile represented by its Office of Communications
(which, in addition to handling media inquiries and managing a state-of-
the-art television studio, issues a glossy annual Guide to Brookings Experts complete with color photographs of its policy experts).[42] The central
point is that Brookings acquires its identity as a think tank, not through
any one of these profiles alone, but rather in their combination.

As the next layer of the figure illustrates, the same set of structural oppositions appears when we take the population of policy experts as our
empirical object. Because think tanks demand of their expert staff members an elaborate skill set that is virtually unattainable in its ideal form,
most policy experts develop one or two of the competencies associated
with their role more fully than the others. The result is that various policy
expert subgroups can be located within the space of think tanks using
the same analytic method. In the folk language of Washington debate,
for example, "wonks" are those policy experts who derive their authority from their technical proficiency and academic credentials; "hacks" are
those who bear more than a passing resemblance to political consultants,
lobbyists, and legislative aides; "policy entrepreneurs" are those with the
keenest eye for marketing their intellectual wares and raising funds; and
"quotemeisters" are policy experts who are more comfortable speaking on
television than writing in an empty office. As the diagram above suggests,
a correlative split is visible across the staff at the Brookings Institution,
which includes the scholarly figure Alice Rivlin, a Harvard PhD holder
and former president of the American Economics Association; the consummate "politico" Stephen Hess, a former staff member and adviser in
four White House administrations; the entrepreneurial Douglas J. Elliott,
who joined Brookings after a two-decade career as an investment banker;
and the journalist Gregg Easterbrook, an MSJ degree holder whose journalistic activities have included writing a regular column for the sports
website ESPN.com.

Yet while policy experts differ in their occupational backgrounds,
styles, skills, and credentials, once they enter the space of think tanks,
their judgments and practices are inevitably shaped by its specific rules

and constraints. To capture this point, we can shift the analysis from the object to the subject, so to speak—or from the think tank's structure to the perceptions, drives, and dispositions of the policy expert. As I will show, think tank–affiliated policy experts face certain pressures to cultivate a complex mixture of skills and reflexes that mirrors the overall structure of their field. Put differently, the ideal-typical policy expert is someone who transcends the four polar types sketched above by merging the intellect of a serious scholar, the procedural know-how and ability to anticipate "hot" policy issues of an "inside the Beltway" player, the willingness to "sell" one's wares of an entrepreneur, and the knack for "talking in sound bites" and writing concise op-ed pieces of a media specialist. Thus, like the think tank itself, a policy expert must exist in "plural" form. The bottom layer of figure 1.2 thus posits that we can observe the same four-sided opposition among academic, political, business, and media logics emanating from within the subjectivity of the policy expert. As a distinguished fellow at Brookings remarked when asked about the competing demands placed upon staff members at that organization: "We're Janus-faced, looking in both directions."[43]

Let me close this section by noting an additional advantage of thinking about think tanks using the image of an interstitial field. I mentioned earlier that the public image of a think tank tends to oscillate between two radically different profiles—on the one hand, the privileged sanctuary for intellectuals, and on the other hand, the mercenary organization or "lobbying firm in disguise." Now I would like to point out that these images of the think tank have their analogues in the scholarly literature as well, most plainly in the pluralist and elite theory approaches described in the prologue. The analytic technique I have outlined allows us to make sense of this opposition by suggesting that it is the product of contrasting *relationships to the space of think tanks* among those who write and talk about them. For example, it should come as no surprise that most of the writers who speak in reverential tones about think tanks, often by emphasizing their ties to academia (as in the phrase "universities without students") are also bound up in the think tank professionally.[44] I would argue that these celebratory depictions of the think tank are not the result of deception or even pure self-interest, but socially conditioned perceptions. Indeed, to anyone whose career is located inside of a think tank, the contrast between a think tank and a lobbying firm or an advocacy group inevitably makes the former appear downright scholarly. By the same token, to a writer who is deeply inserted in the academic field, a think tank will inevitably appear quite different from a university, and probably more like a propaganda mill or an instrument of power brokers. Equally unsurprising, then, is the fact that the writers who have put forward the most critical depictions of think tanks—that is, the Millsian elite theorists—have all been academic scholars, and for the most part, scholars who existed in a region of academic space that is structurally distant from the political field: namely, the discipline of sociology.

In keeping with this spirit of reflexivity signaled in this discussion, let me state explicitly my own relation to the object by reiterating my aims in this study. The purpose of this analysis is neither to celebrate nor to castigate the think tank; nor is it to endorse or to pass judgment on policy experts, or on any other kind of intellectual producer. Instead, its first goal is to provide a sociological analysis of the historical formation of the space of think tanks, which I conceptualize as a hybrid subspace of knowledge production that has emerged recently in the United States at the crossroads of the academic, political, economic, and media fields. After tracing its origins and development, I will report on its interior structure—including the basic "rules" of policy research and the relations of struggle, hierarchy, and partnership that currently obtain among its inhabitants. Finally, I will broaden the analysis by relating the development of think tanks in the United States to a series of wider political, economic, and cultural tendencies in American life.

The Boundary Work of a Think Tank

By way of summary, let me address what I believe is the most likely objection to the approach I have outlined here, particularly my use of the *field* concept. Put simply, doesn't referring to think tanks as a "field" only raise again the problem of demarcation mentioned above, albeit in a slightly different form? In other words, if the real focus of this study is not so much a distinctive breed of organizations per se, but a field-like social space, then don't we still have to decide where the space's boundary lies and which organizations are "inside" and "outside" of it? If so, then aren't we back to square one? Valid as these questions are, I believe they are based on a critical misunderstanding of the field concept. It is important to bear in mind again that a field is not a "thing" per se, only a reminder to break with the substantialist mode of reasoning and reckon with the social world in relational terms. Therefore, I can define the focus of this study in terms of several bundles of social relations, one of which (as I will elaborate below) is the set of relations through which the think tank category came into being, acquired meaning in social and political life, and inevitably changed along the way.

The first bundle of relations, signified by the term *space between fields*, consists of the relations among academic, political, business, and media forces that shape and partially constitute the world of think tanks. I will argue that while each force exists in some degree of tension with all of the others, the resulting set of oppositions is not a truly even one. Overlaying the four-corner structure of the space of think tanks is a master bipolar opposition between a universalist claim to reason and intellectual proficiency (as signified most plainly by the think tank's orientation to the goal of academic proficiency) and the pursuit of worldly power (or what Bourdieu, referring to the ecclesiastical term, calls temporal power). The next bundle of relations, signified by the term *field*, refers to the relations among think tanks themselves, and to the novel social forms (structures, practices, dispositions, and so forth) associated with them. These forms and relations will receive their most extensive discussion in chapter 4. The final bundle of relations, signified by the term *boundary work*, refers to the symbolic relations through which the think tank category acquires meaning in the social world. Central to these relations are the practices of agents who have a stake in the classification itself and actively seek to install it in the social world.

To illustrate this last set of relations, let us look briefly at an actual example of boundary work, which I take from a 2005 essay called "What is a 'Think Tank'?" by National Center for Policy Analysis (NCPA) president John C. Goodman.[45] From a sociological perspective, Goodman's essay can be read as a strategic attempt to defend the coherence and utility of the term *think tank*. How does someone with an interest in the public and political resonance of the category address the problem of demarcation? First, in a section called "Think Tanks vs. Advocacy Groups," Goodman argues that think tanks are not the same as advocacy groups, which are neither "incubators of new ideas . . . [nor] led by intellectuals." Advocacy groups, he says, "are better thought of as lobbyists for ideas," whereas think tanks are involved in expert analysis. Then, in a section called "Think Tanks vs. Universities," Goodman asks, "How are . . . academic institutions different from think tanks?" and the answer deserves to be quoted at length:

> Part of the difference is that the research of tenured professors is unmanaged and undirected. The object of research is up to the whim of the professor. The

goal may or may not be to solve an important social problem. Think tanks, by contrast, tend to be very goal-oriented. They employ or contract with scholars to research specific topics and encourage solutions to well-defined problems. Universities tend to be graded based on the academic prestige of their faculty members. Think tanks tend to be graded based on their success in solving real world problems.

In other words, whereas scholars are insulated in the relative comfort of the academy, think tanks must engage with "real world" problems.

Think tanks are also different from market actors, Goodman insists, because they do not submit to a principle of consumer demand or allow their ideas to be driven entirely by sponsors or market forces. Finally, Goodman writes, a think tank is not a political interest group or a formal agency of the state. In fact, to avoid being drawn too deeply into the muddled thinking of Washington policy debate, he recommends that think tanks establish not just cognitive but also *geographic* separation from Washington politics. As he puts it, "the DC environment stifles creative thought. My view is: If you want to think about what Congress is not thinking about (and is unlikely to think about any time soon), you need to do your thinking away from Washington."

On the surface, this self-presentation seems to boil down to an elaborate game of differentiation. In other words, a think tank must demonstrate that it is not a lobbying firm, a university, a business, an advocacy group, and so on. To do so, it must simply highlight its differences from these organizations. However, if we look more closely, we can find an interesting twist to this game. It is that each "declaration of independence" also establishes a *new form of dependence* for the think tank. Each seeming act of separation is built on a corresponding strategy of affiliation. For example, the main characteristic separating a think tank from the tainted activity of lobbying is its credibility-enhancing *association* with the world of academic research. Thus, even as he contrasts think tanks and universities, Goodman takes care to point out that, "*By their very nature*, public policy think tanks are involved with the academic and scholarly world"— and that think tanks, like universities, "hire scholars, encourage research and provide a *forum for scholarly interaction.*"[46] The relationship between a think tank and a university, in other words, is not one of pure difference, but rather one of managed resemblance. A similar ambivalence marks the think tank's relationship with political institutions such as parties and lobbying firms. Indeed, even while advising think tanks to steer clear of the swamp of Washington, DC, Goodman acknowledges the pressure to be located inside of the nation's capital and "to concentrate on what Congress and the Administration are focused on." After all, "To fail to do so is to risk being characterized as irrelevant"—which is why Goodman's own think tank maintains an "active Washington government affairs office . . . to provide Congress and the administration with NCPA's scholars' research, testimony and advice and to conduct conferences and briefings on issues of direct interest on Capitol Hill." Think tanks, in other words, must orient themselves visibly to the political debate in all of its day-to-day aspects, even to the point of adopting the forms, foci, and practices of legislative aide offices, advocacy groups, and so on.

A think tank's relationship with the business world is equally double-sided, as becomes clear when Goodman notes that a good policy expert is an "intellectual entrepreneur," or "someone who applies *entrepreneurial skills often found in the business world* to the world of ideas."[47] The affinity between a think tank and a business corporation becomes even more apparent from a think tank's written products. For example, unlike scholarly articles, Goodman says, NCPA reports use "bolded headings, bullet points for emphasis, call out sentences and visually pleasing graphics," as well as "executive summaries"—in other words, the distinctive trappings of an executive report. And if any doubt remains as to where these features come from, Goodman dispels it:

> The NCPA introduced all of these techniques and today they are commonplace. But the techniques were not original with us. We simply *copied them from the world of business.* What was original was the insight that ideas can be marketed like products and think tanks could market themselves like a business enterprise.[48]

Indeed, upon its founding in 1983, Goodman says, the NCPA's "job was to find a market niche," just as today the organization "is run as a business."[49]

The overarching point is that a think tank must, as a precondition of its very existence *as a think tank*, engage in a complex balancing act composed of equal parts distancing and affiliation. The performance is at bottom self-contradictory: Whereas the first part of the balancing act differentiates the think tank from each of its parent fields, the second part re-establishes its dependence on the same fields for the material and symbolic benefits they confer. The think tank is thus caught in a never-ending cycle of separation and attachment. It can never fully detach itself from its parent institutions because each association supplies a form of authority that makes its putative separation from the other institutions appear credible. But nor can a think tank simply *become* a university, an advocacy group, a business, or a media organ, because to do so would be to nullify its distinctiveness as a think tank and subject itself to the criteria of judgment specific to those fields. Think tanks must therefore seek to occupy a liminal structural position by gathering and juggling various forms of capital acquired from different arenas: scholarly prestige and credentials, competence in specifically political forms of expression, money and fundraising ability, quasi-entrepreneurial styles, and access to the means of publicity. This game is won, not just by gathering large *amounts* of capital, but by establishing the right mixture.

Conclusion

At this point, it should be clear why it was necessary to establish an epistemological break from both everyday and scholastic commonsense definitions of the term *think tank*, and in particular why it makes no sense to insist on a think tank's "independence," formal or otherwise. Put simply, orphaning the think tank for operational purposes subtly harnesses the scholar to its mission since the think tank's first goal, even prior to that of exercising political influence, is to differentiate itself from its nearest neighbors in social space. I have argued instead for a new way of conceptualizing think tanks based on an extension of the analytic method developed by Pierre Bourdieu, particularly as it is built into the notion of *field*. More than simply a terminological shift, the move from think tank to field represents a different way of constructing the empirical object. The approach allows us to examine both the objective structure of the space of think tanks and the subjective dispositions of the policy expert without in the process creating an analytic rupture. However, the key point is that the various oppositions we see in the space of think tanks—inter alia Brookings versus Heritage, "hacks" versus "wonks," research divisions versus media affairs offices—cannot be reduced to isolated differences between specific agents, offices, or organizations. Instead, each opposition must also be read as a revelator of the *field of power*, the "metafield" in which agents and groups struggle over which forms of power will be considered the most legitimate and valuable in American society. The ultimate goal of this study, then, will be to relate the growth of think tanks to the changing social relations among power holders in the United States.

CHAPTER TWO

Experts in the Making

On the Birth of Technoscientific Reason

The fundamental concept in social science is Power, in the same sense in which Energy is the fundamental concept in physics. Like energy, power has many forms, such as wealth, armaments, civil authority, influence on opinion. No one of these can be regarded as subordinate to any other, and there is no one form from which the others are derivative. The attempt to treat one form of power, say wealth, in isolation, can only be partially successful, just as the study of one form of energy will be defective at certain points, unless other forms are taken into account. . . . To revert to the analogy of physics: power, like energy, must be regarded as continually passing from any one of its forms into any other, and it should be the business of social science to seek the laws of such transformations. —Bertrand Russell

The aim of this chapter is to develop a historical baseline for a theory of the emergence of think tanks. I will argue, first, that this process began in the late nineteenth century with the creation of numerous "proto–think tanks" (a term I will explain shortly), which emerged as the products of tenuous partnerships among variously affiliated elite actors and groups in the United States. Second, I will argue that by the start of the 1960s, the net result of this process was the formation of a large, segmented apparatus of "technoscientific reason" that straddled, and to some degree helped define, the boundary between research and politics in the United States. By the start of the 1960s, technocratic specialists had become the leading experts in American political affairs, a development that set the stage for the formation of the space of think tanks soon after. Before I can fully explain this argument, however, I will need to address some basic questions concerning my own terminology and the mode of historical reckoning on which it is based. For example, why do I insist on using the admittedly awkward term *proto–think tank* to refer to organizations that other scholars might simply describe as the first think tanks? Second, how is my approach different from previous accounts of the origins of think tanks?

Let me begin by identifying what I consider to be the two main weaknesses in the existing body of knowledge about the origins of think tanks. The first is tied closely to the conceptual dilemma sketched in chapter 1. Put simply, the lack of a definitive answer to the question, "What is a think tank?" has given rise to widespread confusion among scholars about how to identify the key agents, groups, and processes involved in the birth of think tanks. In a leading account, for example, James Smith traces the origins of think tanks to an 1865 assemblage of Massachusetts reformers who later formed the American Social Science Association. Patricia Linden, on the other hand, associates the birth of think tanks with the founding of the National Conference on Social Welfare, a public charity group formed in 1873 (an organization Smith never mentions in his extensive study).[1] James McGann then critiques Linden for this choice, calling it arbitrary and stating, "I prefer to trace the origins of these institutions to the Brookings Institution, which was established in 1916." Yet it is not clear how the latter choice is any less arbitrary than Linden's, save for the fact that Brookings later came to be known by the term *think tank*. (And if this is our criterion, then the Carnegie Endowment for International Peace, founded in 1910, would seem to be a better candidate for the title "first think tank.") Meanwhile, Donald Abelson dates the "first wave" of think tanks to the period 1900 to 1945, with the Russell Sage Foundation (formed in 1907) mentioned as the first organization in this wave.[2]

Perhaps the reader will suspect that I am being unfair in pointing out these discrepancies, which the scholars in question might agree are just inconsequential "noise" in the midst of a broader consensus about the origins of think tanks. After all, there seems to be general agreement among scholars that by the close of the Progressive Era, think tanks had arrived on the national scene in something resembling their present-day form. The problem deepens, however, when we consider that all of the references to think tanks listed above are in some sense anachronistic. I am referring, not so much to the use of the term *think tank* per se (although the label did not circulate widely until the 1960s), but rather to the assumption that the organizations in question were always "destined" to become members of the same species. It is tempting to take their affinities for granted, but I believe a better approach would be to preserve a sense of the "taxonomic uncertainty" that actually surrounded these organizations for most of the twentieth century.

Before the 1960s, for example, newspaper reporters typically referred to the organizations listed above on a case-by-case basis, and with no apparent sense of their membership in a common category. In fact, their emphasis often rested on the apparent "uniqueness" of each organization. Thus, a December 1927 *Los Angeles Times* article announced the birth of a new Washington research center in the following terms: "The Brookings Institution, *a unique type of research and training center* in the humanistic sciences, has just been established in the national capital."[3] If our inclination would be to say that Brookings was not a "unique type" (an oxymoronic phrase in its own right), having been preceded by several other think tanks, then this was not the prevailing sentiment in the 1920s. To the early twentieth-century journalist, in fact, Brookings' predecessors were also unique. Hence one finds the following account of the Council on Foreign Relations in the *New York Times* in 1930: "In this vast and evergrowing metropolis of New York, there are hospitals and libraries innumerable, museums and universities, cathedrals, clubs and social settlements of every kind. It is thus a surprise to be told that, on Friday, an institution is to be opened which, even in Manhattan Island, may be described, not inaccurately, as *unique*."[4]

The reader might still wonder why this matters. The main reason is that in the absence of a definitive way of marking the genesis of think tanks, there is no explicit *counterfactual* possibility against which to explain their birth, no criterion for identifying when all possible historical alternatives had been foreclosed. It then becomes impossible to separate the necessary from the accidental features of this process, or to adjudicate among competing explanations. The methodological approach I outlined in the opening chapter was meant to anticipate this problem and offer a solution. My argument was that a rigorous social scientific investigation of think tanks must broaden its focus beyond the organizations themselves and examine also the social relations in which they are embedded, including the network ties that permitted them to mark themselves off from more established institutions (even if their ability to do so always remains a precarious achievement). On this view, it is not just the appearance of certain organizations that inaugurated the birth of think tanks, but also the process by which they became oriented to one another in their judgments and practices, forming a semi-distinct organizational network. I called this network the *space of think tanks*. In chapter 3, I will argue that the space of think tanks did not cohere in the United States in any meaningful fashion until the 1970s, and even then only in a loose and tenuous sense.

The first distinctive feature of my approach, then, is that it treats the formation of the think tank category, not as a simple fact, but as an outcome to be explained. The advantage of this approach is to orient the discussion to a specific counterfactual possibility: namely, the possibility that organizations such as Brookings and CFR might have forever remained a scattered array of "unique," unaffiliated groups. At what point, we can ask, was this no longer a possibility? To push the point a bit further, I would insist that failing to ask this question actually places the scholar in the awkward position of implying that it would not have mattered if the organizations in question had never been classified together. This stance would be questionable at best, and disingenuous at worst, since any discussion of think tanks, scholarly or otherwise, rests already on the assumption that the category has some degree of intelligibility. (It is difficult to imagine writing a book about think tanks, for instance, if the organizations had never been classified together in public and political discourse.) As I suggested, it was only in the 1970s that this category became widely resonant and acquired a meaning closely resembling its present-day one.

The first aim of this chapter, then, is to "denaturalize" the think tank category by describing the complex historical process preceding its formation. With this goal in mind, I will begin by describing five processes of organizational growth that predate the space of think tanks but later became relevant to its formation. Each process, I will argue, was motivated by a specific political circumstance, or set of circumstances, and led by a particular coalition of organizational entrepreneurs. Although some network ties connected the key figures involved in these projects, they can be distinguished from one another by the different goals to which they were oriented, and by the different resources and tactics deployed by their leaders. As we will see later in the book, vestiges of these oppositions survive in the space of think tanks today.

Despite my aim of denaturalizing the think tank category, I do not want to abandon altogether the idea that there was some kind of deeper logic underpinning the emergence of the "proto–think tanks." But what was this logic? This question brings us to what I consider the second weakness in the existing literature on the emergence of think tanks. Put simply, there is a deep-seated disjuncture between idealist and materialist readings of this process. On the one side is the common argument that think tanks originated in a rationalist project to improve political decision-making during the Progressive Era. On this view, the creation of new research organizations was fundamentally a result of the growing use of scientific and technical reason in political affairs during the late nineteenth and early twentieth centuries. Above all, this argument goes, the original think tanks were centers for the production of ideas. Scholars who make this claim usually do so as a backdrop for the more specific argument that think tanks have been somehow adulterated by the rise of "advocacy tanks" since the 1960s. Without denying that a major shift took place after the 1960s, I will argue that this explanation suffers from a double dose of idealism—first, in its idealized rendering of the past, and second, in its misleading assumption that "ideas" were ever the main engine of the work carried out by think tanks. Moreover, this approach cannot account for the distinctive class composition of the proto–think tank founders, or for the highly strategic nature of their actions. Most importantly, it cannot account for the distinctive *content* of their policy recommendations, which generally reflected the interests of their elite sponsors. As I will show, nearly all of the proto–think tanks were founded by elites for quite specific political purposes. Once established, they rarely failed to uphold the worldviews and policy preferences of their founders. The point, then, is that there has been no clear shift from "pure thinking" to "tainted advocacy" among American think tanks, or "from academics to ideologues" (to borrow McGann's phrase).[5]

But if we cannot explain the origins of think tanks without taking into account the material relations of power, it does not follow that we can grasp the process *solely* in these terms. This is the implication of a different set of studies, which argue that think tanks originated in a ruling class project to manage capitalism and direct American foreign policy in the context of the country's growing international power.[6] On this view, which is associated with the elite theory perspective, the birth of think tanks was closely connected with the consolidation of class power in the United States. While this theory is closer to my own view, I believe it remains incomplete. In the first place, I would point out that while all of the relevant parties to the creation of the proto–think tanks were indeed elites, they were not simply the "ruling class" as a whole, but actually a specific fraction of it: namely, a heterogeneous partnership of progressive capitalists and aspiring civil servants, including would-be diplomats and statesmen, operating in conjunction with a technocratic fraction of the American intelligentsia. Furthermore, in some cases this partnership placed its members in strategic opposition to other elites, including entrepreneurs who were committed to an aggressively free market vision of capitalism and intellectuals who were committed to the goal of cognitive autonomy. Once we take these oppositions into account, the elite theory approach becomes tautological since the main cause it identifies for the birth of think tanks—namely, an alliance among certain fractions of the elite—is so proximate to the outcome it seeks to explain as to be nearly indistinguishable from the outcome itself. Put differently, the elite theory approach takes for granted the existence of harmony among certain fractions of the elite while ignoring the fact that other elites were excluded from this partnership altogether.

What is needed, then, is a theory that focuses on how certain elite subgroups brought their interests, resources, and priorities into alignment with one another. To develop such a theory, my approach will be to describe the creation of proto–think tanks in terms of a *precarious encounter among economic, political, and cultural elites in the American field of power*. What do I mean by this? Remember, first, that *field of power* is Bourdieu's term for the system of positions in which powerful agents and groups compete with one another to determine which resources will be considered the most legitimate and valuable in modern societies. I can clarify the purpose of this concept by relating it to the central concept of elite theory. Doubtless one of the main attractions of the concept *elite* is its breadth, or its built-in suggestion that not just capitalists but also professionals, bureaucrats, politicians, intellectuals, and other powerful agents take part in the "labor of domination." To refer to any set of agents as elites, then, is to suggest a certain commonality of interest and outlook among them, as well as the possibility that they might engage in some form of collective action. This idea is useful, so far as it goes, but after a certain point its breadth also becomes problematic. After all, the more we expand our notion of the elite to include all of the relevant fractions, the less we can simply take for granted their affinity. This is where the idea of the field of power becomes useful. It captures the same breadth as the elite concept by depicting the relations among powerful agents and groups using the metaphor of a space structured by the volume and composition of the various species of capital. At the same time, it suggests a more open-ended framework by taking into account the possibility—indeed, the probability—of rivalry and struggle within this space. Central to the concept is a general prediction that actors who exist in close structural proximity to one another are more likely to come into social contact. Yet there is no prediction that they are more likely to collaborate; instead, this must always remain an open question.

By placing the origins of think tanks in this context, I mean to suggest three specific things. First, in line with the elite theorists, I posit the primacy of *class interests* and *class relations* as bases for understanding the origins of think tanks. Second, and also in line with the elite theorists, I argue that the proto–think tanks were unambiguously elite organizations in terms of their social makeup. Third, however, I argue that what was at stake in the creation of these organizations was not simply the accumulation of power, as the elite theorists would have it, but also the *relative values* of the different species of power. Put differently, the modality of the encounter among elites was not one of simple harmony, but rather one of cooperation combined with "horizontal" struggle. As we will see, specific elite subgroups collaborated in the making of proto–think tanks, but they did so partly in the context of struggles with other elites. Furthermore, even their collaborations sometimes involved internecine struggles for control over the agendas of their organizations. In general, while the progressive capitalists played the leading role in the creation of the proto–think tanks, the same organizations could not succeed without the active participation of professionals, scholars, scientists, journalists, engineers, and aspiring political specialists. Broadly speaking, the capitalists saw the proto–think tanks as means of addressing some of the major problems of industrial order and efficiency. More broadly still, they saw the organizations as tools for "becoming modern" and incorporating a scientific worldview into their vision of capitalism. To advance these goals, they recruited the aforementioned groups into their fold. For the most part, however, the latter figures regarded the proto–think tanks as vehicles of professional closure.

Reframing the origins of think tanks in these terms will give us a better understanding of where this process stood at the start of the 1960s. The overarching theme of this chapter will be that a series of tenuous partnerships among elites led eventually to the formation of a large, segmented apparatus of "technoscientific reason," or a semiformal advisory structure that filled the gap left by the absence of a technocratic arm of the federal government. Straddling, and to some degree defining, the boundary between research and politics in the United States, this organizational structure helped to institutionalize a technocratic style of production as the dominant form of intellectual engagement in American politics in the 1950s and 1960s. This argument will become the starting point for the next chapter, which will show that the space of think tanks formed during the 1970s and 1980s through a structural convergence between two sets of experts: first, the technocrats who owed their existence largely to the proto–think tanks, and second, an emerging breed of (mostly conservative) *activist-experts* who put forward a challenge to technocratic authority starting in the 1960s. The activist-experts found their greatest support from a growing movement of free market entrepreneurs seeking to establish control over the economic field.

The rest of this chapter will proceed as follows. First, I will develop a narrative-historical overview of five waves of organizational growth that took place from the late nineteenth century until roughly 1962. The first wave, which dates to the 1890s, consisted of various civic federations created by urban social reformers to address the issues of poverty, labor strife, immigrant assimilation, and urban blight. The central figures in their creation were progressive businessmen acting in concert with fledgling social scientists. The second set of organizations were municipal research bureaus founded by businessmen and accountants starting in the 1900s and 1910s. Their common purpose was to apply new administrative and accounting techniques to the practice of local governance. The third set of organizations, which began to emerge in the 1910s, were foreign policy groups designed to meet the federal government's growing need for knowledge about foreign states and markets. Founded by lawyers, bankers, and aspiring diplomats, these organizations became instrumental in the development of a semiprofessionalized network of foreign affairs specialists. A fourth set of organizations emerged starting in the 1920s largely as the result of the maturation of economics as an academic discipline. Accelerated by the Great Depression, the creation of economic research bureaus such as the National Bureau of Economic Research and the Committee for Economic Development established new technical tools for managing the national economy. Finally, a series of military planning groups began to emerge in the 1940s as a result of the country's growing role as a world superpower and the corresponding increase in federal research and development spending. Led by military personnel and defense-oriented businessmen, these organizations recruited scientists and engineers in the development of a new interdisciplinary science called systems analysis.

In the chapter's final section, I will return to a more analytic discussion meant to elaborate my view that these five waves of organizational development can be read as a series of encounters in the American field of power. I will argue that the formation of proto–think tanks was made possible by a tenuous coalition of groups that came together on the basis of a common faith in technical solutions to the crises of capitalism. By midcentury, their partnership had effectively marginalized from policy debate two groups of elites situated at opposite ends of the American field of power: first, the most autonomous intellectuals, and second, capitalists committed to the most extreme forms of free market ideology.

Proto–Think Tanks: Five Waves of Organizational Growth

Partners in Progress: Civic Federations, 1893–1907

The emergence of organizations dedicated to the goal of improving public policy through social research owed much to the development of a pragmatic social scientific tradition in the United States. By the close of the nineteenth century, the idea that social science could serve as a vehicle of human progress had become a core tenet of the political reform philosophy known as progressivism.[7] The progressives opposed the corrupt machine politics of the Gilded Age and their key institution, the party. Instead they hoped that trained specialists equipped with technical knowledge might aid in the design and implementation of efficient public institutions. In its purest and most ambitious form, the progressive vision was to convert politics into a series of administrative functions that would displace ideological conflict altogether. Some progressives, for example, believed that federal commissions staffed by nonpartisan experts could manage the railroad, banking, and insurance industries more efficiently than legislative bodies or the "invisible hand" of the market. Leading articulators of this vision included sociologist Lester Ward, author of the 1883 book *Dynamic Sociology*; political economist Richard T. Ely, who wrote *An Introduction to Political Economy* (1889); Thorstein Veblen, whose most noted work was *The Theory of the Leisure Class* (1899); and journalist Herbert Croly, who cofounded the *New Republic* in 1914.

If social scientists, journalists, and other intellectuals were among the leaders of the progressive movement (its "true leaveners," in the words of historian Arthur Link), then they were not its sole architects.[8] Also vital to the growth of progressivism were politically moderate businessmen who believed that the application of technical knowledge might hold the key to solving the major problems of industrialism, including labor conflict. A growing pattern of partnership thus developed between owners and experts around this view. The pattern was signaled, for example, by the creation of a new science of industrial management. In 1881, Joseph Wharton founded the world's first management school in Philadelphia, the Wharton School of Finance and Economy, "to provide for young men special means of training and of correct instruction in the knowledge and in the arts of modern Finance and Economy."[9] A distinct field of managerial expertise soon developed through a blending of the knowledge of engineers, economists, and businessmen. Mechanical engineer Henry E. Towne is often credited with proposing the idea of a science of management in his 1886 paper, "The Engineer as an Economist," presented to the American Society of Mechanical Engineers (an organization he would later lead).[10] In the ensuing years, the scientific management movement of Frederick W. Taylor increased the faith of businessmen that rigorous techniques for synthesizing workflows could improve productivity and solve the riddle of class conflict. Managerial experts sought to solidify their status as a group in 1898 through the founding of the American Association of Industrial Management.[11]

The growth of social scientific institutions in the late nineteenth century was another product of the progressive faith in science. In the United States, the American Social Science Association, which was incorporated by a collection of lawyers, philanthropists, educators, and doctors in 1865, became its first significant formal organ.[12] By the end of the nineteenth century, the social sciences were dividing into multiple branches with their own aims, assumptions, and expectations. American sociology, for example, took shape in the context of turn-of-the-century reform movements that were often religious in nature or initiated by social aid administrators to address the problems of poverty, crime, racial division, and immigrant assimilation. Compared with its European counterpart, sociology in the United States tended to focus less on the problem of class conflict and more on issues of race and immigration. American sociology also tended to be more individualistic in its presuppositions and scope.[13] Survey research and urban ethnography, a tradition inaugurated by W. E. B. Du-Bois' *The Philadelphia Negro* in 1899, became the sociologist's preferred data-gathering techniques.

The growing pattern of partnership between businessmen and experts in social and industrial affairs led to the creation of new civic federations designed to address the problems of industrialism.[14] A notable early example was the Chicago Civic Federation, a social reform group founded by journalist Ralph Easley and Chicago banker Lyman Gage during the 1893 depression. CCF brought together leading figures in business, education, and philanthropy to examine the causes of poverty and unemployment, political corruption, and administrative waste. Among CCF's founding figures were Jane Addams and Albion Woodbury Small, holder of the first chair in sociology in the United States and founder of the sociology department at the University of Chicago.

As CCF became a leading voice for education and public health reform, Easley left Chicago to establish a national-level counterpart to CCF, the

National Civic Federation, in 1900. Much like its predecessor, NCF sought to play a mediating role in the conflicts among major societal groups. As one of NCF's officers explained, just as manufacturers, farmers, laborers, lawyers, and church bodies "meet annually or oftener to discuss their various interests . . . the object of NCF will be to provide a national forum by means of which representatives of all these great divisions of society may come together and discuss the problems in which all have a common interest."[15] Despite the potentially limitless scope of this mission, a single issue quickly took precedence among NCF's concerns: namely, the problem of labor conflict. In December 1900, NCF convened its first major conference on the theme of "Industrial Conciliation and Arbitration."[16] The next year, a similar event was dedicated to the goal of "perfect[ing] some kind of an agreement between labor and capital that will prevent strikes and lock-outs, which are so costly to both."[17] NCF sought to find "a peaceable way out of labor difficulties . . . by amicable discussion of the questions at issue between employers and their employees."[18]

NCF quickly gained a reputation as a moderate voice in the labor disputes of the era by convening a wide range of figures, including labor leaders such as Samuel Gompers and philanthropist John D. Rockefeller Jr. Other organizations formed on a similar model included the American Bureau of Industrial Research (1904) and the American Association for Labor Legislation (1906). However, lacking a stable source of material support, most of these organizations were short-lived. The missing ingredient for their survival was the existence of a permanent philanthropic sector, which began to appear in the first two decades of the twentieth century with the creation of new charitable institutions such as the Carnegie Foundation in 1903, the Carnegie Corporation in 1911, and the Rockefeller Foundation in 1913. Although most of the giving of the new foundations was directed toward "civilizing" institutions of higher learning, such as libraries, universities, and museums, a portion of their funding also supported research on matters of social importance. Among the most research-oriented of the new foundations was the Russell Sage Foundation, formed in 1907 with a $10 million bequest from Margaret Olivia Slocum Sage, the widow of politician and banker Russell Sage. Although its founding purpose was to aid "the lowly and unfortunate and any others who do not get the best results out of social conditions," Sage specified that her foundation should not operate as a conventional charity.[19] Instead, its money should be "spent first in investigation" into the causes of poverty and related problems.[20] Among its early projects, the Russell Sage Foundation underwrote the

Pittsburgh Survey, the pioneering study of urban life focused on the living conditions of immigrants and workers.[21]

Apostles of Efficiency: Municipal Research Bureaus, 1907–16

The progressive faith in research and planning found its next major expression in a series of municipal research agencies designed to promote efficiency in government, especially at the local level. As city governments in the United States grew in size, scope, and complexity, problems of waste and corruption became more visible, prompting coordinated efforts to uncover the deepest causes of "graft" and to suggest remedies. The largest and best known of these new organizations was the New York Bureau of Municipal Research (NYBMR), later renamed the National Institute of Public Administration. NYBMR was founded in 1907 with funding from both Rockefeller and Carnegie.[22] Once again, the progressive faith in science was evident in its mission. Although political corruption was its main target, the bureau's aim was not to root out specific cases of misconduct per se, but "to study the conditions and methods that continually generate such misconduct, with a view of securing new and scientific machinery to prevent it."[23] The novelty of this approach was not lost on contemporary observers, who saw in NYBMR's creation signs of a general shift in the nature of social reform. In 1910, for example, the *New York Times* noted approvingly that whereas the "old type" of social reformer was an "exhorting" figure prone to moralistic preaching, the "present type . . . never deals in platitudes, it never rehearses the Ten Commandments, and much of its work is done in silence—excepting when pierced by the cry of an uncovered grafter or incompetent official."[24] "Nowadays," the article concluded, "instead of windy exhortation, we have the expert searching of the records of public service."[25]

As the NYBMR accountants became symbols of prudence and efficiency, reform advocates in other cities took notice. A year after its founding, for example, the *Chicago Daily Tribune* noted with more than a hint of envy, "In New York the bureau has already disclosed wastage in administration so astonishing as obtained the prompt removal by Gov. [Charles Evans] Hughes of one borough president."[26] By 1914, 14 municipal research bureaus acted on similar mandates in various cities across the country.[27]

The local successes of these research bureaus led to the creation of a national-level counterpart in 1916. Rather than fight inefficiency in broad terms, however, the new organization would work toward a specific policy goal: namely, comprehensive overhaul of the federal budget process. Before the creation of an executive budget agency in the United States, fiscal appropriations were made without centralized administration by a morass of congressional committees. This situation appalled the progressive businessmen, who considered sound data to be the prerequisite for effective management. In 1912, the budget reform advocates found a powerful ally in President William Howard Taft, who established the Commission on Economy and Efficiency to devise a reform agenda. Frederick Cleveland, one of NYBMR's founders, led the task force. However, while budget reform had broad bipartisan support in principle, it remained an elusive goal politically, since any conceivable reform measure would end up strengthening the executive branch at the expense of the legislature. Congress balked at the idea, and Taft left office unable to achieve reform. His successor, Woodrow Wilson, was less sympathetic to the cause of budget reform and unceremoniously disbanded the Commission on Economy and Efficiency in June 1913, "explain[ing] to the disappointed commissioners that . . . other issues had priority on his legislative agenda."[28] The reform advocates persisted, however, raising $10,000 from the Rockefeller Foundation to establish a new organization as a base of operations. Joining Frederick Cleveland in this effort were Frank Goodnow, a Columbia law professor, and William F. Willoughby, a statistician with the Department of Labor, both former members of the Taft commission.

Formed in October 1916, the Institute for Government Research (IGR) board brought together leading figures in industry, law, and higher education to pursue the cause of budget reform. Its original members included railroad mogul James J. Hill, AT&T executive Theodore Vail, financier R. Fulton Cutting, and St. Louis household goods manufacturer Robert S. Brookings, as well as the acting presidents of Harvard, Yale, Johns Hopkins, and the University of Wisconsin.[29] Former Harvard president Charles W. Eliot and law professor Felix Frankfurter also sat on the board. The United States' entry into World War I in 1917 brought fiscal concerns back to the forefront of the national agenda, and the budget reform effort gained new momentum. Despite IGR's stated role of providing only neutral facts to aid decision-makers in the project, the institute operated more in the manner of a legislative aide office or a lobbying firm. According to historian James Smith, IGR drafted multiple versions of a new reform bill, coordinated congressional testimony, and campaigned actively in its favor.[30] Another failed attempt at budget reform followed before

Warren G. Harding took office in 1921. Finally, in June of that year, after nearly a decade of struggle by the progressive reform advocates, Harding signed the Budget and Accounting Act into law, creating the Bureau of the Budget (later renamed the Office of Management and Budget) as part of the Department of Treasury. IGR's centrality to the process was such that it housed and staffed the new agency during the first few months of its existence.[31]

Experts in War and Peace: Foreign Policy Groups, 1910–39

The Progressive Era also saw the creation of new research and discussion groups dedicated to foreign policy and international affairs. Andrew Carnegie spearheaded the first major organization of this kind, the Carnegie Endowment for International Peace, with a $10 million bequest in 1910. As set out in its bylaws, CEIP was "to advance the cause of peace among the nations, to hasten the abolition of international war, and to encourage and promote a peaceful settlement of international differences" through the "scientific study of the cause of war and of practical methods to avoid it."[32] To lead the effort, Carnegie assembled a who's who of foreign affairs specialists, including former Secretary of State Elihu Root—then a senator from New York—who became the organization's first president.[33] John W. Foster, another former head of the State Department, served as an executive committee member.

To some observers, Carnegie's new organization amounted to little more than a frivolous expenditure. "This international peace plan beats the free library plan all to pieces," wrote a *Washington Post* editorialist in 1911, referring to Carnegie's earlier project of funding public libraries. "There were limitations to the library plan, but there is no limit to the money that can be poured into the new hole."[34] The same writer predicted that CEIP would fall well short of its lofty aim of "hasten[ing] the abolition of international war, the foulest blot upon our civilization."[35] Instead, the editorialist predicted that the endowment would succeed only in the more modest goals of bankrolling academic scholars, throwing opulent parties, and assuaging Carnegie's conscience: "Of course, human nature will remain about the same, and war will lift its horrid front as of yore, but Mr. Carnegie will have been a good angel to many a deserving and needy professor of international law, and the gayety of nations will have been enhanced by the lavish provision for 'international hospitality.'"[36]

To other observers, however, the Carnegie Endowment for International Peace was anything but "as harmless a method of distributing idle millions as could be devised," as the *Post* editorialist had concluded. In fact, some viewed the organization more negatively, as "an organized lobby working . . . against the interest of the United States," in the words of an unnamed editorialist for the same paper just three years later.[37] Soon after its founding, CEIP came under attack from Congress for lobbying to repeal the tolls exemption clause of the 1902 Panama Canal Act, a rider that excused American vessels from paying the fees charged to other countries for using the canal. Campaigning against the clause, CEIP had distributed more than 700,000 copies of a speech made by Root—then both the organization's president and an acting senator from New York—laying out the anti-exemption argument. The incident provoked a fierce reaction from CEIP's critics, including New York's other senator, James O'Gorman. In March 1914, CEIP secretary James Brown Scott defended his organization before the Senate Lobby Committee, yielding a terse exchange with Missouri senator James A. Reed: "This is a peace organization, isn't it?" Reed asked, to which Scott replied in the affirmative. "Then just what has it to do with Panama Canal tolls?" "Some people," Scott answered, "think that the best way to preserve peace is to smooth out difficulties between nations." "And yield to other countries?" Reed asked. "You will find no yielding to other nations in our attitude," Scott responded.[38] Although CEIP suffered no legal consequences from the incident, the Panama tolls episode posed acutely a question that would eventually become a source of tension among think tanks: Where is the dividing line between lobbying and public education?

By the conclusion of World War I, the United States had become one of the great national powers, even if an enduring strain of isolationism ensured that its leaders entered into international commitments with great hesitation. As foreign policy took on greater prominence in political life, the nation embraced the ambivalent goal of expanding business abroad while avoiding military intervention. However, the federal government remained administratively small and had neither the organizational capacity nor the personnel to support extensive foreign policy planning. For example, although the State Department, which had employed a mere 91 domestic staff members in 1900, was now in the midst of a rapid expansion, its staff of 708 in 1920 was still a far cry from the 8,609 domestic employees it would have by 1950.[39] It was in this context that foreign policy planning and discussion fell increasingly to a network of elites operating outside the formal boundary of the government. Central to this network was a group of advisers to President Woodrow Wilson known as "The Inquiry." Wilson's aide Colonel Edward M. House had conceived the idea for the group, which journalist Walter Lippmann helped assemble in 1917. The next year, Wilson incorporated some of the Inquiry members' suggestions into his Fourteen Points speech and his endorsement of the League of Nations. Together with a set of British diplomats from the Paris Peace conference, the Inquiry members established a joint Anglo-American venture called the Institute of International Affairs (later renamed Chatham House) to develop knowledge about conditions in postwar Europe.[40]

A similar foreign policy group, this one a private club of New York lawyers and businessmen, formed in 1918 under the direction of Elihu Root, still president of the Carnegie Endowment for International Peace (and now a Nobel Peace Prize recipient for his role in arbitrating international disputes as Secretary of State). Like the Inquiry members, the club supported the League of Nations, although its concerns lay squarely with the organization's effects on business. An alliance soon developed between the two groups on the basis of a complementarity of resources.[41] As historian Peter Grose explains, the merger was a case of "academic and government expertise meeting practical business interests."[42] Whereas the Inquiry scholars "could provide diplomatic experience, expertise, and high-level contacts but no funds," the "men of law and banking . . . could tap untold resources of finance but sorely needed an injection of intellectual substance, dynamism, and contacts."[43] In 1921, the two groups merged to form the Council on Foreign Relations. Manifestly elite, the council's fifty-five original officers held a combined seventy-four corporate directorships; thirty-five were Ivy League graduates and three more had studied at Oxford; five were university presidents, including Harold W. Dodds of Princeton and Isaiah Bowman of Johns Hopkins. Wall Street lawyers comprised the largest occupational grouping, although twelve had served in government cabinet or subcabinet positions. Another thirty of the original CFR officers had some other federal bureaucratic experience, most in the State Department. Finally, the majority of the original officers belonged to one or more of the elite New York and Washington social clubs: the Century, Knickerbocker, Cosmos, and Metropolitan.[44] As a CFR-commissioned history acknowledged, "labor leaders . . . might not feel at ease amid the shared assumptions and elite perspectives of the Council."[45]

If CFR had a founding principle, it was the sentiment expressed by Root in the inaugural issue of its journal *Foreign Affairs*: that the United States was now a world power and that its public could no longer afford to be uninformed on matters of international relations. Yet the sense of openness expressed in this mission statement was hardly indicative of the council's later activities. Intensely private, bordering on secretive, CFR members met periodically through a series of study and discussion groups. When they disseminated their ideas publicly, they did so through two primary means. The first was a series of reports and political handbooks authored mostly by Council members, sometimes with the input of outside scholars. The second was its journal *Foreign Affairs*, launched in September 1922 and edited by Archibald Cary Coolidge, a Harvard history professor and original member of the Inquiry. Featuring articles by statesmen, scholars, and foreign policy specialists, including several US secretaries of state and equivalent foreign ministers, *Foreign Affairs* focused on economic and trade issues relevant to the United States, as well as the controversial League of Nations and colonialism in Africa. In the early years of its existence, the journal developed a small but influential readership numbering 5,000 in 1923, 11,000 by the end of the decade, and 17,000 at the end of World War II.[46] Meanwhile, CFR grew steadily, thanks to major research grants from the Carnegie Corporation and the twenty-six business firms that had signed onto its program of corporate support.[47] The money gave the council the means to establish a network of self-governing local committees in cities around the country. Starting at thirteen, the number of committees grew eventually to thirty-seven.[48]

Two other notable foreign policy groups also emerged during the interwar years, although neither would achieve the same prominence as CFR.[49] The first was the League of Free Nations Association, established in New York City in 1918 by a consortium of lawyers, journalists, and statesmen. Journalist Paul Underwood Kellog chaired the organization, which dedicated itself initially to supporting the League of Nations. In 1923, the organization changed its name to the Foreign Policy Association and broadened its focus to include public forums for the debate of a wide range of international issues. In subsequent years, FPA became known for its luncheon series featuring visiting experts on foreign policy, whose speeches were broadcast over the radio as part of NBC's "Air University" program.[50] As the *New York Times* reported in 1927, "Clubs of men and women in suburban towns within radio-reach meet regularly to hear the luncheon discussion, as broadcast through the air, and then conduct their own question periods."[51] By the end of the 1920s, the FPA had established fourteen local chapters around the country.

The second notable foreign policy group formed during the 1920s was the Institute of Pacific Relations, established in New York in 1925.[52] Modeled after existing research and discussion groups of the era, most of which focused on Europe, IPR sought to open "a window on the Far East" by convening informal gatherings of delegates from Pacific Rim countries.[53] The organization's debut event was a July 1925 conference held in Honolulu, Hawaii, and attended by representatives from seven countries, including Japan, China, New Zealand, and Australia. "The genius of this conference," explained Ray Lyman Wilbur, president of Stanford University and head of the American delegation, was that it "had been conceived not as a diplomatic negotiation, nor as bargaining based on national or group aspirations," but as an occasion for "thinking and studying together by experts from each nation upon the problems of greatest mutual interest" to the countries involved.[54] IPR held a second meeting in Honolulu two years later, followed by similar events in Kyoto, Japan, in 1929, Shanghai, China, in 1931, Banff, Canada, in 1933, and Yosemite, California, in 1936. Attendees of the IPR meetings, noted one contemporary journalist, were of sufficient "caliber" to "carry great weight in the influence of thought of their respective countries—a former Secretary of War, a former French Premier, a former Lord of Admiralty of Britain, a former Foreign Minister of Japan, a leading Russian scholar, a leading Chinese philosopher."[55] Among the American delegates to the meetings, for example, were John D. Rockefeller Jr., Harvard president Abbott Lawrence Lowell, and James G. McDonald, chairman of the Foreign Policy Association.

For a brief period, IPR succeeded in maintaining its public reputation as a relatively neutral clearinghouse of facts "with a scientific attitude," as a Korean IPR delegate described it, not a "medium for propaganda."[56] A 1929 *Los Angeles Times* piece emphasized the organization's status as "an entirely unofficial body" whose work thus far "justif[ied] the expectation" that it would provide a "distinct enrichment of cultural contacts and a high level of intellectual . . . co-operation which must inevitably yield far-reaching results of a constructive nature."[57] The same year, a *New York Times* editorialist praised IPR for its "most valuable" role as a "fact-presenting" force in foreign affairs. Whereas mutual ignorance had once enabled "fanatics and propagandists to sow the seeds of distrust" among Pacific Rim countries, the *Times* argued, IPR's dedication to gathering "basic information about the problems of the Pacific" provided a useful public service.[58]

However, as hostilities within East Asia intensified, particularly after Japan's 1931 invasion of Manchuria, and as the debate on US-Japanese relations grew more contentious, it became impossible for IPR to maintain its image as a neutral body. In hindsight, it is difficult to ignore the grim irony in Ray Lyman Wilbur's hopeful prediction, expressed at IPR's inaugural event in Honolulu, that the organization would help the "Island of Oahu" become "spiritually at least, a Gibraltar of international, as well as national, security."[59] Even before the attack on Pearl Harbor, however, IPR's ability to present itself as a font of scientific wisdom waned. In 1934, Asia scholar Owen Lattimore became the editor of *Pacific Affairs*, the first of two journals published by IPR. Lattimore's commitment to presenting a wide range of perspectives in *Pacific Affairs*, including the work of Marxist scholars, brought scrutiny to the organization from anticommunists. By 1936, the *Los Angeles Times* could summarily dismiss IPR as an organization that had "started in Honolulu a little more than ten years ago as a quasi-religious uplift body, and almost immediately shed its outlook and became essentially political and economic in its aims."[60] Lattimore's later involvement in the "China Hands" affair (and Senator Joseph McCarthy's memorable accusation that Lattimore was "the top Russian espionage agent in the United States") further tarnished IPR's reputation.[61] In 1951, when the US Senate Internal Security Subcommittee formally investigated the organization for its alleged role in spreading communist propaganda, IPR's demise was imminent. "In its thirty-five years of existence," IPR scholar and longtime *Pacific Affairs* editor William L. Holland summarizes, the organization "held thirteen international non-official conferences, published two reputable journals on Asian problems, carried out an extensive international research program in most of the Asian and Pacific countries, and published approximately 1,300 scholarly books and popular pamphlets." After the McCarthy fiasco, however, IPR "lost most of its financial support from corporations and foundations," saw its tax-exempt status as an educational body revoked by the IRS, and "dissolved itself . . . at the end of 1960."[62]

Managing the Market: Economic Research Bureaus, 1920–43

The difficult postwar transition years of 1919 to 1921 were marked by high unemployment, layoffs, factory shutdowns, and widespread labor disputes. In 1922, however, these troubles gave way to a partial recovery centered in the auto, steel, and household goods industries.[63] Even so, the majority of Americans continued to lead lives marked by irregular employment and economic insecurity. Ethnic divisions, labor deskilling, and aggressive opposition by employers led to an overall decline in union membership, from five million during World War I to three and a half million in 1929.[64] It was in the context of this economic turmoil and the simultaneous growth of economics as a discipline, that a series of new organizations dedicated to economic research and planning began to form. The first of these was the National Bureau of Economic Research, established in 1920 and headed by Wesley Clair Mitchell, a former Berkeley economist and student of Thorstein Veblen. Under Mitchell's leadership, NBER came to perform a series of technocratic functions. Among its first projects, for example, was a large-scale study of national unemployment carried out in conjunction with the Department of Commerce. The aim of the project was to gather descriptive statistics on unemployment in the United States—virtually unprecedented at the time—in order to diagnose the problem's causes and "recommend a concrete policy and program of control to displace temporary palliatives and emergency measures" for alleviating it.[65]

Meanwhile, the Institute for Government Research, the organization created in 1916 to reform the federal budget process, found new life as a center for economic research. Having achieved its original purpose in 1921 with the passage of the Budget and Accounting Act, IGR soon became an organization "without purpose and without vision," in the words of historian Donald Critchlow.[66] It took the intervention of Robert S. Brookings, a St. Louis lumber and real estate magnate who had served on the IGR board since its inception, to resuscitate the organization. Having departed the business world to pursue his interest in public advocacy, Brookings retooled IGR as part of a three-pronged effort to encourage the development of economic science and accounting methods. As Brookings saw it, IGR would continue to carry out research on administrative efficiency and personnel management with the aim of improving productivity in industry. The second part of the project was Brookings' creation of a sister organization to IGR called the Institute of Economics, which was designed to focus on the issues of trade, tariffs, war debt, and labor policy. Brookings launched the latter organization in 1922 with a $1.65 million grant from the Carnegie Corporation.[67] The final prong of the effort was Brookings' 1924 reorganization of the graduate program of government and economics at Washington University in St. Louis, where he had once served as president of the board of trustees.

Brookings envisioned a synergistic relationship among the three organizations, with the graduate school in particular serving as "a feeder of talent for the two institutes on the firing line of social inquiry."[68] After a few years, however, he became dissatisfied with the three ventures. The graduate school in particular had become internally divided when the school's dean, Walton Hamilton, a former professor at Amherst College, designed a liberal arts curriculum informed heavily by philosophy, history, and political theory. In Hamilton's view, a policy research program that neglected the moral and philosophical bases of political thought would disable itself intellectually and become a mere technical tool in the hands of its sponsors. This stance proved sharply at odds with Brookings' more pragmatic expectations. In 1927, with the graduate school now focusing too much on history and theory for his tastes, Brookings merged the three organizations to form the Brookings Institution. The organization's new charter stated that the center would dedicate itself to research in "the broad fields of economics, government administration and the political and social sciences generally," while interpreting facts "without regard to and independent of the special interests of any group in the body politic, either political, social or economic."[69]

The Great Depression created a major shake-up in the market for policy-relevant knowledge about the economy. In the first place, the depression brought mixed effects for Brookings and NBER, the two largest economic research centers. Both organizations experienced major financial setbacks as the Carnegie and Rockefeller foundations withdrew their support for economic research. To compensate for the shortfall, Brookings took on contract research with the US Chamber of Commerce, the National Transportation Committee, and the American Federation of Labor.[70] However, the depression also represented a positive opportunity for both organizations, since economic experts now found themselves in high demand from policymakers. Franklin Roosevelt in particular became a maverick in his use of experts, most notably in the Brain Trust, the group of informal advisors drawn largely from Columbia and Harvard Universities. Consisting mostly of lawyers and economists, the group included Raymond Moley, professor of government at Barnard College and Roosevelt's confidante since his days as New York governor; Rexford G. Tugwell, professor of economics at Columbia; and Basil O'Connor, a law partner of Roosevelt.[71] The use of academic experts by a president was a "novelty in American political culture," according to historian David Kennedy.[72] Also contributing to the growing political relevance of economic experts was the creation of New Deal federal agencies such as the National Resources Planning Board (formed in 1933), which was staffed partly by economists.

A growing Keynesian orthodoxy in economics decreed that the state should play an active role in the management of demand through market regulation, fiscal policy, and social expenditures. Nevertheless, an oppositional movement dedicated to classical liberal principles endured and gained focus. In the early 1930s, Ludwig von Mises and his Austrian school contemporary Friedrich Hayek began to attract a small but energetic following among American economists centered at the University of Chicago.[73] Marginalized in an American economics profession dominated by Keynesians, the libertarian economists came to rely on various nonacademic centers for organizational support. The first of these was the American Enterprise Association (later renamed the American Enterprise Institute), a small free market organization founded in New York City in 1938 by Lewis H. Brown, chairman of the Johns-Manville Corporation. The outbreak of World War II caused AEA to disband temporarily and reorganize in Washington, DC, in 1943.[74] The organization's early work amounted to an extended critique of the government price and production controls initiated during the depression.[75] A second node in the network of libertarian economists was the Foundation for Economic Education (FEE), a free market educational society formed in 1946 by Leonard Read of the Los Angeles Chamber of Commerce.[76] FEE's principal donor was Kansas City entrepreneur and philanthropist William Volker, who also supported the Mont Pelerin Society, the Switzerland-based conference of scholars founded by Hayek in 1947.[77]

World War II produced additional changes in the landscape of economic research. During the war, defense contracts and government subsidies greatly stimulated economic activity and helped lift the country out of the depression. However, as the war drew to a close, it was plain that these subsidies and contracts would soon be liquidated and thousands of troops would return home jobless. Assuming that the war's end would put millions out of work, newspapers, economists, and government agencies alike forecasted a postwar depression. The problem of how to manage the delicate domestic economy and protect the nation from postwar collapse became the central political question of the day. It was in this context that a new economic research organization, the Committee for Economic Development, was born. CED began on two separate fronts.[78] The first was a postwar industrial program organized through the Commerce Department's National Economics Unit. In 1941, Commerce officials discussed the idea for a project that would allow businesses in related industries to share data on materials and goods production to help forecast consumer demand. However, the officials faced a vexing dilemma related to the project's public credibility. On the one hand, they did not want to oversee the planning unit themselves for fear that "business would cavalierly dismiss it as 'just another New Deal plan,'" in the words of CED historian

Karl Schriftgiesser.[79] Worse yet, they feared the centralized planning committee would appear as a harbinger of creeping socialism. On the other hand, the Commerce Department could not simply hand the project over to existing business and trade associations, such as the US Chamber of Commerce or the National Association of Manufacturers, for fear of the opposite reaction. To earn credibility, the new planning unit would need to maintain the appearance of distance from business. The solution the Commerce officials arrived at was to oversee the creation of the new project, which they would then spin off as a formally independent entity.

Unbeknownst to the Commerce officials, a similar effort was already underway elsewhere. Paul G. Hoffman, president of the Studebaker Company, and William Benton, an advertising mogul and vice president of the University of Chicago, had begun to organize small groups of economists and "literate businessmen," in Benton's words, for weekend seminars in the hope that a scientific solution to the problem of unemployment could be reached by harnessing the country's vast intellectual resources.[80] The two men drew up plans for an organization that would assemble businessmen and economists to converse regularly on matters of economic policy. As the project (which was briefly known as the American Policy Commission) got underway, Hoffman and Benton entered talks with Marion B. Folsom of the Commerce Department to merge the two groups. By late 1942, the nascent American Policy Commission had been folded into the Commerce Department as a research subcommittee.[81] Commerce secretary Jesse Jones then took control of the project and carried through on the plan to disaffiliate the unit, which became known as the Committee for Economic Development.

Formally incorporated in September 1942 with an annual budget of $250,000, CED comprised a diverse group of owners and managers from major American companies, as well as economists and journalists.[82] There was no question, however, which group represented the main force behind CED's activities. Supported by a membership list representing more than $20 billion in corporate assets, CED was, quite simply, the largest-ever collective mobilization of American business.[83] In the words of CED member and General Motors chairman Alfred P. Sloan Jr., its creation signaled "a big broad movement on the part of business to attempt, through the scientific approach, to develop a plan . . . [for] perpetuating free enterprise."[84] During its first few years, more than 50,000 businesses signed on as CED members, and the organization rolled out over 2,000 regional subcommittees to function as liaisons to local Chambers of Commerce and advisory boards to the central committee.[85] At the project's height, nearly every town in America with a population of 10,000 or more had a local CED committee.[86] CED also wrote and commissioned planning handbooks for businesses and trade associations, some of which reached circulations in excess of 400,000.[87] Its biggest project, however, was a wartime effort to gather data from more than 1,400 manufacturers on past, present, and future employment levels. The project culminated in an August 1945 report called *American Industry Looks Ahead* that became notable for its optimism amid forecasts of mass unemployment and economic doom. Although CED had originally been designed to dissolve at the conclusion of the war, its sponsors wagered on the organization's continuing utility and decided not to disband it.

Inventing Systems Analysis: Military Planning Groups, 1942–61

World War II also had important effects on the creation and use of knowledge tied more directly to the military effort itself. From 1940 to 1945, federal research and development expenditures rose fifteen-fold as the government solicited help from engineers, mathematicians, and scientists in the creation of new technical tools and weaponry (see figure 2.1).[88] Several new research centers formed out of this alliance in the nexus between government, business, and academia, including the Center for Naval Analyses (1942), the Mitre Corporation (1958), and the Hudson Institute (1961). However, the organization that would become the main emblem of this movement was the RAND Corporation. Taking its name from the phrase "research and development," Project RAND (as it was first known in 1943) sought to advance the nation's warfare capabilities in light of the ongoing struggle against communism.[89] In the words of its charter, RAND would pursue a "program of study and research on the broad subject of intercontinental warfare . . . with the object of recommending to the Army Air Forces preferred techniques and instrumentalities for this purpose."[90]

   RAND spun off as an independent entity in 1948, but in its early years the Air Force remained its lone sponsor. With a staff of 300 and a budget hovering around $3 million, RAND soon became the most important nonstate instrument of Cold War planning. Its research, much of it covert or classified, ranged widely in subject matter, from civilian defense and international diplomacy to military tactics and the development of weapons systems. Not surprisingly, a large share of its work came to center on the Soviet Union. RAND researchers wrote detailed analyses of Soviet eco-

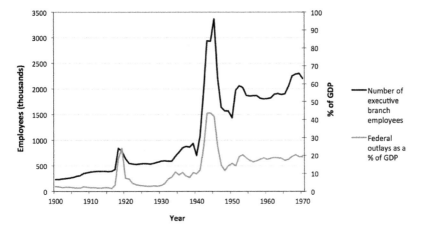

FIGURE 2.1 Growth of US federal government, 1900–70. Sources: Office of Management and Budget, *Budget of the United States Government, Historical Tables,* annual; US Civil Service Commission (currently Office of Personnel Management), *Federal Civilian Manpower Statistics,* http://www.access.gpo.gov/usbudget/fy2004/pdf/hist.pdf. Retrieved on August 15, 2007.

nomics, culture, foreign policy, and military capabilities. As the Cold War arms race escalated, the organization drew up studies related to all aspects of nuclear proliferation, including the anticipated effects of a nuclear blast at home, the strategic aspects of nuclear attacks abroad, and the development of safety procedures to prevent nuclear accidents and sabotage. RAND engineers also carried out technical research that led to the development of radar, reconnaissance, and missile detection systems.

More than any particular discovery or invention, however, RAND's calling card became the method of *systems analysis.* The very height of means-ends rationality, systems analysis is the interdisciplinary science of maximizing efficiency and economy given a particular objective and a set of "system parameters." The procedure usually involved modeling a situation mathematically, be it a sudden crisis of international diplomacy or the accidental detonation of a nuclear weapon, and then simulating the possible courses of action and their effects. Closely interwoven with game theory, the technique later came to be used beyond military strategizing in the areas of space exploration and budgetary and administrative planning. By the 1960s, as RAND's use of systems analysis generated insights that were applicable to other fields, the organization broadened its work considerably. For example, a study of the human eye conducted as part of its research on reconnaissance and missile detection yielded findings with medical implications related to the diagnosis of strokes. The research was eventually spun off into an interdisciplinary project on early stroke detection.[91] In the decades to follow, the organization would conduct myriad studies on computer security and privacy, communication technologies, space exploration, and Third World population control.[92]

RAND, Hudson, Mitre, and their technocratic counterparts became emblems of hyperrational nuclear planning. The popular cultural image of the Cold War defense intellectual, in fact, drew largely from the first two organizations. For example, Stanley Kubrick's 1964 satirical film *Dr. Strangelove* alluded to RAND. (In a pivotal scene, Strangelove cites a study commissioned from the "Bland Corporation.") Even so, the title character himself is often said to have been inspired by Hudson Institute founder Herman Kahn. America's Cold War adversaries also formed their own negative image of RAND. For example, *Pravda*, the official Communist Party newspaper in the Soviet Union, once described the organization as the "American academy of death and destruction."[93]

Partnership and Struggle in the American Field of Power

By the start of the 1960s, a few dozen organizations dedicated to public policy research and planning had emerged in the United States as significant players in the political process. As I have suggested, it is possible to distinguish several waves of organizational growth, each with its own sociohistorical bases. For example, the creation of new civic federations starting in the late nineteenth century reflected the growing political-cultural orthodoxy that neither government action nor private charity alone would be sufficient to solve the problems of poverty, unemployment, labor unrest, and urban blight. Instead, effective remedies would need to come from diverse coalitions of actors organized on the terrain of civil society. Soon afterwards, a set of organizations known as municipal research bureaus, including the New York Bureau of Municipal Research, became visible symbols of a wider movement to apply principles of sound business management to public administration. As with the civic federations, progressive businessmen led the effort, although in the latter cases their main partners were members of an emerging group of accounting and administrative specialists. As one of the major supporters of these organizations, the Rockefeller Foundation, explained in 1916, "advancing the science of administration" offered the best hope for "promoting efficiency in government" and eliminating political corruption.[94]

America's growing military and diplomatic engagement with the rest of the world during the 1910s and 1920s prompted the creation of a third set of organizations dedicated to foreign policy research and planning. The most important of these was the Council on Foreign Relations, which became a way station for the members of an emerging foreign policy establishment. These would later include the so-called "wise men" on whom President Harry Truman relied during his presidency.[95] The Great Depression and the development of economics as an academic discipline soon gave rise to new organizations devoted to the management of national economic affairs. Among them, the Committee for Economic Development was the most influential as the planning tool of a consortium of American business firms. Finally, the Cold War and the nation's growing military capacity supplied the main contexts for a handful of defense-oriented technocratic research centers, most notably the RAND Corporation.

Even if it is useful to disentangle these waves of organizational growth, however, it is also possible to treat them as components of a single process. The purpose of thinking about the organizations described here as "proto–think tanks" is to identify the common causes and effects of their development and their shared characteristics. Earlier in the chapter, I noted two imperatives that a good social scientific analysis of this process should obey. First, it must not presuppose that the research centers in question would inevitably cohere into a single organizational species. Instead, I argued, let us treat their eventual convergence (and the formation of a mental category for think tanks in American political discourse) as *outcomes* to be explained. Second, I argued, a proper explanation should find the sociohistorical bases of the process without reverting to either a purely materialist or an idealist logic. As I noted, the opposition between materialism and idealism is reflected in the early scholarly literature on the birth of think tanks. On the one side were the pluralists, who argued that the main catalyst for the emergence of think tanks was the growing use of scientific and technical reason in American political affairs. On the other side were the Millsian elite theorists, who depicted think tanks as the machinery of a small ruling elite, or a closed network of corporate, financial, and political power holders intent on consolidating their resources.[96]

Without denying the empirical facts underpinning either theory, I would argue that neither is sufficient on its own and that the opposition between them leads ultimately to a futile debate over what kinds of organizations the proto–think tanks "really" were. To see why this is a problem, consider the specific case of the RAND Corporation. How would we characterize RAND with respect to the opposition between pluralist and elite theory explanations? Channeling the pluralists, it would be possible to emphasize that RAND was neither an official arm of the state, nor a for-profit corporation subject to the forces of the market. For this reason, one could argue that RAND was an independent organ of civil society, not a creature of the state or the market. To bolster this argument, one could also point to the occasional (albeit overpublicized) instances of RAND's "intellectual rebelliousness," or those cases in which the organization asserted its cognitive autonomy by questioning the basic premises of its research assignments.[97] On the other hand, channeling the elite theorists, it would also be possible to make nearly the opposite argument. With equal conviction, one could point out that RAND was founded as a joint project of the US Air Force and the Douglas Aircraft Company to conduct strategic defense analyses on behalf of the US Defense Department. Furthermore, the dense network of personnel ties connecting RAND to the upper echelons of the US military and private defense contractors would seem to strengthen the impression that RAND was actually a camouflaged creature of the state and the market.

I would argue, however, that neither description sufficiently captures the "ultimate truth" of the RAND Corporation, or by extension, of the proto–think tanks in general. In the first place, the pluralist approach arbitrarily privileges a set of folk and official bureaucratic categories over properly analytic categories in classifying RAND. In doing so, it misses any possible "will to class power" among the creators of the proto–think tanks. On this count, the elite theory perspective has a certain advantage over its counterpart. Nevertheless, the elite theory approach unjustifiably dismisses the formal separation between the proto–think tanks and the state and market as somehow "false," or as the result of a kind of Machiavellian strategy orchestrated by a small ruling elite. More to the point, I would argue, the elite theory approach tends to presume what it should explain by taking for granted the "group-ness" of the upper class coalition behind the creation the proto–think tanks. In doing so, it misses both the specificity of this coalition and the existence of "horizontal" struggles among its members.

In the opening section of this chapter, I suggested that we could overcome these problems by describing the prehistory of think tanks in terms of a series of partnerships and struggles within the American field of power. This approach integrates the key insights of the two theories sketched above while avoiding their main flaws. What are the defining marks of this framework? First, like the elite theory approach, it locates the creation of the proto–think tanks explicitly on the terrain of *class formation* and *struggle*. This is a necessary starting point for a properly social scientific theory of think tanks, I would insist, because the key agents and groups in their creation were drawn almost invariably from the uppermost regions of the American class structure. As we have seen, the founders and directors of the proto–think tanks were unambiguously elite. However, in contrast to the elite theory approach, the framework I have suggested makes use of a highly open-ended concept of class. The main difference, as signaled in the concept *field of power*, lies in the proposition that the class structure has both vertical and horizontal dimensions. Terms such as *ruling class*, it suggests, are potentially misleading for the image they invoke of multiple, preexisting groups automatically merging together to consolidate their power—or, worse, the image of a single pre-constituted "elite" driven by the same impulse. In the case of proto–think tanks, the problem with these images is that they obscure what was actually the main attraction of these organizations for their founders: namely, their *group-making* function.

The idea of the field of power, on the other hand, does not take the existence of a cohesive upper class for granted. By suggesting that social relations within the highest regions of social space inevitably have both competitive and collaborative dimensions, it identifies the formation of specific class coalitions as the main *stake* in the process we are describing. My argument, then, is that it was not the "ruling class" as a whole that created the proto–think tanks, but instead a tenuous coalition composed of specific elite subgroups located at proximate positions in the field of power. Their affinity was based on a common faith in science and reason as vehicles of human progress. The leading figures in this coalition were a subset of politically moderate capitalists who, having rejected a purely laissez-faire philosophy, became convinced that scientific and technical planning could solve the major problems of the industrial era. Their partners in this project were members of an emerging American intelligentsia already predisposed to the search for technical means of reforming capitalist society. If we narrow our analytic lens somewhat, however, we can see that the aims of these two groups—the moderate capitalists and the technocratic intellectuals—were not identical. Above all, the progressive capitalists were engaged in an effort to "become modern" by incorporating a rational or scientific worldview into the capitalist system. Their actions were based on a particular understanding of what it meant to advance their class interests and to facilitate human progress. The technocratic intellectuals, on the other hand, were engaged in their own separate professionalization projects. Organizations like the National Bureau of Economic Research, for example, served as vehicles for economists to develop economic science and thus demonstrate their own utility in modern society.[98]

The proto–think tanks were thus both organs of class power and expressions of a growing rationalist tendency in American politics. However, while the increasing use of scientific and technical argumentation in politics was a tendency common in much of the advanced industrialized world, the emergence of proto–think tanks was not. What was distinctive about the American experience that led to this outcome? Doubtless the first factor was the ability of capitalists to create their own machinery of intellectual production, a power made possible by the enormous concentration of wealth during the industrial era. Following a period of rapid economic growth, businessmen were unusually well equipped to direct the form and content of policy-oriented research. A second enabling factor in the emergence of the proto–think tanks was the rapid expansion of the American higher educational system during the first half of the twentieth century. Universities supplied a new cadre of credentialed experts in the fields of administration, accounting, economics, finance, and foreign affairs.[99] Third, the emergence of the proto–think tanks depended on the presence of a highly technocratic culture within the American intelligentsia, especially among social scientists. In the view of historian Dorothy Ross, American social science in the late nineteenth century bore "the distinctive mark of its national origin," especially in its "liberal values, practical bent, shallow historical vision, and technocratic confidence."[100] In keeping with a political orthodoxy that valorized private over public solutions to social problems, early American social science blended seamlessly with the work of settlement reformers by focusing on the goal of making private charity more effective.[101]

The creation of proto–think tanks thus depended on a tenuous coalition between holders of economic and cultural capital, with the former generally taking the dominant role. This is not to suggest, however, that the holders of cultural capital always followed the lead of their capitalist sponsors or accepted their status as "junior partners." In fact, credentialed experts always had some measure of control within these partnerships, since the credibility of the proto–think tanks depended on their ability to distinguish themselves plausibly from trade associations and other business groups. In some cases, then, the holders of cultural capital succeeded in wresting a considerable degree of autonomy from their capitalist sponsors.

Consider the case of Harold Moulton, the economist and first president of the Brookings Institution, who had originally been reluctant to leave his post in the economics department at the University of Chicago to lead one of Brookings' predecessor organizations, the Institute of Economics. Understandably, Moulton feared that the position would bring intellectual restrictions from which his academic post protected him. (In the words of a Brookings historian, Moulton was "wary of a research institution with so many businessmen on its board. He worried about the constraints of seeking philanthropic support for scholarly research. And he bluntly told Robert Brookings that he did not want to manage an organization that would simply operate as a front for business interests."[102]) Nevertheless, Brookings was able to provide Moulton the assurances he needed, and the economist began a 25-year stint as the organization's president.

A skilled fundraiser, Moulton was able to amass a considerable endowment for the Brookings Institution, and in 1942 he wrote to Vannevar Bush, the celebrated statesman and Brookings trustee: "Dear Mr. Bush, You will be interested to learn that, on May 14, the Carnegie Corporation made a grant to the Brookings Institution in the amount of $50,000; and that on May 15 the Rockefeller Foundation made a two-year grant of $75,000 a year. This is better than I had dared to hope; and in consequence our financial situation is excellent for the next two years."[103] Bush replied, "I am very happy about it, for it seems to me that you are in decidedly sound financial condition and able to work out a constructive program with a bit of freedom, all of which is much to be desired."[104] The money gave Moulton the freedom to hire academic scholars and direct research projects meant to advance the science of economics. Nevertheless, the Brookings Institution encountered considerable difficulty maintaining the image of scientific detachment, owing mainly to its capitalist pedigree and its consistent opposition to the New Deal and Fair Deal programs. As James Smith points out, skeptical journalists took to calling the organization the "Rockefeller Inquiry," while the UAW-CIO described Brookings as "a research center which usually assembles a lot of rubber facts to prove that the planks in the Republican Party platform are based on natural and divine law."[105]

Thus, even if businessmen consistently enjoyed the upper hand in their partnerships with experts, the success of their organizations always depended on their willingness to grant the holders of cultural capital some measure of autonomy. It would be problematic also to overlook the internal conflicts that frequently marked the creation of many proto–think tanks. During its initial planning stages, for example, the Committee for Economic Development was riven by disagreements as to what function the organization should serve. According to Schriftgiesser, Hoffman and Benton wanted the organization to carry out a program of empirical research, whereas Folsom "was opposed to research per se . . . [by] what he conceived to be fundamentally a propaganda machine formed to spread the necessity of practical, plant-by-plant thinking about industrial postwar planning."[106] Conflicts affected personnel decisions, as when Commerce Secretary Jesse Jones vetoed the candidacy of General Electric's Owen D. Young for the chairmanship of CED because of Young's view that CED should incorporate labor and agriculture representatives.[107] More broadly, the creation of proto–think tanks depended ultimately on a series of delicate partnerships between businessmen and experts that gave rise to a complex dynamic of affinity and struggle.

How should we summarize this double-sided point? The simplest answer, I believe, is that while the proto–think tanks were unmistakably elite in character, they were also constitutively *hybrid* in their design and construction. It is no coincidence, in fact, that most of the organizations described in this chapter were formed through the mergers of multiple preexisting groups, and that in each case one of the originating groups was plainly the more intellectual while the other was more moneyed and politically connected. For such mergers to take place, a series of fragile compromises between businessmen and experts had to be forged. The partners to these projects were therefore neither the most extreme proponents of free market ideology, nor the intellectuals most committed to the principle of cognitive autonomy. Instead, they were capitalists known for their faith in research and planning and technocratic intellectuals willing to aid in the search for market-oriented solutions to political problems. Put differently, the formation of the proto–think tanks was the result of an elective affinity and unstable convergence among elites at the center of the American field of power.

Even these factors are not sufficient to explain the emergence of the proto–think tanks, however. Another necessary condition for their growth was the relative absence of formal political institutions in the United States that might have rendered these organizations superfluous. I am referring especially to the lack of both a formal technocratic arm of the state and a highly professionalized civil service in the United States. It is also worth noting the relatively limited policy-planning capacities of American political parties.[108] In other Western countries, by contrast, expert participation in political decision-making grew during the first half of the twentieth century as well, but it took different institutional forms. Compared with their European counterparts, American social scientists were generally more willing to accept the pro-capitalist premises of their sponsors, but the former were more likely to be incorporated into the formal apparatus of the state or the party. The weakness of the latter institutions in the United States created opportunities for experts to exist in organizations that remained outside the formal reach of the state.

Formal independence did not always translate into cognitive independence, however, since the influence of the proto–think tanks in political affairs depended ultimately on the material support of businessmen and the recognition of politicians. A good illustration of this point can be found in the history of the Council on Foreign Relations, which saw its influence grow as a result of the American federal government's limited foreign policy planning capabilities during World War II. In September 1939, the State Department initiated a covert partnership with CFR to carry out research on foreign states and markets. Assistant Secretary of State George S. Messersmith set up the project, known as the War and Peace Studies division, with two CFR directors, Hamilton Fish Armstrong and Walter Mallory. The Carnegie Corporation and Rockefeller Foundation were then recruited to assist financially in the effort, with the former supplying $350,000. Over the next five years, the War and Peace Studies project generated hundreds of classified memoranda related to the war's anticipated effects on security, trade, finance, and geopolitical relations. A study on postwar Asia, for example, suggested that in the event of a Japanese defeat, China could become both a major market for American exports and a source of raw materials. Another study developed contingency plans for the federal government in the event of a German invasion of Great Britain. Finally, the decision to establish American military bases in Greenland was a direct result of a War and Peace Studies memo.[109] When the project concluded, most of those affiliated with it either entered or returned to government service in the military, the State Department, or the Office of Strategic Services (a wartime intelligence agency and precursor to the CIA).

The CFR example points again to the advantage of a theoretical model that remains attentive both to the group-making function that the proto–think tanks performed for a particular segment of the American elite and to the rationalist underpinnings of these projects. Consider, for example, the motley collection of lawyers, journalists, bankers, and scholars who formed CFR in 1921. Rather than describe these founders simply as elites who created a vehicle of class power "disguised" as a purveyor of expertise, it would be more accurate to characterize the project in terms of the *creation of a new form of expertise* itself. What better way to describe CFR's journal, *Foreign Affairs*, for example, than as an organ through which aspiring foreign policy experts could develop their own language, their own criteria of judgment, and their own body of knowledge—and thus constitute themselves as experts of a new breed? CFR thus operated, not simply as an instrument for the accumulation of class power, but also as a terrain on which a new form of expertise could be developed. More broadly, we can say that CFR and organizations like it were settings in which the *relative values* of the different media of power—money, information, credentials, social capital, and so forth—could be hammered out. The alliances among their members formed *through*, rather than in spite of, the growing use of rationality in political affairs.

Conclusion: Proto–Think Tanks in the Social Structure

An elective affinity between politically moderate capitalists and technocratic intellectuals—itself enabled by the weakness of alternative political institutions—led to the growth of a large, segmented apparatus of technoscientific reason in the United States. What effects did this process have on the American social structure? I would argue that, in addition to facilitating a specific elite coalition, the process marginalized or excluded from the policy-making process two fractions of the elite. I am referring, first, to the most autonomous American intellectuals, or those intellectuals whose distance from politics predisposed them to analyze, historicize, and contextualize the basic premises of policy debate. In the "proto–think tanks" I have just described, there was little room for those who refused to take into account the preferences of wealthy donors or the need to earn recognition from politicians. Even before midcentury, signs of mutual enmity between intellectuals who valued their cognitive autonomy and the organizations described here were apparent. In 1947, for example, historian Charles A. Beard famously castigated the Council on Foreign Relations for its self-subordination to the needs of the federal government during World War II. Writing in the *Saturday Evening Post*, Beard criticized CFR for discouraging "journalists or any other persons" from "question[ing] too closely or criticiz[ing] too freely the official propaganda and official statements relative to our basic aims and activities during World War II."[110]

The second elite subgroup marginalized by the formation of new technoscientific machinery was the most conservative segment of the American capitalist class, or those steadfastly committed to policies of unrestricted free trade and commerce. Sitting at the opposite end of the American field of power, the latter were largely excluded from the "New Deal coalition." Even when the promoters of laissez-faire policies did begin to form their own research and discussion groups during the 1930s and 1940s—as in the case of the American Enterprise Association—the organizations generally occupied a marginalized position in the nascent technoscientific establishment. The creation of proto–think tanks during the first half of the twentieth century was thus part and parcel of a wider corporatist bargain, or a tenuous class compromise between American owners and workers that was mediated largely by technocratic specialists. This observation offers a useful starting point for the next chapter, in which I will trace the reassertion by free market capitalists of their power over economic decision-making through the creation of new organs of intellectual production. As I will argue, the market dislocations of the 1970s motivated free market capitalists to carry out a full-scale invasion of the space of technoscientific production that had once been dominated by their corporatist counterparts. This invasion led to major transformations in the American field of power with significant ramifications beyond the United States. However, the main focus of my argument will be to show that this transformation helped bring the *think tank* category itself into being.

In closing, let me note a final structural effect produced by the emergence of the proto–think tanks during the early twentieth century. To illustrate the point, we must return again to the question of organizational classification, particularly with respect to the commonsense division of the social world into three spheres: state, market, and civil society. As I suggested earlier, to ask which of these spheres think tanks originated in or "belonged to" is to introduce a red herring into the discussion—one that actually calls into question the utility of this tripartite model of the social world. Even the most nuanced answer to the question—namely, that the proto–think tanks managed to exist in all three domains at once—is in some ways unsatisfying. In certain contexts, it might indeed be useful to suggest that the organizations described here spanned the boundaries between state, market, and civil society. However, I would also like to suggest that this formulation misses a key dimension of the proto–think tanks' sociohistorical significance. Consider again the case of the RAND Corporation. The main problem with calling an organization like RAND a "boundary spanner" is that the description reifies the institutional boundaries in question. It implies, in other words, that the boundaries between state, market, and civil society were already "there" to begin with. Broadening our lens beyond the United States, however, shows that the exact reach of the state, the market, and civil society is not always and everywhere the same. In some countries, for example, organizations quite similar to RAND exist *inside* of the formal apparatus of the state. RAND's closest counterparts in Canada and France, for example—the Defense Research and Development Canada and the Defence Procurement Agency, respectively—are both official government agencies. Furthermore, as the previous discussion implies, historical and cross-national differences such as these do not develop simply at random, but emerge partly as the result of "boundary work" performed by the organizations, their clients, and their sponsors. As we have seen, organizations like RAND must go to elaborate lengths to create and maintain the perception that they are independent from the state and the market, especially in light of their profound dependence on the same institutions for their material support, relevance, and personnel.

Recast in this light, the question of the location of the proto–think tanks with respect to the state, the market, and civil society takes on a new significance. In particular, we can see now that the location of the boundary is less a straightforward fact than a partial *effect* of the presence or absence of specific institutions that create the boundary. The proto–think tanks, I am suggesting, lay at the heart of this process. Thus, we can identify another effect of the emergence of proto–think tanks, one very similar to the "state effect" described by Timothy Mitchell in his analysis of the dilemmas involved in theorizing the state.[111] In short, the growth of a "non-state" apparatus of technoscientific production in the United States was pivotal in institutionalizing a boundary between the state, the market, and civil society. The entire process helped to establish a particular understanding of where politics ended and research began in the United States—one that remained open to contestation but nonetheless exhibited a patterning effect on future struggles. The question of the boundary's location is not just an idle theoretical question, especially for the politicians and bureaucrats who use the work of technocrats. To return to the case of the RAND Corporation, for example, it is easier for a Pentagon official intent on a particular course of military action to cite a RAND study as corroborating evidence for an argument if he can also plausibly claim that the study was conducted "outside" of the state. The fact that the research may have been commissioned by the Pentagon, carried out by ex–Defense Department officials, and circumscribed on all sides by rigid guidelines that shaped its results has no bearing on the fact of RAND's formal autonomy. Put differently, even if a technocratic organization's work is carried out under conditions that are objectively similar to those of its foreign counterparts, the fact of its formal separation from the state can have significant consequences with respect to its legitimacy.

CHAPTER THREE

The Crystallization of the Space of Think Tanks

[Activists] took the existing network of expertise apart and wove a wholly new and alternative network of knowledge production and dissemination. It was not a mere teaming-up of adjacent groups. . . . Rather, it involved the hybridization of identities, blurring of boundaries between expert and layman, and crucially "co-production" of common objects of inquiry and treatment. —Gil Eyal, *The Autism Matrix*

The previous chapter traced the think tank's precursors to a complex encounter in the American *field of power*—Bourdieu's term for the "system of positions occupied by the holders of the diverse forms of capital" and the struggles over their relative values.[1] I argued that several waves of organizational growth occurred through specific partnerships among economic, political, and cultural elites seeking to align their interests and resources. The overarching result of this process, I argued, was the formation of a large, segmented machinery of "technoscientific reason" in the United States, some parts of which would later come to be known as think tanks. At the same time, I insisted that we separate this process analytically from the formation of the think tank category itself, since the latter became meaningful only when a specific organizational network had formed, and only when the members of this network had developed novel products and practices to distinguish themselves from the more established institutions of academia, politics, business, and journalism. In short, the birth of think tanks depended on the development of a particular mode of *social and organizational relations*.

The purpose of this chapter is to explain the latter process, which I will refer to as the crystallization of the space of think tanks. My argument is that the space of think tanks formed in the United States starting in the 1960s through a process of structural convergence between two formerly

distinct sets of experts: first, the technocrats described in the previous chapter, who had by the mid-twentieth century become the leading
providers of strategic policy advice, and second, an emerging breed of
activist-experts who issued a significant challenge to the technocrats, and
to technocratic rationality more broadly, starting in the 1960s. Drawn first
into conflict and subsequently into a kind of tacit collaboration, the organizations staffed by the technocrats and activist-experts became increasingly oriented to one another in the 1970s and 1980s, giving rise to a new
organizational category: the think tank. In developing this argument, I
hope to clarify why I have insisted on treating the formation of the think
tank category as an object of explanation rather than as a straightforward
fact. Put simply, it is only by holding this category at arm's length that we
can see the new alignments and oppositions that developed among social
actors and groups with different claims to expertise after 1970.

   In contrast with the last chapter, which was set analytically within the
field of power, this chapter focuses more narrowly on the struggles and
partnerships among expert groups in the United States starting in the
1960s. Accordingly, I will need to use a different theoretical tool for the
discussion. Before moving to the main part of the chapter, then, let me
explain the key concept that will guide my analysis: *field of expertise*. The
purpose of the following section is to clarify this concept and its uses in
the chapter.

What Is the Field of Expertise?

Field of expertise is a term I take from the work of Gil Eyal, who uses it
to describe the dilemmas and constraints faced by expert groups in their
encounters with the consumers of their knowledge and with one another.[2]
Derived from Bourdieu's field theory, the concept nonetheless departs
from a conventional reading of Bourdieu in a few respects. The key difference is that Eyal defines the two dimensions of the field of expertise in
terms of a pair of strategic dilemmas that arise for expert groups. As figure 3.1 shows, the field's horizontal axis refers to the opposition between
autonomy and heteronomy, or independence from the consumers of one's
knowledge and dependence on them. Building on Bourdieu's reconstruction of Weber's sociology of religion, Eyal argues that all expert groups
face an important choice: They can either seek autonomy from the consumers of their knowledge by attempting to define the consumers' needs

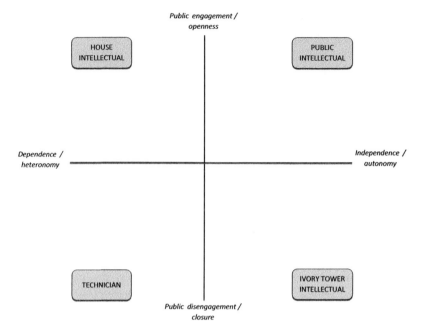

FIGURE 3.1 The field of expertise. Adapted from Gil Eyal. 2006. *The Disenchantment of the Orient: Expertise in Arab Affairs and the Israeli State.* Stanford: Stanford University Press, 29.

for them, or they can tailor their products and practices to the preferences of the consumers. A good example of expert autonomy is the ability doctors have to evaluate the needs of a patient and determine the best course of treatment, independently of the patient's own opinions of his or her medical needs. Of course, this example also illustrates the fact that the choice between autonomy and heteronomy is not simply an either-or decision. The same doctors, after all, face certain pressures to take into account the preferences of their patients before deciding which treatment to administer. We can therefore think of the opposition between autonomy and heteronomy in terms of a spectrum, and an expert group's position on the spectrum as subject to change over time.

The main purpose of this opposition becomes clear when we consider how it comes to bear on the question of an expert group's power. Among social theorists, the conventional approach has been to assume that cognitive autonomy constitutes an unqualified "plus" to an expert group's power, whereas dependence on clients is simply a form of constraint. On this view, the best way for an expert group to gain power is to enforce positive standards of rigor and competence on its own members in exchange for the right to dictate its consumers' needs to them. Eyal's first contribution, then, is to point out that the opposition between autonomy and heteronomy is more complex than the classical approach has typically assumed. In fact, the opposition is better thought of as a perennial *dilemma* demanding constant attention and maintenance. After all, since the theoretical case of perfect autonomy is one in which the members of an expert group are the sole judges of their own competence (in Bourdieu's words, they alone control the "means of production and evaluation" of their own work[3]), a strategy of uncompromising autonomy always puts the group at risk of isolating itself from its clients. Highly autonomous experts open themselves up to competition from rival experts who are more willing to tailor their products and services to consumer demand. However, it should also go without saying that a strategy of total subservience to one's consumers is never an ideal strategy either. No group of experts, in other words, can become entirely deferential to its clients without also losing the quality that makes it "expert." A doctor who is willing to prescribe any drug to his patients, for example, does not become a better or more powerful doctor for that fact, but actually begins to undermine his or her own authority as a medical expert. The overarching point is that the opposition between autonomy and heteronomy demands an ongoing balancing act.

A separate dilemma obtains with respect to the vertical axis of the field of expertise, which refers to the choice between "openness" and "closure." In this usage, which derives from Max Weber, the term *closure* refers to mechanisms such as credentialing and training that allow experts to control the means of entry into their own ranks and exercise proprietary control over their knowledge. To extend the medical example, we could say that doctors derive a certain power from their ability to limit entry into their group and thereby control the use and attribution of their knowledge. If everyone knew how to diagnose a malady and administer treatment, in other words, then medical knowledge could not function as a source of power. Closure is thus a strategy by which expert groups collectively safeguard their prestige and their ability to extract rents for services. Once again, however, we can see the limits of this strategy, since an expert group that "closes" its knowledge too much risks becoming too esoteric and isolating itself from consumers.

Put differently, an expert group's power depends also on its *openness*, or its ability to generate ideas and concepts that are accessible and useful to a nonexpert "laity." Again, the point operates in tension with the classical social scientific approach, which usually presumed that intellectuals, professionals, and other experts gain power by maximizing social closure. Shadings of the opposite point can be found in the more recent work of Michel Foucault, for example, who suggested that the very height of intellectual power came, not when experts closed ranks, but when they *lost* proprietary control over their knowledge, which then became part of the general *episteme*. A psychologist who wonders whether he is in a "codependent" relationship, for example, or asks himself whether he is truly "purpose-driven" (to borrow two terms from recent pop psychology) has become both the object and the subject of his own expert discourse, in Foucault's sense. In such cases, Foucault might say, it would make little sense to describe the "power effects" of expertise in terms of closure, since no one is exercising monopolistic control over its application.

Foucault's work has been criticized for stretching the concept of power beyond the limits of its coherence, and perhaps rightly so. However, as Eyal points out, this is no reason to abandon the idea that an expert group's power depends also on its openness, or its ability to generate knowledge that is accessible and useful to clients. Eyal synthesizes these two points—the Weberian and the Foucaultian—by reframing the opposition as a second dilemma faced by experts, which I can summarize as follows: To maintain its audience, an expert group must exhibit some degree of openness in its writings and speech (i.e., it cannot be too esoteric, and its knowledge must have some practical utility beyond the world of its production). And yet to capitalize on its knowledge, the same group must also achieve some degree of closure, "mystery," or proprietary control. Once again, the strategic importance of balance becomes apparent. Too much openness leads to a situation in which the group cannot claim any material or symbolic rewards for its knowledge, which then becomes freely available to everyone. (Think, for example, of most everyday folk wisdom, or of certain truisms of pop psychology, which are "owned" by everyone and therefore no one.) At the same time, too much closure leads to pure esotericism, which undermines the utility and marketability of the expert group's knowledge. (Think, for example, of the mathematics subfield of number theory, which has almost no practical uses whatsoever—or of the Laputans of *Gulliver's Travels*, who possess advanced theoretical knowledge that is of no use to anyone outside of the immediate world of its production. The point is that neither group has many clients.[4])

For heuristic purposes, the labels on figure 3.1 build into this framework some common terms used by scholars to describe various kinds of experts. For example, in the upper right-hand corner associated with high autonomy and high openness, I have placed the so-called "public intellectual," or the ideal-typical thinker who combines cognitive autonomy with a willingness to "give away" his or her knowledge by making it accessible to the lay public. (Quoting Nikolas Rose, Eyal refers to this latter characteristic as "generosity.") The structural inverse of the public intellectual is the expert who combines a high level of closure with heteronomy, by which I mean dependence on clients and responsiveness to their demands. This pair of attributes is captured in another ideal-type, which I will, following Robert Merton, call a technician.[5] While technicians reap all of the rewards associated with group closure (via their credentials, formal training, and technical skills), they do not enjoy much autonomy because they are under constant pressure to demonstrate their worth and effectiveness to clients. The lower right-hand corner of the figure indicates a third ideal-type, the proverbial ivory tower figure, who belongs to an expert group that monopolizes the evaluation of its products while remaining "closed." In the conventional image, ivory tower intellectuals are both autonomous and disengaged from public debate because of their esotericism, their self-absorption, or some other form of social closure. Finally, the expert who tailors his or her products to the demands of clients while remaining "open" and actively engaged in public debate is what I will call, following Amitai Etzioni, a "house intellectual."[6] The essence of house intellectualism, in Etzioni's description, is the practice of making public arguments on behalf of self-interested clients. Public relations spokespeople, for example, must dispense knowledge that is both non-esoteric and available to everyone, even as they remain highly dependent on their clients.

At this point, however, I will follow Eyal in making an important qualification to this discussion. While the labels on figure 3.1 may be useful for heuristic purposes, in another sense they miss the point entirely. After all, once we begin to think in terms of the relations among experts, the labels themselves become more of a hindrance than a benefit. In the first place, they describe only the most extreme, unstable locations in a field of expertise, or the positions at which experts become most vulnerable to the loss of clients and the challenges issued by other experts. Furthermore, they miss the fact that struggles in the field of expertise obey a somewhat predictable pattern. Because the center of the field is the best position from which to fend off challenges from outsiders and maintain one's clients, the interior dynamic of the field is typically one of "constant migration toward the center and challenges from the margins."[7]

To see how this framework helps illuminate the history and role of think tanks, recall the story of Charles Murray's role in the welfare debate of the 1980s and 1990s as told in the book's prologue. The key point was that Murray's power flowed, not from his ability to embody a particular expert "type"—that is, not by locating himself in one of the four corner locations of the field of expertise—but by merging the characteristics associated with each type and existing near the field's *center*. More broadly, since the precise meanings of "centrality" and "marginality" depend at any given moment on the totality of the relations constituting the field of expertise, we cannot find the source of any expert's power in his or her individual characteristics alone. Skills, credentials, and knowledge, for example, are never enough to explain a given expert's influence. Instead, we must think in terms of the current structure of the field and its location within the wider field of power.

Where Did the Space of Think Tanks Come From?

The purpose of this theoretical digression was to establish an analytic terrain on which to locate my argument about the formation of the space of think tanks. My argument is that by the 1960s and 1970s, several expert groups vied for the capacity to represent the prototype of the politically influential expert in the United States. Moreover, the relations among these groups can be described in terms of a struggle in the field of expertise as sketched above. Focusing on the role of knowledge and expertise in this way gives us a novel picture of the recent history of American politics.

The empirical starting point for my argument is the conclusion I reached in the last chapter: namely, that by the early 1960s, a set of technocratic specialists had secured for themselves a major role in American politics, especially in matters related to foreign policy, economics, social policy, and military affairs. A group of semi-autonomous technocrats enjoyed a brief but relatively uncontested period of dominance in the field of expertise. However, two major challenges to technocratic authority soon developed. The main challenge, I will argue, came from an emerging set of *activist-experts* who sought to undermine the power of technocrats from a standpoint of greater openness in the field of expertise. Implicit, and sometimes explicit, in their work was the suggestion that the technocrats were too esoteric, too driven by professional self-interests, and too unaccountable to public needs and democratic principles. (In a word, they were too *closed* in the Weberian sense.) Let me point out immediately what is surely the most idiosyncratic feature of this argument: It treats political activists of the left and right as homologous expressions of the same tendency. Later in the chapter, I will discuss the differences between conservative and progressive activists of the 1960s and 1970s. However, for now I would like to point out a key *similarity* between them. Put simply, both groups were deeply suspicious of professionalized rationality and its main carriers in American politics. Furthermore, major segments of both groups framed their political grievances against technocrats. To be sure, conservative and progressive warnings about the dangers of technocratic power took very different forms and had different targets during the 1960s. Whereas activists of the left found one of their major adversaries in the Cold War military planner, for example, those of the right aimed much of their skepticism toward government bureaucrats and planners, especially the technocratic experts of the New Deal welfare state.

How, we might ask, did the 1960s activists become "activist-experts"? The next part of my argument concerns the relationships that developed between the technocrats and their challengers during the 1970s, which I can explain using the concept of the field of expertise. First, it is crucial to recognize that in challenging the authority of technocrats, the activists faced a basic problem. With virtually no credentials or academic titles to speak of, and no recognized body of knowledge at their command—that is, no form of *expertise*—they could not easily constitute themselves as authoritative critics in political debate. Nor could they exercise any proprietary control over their knowledge, or by extension, lay claim to any of the symbolic or material dividends normally paid an expert. Consequently, their knowledge was always in danger of being co-opted by other experts, including technocrats. With respect to their position in the field of expertise, the activists faced a problem of excessive *openness*. As a result, many of their activities during the 1960s and 1970s can be read as elements of a closure strategy, or an attempt to "certify" their knowledge and constitute themselves as experts of a new species. The centerpiece of their strategy was to establish a set of nonprofit, politically oriented research centers that served a kind of self-credentialing function. Organizations such as the Institute for Policy Studies (formed in 1963) and the Heritage Foundation (1973) exemplified this strategy. By the mid-1980s, hundreds of such ideologically oriented policy research centers had emerged in the United States.

By the end of the 1970s, the growing presence of activist-expert organizations in American politics constituted a legitimate threat to the technocrats. As I noted in chapter 2, the major technocratic networks of the mid-twentieth century were composed of economic, military, and foreign policy specialists operating outside of the formal boundary of the state and within organizations such as the Brookings Institution, the RAND Corporation, and the Council on Foreign Relations. By the start of the 1970s, these organizations found themselves increasingly under public attack for their esotericism, their professional self-absorption, and their civic unaccountability. The emergence of rival organizations meant that the technocratic groups faced a problem directly opposite that of the activists: namely, too much closure. Having long sought to operate behind the scenes, they were forced to respond to this pressure by making their knowledge more accessible to the general public. The goal of achieving news media visibility, for example, once abjured by these organizations, became central to their missions. In other ways too, organizations such as Brookings, RAND, and CFR "opened up" their knowledge by altering its form and content to enhance its accessibility. In terms of the theoretical model I have sketched above, their strategy was to move vertically toward the center of the field of expertise (see figure 3.2).

The central argument of this chapter, then, is that *the space of think tanks formed in the United States as the two sets of organizations—the technocratic research centers and their activist-expert challengers—undertook convergent strategies in the field of expertise.* It is important to recognize that the two horns of their respective dilemmas had little to do with the opposition between autonomy and heteronomy. Indeed, I would argue that both groups already occupied relatively stable central locations along the horizontal axis of the field. Put differently, neither group was especially autonomous, and yet neither was completely heteronomous. The technocrats, for example, had a built-in clientele of government agencies (which, to be sure, placed considerable limits on their cognitive autonomy), even as they enjoyed a degree of formal separation from the state, which functioned as a guard against total subservience. While they could not choose the ultimate aims of their studies, neither were they completely at the mercy of their clients. The activist-experts were in a similar boat. Standing further outside the official halls of power, they could lay claim to a kind of independence, and yet they remained highly accountable to clients of their own—namely, sympathetic activists, journalists, media organs, and donors, the latter consisting (especially for the organizations of the right) largely of business corporations.

I mentioned above that two main challenges to the authority of technocrats emerged during this period. Of these, the one that has received the

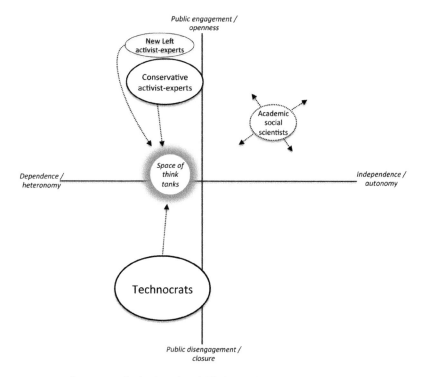

FIGURE 3.2   Convergence in the American field of expertise, 1960s to 2000s.

most attention from scholars is the so-called "public intellectual" challenge mounted by social scientists and journalists during the 1950s and
1960s. I am referring to the relatively small set of scholars and other intellectuals who, having accumulated a degree of cognitive autonomy through
decades of debate centered in the academy, sought to intervene in public
affairs from a privileged standpoint of autonomy and openness. Starting in
the late 1950s, for example, economists such as John Kenneth Galbraith,
sociologists such as C. Wright Mills and David Riesman, political scientists
such as Seymour Martin Lipset, and historians like Richard Hofstadter
occupied the leading edge of a movement to reinvest their scholarly authority in the public sphere. By writing books and periodicals aimed at an
educated lay public, they were, like the technocrats, also engaged in an
effort to "open up" their knowledge. Journalists such as Dwight MacDonald, Michael Harrington, and Jack Newfield represented the journalistic
face of this movement. In terms of the theoretical model I am using, they

located themselves within the quadrant of the field of expertise associated with high autonomy and openness.

While the political interventions of these intellectuals have garnered a great deal of attention from scholars—including those who lament the death of the "public intellectual" (a topic I will address in the book's conclusion)—my purpose here is to emphasize the extreme *limitations* of their project. Compared to the activist-experts, the public intellectuals of the 1950s and 1960s represented the lesser of the two challenges to professionalized rationality that developed during this era. Meanwhile, the greater challenge—that of the activist-experts—has gone largely unnoticed by scholars. Among my goals in this chapter, then, is to direct more scholarly attention to this important aspect of American political and intellectual history.

The final part of my argument in this chapter concerns the convergence between the technocrats and the activist-experts in the field of expertise. As the two groups met at the center of the field, they became more interconnected, and the distinctions between them grew muddier. To the degree that the activist-expert organizations succeeded in having their policy recommendations taken seriously by politicians, for example, they became more like the technocrats. Competition continued to shape the relationship between the two sets of organizations, but in many ways growing contact led also to a kind of tacit collaboration. By the 1980s, the organizations had coinvented certain hybrid intellectual products such as the "policy brief" (i.e., short, synthetic memos written for journalists and politicians) and the presidential transition manual (i.e., policy guides written for incoming presidential administrations), which in turn became effective means of marking their difference from academic scholars. Increasingly, the technocratic and activist-expert organizations oriented their judgments and practices to one another, so that eventually it became possible to speak of them as occupying the same semidistinct space of intellectual production. The growing use of a new political folk category, *think tank*, was the cultural corollary of this structural transformation.

Up to this point, the discussion has treated the conservative and progressive activist-experts as two sides of the same coin. However, to anyone familiar with the current landscape of American think tanks, it is obvious that the respective fates of the two groups were actually quite different. While the activist critique of technocracy received its first clear expression from organizations of the left, such as the Institute for Policy Studies and the Worldwatch Institute, by the 1980s this region of the field of expertise was dominated by conservative organizations. How and why did the right take control of the space of think tanks? In the last section of this chapter, I will argue that the dominance of conservatives in the space of think tanks can be traced to three main causes: first, an enormous advantage in financial support from American business; second, relative freedom from state repression (a luxury the progressive activist-experts could not always count on); and third, greater absorption of the progressive activist-experts by the university.

The remaining sections of this chapter will put some empirical flesh onto these theoretical bones, first, by offering a narrative history of four specific organizations that I take to be emblematic of the tendencies I have just described: the Institute for Policy Studies, a progressive think tank founded in 1963; the Heritage Foundation and the American Enterprise Institute, two major conservative think tanks; and the Brookings Institution, a model of technocratic rationality forced to adjust to a changing institutional environment. I will describe the strategies, resources, and trajectories of these organizations during the period from 1963 until the mid-1980s. At various points, I will supplement this discussion with observations about parallel developments among other organizations. The unifying thread of my narrative will be that, through their growing interconnectedness, the technocratic and activist-expert organizations gradually merged, forming a new subspace of knowledge production at the crossroads of the academic, political, bureaucratic, economic, and media fields. The final section of the chapter will then extend the discussion to the present day by tracing the formation of the space of think tanks along three dimensions: first, the growing density of network ties and partnerships among think tanks; second, the invention of new intellectual products; and third, the creation of folk, professional, and academic knowledge about think tanks.

Specialists without Spirit: The Activist Critique of Technocracy

During the first half of the twentieth century, experts came to play a pivotal role in American political affairs. By the end of the 1950s, experts of various kinds had devised and implemented the social programs of the welfare state, supplied technical assistance to the defense industry, staffed the economic administration, brokered deals between management and labor, and presided over key decision-making processes related to health,

well-being, and the management of deviance. By 1962, when President
John F. Kennedy famously predicted in his Yale commencement address
that the political struggles of the coming era would be marked, not by
"some grand warfare of rival ideologies which will sweep the country with
passion," but by concrete problems demanding "technical answers," the
authority of the technocrat appeared secure. As the *New York Times* put
it the following year, "Never before have so many scholars and scientists
been in the business of giving the Government advice." For example, when
it came to military affairs, argued the *Times*, "the most important fount of
strategic wisdom is what the lingo calls the 'think factory,' like the RAND
(Research and Development) Corporation."[8]

Other technocratic organizations had come to play a major role in political affairs as well. In the realm of economic decision-making, for example, the Brookings Institution and the National Bureau of Economic
Research had become leading voices. Brookings assisted in the development of the Marshall Plan and the Kennedy wage and price guideposts of
1962, while NBER's work became the basis for the government's official
measure of the gross national product. In foreign affairs, the Council on
Foreign Relations had positioned itself as the leading supplier of diplomatic advice and talent.

While it is difficult to generalize about the prevailing mood of any era,
it is safe to say that the growing role of experts in American life was initially met with a considerable degree of optimism. During the 1930s, for
example, major advances in medical, atomic, and automotive technologies had contributed to a widespread sentiment that experts represented
a positive force in social life.[9] By the next decade, however, a series of
negative possibilities had already begun to attach to the public profile of
the technocrat. In 1944, a *Wall Street Journal* editorialist weighed in on
"the curious phenomenon known, where it is known, as *Technocracy*" as
a kind of wolf in sheep's clothing: "If anything could typify the state of
mental confusion existing in some of our people it is this movement," the
editorialist wrote. "Its admitted object is to turn the lives, liberties and
properties of the citizens over to the complete control of a body of self-
selected 'technocrats' to do with as they please."[10]

Of course, suspicion toward intellectuals was nothing new in America,
where a longstanding cultural tradition exalted common sense over specialized knowledge and practical know-how over theoretical wisdom. In
the 1950s, this tradition found its most notorious political expression in
the person of Joseph McCarthy, whose anticommunist campaign aimed

to discredit intellectuals as threats to the national order. Relatedly, Adlai Stevenson's reflective, eloquent style during the 1952 presidential campaign famously earned him the nickname "egghead" and contributed to the public perception that his seeming populism concealed the heart of a patrician.

Suspicion toward technocratic authority in particular became a major theme in the political upheavals of the 1960s. For activists of the left, fears of nuclear catastrophe and environmental destruction became bases for a more general mistrust of experts affiliated with government and corporate bodies. For example, disillusionment with experts was a major theme in the Port Huron Statement, the 1962 declaration of the Students for a Democratic Society and to some the signature manifesto of the New Left. The statement's authors lamented "the use of modern social science as a manipulative tool" and decried "social and physical scientists," who, "neglecting the liberating heritage of higher learning, develop 'human relations' or 'morale-producing' techniques for the corporate economy, while others exercise their intellectual skills to accelerate the arms race." The core problem, the SDS authors argued, was not so much the use of rationality itself, but the tendency of experts to place their professional self-interests ahead of their concern for the public good. Contrasting the 1960s with the preceding historical period, they argued that if "our liberal and socialist predecessors were plagued by vision without program," then "our own generation is plagued by program without vision. All around us there is astute grasp of method [and] technique . . . but, if pressed critically, such expertise is incompetent to explain its implicit ideals."[11]

A parallel critique of technocratic authority was growing on the political right. Since the 1950s, conservatives in the United States had subjected themselves to a considerable degree of self-scrutiny, much of it on the pages of periodicals such as *Commentary*, *The Public Interest*, the *National Review*, and *Human Events*. The publishers of these journals—men such as Frank Meyer, M. Stanton Evans, and William F. Buckley Jr.—had recently become the architects of a project known as fusionism, which sought to reconstruct conservative philosophy by synthesizing its various strands.[12] During the 1950s, the main ideological fault line on the right was between libertarian and traditionalist varieties of conservatism.[13] Whereas the libertarians identified economic individualism as their central creed, the traditionalists emphasized the need for greater moral order. While the fusionist project would require the articulation of positive conservative principles on which to build consensus, its ultimate success lay also in the identification of a common enemy, or an ideological foil against which the various segments of the right could define themselves. Buckley in particular recognized that, their disagreements aside, the different kinds of conservatives could rally around a common distaste for bureaucrats, technocrats, "pointy-headed intellectuals," "secular humanists," and other experts who had become the architects of liberal reform. Among conservatives, discontent with the social engineering programs of the New Deal had become part of a larger theory about the emergence of a "New Class," or a growing professional elite whose technical knowledge functioned principally as means of self-advancement. Ironically, the New Class concept itself derived from Marxist theory, but the idea had been a recognizable theme in conservative thought at least since 1944, when Friedrich Hayek's *The Road to Serfdom* warned that the self-interests of government bureaucrats were the wellspring of totalitarianism.[14]

By the 1960s, the idea that the growing power of experts represented a threat to the American way of life had gained a firm foothold on both sides of the political spectrum. But progressive and conservative activists alike would soon recognize the peculiar dilemma built into any attempt to undermine or challenge the legitimacy of an expert. To call into question the authority of an expert inevitably meant constituting *oneself* as a kind of expert. As the following organizational vignettes illustrate, the 1960s and 1970s saw the growth of a new breed of "activist-expert" organizations designed to challenge technocratic authority on the terrain of knowledge production. These organizations intensified the struggle in American life over the dominant model of the expert.

"On the Bare Edge of Custom": IPS and the Progressive Critique of Technocracy

In 1963, two progressive activists, Marcus Raskin and Richard Barnet, both lawyers and former Congressional aides, established a new organization to oppose what they viewed as an authoritarian tendency in American politics. Raskin had served as a legislative counsel for several Democratic congressmen and as an aide to McGeorge Bundy, then head of the National Security Council. Barnet had been a foreign affairs officer with the US Arms Control and Disarmament Agency, which later became part of the State Department. While working for the federal government, both men had become disillusioned with what they considered to be harmful abuses of power and a lack of responsiveness to public needs. Raskin later outlined his still-developing "political philosophy of reconstruction" by suggesting that "the basic situation in the United States—and in the twentieth century—can be best described as authoritarianism, and . . . what the resisters are attempting to build is non-hierarchic, and anti-authoritarian institutions."[15] One of the main pillars of Raskin's thought was the idea that American intellectuals, especially academic scholars, had abandoned their moral duties to serve the public good. Barnet concurred: "I was quite struck by the relationship between academics and the government," he told an interviewer about his stint at the State Department. "They were essentially servicing the bureaucracies, not challenging the assumptions. It was a narrow group."[16]

According to Raskin and Barnet, the existing channels through which experts could participate in politics, especially consultancies and contract research, tended to transform them into de facto "supporters of government policies, rather than critics."[17] Experts, they wrote, were never "invited to challenge existing policy (especially the basic premises) much less to suggest or prepare alternatives."[18] Hoping to provide a positive model for public intellectual engagement, Raskin and Barnet created the Institute for Policy Studies in 1963. According to their plan, IPS could not remain content merely to imitate existing technocratic organizations; instead, it must fuse concrete proposals for political action with a broader inquiry into "the nature of scientific, technical and social knowledge" itself.[19]

Raskin and Barnet gathered $200,000 in startup funding for IPS from a collection of foundations before formally launching the organization in October 1963.[20] Arthur Waskow, a historian and IPS fellow, captured the organization's distinctive spirit in these terms: "The Institute is not just an ordinary research center because it's committed to the idea that to develop social theory one must be involved in social action and in social experiment. And therefore, the Institute stands on the bare edge of custom in the United States as to what an educational research institution is, as against what a political institution is. By standing on that bare edge, it creates tension."[21] Raskin was similarly explicit about the need for an ambitious rethinking of the relationship between social thought and public action. In 1968, he wrote that the knowledge needed to construct "non-hierarchic, anti-authoritarian institutions . . . must stem from a nonobjective base—at least as objectivity has come to be understood in the social sciences."[22] His interest in epistemological problems was also signaled in an approving review of Michel Foucault's *The Order of Things* published in July 1971—years before Foucault would become well known outside of a narrow circle of academic scholars, and only one year after Foucault's first visit to the United States.[23]

IPS achieved modest early successes in the 1960s, positioning itself as an occasional consultant to liberal members of Congress and other public officials. For example, the organization sponsored a seminar series that led to the creation of an antiwar congressional caucus called the Members of Congress for Peace Through Law. With support from several foundations, chief among them the Samuel Rubin Foundation, its staff grew to 53 by 1973. During these years, the organization made radical policy proposals on issues such as human rights, homelessness and poverty, race relations, and urban unrest in America.[24] However, as I will discuss below, the organization would soon encounter major financial, legal, and administrative difficulties in its effort to fuse social theory and political action.

Raskin and Barnet were not alone among activists of the left in their attempt to establish new forms of expertise built on moral as opposed to purely technical foundations. In 1970, for example, a coalition of black scholars and politicians founded the Joint Center for Political and Economic Studies to offer training and assistance to aspiring black elected officials. JCPES later expanded its operations to include the study of civil rights issues, especially those related to political participation, the economic advancement of blacks, and the racial dimensions of health policy.[25] Another progressive activist-expert organization was the Worldwatch Foundation, established in 1974 by environmentalist Lester R. Brown. Worldwatch dedicated itself to supporting the nascent environmental movement. Like the other activist-expert organizations of its era, the novelty of its approach rested on a strategy of aggressive public engagement. As one early Worldwatch staff member explains, "We were really one of the first think tanks to really go after [media attention] with a vengeance. We had a theory—it was Lester Brown's theory because he was the founder of Worldwatch—that you should spend half of your time and money" on communications.[26] "That was kind of the overriding theory: communicating to the world your ideas [and] that the Brookings of the world spent ten percent or less of their time and money on communication. And the best ideas in the world were worthless if you couldn't get them out and get them into circulation."

"To Enlighten Public Thinking": The Heritage Foundation and the Conservative Critics of Technocracy

Like their counterparts on the left, a subset of conservative activists dedicated themselves to developing new forms of expertise founded on moral principles. Two key figures in this effort were Paul Weyrich and Edwin Feulner Jr., both Republican legislative aides. Weyrich had begun his career as a newspaper and radio journalist in his home state of Wisconsin before becoming the press secretary to Senator Gordon Allott of Colorado in 1967. Feulner, a PhD recipient from the University of Edinburgh, held a variety of political posts, most notably as an aide to Secretary of Defense Melvin R. Laird and Illinois Congressman Philip Crane.[27] To Weyrich and Feulner, the embodiment of expertise run amok in the 1960s was the Brookings Institution, by then an emblem of Keynesian economic thinking.

Brookings' power was illustrated vividly for Weyrich one day in 1969 when, through an unusual set of circumstances, he found himself sitting in a coalition meeting of civil rights groups.[28] "I just went and nobody asked me who I was or anything. I sat in the back. And there before my eyes was unveiled exactly how the left operates. I saw the effects of it, but I never understood the mechanics," he explained.[29] As Weyrich remembered, the civil rights activists had heard that President Nixon was planning to roll back the civil rights bill on housing. "And so right there before my eyes, they put together a bipartisan amendment between [Indiana senator] Birch Bayh and [Maryland senator Charles] 'Mack' Mathias, who had just been elected." Weyrich watched as the coalition members hammered out an agreement: "Somebody was there from the Brookings Institute [*sic*], and they said, "We've got a study coming out on segregation and housing, and we can do a preprint of the study . . . [to] help you frame the issue." To Weyrich, the presence of a Brookings-affiliated expert at a civil rights strategy meeting represented a major problem for Republicans on Capitol Hill. Above all, it meant that Democrats could draw on the authority of a trusted, seemingly independent group of experts to bolster their arguments.

Weyrich's first impulse was to establish ties with an equivalent organization on the right. At the time, however, the closest conservative counterpart to Brookings was the American Enterprise Institute, an organization first established in 1938 to oppose Depression-era government price and production controls and defend the free enterprise system.[30] Yet with no full-time experts on its staff and an annual budget hovering around $1 million, AEI was a modest operation. Adding to its relative ineffectiveness was the fact that the IRS had recently conducted an investigation into AEI's alleged partisan activity.[31] With his organization's tax-exempt status in jeopardy, AEI president William Baroody had become careful to avoid any hint of partisanship. Weyrich described his first encounter with AEI in 1971: "Among the things that [Senator Allott] had me do was transportation appropriations work. And I one day received an excellent piece of research on the supersonic transport [from AEI]. It had tabs on it, you know, to distinguish the different sections. It was well researched. It had a lot of data, a lot of testimony, if you will, from scientists and so on. There was only one problem with it. It arrived two days after the vote on the SST that killed it." Frustrated by the impracticality of the report, Weyrich and Feulner approached Baroody to try to forge a working partnership: "We went to Bill Baroody, Sr. at American Enterprise Institute and said, 'Are there things that we can work with you on that will produce timely material?' And he said, 'Oh, no, we don't want to produce timely materials. We got in trouble once with the IRS when Lyndon Johnson sicced them on us and so we don't do anything that could be construed as influencing legislation.' And I said, 'Well, then, what are you doing this stuff for? Are you preparing it for libraries? For what?'"[32]

Perplexed by the sight of a conservative organization unwilling to aid its supposed allies in Congress, Weyrich and Feulner decided to form their own organization.[33] "What was needed," Weyrich later wrote, "was an outside operation that could provide timely information to Members of Congress from a principled perspective [and] supply witnesses for hearings and experts to privately brief senators and congressmen."[34] Weyrich and Feulner joined forces with two other young conservatives, Victor Fediay of the Library of Congress and Jim Lucier Sr., an aide to South Carolina Senator Strom Thurmond, in an effort to raise startup money.[35] A key breakthrough came when Weyrich read a letter sent to Allott's office from a man named Jack Wilson. As Weyrich remembers, "The letter said, 'You may remember me, Senator, I used to be news director at KBTR in Denver and I have now been hired by Joe Coors to find out where is the best place to put his money to help the conservative movement.'"[36] Weyrich invited Coors to Washington to hear the group's pitch:

> So Joe [Coors] came up, and we had him meet with two congressmen and two senators and the administrative assistant to the vice-president, and Lyn Nofziger, who at that time was Reagan's man in the Nixon White House. I had them all wired, and they all said we've got to have an operation that gets us information at strategic times. We are not getting it now. There is nobody that is providing it. Brookings is very, very active on the left—they are omnipresent—but we don't have anything on the right. And so eventually Joe bought that and we started up what is now the Heritage Foundation.[37]

Coors supplied $260,000 in start-up funding for the organization, and the Heritage Foundation opened its doors in 1973 with Weyrich serving as its first president.

The founding of Heritage took place at a pivotal moment in American economic history. Although big business had been successful in resisting the New Deal's expansion for roughly a generation, so far it had failed to challenge the basic orthodoxy that state intervention in the economy was both legitimate and necessary. The economic dislocations of the early 1970s, however, intensified the issue's urgency in the minds of American business leaders. As supply shocks led to an extraordinary combination of high inflation and declining productivity, wage, and gross domestic product (GDP) growth, the competitive status of American goods declined overseas and negative trade balances emerged in various industrial sectors. The members of a growing "business conservative movement" made the argument that the New Deal era measures once designed to protect workers, consumers, and the environment were no longer viable in an era of floating exchange rates and heightened international competition.[38]

Sensing a major political opportunity, several key conservatives urged business leaders to fund new organs of conservative thought. In 1971, for example, attorney (and soon to be Supreme Court justice) Lewis F. Powell Jr. famously warned the US Chamber of Commerce that "the American economic system is under broad attack" from "perfectly respectable elements of society," including the "college campus, the pulpit, the media, the intellectual and literary journals, [and] the arts and sciences."[39] In Powell's view, business leaders in the United States had long shown "little skill in effective intellectual and philosophical debate," resulting in a pitiable state of political exclusion. In fact, Powell argued, "few elements of American society today have as little influence in government as the American businessman, the corporation, or even the millions of corporate stockholders." Worse yet, he argued, through their taxes, contributions, and personal service as board members, businessmen actively supported the very cultural institutions that, if given the chance, would see to their demise. Only a vigorous campaign of intellectual self-defense could rehabilitate the image of free enterprise. More than mere public relations, the effort would require "careful long-range planning" and the implementation of "educational programs . . . designed to enlighten public thinking."

The call for a conservative "counter-intelligentsia" was echoed in other quarters as well. Another leader of the effort was William E. Simon, a businessman and Treasury secretary under Presidents Nixon and Ford. Like Powell, Simon became a vocal proponent of the idea that business should fund new intellectual organs aimed at changing the basic "assumptions and goals presently underlying our political life."[40] Also joining the campaign to win business support for conservative thought was Irving Kristol, a member of the loosely connected circle of New York intellectuals known as the neoconservatives.[41] In the early 1970s, Kristol wrote a series of op-ed pieces for the *Wall Street Journal* urging businessmen to sponsor new organs of conservative research and discussion. In one piece, for example, he chided corporations for their unprincipled giving patterns and suggested that supporting conservative causes was less a choice than a duty: "When you give away your money, you can be as foolish, as arbitrary, as whimsical as you like," Kristol wrote. "But when you give away your stockholders' money, your philanthropy must serve the longer-term interests of the corporation. Corporate philanthropy should not be, and cannot be, disinterested." In another piece, Kristol echoed Powell's views about the underdog status of big business by calling the American corporation "largely defenseless, a nice big fat juicy target for every ambitious politician and a most convenient scapegoat for every variety of discontent."[42]

A series of major conservative donors were emerging during this era, including Richard Mellon Scaife, Lynde and Harry Bradley, John M. Olin, Joseph Coors, and members of the Koch and Richardson families. Mostly second- and third-generation businessmen from successful entrepreneurial families, they created a systematic program of support for organizations dedicated to promoting the philosophy of free enterprise. Olin, for example, an Illinois chemical and munitions manufacturer, directed his philanthropic giving to conservative causes after antiwar activities at his alma mater, Cornell University, convinced him that left-wing radicalism posed a major threat to the free enterprise system. Before closing its doors in 2005, the Olin Foundation made nearly $400 million in contributions, much of it to think tanks and academic programs dedicated to free market thought—most notably the John M. Olin School of Business at Washington University. Headed by William E. Simon for 23 years, the foundation also supplied grants to individual conservative thinkers, such as William Bennett, Allan Bloom, Robert Bork, Dinesh D'Souza, Samuel Huntington, Irving Kristol, and Charles Murray.[43]

Together the conservative philanthropists underwrote a multifaceted institution-building project that supported the growth of legal foundations, television programs, magazines and journals, and political action committees (see table 3.1). In addition to the Heritage Foundation, key beneficiaries of this project included the Cato Institute and the Manhattan Institute. Cato, a libertarian organization founded in 1977 by Edward H.

TABLE 3.1 **Major beneficiaries of conservative philanthropy. Source: Jerome L. Himmelstein. 1990. *To the Right: The Transformation of American Conservatism*. Berkeley: University of California Press.**

Organization Type	Examples
Political action committees	American Conservative Union (1964) GOPAC (1978)
Public television shows	Milton Friedman, "Free to Choose" (1980) Ben Wattenberg, "In Search of the Real America" (1977)
Magazines and journals	*The Public Interest* (1965) *The American Spectator* (1967) *The New Criterion* (1982)
Foreign policy groups	Committee on the Present Danger Committee for the Free World
Legal foundations	Pacific Legal Foundation (1973) National Legal Center for the Public Interest (1975)
Lobbying & trade associations	Business Roundtable (1972)
University outreach	Endowed professorships for probusiness faculty University research centers (eg, Mercatus Center) The Collegiate Network (campus newspapers) (1979)
Independent scholars	Jude Wanniski, *The Way the World Works* (1978) George Gilder, *Wealth and Poverty* (1981) Bruce Bartlett, *Reaganomics* (1981)
Think tanks	American Enterprise Institute (1938) Center for Strategic and International Studies (1962) Heritage Foundation (1973) Cato Institute (1977) Manhattan Institute (1978) Competitive Enterprise Institute (1984)

Crane, a financial analyst and former vice president at the Alliance Capital Management Corporation, was bankrolled largely by Kansas businessmen Charles and David Koch. Another major recipient of conservative funding was the Manhattan Institute, formed in New York in 1978 by British businessman Antony Fischer and former Nixon administration official William J. Casey. Conservative philanthropists also supported the expansion or refurbishment of older policy institutes such as the Hoover Institution (founded in 1919), the Hudson Institute (1961), and the Center for Strategic and International Studies, created in 1962 as a research institute at Georgetown University. However, it is another conservative organization whose fortunes rose dramatically in the 1970s, the American Enterprise Institute, that I will now consider in greater detail.

*"We Were All Friends, and It Sparkled": The American Enterprise Institute
in the 1970s*

The 1970s was a prosperous decade for the American Enterprise Institute,
the organization that Paul Weyrich and Edwin Feulner had once considered too timid to count on for ideological support. During the first half of
the decade, sponsorship from the growing business conservative movement transformed AEI into a major player on the policy research scene.
The organization saw its budget quadruple from $1 million to more than
$4 million, largely on the strength of corporate donations. With an original
trustee list that included executives from General Mills, Bristol-Myers,
Eli Lilly, Chrysler, and Chemical Bank, AEI had long been positioned
to benefit from an increase in corporate giving. As the 1970s continued,
executives from Mobil Oil, Standard Oil of California, Continental Can,
Procter & Gamble, Rockwell International, and Libbey-Owens-Ford also
signed on to AEI's board.[44]

The flood of money allowed AEI's president, William Baroody, to expand his organization's research and communications functions considerably. The year 1972 marked a particular turning point, as AEI named
its first resident scholar, Gottfried Haberler, a Harvard economist and
longtime member of the institute's advisory board. Other notable staff
additions during this time included Irving Kristol, political scientist Ben
Wattenberg, future Supreme Court justice Antonin Scalia, and Jude Wan-
niski, who came aboard AEI while on leave from the *Wall Street Journal*
to write the supply-side economics bible, *The Way the World Works*. In
1974, AEI started the first of several new research divisions, the Center for
Health Policy Research. The organization also began publishing two new
magazines, *Regulation* and *Public Opinion*.

As the Ford administration ended in 1977, more talent flowed to AEI,
including Gerald Ford himself, who was named an AEI distinguished fellow. Other members of the new cohort included economists Arthur Burns
and Laurence Silberman and future Supreme Court nominee Robert H.
Bork, who headed AEI's Legal Policy center.[45] Silberman described the
influx of thinkers in terms of a "synergistic impact": "We were all friends,
and it sparkled. A cross-pollination took place."[46] By the end of the decade, AEI's annual budget had grown ten-fold and now approached the
$10 million mark. Longtime AEI fellow Norm Ornstein reflects on the
significance of this period: "The real initial flowering of AEI was during
the Carter years, when the business community . . . felt the need to have

some center for ideas and believed at the time, and I think legitimately so, that most universities were not going to fit that bill because they were more liberal in their orientation."[47] As the decade drew to a close, AEI received $1 million bequests from each of four companies—Weyerhaeuser, Potlatch, Ford, and Reader's Digest—to create endowed chairs.[48] By 1981, the share of its revenue drawn directly from corporations had grown to 40 percent, up from 25 percent five years earlier.[49]

"One Had Better Be Aware of One's Competition": Brookings Opens Up

The 1960s and 1970s saw a proliferation of new "activist-expert" organizations meant to challenge technocratic authority from a position of greater public openness. But what effect did this development have on the technocratic research organizations that had emerged during the early and middle parts of the twentieth century? Let me address this question by offering a snapshot of the organization that had become the quintessential supplier of technocratic knowledge in American politics: the Brookings Institution. Targeted by activists of both the right and the left, Brookings found itself in a position of unexpected adversity by the end of the 1970s. My argument in this section is that Brookings, like other organizations of its ilk, responded to these challenges by "opening" up its knowledge, or becoming less esoteric and more responsive to an audience consisting of journalists and mass media institutions.

The 1970s had begun on a positive note for Brookings. Longtime fellow Stephen Hess remembers that when he came aboard the organization in 1972, "Brookings was rich," and in some ways, "the only game in town."[50] As the decade began, Brookings held fast to the technocratic principles that had long sustained it. In 1972, for example, a memorandum circulated within the organization reminding Brookings staff members that its reputation was enhanced when its experts provided "substantive information and technical assistance" directly to policy makers. Brookings fellows succeeded, the memo said, by "serving on government commissions or task forces, participating as consultants to government departments, testifying before legislative committees, briefing legislative groups or their staffs on specific public policy issues, and speaking to or advising private organizations."[51] Public visibility, on the other hand, was not central to the Brookings mission. "We worked on books and studies," says Brookings fellow Alice Rivlin, "but we were not so oriented to getting a message out. In fact, it was almost negative. . . . It wasn't somehow quite seemly for a scholarly organization to be pushing its products. Something like that. You should do research, you should publish, you should go to conferences, but you shouldn't be too focused on the media."[52]

In fact, Rivlin remembers doing a stint as an editorialist for the *Washington Post* in the early 1970s:

> That was viewed with some—well, I'm not quite sure what the word is, but it was viewed negatively. My then boss, Joe Pechman, said, "You shouldn't be doing so much newspaper writing. You'll lose the respect of your professional colleagues." I was relatively young and he was a sort of mentor relationship. It was a friendly "For your own career's sake, you should be focusing more on books and journal articles and not so much on newspaper writing."

As Stephen Hess explains, even the most intellectually serious forms of news media engagement were frowned upon at Brookings. For example, Hess remembers reluctantly declining an invitation from journalists Jim Lehrer and Robert McNeil to join the PBS television coverage of the Watergate hearings when his boss, Brookings president Kermit Gordon, disapproved of the idea.[53]

Soon, however, Brookings was compelled to change its strategy. The first setback it faced was a financial loss incurred in the 1973–74 stock market decline that lowered the organization's endowment from its 1972 high-water mark of $50.1 million to $33.4 million in 1978.[54] In 1976, Gordon, the organization's third president, died after nine years in office, the shortest term of any Brookings leader to date. In choosing his successor, the Brookings trustees saw a need to address the organization's unwanted reputation as a "government-in-exile" for Democratic Party officials. They selected Bruce K. MacLaury, a Republican and former Nixon Treasury official. As one Brookings fellow explains, MacLaury "was chosen because he was a moderate conservative, a former Federal Reserve Bank chair. And his tenure was keeping the boat more or less on an even keel and sailing straight."[55] The most immediate threat to Brookings, however, was growing competition from its surging rivals—especially the American Enterprise Institute. By 1977, the *Washington Post* could already argue that AEI had "eliminated the monopoly Brookings had held for decades as the nation's premier think tank."[56] Three years later, Ronald Reagan's election to the presidency marked the Heritage Foundation's entry into the policy research big leagues. Heritage supplied eleven members of Reagan's transition team and numerous administration officials. Nevertheless, its most important contribution to the Reagan presidency was *Mandate for Leadership*, a 1,000-page transition manual for the new administration.[57] The hefty guide, which the *Post* later called "the bible of the Reagan transition," laid out a series of policy prescriptions that touched on every agency of the federal government.[58] According to Weyrich, "Reagan, at his first cabinet meeting, handed out the book and said, 'This is a blueprint to run the administration. I want you to follow it.' And it was at that point that Heritage's credibility just soared. I mean, word of that got around and all of a sudden Heritage was an important institution."[59]

Recognizing its newly embattled position, the Brookings Institution entered a period of administrative soul-searching and active reorganization. In September 1981, the trustees retained the services of a management consulting firm, Barnes & Roche, to carry out a study of Brookings' plans and programs, considered "in the broadest terms."[60] According to internal documentation from the period, the move was prompted by a "recognition that straitened financial circumstances may make Brookings less competitive" in the near future, carrying "pervasive implications for long term fund-raising potential."[61] The consultants interviewed Brookings staff members at all levels and issued a diagnostic report. Its main conclusion was that Brookings was now operating in "a substantially changed climate in which measures from the 'old times' are no longer applicable." In particular, the consultants argued, there were two areas in which Brookings was now at a disadvantage. The first was fundraising. Whereas Brookings could once count on recurring donations from large philanthropic foundations, the growing trend among donors was toward shorter-term, more targeted giving. Since Brookings had only a "limited file" on prospective donors, the consultants advised, it would benefit from a more "centralized, coordinated" approach. The consultants also urged Brookings to broaden its donor base, especially by targeting corporations.

The second problem the consultants noted involved "the repeated failures of Brookings to communicate effectively with various segments of its constituency." More to the point, the consultants were recommending that Brookings create a *new* constituency by engaging the general public. "By contemporary standards," they wrote, "the Brookings Institution does not have a public relations program." To earn widespread attention, Brookings should adapt its work to the needs of journalists, especially by shortening the length of its studies. As the consultants wrote, "One commentator characterized it succinctly, 'In 1931 the way to communicate one's analysis of a problem was to write a book. And, in 1981 we are still writing books.'" The presence of rival organizations more willing to take part in public debate made Brookings seem comparatively detached and exclusive. The overall tone of the Barnes & Roche report was distilled in its final sentences: "The Brookings setting is at a point of significant change. The research staff keenly feels the changes and the pressure of transition which press on their organization."

MacLaury responded to the consultants' report by instituting a series of corrective measures. He appointed a full-time public relations officer to help Brookings become, in his words, "more professional in our outreach to the public and the press."[62] Brookings also increased the number of its public briefing sessions and instituted a weekly lunch series for members of the Washington press corps. In 1982, the organization began publishing the *Brookings Review*, a quarterly journal featuring articles and commentaries from its fellows. Brookings also started a "Discussion Papers" series and a periodical called the *Brookings Dialogues on Public Policy*, which ran excerpts from its books. The threat posed by the new policy institutes, especially those of the ideological right, was an explicit motivation for the shift in strategy. As MacLaury told the *New York Times*, "One had better be aware of one's competition. We saw that in certain areas we were not up to speed. . . . We had to take some lessons from our more aggressive competition, like AEI, in the public affairs field."[63]

The consulting firm's advice had come as no surprise. Two years earlier, the Brookings directors had already begun a gradual about-face in their attitude toward news media coverage. For example, the minutes of a January 1979 program directors' meeting summarized an official change in organizational policy toward public outreach: "It was agreed that . . . research staff members be encouraged to write newspaper op-ed pieces and articles for magazines such as *Harper's, Atlantic, Saturday Review*, etc., based on congressional testimony, work in progress, and work recently completed."[64] An accompanying memo instructed the Brookings program directors to "inform their staff . . . that writing for publication in mass media is a legitimate use of their time."[65] In 1983, Brookings fellow Gilbert Steiner told the *New York Times*, "The new competition of recent years . . . has in very overt fashion changed the character of our product. There is less a disposition to produce complete analyses in book form, and a more pronounced disposition to comment in either testimony, short form or very brief monographic form."[66] At the same time, the shift in strategy led to a greater dependence on corporate funding, which in turn gave rise to fierce disputes within the organization over the protection of academic freedom. The *Times* reported on the rift in 1985: "This is a university without students," said Herbert Kaufman, a [Brookings] political scientist. "But at a university, the trustees don't say, 'Why don't you do this or that?'" Mr. MacLaury responded: "There is always the question about the role of the trustee, particularly with regard to academic freedom. But we are a think tank. We are not a university."[67]

As Brookings reoriented itself, the Heritage Foundation continued to grow. By 1983, the Heritage budget reached $10 million, a milestone the organization celebrated by moving into a new eight-story, $9.5 million building on Capitol Hill. In just a decade, Heritage had grown from a "total upstart," in Paul Weyrich's words, to one of the leading conservative organizations in the country. In 1983, William Rusher, the publisher of the *National Review*, called Heritage's rise "probably the biggest development in the conservative movement during the decade of the 1970s . . . absolutely indispensable."[68] New York congressman Jack Kemp expressed a similar sentiment in a message to Heritage trustee Clare Boothe Luce: "I'm convinced that the Heritage Foundation is the single most important intellectual 'bank' for our growing 'positive conservatism' in America and the world."[69] Recognizing an opportunity for further growth, Heritage launched an aggressive fundraising campaign known as "Heritage 10: Funding the Conservative Decade" designed to raise $35 million for an operating reserve, a building fund, and an endowment for the organization's Asian Studies Center. The initiative succeeded even beyond its planners' expectations, bringing in $37 million by 1986. At a black-tie gala celebrating the campaign's success, Shelby Cullom Davis, chairman of the Heritage Board of Trustees, called the money "a solid financial base that allows us to look forward to the next decade with greater optimism."[70]

The Birth of the Think Tank: A Reinterpretation

At one level, the preceding narrative may seem to fit quite well with the existing body of knowledge about the recent history of think tanks. After all, among scholars and journalists there is general agreement that American think tanks underwent some kind of major transformation starting in the 1960s. Not only was there a dramatic growth in the number of think tanks, on this view, but the new organizations exhibited a different *style* of intellectual production as well. Newly founded think tanks such as the Heritage Foundation and the Cato Institute were more oriented than their predecessors to the news media, more likely to adopt ideological positions, and better equipped for the rapid-response production of short, synthetic materials as opposed to long-term research. Partly in response to their new competitors, but also in reaction to wider changes in the sociopolitical environment, many older think tanks began to adopt the tactics pioneered by the newer "advocacy tanks" (to use R. Kent Weaver's expression).[71] While maintaining their claims to ideological neutrality, certain long-established think tanks, such as the Brookings Institution and the Council on Foreign Relations, also shifted toward faster, shorter, and more media-oriented production.

Repeated in various forms, this "transformation thesis" has become the standard scholarly narrative about the recent history of think tanks. Without denying any of the basic facts on which it is built, I would argue that the story is incomplete in two ways that tend to impede our overall understanding of think tanks. The first, which was signaled in chapter 2, is that the transformation thesis rests on an anachronistic think tank concept. Put differently, any story of transformation implies the prior existence of the thing being transformed. And yet I would argue that in an important sense, the process I have just described is better understood as the birth of think tanks, or better still, as the *genesis of the space of think tanks*. There was something appropriate in Brookings president Bruce MacLaury's defense against the charge, made largely by members of his own staff, that Brookings had abandoned its commitment to academic freedom: "But we are a think tank," he said. "We are not a university."[72] The point I would like to make is that in a sense both parties to this dispute were correct. Brookings had undeniably become less oriented to the norms of academic production than it had been in the previous era. In the 1970s a new set of forces compelled the organization and its technocratic cousins to angle their work more to the market and the media. Yet Brookings' transformation was neither the result of a deliberate abandonment of its academic principles nor an isolated, organization-level shift. Instead, its reorientation must be understood as the result of the imposition of market and media forces by other organizations in the context of their growing mutual orientation. At once competitive, collaborative, and mimetic, this mutual orientation gave rise to a new organizational category in political, folk, and academic discourses. Brookings, in a sense, *became* a think tank as the organizational species was created through a process of intensifying competition over the prototype of the politically relevant expert in the United States. In terms of the theoretical model sketched above, this process took the form of a "race to the center" of the field of expertise.

The second problem with the conventional scholarly narrative about the recent history of think tanks lies in its rather superficial focus on surface-level changes, such as organizational proliferation, and the corresponding neglect of the social logic underpinning these shifts. Insofar as scholars have tried to identify any unifying tendency in the process described here, their focus has rested on the so-called "politicization" of think tanks—or their tendency to embrace ideological advocacy over neutral, disinterested inquiry. This argument is signaled, for example, in the title of McGann's article, "From Academics to Ideologues," and in Rich's argument that the role of think tanks "has become one focused more on providing skewed commentary than neutral analysis."[73] I believe these claims are problematic because they falsely imply that think tanks were ever neutral to begin with. As we saw in chapter 2, most of the precursors of the think tank were also founded by activist sponsors for quite specific political purposes. Brookings, for example, was established by budget reform advocates during the height of the Progressive Era with a specific policy goal in mind. And while it is certainly true that the post-1960s organizations were more "ideological" by a contemporary definition of the term, when pressed too far this argument becomes tautological. After all, from a broader standpoint, the new organizations reflected a historical shift in what it meant to be "ideological." On this view, it was the content—not the degree—of ideological position taking that changed. One could argue, for example, that the research centers established during the Progressive Era were equally "ideological" in their adherence to the dominant political ideology of that period: namely, the ideology of pragmatic social reform guided by technical expertise. Likewise, the military planning groups of the postwar period embodied the technocratic ideology of the Cold War era, itself built on a belief in the superiority of capitalist democracy over its political-economic alternatives. From this standpoint, it makes little sense to speak of any period in the history of think tanks in terms of "politicization." Instead, it is better to think of their history as a sedimentary layering of ideologies, each representing a specific understanding of the proper political role of experts.

The theoretical framework I have outlined for this chapter avoids both of these problems by changing the explanandum of the discussion, or the thing being explained. First of all, it suggests that we understand the term *think tank* as referring to a *political folk category* corresponding to the formation of a new subspace of knowledge production situated at the crossroads of the academic, political, bureaucratic, media, and economic fields in the United States. How did this subspace form? My answer has been that the main process leading to its development was a structural convergence between the technocratic research organizations of the early and mid-twentieth century and the emerging activist-expert organizations, which challenged their authority from a standpoint of greater "openness" in the field of expertise. Whereas the activists aspired to be experts as part of a strategy to certify or "close" their knowledge, the technocrats needed to "open" their knowledge to offset the charge of civic disengagement made possible by their close ties to the state. The activists thus posed themselves as representatives of a new form of expertise that valorized public engagement and moral argumentation over pure technical proficiency. The technocrats, meanwhile, were compelled to pursue a strategy based on increased public engagement. Once media-shy, most began to shorten their written work, accelerate the pace of its production, and shift their resources toward promotion and dissemination.

I have focused on how this process unfolded at the Brookings Institution in particular, but it is important to see that parallel changes were taking place at the other technocratic organizations as well. Not surprisingly, the longest holdout was the policy research organization marked by the highest level of closure—the Council on Foreign Relations. But even at CFR, a process of opening occurred. By 1988, the organization was engaged in what it described as a comprehensive effort "to cover more 'hot' issues and to bring a diversity of views to these issues" and "to launch a program of 'reaching out' more to the public at large."[74] As CFR's annual report summarized, "We have added our first full-time Public Affairs Director, who has already dramatically expanded media coverage of our various activities."[75] CFR also began staging town hall meetings and shortening the length of its publications: "Over time . . . the number of book-length publications probably will decline as Senior Fellows concentrate more on articles, monographs, and occasional papers."[76] The next year, CFR reported on its efforts to open up its knowledge in a different way: namely, by expanding its membership list, both numerically and in terms of social representation: "the Board of Directors charged the Membership Committee with a mandate to strengthen significantly certain demographic segments of the membership currently underrepresented—in particular, women, minorities, labor leaders, and members of the scientific community—as well as to broaden the geographic base beyond the East Coast."[77] The impact of the initiative, CFR noted, "has been dramatic: . . . The numbers of women and minorities elected in 1989 (31 percent and 16 percent, respectively, of the 170 new members) are both records in the history of the Council."[78]

It is worth pointing out another advantage of the model I have suggested. Although much of this discussion has rested on a distinction between technocratic and activist-expert organizations, let me emphasize that I do not mean these terms to stand for wholly distinct organizational "types," but rather for a set of positions in the field of expertise. A typological representation would be at once too static and too essentialist to capture the subtleties of this process. After all, as chapter 2 showed, the technocrats were once "activist-experts" themselves, having originally been more open in their intellectual production. Many of their organizations were founded with the express purpose of "enlightening public debate." They closed their knowledge gradually by developing new forms of expertise (such as systems analysis) and establishing close ties to the state. Likewise for the activist-expert organizations of the 1960s and 1970s, "success" meant migrating toward the center of the field of expertise, or becoming more technocratic. The Heritage Foundation, for example, which had once been able to portray itself as an "outsider" organization because of its formal separation from the state and the party, quickly became more of an "insider" organization as conservatives took over the White House and the Republican Party.

Indeed, it would be a mistake to overstate the degree to which Heritage was ever truly composed of "outsiders," since its main difference from other activist-expert organizations was always its comparatively close ties to conservatives in Congress. As Paul Weyrich explained, Heritage's early strategy was to exploit these ties:

> We targeted the Hill and our niche was to be very responsive to whatever need was expressed. In the meantime, I went and helped organize the Republican Study Committee and it became a generator of [research] requests. Likewise, in 1974, Dick Thompson and I, along with Senators Curtis and [James A.] McClure, organized the Senate Steering Committee, and again, it became a generator of requests. Both of these are caucuses of conservative members, and so when they knew that there was an institution that was available, they would write us a letter and say, "Can you do a study on such-and-such?" Very quickly, the number of requests far exceeded our ability to meet them. And so we had the problem of picking and choosing which we were going to answer positively.[79]

Put differently, Heritage was able to balance openness and closure in the field of expertise by portraying itself as an outsider organization while nonetheless maintaining ties in the government. The Republican Study Committee in particular played a key role in its early success. In 1983, for example, RSC director Don E. Eberly described the caucus as "basically a conduit . . . from the Heritage Foundation to and from conservative members of the House."[80]

Terra Obscura: Think Tanks as an Interstitial Field

In sum, then, the think tank category developed through the formation of a field-like network of organizations with its own interior structure and dynamic, albeit one that was nonetheless highly dependent on the more established spheres of academia, politics, business, and the media. To round out this historical picture, let me turn now to three specific aspects of the crystallization of the space of think tanks that continued into the 1990s and 2000s: first, the growth of network ties and formal linkages among organizations; second, the invention of new intellectual products and practices by the members of this network; and third, the creation of bodies of folk, professional, and academic knowledge about "think tanks." Together these processes contributed to the installation of the think tank category in the social world.

Network Ties and Formal Linkages

As we have seen, the explosion of policy research centers after 1970 increased the competition for funding, media visibility, and political attention. However, to focus only on this competition would be to miss the concurrent tendency toward collaboration among think tanks. As the *New York Times* pointed out in a 1982 article on the recent proliferation of think tanks in the nation's capital,

> There is much cross-fertilization, or what [C. Fred] Bergsten calls "synergism," among the senior staff members of the competing institutions. They attend each other's meetings, go to each other's lunches, keep track of each other's studies. There is also some crossover. William R. Cline, a senior fellow at Brookings, was one of the first staff members hired [at IIE] by Mr. Bergsten, who himself had been at Carnegie and Brookings.[81]

The tendency was also apparent in the multiplication of formal ties among think tanks during the 1990s. In 1992, for example, the Heritage Foundation established the State Policy Network, a concatenation of state-level conservative think tanks united in the mission of "working in the trenches at the forefront of the movement for free market policy solutions."[82] (As of 2011, this network consisted of 59 think tanks in all 50 states and more than 150 "associate member" organizations.[83]) Other prominent partnerships also developed among think tanks in the ensuing years. In 1998, for example, AEI and Brookings joined forces to form the AEI-Brookings Joint Center for Regulatory Studies, and in 2002 the Urban Institute and Brookings Institution cofounded the Tax Policy Center, a group of experts in tax, budget, and social policy.

More numerous still were the many short-term partnerships among think tanks through jointly sponsored conferences, symposia, and publications. For example, in May 2004, no fewer than eight major think tanks, running the full ideological gamut from the liberal Center on Budget and Policy Priorities to the conservative Heritage Foundation, co-sponsored a conference called "Restoring Fiscal Sanity—While We Still Can."[84] As the president of the Committee for Economic Development, one of the event's co-sponsors, explained in an interview, "We have friends and colleagues at virtually every one of the think tanks you can mention. . . . I mean, it's a friendly, collaborative community, in my view. It's not a zero-sum game."[85] Another sign of interconnectedness can be found in the considerable level of personnel movement among think tanks. Figure 3.3 offers a partial illustration of this traffic based on the past organizational affiliations reported by the staff members at 22 major think tanks, as drawn from a database of educational and career backgrounds compiled in 2004. A few notable patterns emerge from the data, such as the tendency of certain think tanks to recruit from others (e.g., Brookings from the Council on Foreign Relations, and the Institute for International Economics and Hoover from Brookings; CSIS from the London-based International Institute for Strategic Studies). Second, we can see that certain think tanks are major nodes in this network, while others exist at its periphery. Brookings, for example, connects several organizations not otherwise linked via direct personnel movement. The data also suggest the importance of geography in the recruitment patterns of think tanks. For example, RAND and Hoover (both located in California) share a strong personnel connection, despite their structural dissimilarities, and each is tied more weakly to the main Washington think tanks.

As the space of think tanks became more internally cohesive, its center of gravity shifted to the nation's capital. Accordingly, many think tanks founded outside of Washington—such as the Hudson Institute, the

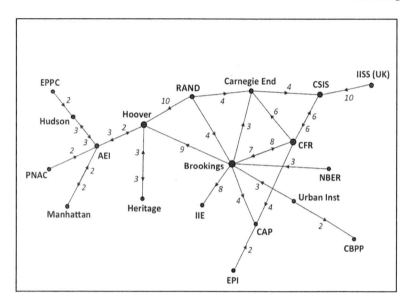

FIGURE 3.3 Personnel movement among major think tanks.

Council on Foreign Relations, the National Center for Policy Analysis, and the Century Foundation—either moved to or set up branches in the District of Columbia. Given the increasing concentration of think tanks in Washington, it should come as no surprise that there is a rough intelligibility to the physical layout of think tanks within the city. To anyone familiar with the world of Washington think tanks, in fact, the patterns are fairly obvious (see figure 3.4). For example, located side by side along the famous "Think Tank Row" in Dupont Circle are several older think tanks with extensive ties to academic institutions and philanthropic foundations, including the Carnegie Endowment for International Peace and the Brookings Institution. Moving south toward Foggy Bottom, the neighborhood long associated with the diplomatic and foreign policy communities, one finds several foreign policy think tanks clustered around the US State Department. These include the Washington Institute for Near East Policy, the Stimson Center, and the Washington branch of the Council on Foreign Relations. Meanwhile, on or near K Street, the downtown thoroughfare widely known as the headquarters of the lobbying industry, are several think tanks that bear more than a passing resemblance to lobbying firms. As the figure shows, organizations such as the Cato Institute and the

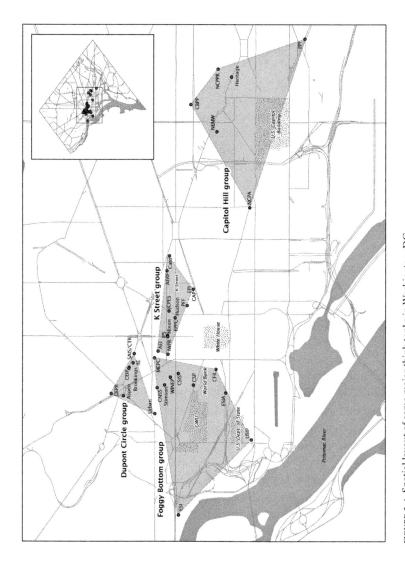

FIGURE 3.4 Spatial layout of some major think tanks in Washington, DC.

Center for American Progress are situated in this cluster. Finally, located on Capitol Hill is a small set of think tanks that are oriented to direct legislative action, such as the Heritage Foundation and the Center on Budget and Policy Priorities.[86]

The purpose of this figure is not to suggest that the world of think tanks has a perfectly intelligible spatial structure. Neither is it to imply that think tanks divide cleanly into types. (Indeed, I will argue against this point in the next chapter.) Instead, its purpose is to show that a degree of coherence marks the geographic arrangement of think tanks in Washington, which in turn contributes to the overall sense of their embeddedness in a field-like system.

Distinctive Products and Practices

As think tanks became more interconnected, they converged on certain modes of intellectual production distinct from those of academia. For example, most think tanks turned to writing shorter, synthetic policy reports (known variously as "policy briefs," "backgrounder reports," or "issue briefs") on faster schedules, rather than conducting original empirical research.[87] In contrast to the length, rigor, and technicality of a scholarly book or article, the defining marks of the policy memo were its brevity, accessibility, and utility to journalists and politicians. More than any other organization, it was the Heritage Foundation that pioneered the invention of policy memos, through its *Backgrounder Report* series. The key innovation was to establish an informal yardstick for establishing their proper length: the so-called "briefcase test." As one Heritage fellow puts it, "The test was if the Congressman could put it in his briefcase and read it going to National Airport . . . then, okay, he might find some use in it and take the arguments and rely upon those in the debate about a particular issue."[88] Other think tanks have established formal templates and guidelines for the production of policy memos. One example is the Competitive Enterprise Institute, which issued a reference manual called the *Field Guide for Effective Communication* to its staff members.

The other major intellectual genre pioneered by think tanks was the presidential transition manual. Again, it was the Heritage Foundation that led the way in this development. By all accounts, Heritage's watershed moment was the 1980 publication of *Mandate for Leadership*. As Paul Weyrich explained, the idea for *Mandate* came from a story Weyrich heard from J. William Mittendorf, a Heritage trustee and former Secretary of the

Navy. According to Mittendorf, on the night of Richard Nixon's election in November 1968, former Secretary of Agriculture Fred Seton and former Attorney General Herbert Brownell brought Nixon "a briefing book, a blueprint, if you will, of how the administration should proceed on practically every issue imaginable."[89] Weyrich relayed the story to Robert J. Perry, a Houston homebuilder and Republican donor, who gave Weyrich the money to put together a similar briefing book. (Perry later funded the Swift Boat Veterans for Truth organization whose criticism dogged John Kerry's 2004 presidential run.) Personal contacts in the White House then helped Heritage disseminate *Mandate* to Reagan officials. Reagan advisor Edwin Meese III, a personal friend of Joseph Coors and a Heritage supporter since the organization's inception, became the manual's leading promoter in the White House.[90]

To other organizations, *Mandate*'s success suggested that a well-constructed transition manual could quickly catapult a relatively new organization into the elite tier of think tanks.[91] "Four years ago, we started a fad," a Heritage staff member told the *Washington Post* in 1984 as the Cato Institute, the Hudson Institute, and AEI all released major policy documents to coincide with Reagan's second inauguration and the start of the Ninety-Ninth Congress."[92] Referring to Heritage's success with *Mandate*, Cato president Edward H. Crane acknowledged, "I guess maybe it did give us the idea."[93] The transition manual blitz continued in 1988, with no fewer than thirty-six policy guides written for incoming President George H. W. Bush, most of them by think tanks.[94] A week after the election, the *Washington Post* reported that, "Self-appointed advisers to the transition team are Washington's latest cottage industry, publishing policy guides, holding workshops and setting up press conferences complete with dinners and dazzle in an effort to sway policy and personnel decisions in the coming administration."[95] The end of a 12-year run of Republican presidents in 1992 gave think tanks aligned with the Democratic Party a chance to participate in this trend. As Bill Clinton took office, the Progressive Policy Institute released its foundational document, *Mandate for Change*. William Galston, a central figure at PPI and later a domestic policy adviser in the Clinton White House, acknowledges PPI's debt to Heritage:

INTERVIEWER: So do you think [PPI's] significance was comparable to Heritage Foundation in the early '80s?

RESPONDENT: Very much so. And, as a matter of fact, our most significant official contribution to the Clinton campaign was conceived very much on the same lines as Heritage's *Mandate for Leadership* twelve years earlier. And this is right down to the selection of the title, right? So absolutely.[96]

While other scholars have documented many of these specific changes, the conventional scholarly approach offers an insufficient account of its central logic. Put simply, my argument is that the formation of an organizational network of think tanks gave rise to common criteria of judgment, which in turn gave rise to standard products and practices that were useful in differentiating policy experts from potential rivals in the field of expertise, including academic scholars. Think tanks carved out an institutional niche located structurally in between academia, politics, the media, and the market.

The Growth of Knowledge about Think Tanks

Finally, I would point out that as the space of think tanks acquired field-like properties, new bodies of folk, professional, and social scientific knowledge about them began to develop. We can begin by noting the growing use of the term *think tank* itself in public discourse. Figure 3.5 illustrates a dramatic rise in the term's use in major American newspapers after 1980. It is no coincidence, I would argue, that this lexical shift took place concurrently with the changes described above. However, I would argue that the pattern illustrated here was more than simply a lexical shift. To explain the growing use of the term *think tank*, we can refer to the classic hypothesis of *Primitive Classification*, in which Durkheim and Mauss "sociologized" what was until then a strictly philosophical problem by arguing that systems of classification, rather than being invariant, transhistorical, or God-given, have a social genesis. Mental categories, Durkheim and Mauss suggested, tend to mirror the social organization of the groups in which they find resonance. Applied here, the point is that the formation of the *think tank* category in American political discourse was not simply a linguistic phenomenon, but one that also reflected a structural shift in patterns of intellectual jurisdiction and association in the United States.

As think tanks came to appear more distinct from other organizations, the practice of gathering knowledge about them became more common. For a small group of scholars, journalists, and professionals, in fact, think tanks became a recognized area of expertise. By the turn of the twenty-first century, a handful of consultants had emerged to dispense specialized knowledge and advice about the business of running a think tank. In 2003,

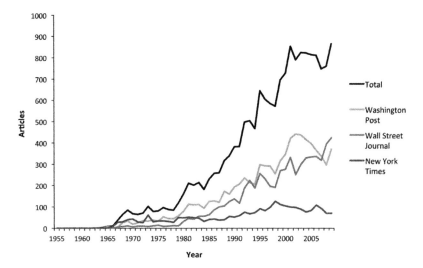

FIGURE 3.5 Use of the phrase "think tank" in major American newspapers, 1955–2010. Sources: LexisNexis, ProQuest Historical Newspapers. Search excludes references found in obituaries, letters to the editor, advertisements, and photo captions.

for example, Urban Institute fellow Raymond J. Struyk wrote the book *Managing Think Tanks: Practical Guidance for Maturing Organizations*, an advice manual for think tank managers based on the author's experience as an adviser to think tanks in Europe and the former Soviet Union. The book covered a number of practical issues faced by think tank directors, such as how to motivate staff members, how to diversify an organization's funding base, how to communicate one's intellectual agenda to policy actors and the wider public, and how to establish a niche in the crowded think tank "market."[97] Meanwhile, the Mackinac Center for Public Policy, a Michigan-based free market think tank, ran a series of twice-annual Leadership Conferences on the topic of think tank managerial strategies. In a summary article called "Thinking Through a Successful Think Tank," Mackinac president Lawrence Reed advised think tank managers on how to cultivate personal contacts with journalists as a way of courting media attention and how to identify competitors and "like-minded" allies in the crowded world of think tanks.[98]

As figure 3.5 showed, journalists wrote about think tanks with growing frequency during the closing decades of the twentieth century. From 1999 to 2003, the *Washington Post* ran a weekly column about think tanks called "The Ideas Industry." The punchy feature, which typically strung together several short items, was soon replaced by "Think Tank Town," a series of columns submitted on a rotating basis by 13 major think tanks.[99] In 2010, the *Post* began publishing a blog called "Think Tanked," by Allen McDuffee, a political journalist and ex–think tank fellow. Knowledge about think tanks became a purchasable commodity as well. For example, in June 2004, PRM Consulting, a Washington-based consulting firm, released the fourth edition of its *Research Organizations: Total Compensation Study*. The report compiled detailed data on the pay of expert and nonexpert staff members at major think tanks.[100] Each year since 2007, the Foreign Policy Research Institute has released a new edition of The Global Go-To Think Tanks Report, a 90-plus-page guide to "the leading public policy research organizations in the world."[101] Finally, I would point out that the growth of a substantial academic literature on think tanks—including this book—further contributed to the institutionalization of *think tank* as a meaningful category in the social world.

Think Tanks and the Rise of the Right

The main argument of this chapter has been that the space of think tanks formed largely in response to struggles and partnerships among expert groups that originated in the political upheavals of the 1960s. In making this argument, I have deliberately emphasized a crucial point of similarity between activists of the right and left: namely, that both were highly critical of, and initially posed themselves in opposition to, technocrats. However, beyond this similarity lay many differences—most glaringly the enormous success of the conservative think tanks during the 1970s and 1980s and the stalled development of the progressive ones. What accounts for the divergent fates of the two sets of organizations? My view is that the relative success of the conservative think tanks can be traced to three causes: first, an enormous advantage in the receipt of material support from big business; second, relative freedom from state repression, which sometimes beset think tanks of the left; and third, relative freedom from absorption by the university, which also forestalled the development of progressive think tanks.

To illustrate these points, consider the respective fates of two specific organizations that can be taken as emblematic of this pattern: the Heritage Foundation and the Institute for Policy Studies. It is worth remembering that the origins of the two think tanks were in many ways similar. Each organization was founded by a pair of ex-legislative aides who identified themselves as 1960s activists and wished to advance a moral critique of the technocratic "establishment." Both sets of founders, furthermore, sought to constitute themselves as experts of a new breed by forming organizations that could serve a kind of self-credentialing function. Yet here is where the similarities end and the differences begin. Despite IPS's 10-year head start, it was the Heritage Foundation that saw its budget, visibility, and influence grow exponentially during the 1970s and 1980s as IPS teetered on the edge of bankruptcy and collapse. Why did Heritage flourish and IPS falter?

It is important to recognize, first, that Heritage enjoyed a major advantage when it came to corporate and individual fundraising. As chapter 2 showed, business sponsorship had always been instrumental to the creation of civil society–based research organizations in the United States. After the 1960s, the situation was no different. What changed, however, was the political orientation of the business leaders themselves. In particular, a once-marginalized libertarian flank of the capitalist class grew and asserted itself forcefully in the political sphere. Starting in the 1970s and 1980s, the members of this business-activist movement put forward a concerted challenge to the taxes and government regulations of the New Deal era. Conservative critics of technocratic capitalism therefore became the primary beneficiaries of business philanthropy, whereas the activist-experts of the left found fewer moneyed sponsors.

Although the Heritage Foundation has often suggested that its funding comes from an army of small-money contributors, in fact most of its support actually came from a limited set of wealthy donors. Internal documentation summarizing the "Heritage 10" campaign, for example, lists 166 donors of $10,000 or more, 44 of whom gave at least $100,000. Of the large contributors, 71 were corporations or corporate foundations, 41 were individuals or couples, and 39 were philanthropic foundations.[102] There was also a core elite group on Heritage's top-donor list, whose contributions accounted for a disproportionate share of its overall funding. Most notably, Richard Mellon Scaife alone gave the Heritage Foundation more than $23 million (or $34 million in inflation-adjusted dollars) from 1974 to 1998.[103] The son of Pittsburgh steelmaker Alan Scaife and heir to the Mellon fortune, Scaife also funded the Hoover Institution, the Manhattan Institute, CSIS, and the Institute for Contemporary Studies, as well as conservative legal foundations and academic centers for promoting free-market thought, such as Emory University's Law and Economics Center.[104]

By 1981, the *Washington Post* could argue that Scaife, who had already given more than $100 million to conservative causes, might "have done more than any other individual in the past five or six years to influence the way in which Americans think about their country and the world."[105]

Scaife was only one member of a growing set of philanthropists who ramped up their giving to conservative causes during the 1980s and 1990s. By the end of the century, the country's largest conservative philanthropy was the Lynde and Harry Bradley Foundation, a Milwaukee-based institution with assets totaling $715 million. By 2005, the Bradley Foundation had given more than half a billion dollars to a wide range of organizations and individuals, including more than $13 million each to AEI and Heritage.[106] Also notable among donors of the right were Charles and David Koch, the sons of Wichita-based oil magnate Fred C. Koch.[107] In 2011, *Forbes* listed the Koch brothers as the fourth and fifth wealthiest Americans, with a combined net worth of $50 billion.[108] Charles Koch cofounded the Cato Institute in 1977 and remained its principal sponsor at least until 1985.[109] The Koch brothers also established the libertarian think tank Citizens for a Sound Economy in 1984.

IPS, meanwhile, obtained almost no support from American business corporations and only a small fraction of the money Heritage received from wealthy individuals. Accordingly, while the organization got off to a relatively auspicious start in the 1960s, IPS quickly became dependent on a few key donors, leading to fiscal problems and internal dissent. Already by 1973, the year of Heritage's founding, an IPS trustee report described the organization as "at a crisis point, both intellectually and institutionally."[110] The previous year, with IPS facing a $125,000 budget deficit, one staff member circulated a memorandum charging that more than half of all IPS expenditures were under the personal control of its codirectors, with no "corporate or fiscal controls upon them."[111] As the staff member wrote, "the present approach, depending as it does on private deals and personal favors, is both fiscally irresponsible and destructive of the internal cohesion of the Institute." By 1975, nearly half of the IPS budget came from a single source, the Samuel Rubin Foundation, a proportion that increased to 55% by 1978.[112]

The second advantage Heritage had over IPS was a set of powerful allies in the Republican Party and the federal government, which gave the organization relative freedom from state repression. Paul Weyrich, for example, described Heritage's early strategy in terms of its close connections to Republican networks in Congress, especially the Senate Steering and Republican Study Committees. "We did have friends on the Hill," Weyrich said in an interview. "I had worked on the Hill for not only Senator Allott, but also then for Senator [Carl T.] Curtis of Nebraska, and both were members of the Senate leadership, so you get to meet lots of people when you're in the leadership."[113] IPS, meanwhile, not only lacked "friends on the Hill" or virtually anywhere else in government, but also found itself the target of two aggressive cases of government harassment, each of which led to a costly, demoralizing, and time-consuming legal battle. In late 1971, the IPS directors discovered that their organization was the target of ongoing government surveillance when a disaffected ex-FBI agent named Robert Wall went public with the story of his secret life as a Counter Intelligence Program (COINTELPRO) operative.[114] Wall filed an affidavit stating that while working as an FBI agent, he had obtained the banking records of several New Left organizations, including IPS, ostensibly to determine whether or not they were training extremists to incite violence.

IPS spent much of the next year conducting its own internal investigation and preparing a lawsuit against the FBI.[115] Court records from the era show that, over a span of six years, the bureau had used more than 60 informants to gather information on IPS, monitored its mail, and collected garbage from outside of its building.[116] In July 1979, the two parties reached a settlement in which the FBI admitted wrongdoing, paid IPS's legal expenses, and agreed to limit access to its IPS files.[117] Even so, IPS was unsuccessful in its attempt to claim monetary damages. Nor did the organization's problems with the federal government end there. In October 1972, the IRS charged the organization with a series of tax code violations and attempted to revoke its tax-exempt status retroactively to October 1966, a move that, if successful, would have effectively put the organization out of business.[118] IPS lawyers alleged a systematic campaign of harassment.[119] Once again, it ultimately prevailed in the matter, albeit at considerable costs of time, money, and effort. By contrast, few conservative think tanks faced major threats from opponents in the government. To be sure, the American Enterprise Institute was the target of an investigation by the IRS during the Lyndon Johnson administration, although its experience was mild compared with that of IPS.

Another challenge IPS faced during this calamitous period was a series of public attacks by conservatives, who portrayed the organization as a pro-Soviet propaganda group. Notable among them was the Heritage Foundation, which in 1980 singled out IPS as an organ of radical insurgency

and recommended that the Reagan administration reinvigorate its counter-
intelligence capabilities to suppress the organization. As right-leaning
periodicals such as *Fortune*, *Barron's*, and *Human Events* added to the
onslaught by publishing unfavorable profiles of IPS, the organization's
president Robert Borosage complained to the *Washington Post* that his organization had "become a popular target for the McCarthyite right, which
is searching for a metaphor for a communist party."[120] Perhaps the most
damaging news media article, however, was an April 1981 *New York Times*
magazine piece by Joshua Muravchik that mused about whether IPS fellows could be prosecuted for treason.[121] The conservative attack against
IPS continued in May 1981, however, when Senator Jeremiah Denton, a
Republican from Alabama, circulated a letter on Capitol Hill denounc-
ing IPS as a source of "anti-American propaganda." The next year, Avon
Books published a spy thriller novel called *The Spike*, depicting a thinly
veiled version of IPS as a KGB disinformation front. IPS threatened legal
action against the publisher, which eventually agreed to change the text to
reduce any similarities between IPS and the organization depicted in the
story.[122] IPS limped into the 1980s a shell of its former self. In the heady
days of the late 1960s, Raskin and Barnet could devote their energies to
spinning grand theories about the proper role of experts in politics. As the
1970s began, however, they faced a series of challenges that threatened to
destroy their organization.

The third cause of the left's relative weakness in the space of think tanks
was the partial absorption of progressive activist-experts by the university. While conservative activists and intellectuals made some attempts to
gain a foothold in the academy as a means of certifying their knowledge,
for the most part conservative movement leaders had come to regard the
university as a hostile territory. The sentiment was clear already in 1951,
when William F. Buckley argued in *God and Man at Yale* that his alma
mater—and by extension the rest of the university system—had been
overrun by liberal faculty members who imposed their political views on
students under the guise of academic freedom. Accordingly, conservative
activist-experts focused their closure strategy outside of academia.

The left-wing critics of technocracy, on the other hand, had a more
ambivalent relationship with the university. Like the conservatives, some
progressive activist-experts of 1960s and 1970s regarded the university as
complicit in the technocratic system that undermined democratic ideals.
Other activist-experts of the left, however, found the academy a more con-
genial environment and pursued university careers. Numerous biographi-

cal and autobiographical accounts, in fact, have documented every step along the path from 1960s student-activist to 1980s professor. And while these accounts vary in their details, they tend to converge on one particular theme: namely, the process of turning away from one's activist ideals in favor of a new set of professional obligations and incentives. The editors of one book on the topic, *The Disobedient Generation: Social Theorists in the Sixties* describe the pattern in this way: "Within a few years [after 1968], their initial enthusiasms, often politically anchored, were converted into energy for the long climb up the academic ladder."[123] Ensconced in an academic world marked by growing professionalization, the "'68 cohort" of progressive activist-intellectuals could not reconcile the goals of civic engagement and occupational success as effectively as their conservative counterparts did. In terms of the theoretical framework I have used, the key point is that the activist-experts of the left did not balance openness and closure in the field of expertise as well as their ideological opponents.

It is worth contrasting this argument with that of the conservatives themselves, who have typically tried to account for the success of their think tanks in terms of the inherent "power" of their ideas. (Indeed, it is not for nothing that Lee Edwards' authorized history of the Heritage Foundation is titled *The Power of Ideas*.) Doubtless it is true that the success of Heritage and other conservative think tanks was "ideas-based" in two senses: first, it depended on their ability to disseminate ideas in novel forms and combinations that helped mark their activity as separate from that of academic scholars. (Put differently, the conservative activist-experts played the leading role in inventing "policy research.") Second, their ideas turned out to be more in step with the dominant political orthodoxy of the era, which ultimately reflected the interests of powerful clients in the political and economic fields. Yet the argument that the conservative think tanks succeeded simply because of the inherent power of their ideas is at once too vague and too celebratory to provide a satisfying explanation on its own. As an alternative to this argument, I have suggested that the success of conservative think tanks was based on an elective affinity between the content of their policy prescriptions and the interests of their allies in the market and the state, who sustained them financially and conferred on them the recognition needed to appear influential.

CHAPTER FOUR

The Rules of Policy Research

I use the analogy—I've used it for years—public policy [research] is . . . like having a vaudeville act or something. You go up on the stage and you're juggling and you're singing and
you're balancing. And then you run behind the curtain and run up in the audience and applaud
madly. And then you run back up on the stage and you juggle. And then you run back and
applaud madly. If you do it right, all of a sudden other people start applauding and you've got
a hit.—Fred Smith Jr., Competitive Enterprise Institute[1]

T he two preceding chapters have traced the formation of a hybrid institutional niche that I have called the *space of think tanks*. As the
reader will remember, the original purpose of this discussion was to answer the seemingly prosaic question, "What is a think tank?" In the book's
opening chapter, I argued that no purely theoretical definition, regardless
of how rhetorically precise or operationally sound, can avoid creating the
false impression that a think tank is a ready-made object or a "thing."
To overcome this problem, I insisted that we would need to examine the
historical process through which a formerly disparate array of organizations became oriented to one another in their judgments and practices and
eventually cohered into a new subspace of knowledge production. In the
previous chapter, I argued that the main process leading to this outcome
was a structural convergence between two sets of experts and the organizations at their command: first, the technocratic research institutes of the
early twentieth century, which had already established for themselves a
major role as suppliers of advice and expertise in American politics, and
second, the activist-expert organizations that emerged as their main challengers starting in the 1960s. After 1970, I argued, the two sets of organizations entered into a more collaborative set of relations and developed
novel, albeit hybrid, intellectual forms and products. In the process, they
collectively acquired a weak form of autonomy akin to that of a field, in
the term's sociological sense.

Having traced this process to the present day, we can now look at the current structure of the space of think tanks, its interior rules of functioning, the intellectual practices carried out within it, and the social characteristics of its inhabitants. My argument in this chapter sets out from the curious analogy suggested to me by a think tank president and quoted in the epigraph above. According to this analogy, the practice of policy research is like a vaudeville act in which a performer juggles, sings, runs to and fro, and then applauds his or her own performance. At one level, the comparison is meant to convey a sense of the difficult combination of styles and skills needed to excel in the world of think tanks. Just as a vaudevillian must fuse the artistry of a singer with the dexterity of a juggler and the timing of a comedian, so a think tank–affiliated policy expert must blend an assortment of seemingly disparate skills: intellectual proficiency, political savvy, self-promotional ability, and entrepreneurial drive. The vaudeville analogy, however, does not end there. I will argue that it can also be extended to the organizational repertoire of the think tank. To succeed in its mission, a think tank must reconcile its pursuit of intellectual credibility with the pursuit of three "temporal" forms of power: political access, public visibility, and financial support.

The reader might also notice that shadings of the vaudeville imagery have already informed my account of the *boundary work* carried out by actors with a direct stake in the think tank classification. In the opening chapter, I argued that to be counted as a think tank in the first place, an organization must differentiate itself from a lobbying firm, a university, an advocacy group, and any other kind of organization for which it might plausibly be mistaken. This is a kind of metaphorical vaudeville act, too, because it draws the think tank into a complex game of distancing and affiliation from which it can never fully escape.

The image of a balancing act thus offers a *layered metaphor* for describing various social forms and practices found in the space of think tanks, including the styles and dispositions of the policy expert and the strategies of the think tank. Each of these forms and practices entails a four-sided encounter between the logics of academic, political, economic, and media production. In this chapter, I will argue that the formation of the space of think tanks has institutionalized a new form of intellectual practice in the United States known as "policy research." This discussion will begin with a critique of the standard conceptual device used by scholars to describe think tanks: organizational typologies. The problem with typologies, I will argue, is that they lock us into a mode of reasoning that reduces think tanks to expressions of purely external forces

and interests. To grasp the space of think tanks in all of its specificity requires taking into account its unique rules of functioning. The chapter's
next section will examine the specific form of *interest* made possible by
think tanks, as well as the distinctive dispositions and drives of the policy
expert.

This discussion will lead to a new question: What is to be gained by existing as a think tank? What forms of power, social leverage, or influence
are available to the organizations that exist under this rubric? I will argue
that a think tank's "quadruple bind"—that is, the challenge of existing
simultaneously in four fields at once—is not merely a form of constraint.
Rather, it also functions as a curious source of freedom, flexibility, and indeed, power, for a think tank. By occupying a crucial point of interchange
in the social structure, think tanks claim for themselves an important mediating role in the relations among elite actors and groups. The chapter's
final section will then return to a "big picture" view of the space of think
tanks and its role within the wider system of knowledge production in the
United States.

Typological vs. Topological Representations of Think Tanks

One of the main premises of this book has been that it is analytically useful
to depict think tanks as embedded in a four-cornered space of forces and
relations divided internally by the logics of academic, political, bureaucratic, economic, and media production. A key implication of this model
is that the identities of specific think tanks can be ascertained largely from
their relationships to these anchoring fields. Each think tank, in other
words, sits in a particular relation of proximity to, and distance from, the
field's surrounding institutions. Some think tanks, for example, reside in
the economic region of the field, or the sector that borders and overlaps
the market. Others are inserted in the bureaucratic field, or the array of
public institutions "entrusted with the maintenance of the economic and
legal order . . . [and] the sustenance of the dispossessed and the provision of public goods."[2] Other think tanks are more clearly embedded in
the political field, by which I mean the system of struggles among parties,
politicians, political specialists—including pollsters, campaign advisers,
political aides, and activists—over the powers of delegation and representation.[3] Finally, some think tanks derive their main identities from
their relationships to the major cultural institutions of American society,

including universities and the media. These organizations can thus be said to exist within the field of cultural production.

Later in this chapter, I will revisit and extend this point by developing a *social topology*, or analytic mapping, of the space of think tanks meant to elaborate these differences. However, at this point the reader might ask a more basic question: Why would I insist on describing think tanks in topological terms rather than simply use one of the many *typologies* already developed by other scholars to describe the same organizations? In the existing scholarly literature, the most common approach to describing the differences among think tanks is simply to label each organization according to its external affiliations—for example, by calling the most academic think tanks "universities without students," the most activist ones "advocacy tanks," the bureaucratic think tanks "government contract tanks," and so on. Weaver's typology, in particular, has become part of the standard vocabulary for describing think tanks, even among some think tank-affiliated actors themselves.[4] On the surface, this approach might seem essentially the same as the one I have just described. However, I would disagree. To explain the differences between the two approaches, let me first identify some shortcomings of typologies and then discuss the advantages of a topological approach.

The Drawbacks of Typologies

The first sign of a problem with think tank typologies is that they make it difficult to represent change over time. Given the dynamism and uncertainty surrounding think tanks, it should come as no surprise that they change constantly, and usually without any identifiable moment of rupture to signal their switch from one "type" to another. Remember, for example, the story of the Brookings Institution's transformation in the 1970s and 1980s as told in chapter 3. Faced with mounting pressures from new competitors, Brookings strategically reoriented itself by increasing its focus on news media attention and corporate fundraising. A typology would offer us no way of representing either of these changes, only confusion. After all, Brookings is usually held up as the prototypical "university without students." However, it would be pointless to ask whether Brookings ceased to represent this type during the 1970s, just as it would be problematic to ignore its transformation altogether. By contrast, a topological model invites us to think about each organization, not as representing a particular type, but as occupying a position within a dynamic field of

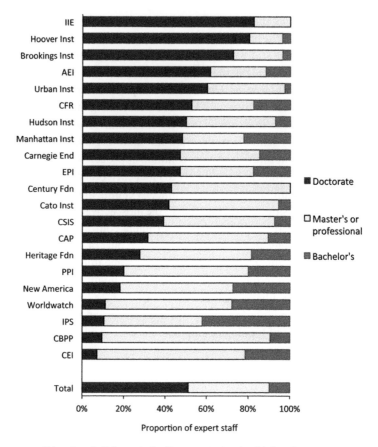

FIGURE 4.1 Educational attainment of policy experts at major think tanks, 2005.

relations. Using such a model, I would posit that Brookings migrated in social space away from the academic and bureaucratic fields, even as it extended its reach into the economic and media fields. The topological approach also underscores the broader structural tendencies of which this transformation was a part, since it was not just Brookings that adopted this strategy, but several other think tanks as well.

A second drawback of typologies is that they force us to establish arbitrary lines of separation among think tanks, which do not actually cluster into distinct types. Figure 4.1 supports this point using one measure of an organization's orientation to the academic field: the proportions of doctorate, master's/professional, and bachelor's degree–holders on its expert staff. The figure illustrates two key points: first, as either a typological or a topological framework would predict, there is considerable variation among think tanks with respect to academic orientation. In fact, they run the full gamut from organizations with few PhD-holders to those in which holding a PhD is a virtual prerequisite for employment. However, despite all the variation, there is actually no discrete category of academic think tanks, only a series of gradational differences. Indeed, where would we draw the line between the "universities without students" and the rest of the think tanks?

I can illustrate this point further by referring to a specific think tank not included in figure 4.1 but often described as an academic think tank: the National Bureau of Economic Research. While it is true that NBER derives much of its reputation and influence from its scholarly resources, especially the vast network of academic economists it coordinates, this fact alone does not tell the whole story about NBER. It is also worth noting, for example, that NBER performs a quasi-bureaucratic function by carrying out federal contract research and supplying the official determination of whether the United States has entered or exited an economic recession. To put the point succinctly: NBER is not *just* an academic think tank, but also a bureaucratic one. A typology would not be able to capture this point unless we were to hedge our bets by treating NBER as a "hybrid" case.

However, this last observation points to what is ultimately the chief inadequacy of think tank typologies. Put simply, in their hybridity, organizations such as NBER are the *norm* rather than the exception among think tanks. Most real-life think tanks, in other words, do not clearly belong to any type at all, but exist in the murky "spaces between types." As the case of NBER suggests, coming up with examples of "universities without students" requires glossing over important details about each organization. I will not belabor the point here, but a similar observation could be made about virtually any other think tank type, since along any relevant measure one finds continuous rather than categorical variation. (See the supplementary tables and figures in the appendix, which offer some sense of the distribution of other resources among think tanks.) The main problem with think tank typologies, then, is not just that they mask the nuances and complexities of individual think tanks, but that they hide a common propensity among think tanks to "become hybrid." This propensity, I would argue, is not a secondary feature of a think tank's existence, but a primary one. A topological approach that depicts think tanks as occupying a structural location in between more established fields therefore makes for a more appropriate starting point for a theory of policy research than a typological approach.

Let me extend this point with another example. Consider a well-known think tank often described as a "labor-backed" organization: the Economic Policy Institute. To anyone familiar with EPI's history, it is obvious that the organization has a complex relationship with the labor movement—and indeed with the label "labor-backed" itself. At one level, the association is an albatross around EPI's neck. The organization's conservative opponents in particular are often keen to point out that labor unions supply a significant share of EPI's funding, the implication being that EPI is simply a mouthpiece of the labor movement, not a bona fide supplier of expertise. (Thus, a 2009 Heritage Foundation *Backgrounder Report* titled "Big Labor Admits Employer Violations Rare in Elections" peremptorily dismisses EPI as "a union-funded think tank," while a 2011 article by the *Weekly Standard* is simply titled, "Just a Reminder: The Economic Policy Institute is Dominated by Labor Interests."[5]) Given the drawbacks of this association, it should come as no surprise that EPI spends considerable time and energy fighting off the appellation "labor-backed." A section of its website, for example, advises journalists on the organization's preferred public description: "Is it accurate or appropriate to call EPI labor-supported or labor-backed? No. Foundations provide about twice as much of EPI's funding as unions do, so 'foundation-supported' would be accurate but 'labor-backed' is not."[6]

However, to stop the analysis here would be to miss the key fact that, in other contexts, EPI's ties to the labor movement serve a salutary function for the organization. Many of EPI's practices, in fact, are manifestly designed to bolster its public ties to organized labor. In 2000, for example, EPI cofounded the Global Policy Network, a set of "policy and research institutions connected to the world's trade union movements," which lists among its goals "forging links between institutes connected to unions and labour movements in developed and developing countries" and "furthering international solidarity and engaging the common challenges posed by globalization."[7] EPI's *Briefing Papers* suggest another facet of the organization's complex relationship with organized labor. In certain cases, EPI makes a direct claim *to speak on behalf* of labor unions to an audience of policymakers. (The *Briefing Papers* series includes such titles as "How Unions Help All Workers" and "Still Open for Business: Unionization Has No Causal Effect on Firm Closures."[8]) From this vantage point, EPI's connection to organized labor is not an albatross around its neck at all, but actually the organization's calling card. In particular, it is a signal to journalists that EPI will always be ready with a quotable expression of the prolabor side of a debate, a cue to labor unions that EPI is an ally (and thus a worthy recipient of donations), and a pointer to prolabor politicians that they can always count on EPI for a useful statistic, a private briefing, or an expert witness for a legislative hearing. Thus, in a crowded "marketplace of ideas," EPI has what every think tank needs: a recognizable identity and a corresponding set of clients for its products.

This observation raises an interesting puzzle: Given the complexity of its relationship with the labor movement, how can we describe EPI without either oversimplifying it or becoming ensnared in the discursive battles among think tanks over the ultimate "truth" of its identity? In my view, the question poses a theoretical problem only if we insist on depicting EPI in static or essentialist terms. A better approach is to describe the organization as engaged in a dynamic *balancing act*, each element of which is constitutive of its identity. Contained in this point is a general lesson about think tanks that typologies cannot capture. Put simply, all think tanks must carry out a balancing act that involves establishing certain ties and relations of exchange with other institutions. These ties allow the think tank to gather various institutionalized resources and assemble these resources into unique packages. The theoretical framework I have suggested is meant to capture these core points. First, by locating think tanks in between more established fields, it allows us to depict hybridity as the norm rather than the exception among think tanks. Second, by suggesting that think tanks have developed certain field-like properties of their own (and here it is important to keep in mind that the first metaphor on which the field concept is based is that of a *magnetic field*), it suggests that a set of quasi-magnetic forces "pulls" think tanks toward a particular location in the social structure. The main upshot of these points is that before we can properly grasp the differences among think tanks, it is necessary to understand the general force that compels them to become "hybrid."

The Space of Think Tanks as an Interstitial Field

I can clarify my argument by contrasting it with the standard way scholars have understood think tanks and their missions. As a representative example, consider Andrew Rich's definitional characterization of think tanks as "institutions that actively seek to maximize public credibility and

political access to make their expertise and ideas influential in policy making."[9] My purpose in citing this description is not to *refute* it per se, but
rather to use it as a way of clarifying my own argument, and ultimately
to contribute something new to the scholarly discussion. For example, I
would begin by noting some of the conspicuous questions raised by Rich's
formulation. What does it mean to say that a think tank tries to "maximize public credibility"? The idea of credibility itself is already ambiguous, and all the more so after speaking with think tank representatives on
the topic.

Consider the notion of credibility implied in the following interview
exchange with Fred Smith Jr., president of the Competitive Enterprise
Institute:

INTERVIEWER: So is there some form of scholarly credibility that you have to have
in order to be successful?
FS: I'm not sure "scholarly" is a term I'd use. Credibility is certainly something you
have to have.
INTERVIEWER: Credibility based in evidence?
FS: Generally, groups like ours, how do we earn our credibility? Well, we have very
strong bright-line standards. We have a very strong point of view and we have
never deviated from that point of view. . . . If you're a free market group whose
position keeps changing, you don't have any credibility.[10]

Smith makes two interesting points. First, whatever form of credibility
CEI seeks to maximize, it is not the same kind that academic scholars
typically recognize as legitimate. Second, CEI's credibility does not rest
on its ability to disguise its unwavering commitment to free market ideology. On the contrary, Smith says, his organization's ideological clarity
and consistency are the wellsprings of its credibility, since they enhance its
reputation with a particular audience.

A similar idea emerges in the description offered by former Heritage
Foundation vice president Adam Meyerson of the organization's novel
direct-mail fundraising strategy: "The significance of the Heritage model . . .
is that the 200,000 or so [donors] gave Heritage a certain credibility with
the audience, including their political audience. That is to say, members of
Congress would respect any organization that had 200,000 donors, whatever its political ideology. They would respect that. It gave Heritage, I
think, more credibility with its number one audience."[11] Like Smith, Meyerson uses the term *credibility* in a curious way. On this view, credibility is

not an attribute that can be measured in universalistic terms, but a practical achievement rooted in the ability to coordinate specific social ties and relations. Both responses imply that the definition of credibility itself will vary from one organization to the next. In Heritage's case, for example, to earn credibility means to demonstrate to an audience of policy makers that the organization can speak on behalf of a large constituency of conservative voters and activists.

As we have already seen, the notion of credibility put forward by EPI rests on an appeal to a different constituency. Of course, none of these observations forecloses the possibility that some think tanks subscribe to a more universalistic notion of credibility. However, they do show that the specific kind of "public credibility" a think tank will try to maximize depends on the particular *public (or publics)* to which it is oriented. (Here it is useful to remember that the word credibility derives from the Latin word *credere*: "to believe." The question, in short, is: "*Who* is meant to believe?") Put differently, the relevant definition of credibility is one of the stakes of competition among think tanks.

This point brings me to the second part of Rich's formulation—the claim that think tanks also attempt to "maximize . . . political access." In one sense, this point is irrefutable. There is no question that think tanks must cultivate access to policy makers and other political insiders as a means of exercising influence. However, I believe the point is also partial and potentially misleading in that many think tanks also *turn down* certain opportunities to increase their political access. The Heritage Foundation, for example, has long been careful to maintain a certain distance from the Republican Party. The reason is clear: To remain a standard bearer of American conservatism, Heritage must reserve the right to critique Republicans who stray too far from conservative principles. Of course, this is not to say that Heritage lacks ties to the Republican Party, only that it must take care to moderate these ties, or to balance them with other institutionalized resources to avoid appearing like an appendage of the party. The general point is that there is a certain danger in achieving "too much" political access, or in achieving access in the wrong forms.

In fact, the history of think tanks is filled with examples of organizations that enjoyed a brief moment in the sun by virtue of some privileged form of access to a specific political network or agency, only to be pushed to the margins of the field when this access either evaporated or lost its value. The Progressive Policy Institute, for example, a think tank once regarded as the intellectual base of the New Democrat movement, is a notable case in point. By the close of the Clinton presidency, PPI's status among think tanks had fallen considerably, along with that of the Democratic Leadership Council that sustained it. (Not surprisingly, PPI recently disaffiliated itself from the DLC in an effort to refashion its public image.) Together, these points suggest a set of basic revisions to the conventional way of describing a think tank's mission. First, rather than think of credibility as a homogeneous resource to be "maximized," we should recognize the plurality of its forms, which in turn corresponds to a plurality of audiences. Second, the pursuit of credibility is neither wholly distinct from the pursuit of political access, nor are the two locked in a simple relation of opposition. Instead, political access can be thought of as its own form of credibility, albeit one that operates in tension with other forms. There is no point, then, in describing think tanks as engaged in an attempt to "maximize" credibility or access.

A more useful approach, I would suggest, is to depict the basic mission of a think tank as a game of gathering, balancing, and assembling various institutionalized resources or forms of capital, especially academic, political, economic, and media capital. In keeping with the usage associated with Bourdieu, I use the term *academic capital* to refer to visible markers of scholarly proficiency, especially academic degrees and titles. By the same token, *political capital* refers to competence in specifically political forms of expression, including the capacity to generate knowledge and make pronouncements that are effective in the competition for control over the state (e.g., polling data, demographic statistics, "talking points" memoranda, speeches, slogans, and strategic advice); *media capital* refers to direct or indirect access to the means of publicity, as well as the styles and skills needed to assist journalists and media institutions in their work; and *economic capital* refers not just to money per se (which think tanks typically raise in the form of donations), but also to the means of obtaining it, including the skills needed to raise funding and "sell" one's intellectual products to politicians, activists, and other "buyers."

Policy Research as a Dynamic Balancing Act

Let me develop this alternative model, first, by looking at how think tanks present themselves to their main publics. Here my central claim will be that think tanks must actively signal both their autonomy (or cognitive independence) and their heteronomy (or their dependence on clients for resources and recognition) through a complex balancing act. Understanding this balancing act is the starting point for grasping policy research as a distinctive form of intellectual practice.

First, as any survey of the annual reports and mission statements of think tanks will attest, the outermost layer of a think tank's public self-presentation is typically an announcement of its own intellectual rigor and independence. To mention just a few examples, the Brookings Institution states that its "scholars provide the highest quality research, policy recommendations, and analysis," and that the "independence, professional integrity and objectivity of Brookings research are among the Institution's principal assets."[12] The Century Foundation similarly notes, "Political forces have swung dramatically during the passing decades and surely will again in the future. But our commitment to offering reason and facts in the pursuit of national progress endures."[13] Meanwhile, the Urban Institute lists among its goals, "bring[ing] sound objective evidence to public policy decisions." RAND likewise cites its "dedication to high-quality and objective research and analysis."[14] It is worth noting that claims like these are nearly as common among think tanks with stated ideological missions. Thus the conservative AEI says that its "trustees, scholars and fellows, and officers and staff are responsible for maintaining the highest standards of integrity, intellectual rigor, and excellence—and for sustaining AEI's founding commitment to open inquiry, lucid exposition, [and] vigorous debate."[15] The liberal Economic Policy Institute similarly announces that it "adheres to strict standards of sound, objective research and analysis."[16] Finally, in an interview, a Heritage Foundation representative answers the question, "What are the marks of a good research product in the context of the policymaking process?" with the following rejoinder: "Good research is good research, whether it's policy-oriented or not. It's transparent, it's replicable."[17]

The basic message contained in all of these claims is that think tanks enjoy a certain degree of cognitive autonomy. Their argument, in other words, is that the contents of their studies are determined first and foremost by standards of rigor established by communities of experts who enjoy a degree of insulation from political, economic, and cultural pressures. Of course, there is nothing especially surprising in these claims, since assertions of cognitive independence are more or less ubiquitous among experts. What is noteworthy, rather, is that even as think tanks proclaim their cognitive autonomy in certain contexts, they also actively signal their *heteronomy*, or their dependence on clients for the resources and forms of legitimacy they confer, in others. In particular, think tanks consistently depend on three kinds of clients: first, political clients (especially policy makers, parties, and activist networks) for the political access they can provide; second, economic clients (especially foundations, corporations, and wealthy donors) for financial support; and third, media clients (especially journalists and media organs, such as newspapers, periodicals, and radio and television programs) for public visibility. Let me discuss each of these forms of dependence in turn.

Political Dependence

How do think tanks signal their dependence on political clients? Undoubtedly, the most effective way for a think tank to have its work taken seriously by policy makers is to make a plausible claim to solve some preexisting political need. We have already seen some evidence to support this point in chapters 2 and 3. Among the early twentieth century forerunners of the think tank, for example, the most successful organizations were those that responded to preexisting political needs, including the demand for strategic knowledge about foreign states and markets during the interwar years and the need for technical tools for managing the domestic economy, especially during the Great Depression. By the same token, think tanks that have advocated policy ideas that were radical or unpopular, or that required a significant reframing of policy debate, have been fewer in number and generally doomed to marginality in the space of think tanks. For example, if socialist economic policies, aggressive wealth redistribution, or a major political role for organized labor were ideas that lay beyond the political pale in American political debate for most of the twentieth century, then they also lay beyond the intellectual pale in the space of think tanks.

A notable counter-example to this point is the Institute for Policy Studies, the radical organization that has been exceptional among think tanks for aligning itself with left-wing causes, including the anti-apartheid, civil rights, women's, environmental, and anti-globalization movements. However, from a wider perspective, IPS's experience only tends to confirm the general rule, since for its radicalism the organization has been demonized by its political opponents, infiltrated by the FBI, investigated by the IRS, and consistently pushed to the margins of the space of think tanks. IPS's marginality, in other words, can be explained partly in terms of its insistence on challenging the orthodoxy of policy debate.

Of course, the reader might ask whether the success of conservative think tanks over the last four decades contradicts my point in this discussion. After all, some conservative think tanks have thrived even while challenging certain longstanding political orthodoxies. As I have noted, think tanks of the right carried out a sustained antiwelfare campaign during the 1980s and 1990s that challenged mainstream assumptions about the necessity of social provisions in the United States. Is it fair to say, then, that these think tanks enjoyed autonomy from political demand? I would argue that any answer in the affirmative must be qualified in two major ways. First, we should recognize the degree to which the success of conservative think tanks depended on a strategy of self-subordination to political demand. Consider the early tactic adopted by Heritage cofounders Paul Weyrich and Ed Feulner as discussed in chapter 3. Weyrich described his organization's approach in this way: "Our niche was to be very responsive to whatever need was expressed" by the organization's conservative allies in Congress.[18]

A current Heritage public relations officer gives a similar account of Heritage's early success: "Before [Heritage], think tanks tended to be the standard 'universities without students' where people would write about whatever struck their fancy, whatever they found intellectually stimulating and interesting. Write it up and send it over to the staff on the Hill or whoever, and that was kind of the end of it." Weyrich and Feulner, however, adopted a different tactic: "They [said], 'Let's address the topics that—not what we determine, but what the opinion leaders of the country—political, media, whatever—have determined are the important issues of the day.'"[19] Restated in theoretical terms, Heritage relinquished a major share of its cognitive autonomy by orienting its work to the pre-established needs of political and media actors. It is worth noting that Weyrich and Feulner did not likely *experience* their work as a form of political servitude, however, because as former legislative aides they were already oriented to the needs of Capitol Hill legislators and, to a lesser degree, the media. Regardless of their experience, though, the central point is that the Heritage cofounders were predisposed to exist in a space of knowledge production dominated by political and media demand.

Economic Dependence

The second qualification we must make is that much of the political autonomy demonstrated by the conservative think tanks was made possible by a different sort of dependence: namely, dependence on financial sponsors. As I noted in chapter 3, conservative think tanks were among the main beneficiaries of a business activist movement intent on rolling back the taxes and regulatory mechanisms of the New Deal era. Their dependence on this movement placed decisive limits on the range of intellectual stances open to them.

The situation of financial dependence is hardly limited to conservative think tanks, however. Nearly all think tanks, in fact, rely heavily on short-term donations and must therefore orient their work to the market for funding. To list a pair of prominent examples: the Brookings Institution runs both a series of corporate Executive Education courses ("designed to demystify Capitol Hill," according to its description) and a Custom Corporate Program, which promises enrollees that Brookings "experts will work with you to craft a curriculum tailored to your company's needs."[20] The Council on Foreign Relations similarly maintains a program that "serves an international membership of prominent global corporations."[21] All enrollees in the three-tiered program receive "private briefing[s] by a CFR fellow tailored to the company's interests," discounts on advertising and rental rates for CFR facilities and services, and invitations to special briefings and events, including the organization's annual Corporate Conference, "a yearly summit on geopolitical and geoeconomic challenges."[22] Second-tier program members are promised additional private briefings, "invitations for senior executives to attend two to three small, private events with world leaders," invitations to "select in-depth study groups and roundtables," and "complimentary use of the prestigious Harold Pratt House ballroom and library for a single corporate event." Membership in the program's highest tier earns the subscriber a "private briefing by CFR's president tailored to the company's interests." On its website, CFR currently lists eight corporations as upper-tier members, thirty-seven second-tier members, and 128 third-tier members. Assuming that each corporation paid the advertised fee associated with its membership level ($100,000, $60,000, and $30,000, respectively), these subscriptions netted CFR roughly $6.9 million during the last year.[23]

The extent to which sponsors can determine the boundaries of permissible action among think tanks must always remain an open question. However, in much the same way that a sociological "breaching experiment" can reveal the unspoken rules regulating a particular social situation, moments of conflict and disjuncture between think tanks and their sponsors suggest that money often has considerable power in the space of think tanks. Among many possible examples, consider one from the recent past. In 2003, the Center for Strategic and International Studies convened a policy conference featuring an economist who presented a paper advocating that patent protections be lifted on drugs in poor countries to reduce their costs.[24] Soon afterwards, one of CSIS's donors, the Pharmaceutical Research and Manufacturers of America (PhRMA), an industry trade association and energetic opponent of such measures, discontinued its annual grant to CSIS. The incident created a minor ripple in the local press because of the seemingly punitive nature of PhRMA's actions, especially given the highly indirect linkage between the trade association's money and the offending paper. (The economist in question had no formal ties to CSIS, and PhRMA's grant actually supported a division of CSIS separate from the one that had convened the conference. Moreover, CSIS had made certain to include a critic of the report on the conference panel.)

None of these measures was enough to stop CSIS's sponsor from halting its support, however. And although PhRMA's response was notable for its severity, policy experts themselves occasionally acknowledge the constraining effects produced by their financial dependence. Sometimes these constraints are posed as a form of virtuous "accountability," however, as the president of the Committee for Economic Development suggests when asked about the intellectual limitations imposed by the need to engage in continuous fundraising. "Accountability is a good thing, in my view," the respondent notes. "It's important to be able to go back to our funders and also to the people who support us with time and/or money, and say, 'Here's what we did and here's the impact that we had.'"[25] A Brookings Institution fellow relates a story with a similar point: the "head of Cato, and this is a quote, he said it to me, 'I don't want an endowment because I want to be on a short tether with my funders.' Fundamentally, it was to keep ideological purity in the institution. And they have."[26] Other policy experts refer to the influence of financial sponsors as the corrupt or "sleazy" side of their business. As the president of one think tank explains, "I've . . . been at meetings where you can see think tank folks basically milking trade associations or businesses. Essentially, 'Give me more money and I'll say more things.' And it's a little sleazy."[27]

Perhaps the most systematic discussion on this point from a think tank-affiliated actor came in 2003, when Steven Clemons, vice president of the New America Foundation and a veteran of several think tanks, published an essay called "The Corruption of Think Tanks." In striking fashion,

Clemons argued that think tanks had become willing accomplices in "the development of an underground, or 'second,' economy of political influence" in which donors "increasingly expect policy achievements that contribute to their bottom line."[28] Speaking from experience, Clemons acknowledged the difficult balancing act a think tank must perform to survive: "To grow as an institution means struggling to some degree with a Faustian bargain—taking money from donors and, while maintaining the guise of policy objectivity and seriousness, doing the bidding of the lobbyist." In an increasingly competitive environment, Clemons argued, "think tanks are less and less committed to genuine inquiry designed to stimulate enlightened policy decisions and more and more oriented to deepening the well-worn grooves of a paralyzed debate, frozen in place by the contending power of potential winners and losers with armies of lobbyists at their heels."

The most egregious instances of corruption, Clemons maintained, involved the practice known as "deep lobbying," in which lobbyists effectively funnel the money of private interest groups through think tanks as a way of skirting federal lobbying regulations. Because congressional ethics rules permit members of Congress and their staffs to accept meals, trips, and gifts related to their official duties so long as they come from nonprofit entities, ambiguous conflicts of interest often arise. As Clemons explained,

> if the Biotechnology Industry Association wanted to lay out the reasons why Europe's "precautionary principle" regarding genetically modified foods and products was a violation against science, free trade, and modernity itself, then these interests might try to secure an organization like the New America Foundation, or the Heritage Foundation . . . to host a luncheon or a conference to provide "education" for public officials about these issues.

According to Clemons, the corruption of think tanks is enabled by a "lack of IRS resources to investigate the non-profit sector in any serious way," and "the inherent fuzziness in differentiating between 'public education' and lobbying." Elaborating on his thesis, Clemons later told the *Washington Post*, "We've become money launderers for monies that have real specific policy agendas behind them. . . . No one is willing to say anything about it; it's one of the big taboo subjects."[29]

Clemons' emphasis on "corruption" obscures the highly systematic nature of the influence of financial sponsors over think tanks. But the vi-

cissitudes of specific organizations' histories vividly illustrate the degree
to which a think tank's fate inevitably depends on its ability to provide
useful services to financial sponsors. Consider the case of the American
Enterprise Institute. For the first three decades of its existence, AEI was
a minor player in the policy research world, its marginality guaranteed by
its miniscule budget and its lack of full-time policy experts. However, as
I noted in chapter 3, AEI's fortunes improved dramatically in the 1970s
when the organization became a favored beneficiary of the business conservative movement that grew during the period. What I did not mention,
though, was that for a brief period in the 1980s, AEI fell out of favor with
the donor network that sustained it, precipitating a brief but major organizational crisis. The catalyst for the episode was the retirement of AEI's
longtime president William J. Baroody in 1978 and his son's succession
to the presidency. As the younger Baroody took over, a perception grew
among conservative donors that AEI was abandoning its conservative
principles. In 1986, *Reader's Digest*, a consistent supporter of conservative
causes, abruptly cut off its funding to AEI. The magazine's editor William
Schulz told the *Washington Post*, "AEI has lost sight of what its mission is
or was. Baroody [Jr.]'s desire to move the organization to the center and
appeal to foundations and corporations not thought of as conservative
has alienated the original supporters."[30] The same year, the John Olin and
Smith-Richardson Foundations—both major conservative donors—also
drew back their support for AEI. As longtime Olin Foundation president
William Simon explained, "We have ceased giving grants [to AEI]. . . .
Suffice it to say, they've gone very far downhill, on a managerial and a
philosophical basis."[31]

In their defense, the AEI trustees argued that, far from having moved
toward the political center, they had simply failed to move further to the
right. Now faced with more stridently conservative competitors, such as
Cato and Heritage, the organization had become a less viable "investment" for conservative donors. An anonymous AEI fellow summarized
the problem in these terms in 1986: "There's so much diversity at AEI.
That's what the conservative foundations see as the problem. . . . A lot of
corporations and foundations willing to give to anything a few years ago
want more bang for their buck now."[32] AEI managed the problem by visibly reaffirming its conservative credentials. In an attempt to restore the
confidence of donors and quell the crisis, the AEI trustees fired Baroody in
1986 and replaced him with Christopher DeMuth, former Reagan administration "deregulation czar" at the Office of Management and Budget.[33]

In the ensuing years, DeMuth successfully managed AEI's recovery and tripled its budget.[34]

Media Dependence

Policy makers and donors are not the only clients with whom think tanks must establish durable ties and partnerships in order to succeed in their missions. In a political setting increasingly structured around and responsive to the news media, journalistic and media organs constitute a third source of dependence for think tanks. Accordingly, many think tanks strategically orient their work to the needs of journalists and the media to gain public attention. In the most conspicuous cases, this involves explicitly offering a free service to reporters, as illustrated by the title of a 2005 daily *Progress Report* memo from the Center for American Progress: "We Do The Research So Reporters Don't Have To."[35] More often, however, think tanks tailor their work to the needs of journalists and the media in subtler ways. For example, many encourage their policy experts to publish op-ed pieces in the newspaper or to write articles for magazines. Television and radio punditry are also increasingly prized among think tanks for the visibility they bring. Many think tanks likewise distribute press guides to media outlets and maintain their own radio and television broadcasting equipment. Brookings, for example, is known for having a state-of-the-art television studio on its premises, while Heritage has a small radio studio.[36] Some think tanks hold symposia and press conferences designed for broadcast on cable television (especially C-SPAN), while others have fashioned themselves as convenient venues for political speeches. The importance of publicity is also evident in the fact that many think tanks meticulously catalogue their own press clippings and keep careful track of traffic to their websites. Finally, when asked to describe the marks of a good policy argument, a CAP fellow emphasizes the importance of media friendliness: "First of all, it has to be intelligible. It has to be brief, and digestible. . . . By and large what we produce is less than ten pages and our talking points are one page. And our columns are 750 words. They're op-ed length."[37]

Broadly speaking, the relationship between think tanks and journalists is a symbiotic one. On the one side, journalists face what one interview respondent calls an acute "time scarcity and resource scarcity."[38] Many reporters therefore rely heavily on experts who can provide brief, quotable explanations to flesh out their stories: "If you're writing a story and you have one afternoon to write the story, it's hugely important whether—if you call Heritage, you find out who their health care policy person is—if that person is someone who is articulate in a media sense."[39] Crucially, think tanks with stated ideological agendas are often no less valuable to reporters than ideologically neutral think tanks since reporters "are dependent on finding two sources of expertise to cover both sides of the question. And a lot of what happens in this city is defining the two poles. What's the conservative position? What's the liberal position?"

For its part, media coverage has two main benefits for a think tank. First, in the absence of direct access to policymakers, publicity can function as a secondary means of political influence. Second, publicity generally has positive effects on a think tank's fundraising efforts. As many think tank directors emphasize, financial donors typically prefer to see some evidence of past success before they dole out money to a think tank, and since direct policy influence is difficult to prove, publicity has become a standard marker of success in fundraising meetings and grant proposals. As one policy expert puts it when asked why think tanks seek publicity, "It's partly a fundraising thing. Funders need to know that somebody is paying attention to the product. And the way you convince them that somebody is paying attention to the product is to show them the newspaper headline or the talk show appearance."[40] The president of another think tank explains, "The big thing in the MacArthur Foundation right now is measuring impact. I think it is next to impossible to measure. I mean, there are things that you can do to measure impact. Media hits, that's a way to measure impact."[41] Another policy expert worries that the impossibility of measuring policy influence "leads to measuring what's measurable," which in turn creates an incentive to generate superficial forms of publicity: "You can demonstrate that you've generated so many press stories or so many evening news stories. . . . [But] I think one of the problems in this nebulous environment is that tangible beats intangible often, even if the tangible is arguably not worth very much."[42]

The Temporality of Policy Research

Political, economic, and media demand shape not just the content of a think tank's work, but also its *temporality*. By this term, I mean the pace at which intellectual products must be generated in order to be deemed useful by policymakers, donors, and journalists. The fact that think tanks must adhere to a political time frame has become a taken-for-granted feature of the think tank universe. For example, one think tank veteran contrasts the elongated cycles of academic debate with what he calls the "real time" of policy debate. Asked to name a think tank's main priorities, he answers, "Well, the policy process occurs in real time, and so coming out with a really useful study two years after the reauthorization of the bill is of no earthly use to anyone who is engaged in the real policy process. So one thing think tanks are aware of is the policy schedule."[43] The director of another think tank answers the question, "What are the marks of a good researcher here?" with a similar point: "Timeliness. It's not just seeing something, but it's also getting it out fast. I think the value here is being able to rip things out in a hurry. The staff here is really good at that."[44] On this point, remember also the claim made in chapter 3 about the temporal aspect of the Heritage Foundation's early strategy. In the view of the Heritage cofounders, a major problem for Capitol Hill Republicans in the early 1970s was that the work of AEI—then the major conservative policy institute—often lagged behind the policy cycle. As one current Heritage fellow puts it, AEI had "gotten into the habit of doing big long studies, fat studies and volumes, and so forth. Being a little too, in their writing, perhaps a little too scientific."[45] Put differently, AEI's weakness was an overabundance of autonomy with respect to the temporal dimension of its work (which in turn signaled excessive resemblance to an academic institution), leaving the organization vulnerable to competition from other think tanks more willing to subordinate their production to the preestablished rhythms of Washington debate.

Agent Non-Provocateur: The Practical Sense of the Policy Expert

The point of this discussion so far has been that, to succeed in its mission, a think tank must carry out a complex balancing act that pairs a general announcement of intellectual autonomy with a more subtle willingness to abide by the established rules of the political, economic, and media fields. At times, this mixed stance turns positively cumbersome, as indicated by the Manhattan Institute's stated mission of "Combining intellectual seriousness and practical wisdom with intelligent marketing and focused advocacy."[46] At other times, the balancing act I am describing gives rise to apparent hair-splitting, as when the Carnegie Endowment for International Peace describes its mission in the following terms: "We think of ourselves not as an advocate of certain policies or positions, but as a facilitator of significant advocacies by conflicting contributors to the dissensus."[47] In each case, the strategy involves cultivating various ties to more established institutions for the resources and forms of credibility they confer.

While each element of this balancing act operates in some degree of tension with the others, the result is not a truly even set of oppositions. Rather, the pursuit of political access, money, and media visibility can be more easily brought into line with one another than any of these can be reconciled with the pursuit of intellectual credibility. Political access, for example, is often a boon to a think tank's public visibility, which can in turn increase its fundraising capacity. By the same token, a think tank with ample financial resources can hire policy experts with all of the proper political competencies and connections or recruit journalists or media specialists who can help the think tank earn publicity. The goal of demonstrating intellectual autonomy, on the other hand, tends to operate at loggerheads with all of the other forms of credibility because it demands insulation from commercial pressures, freedom from political constraint, and relative indifference to publicity. In this sense, then, the think tank's balancing act can be thought of as a case of "three against one."

At this point the reader might raise two objections, if not to the actual content of my argument, then at least to its spirit and the implied image of the think tank–affiliated policy expert. The first objection is that by portraying the work of think tanks as shaped by so many outside interests, I have committed one of the errors that I warned against at the outset of this book: namely, that of depicting policy experts as powerless functionaries in the hands of political, economic, and media elites. The question is whether I have left any room in my account for the will or agency of policy experts. It would be problematic, after all, to suggest that policy experts have no agency, not least because they typically portray themselves as acting relatively free of outside constrains. "No one is asking me to trim anything I want to say," one policy expert tells me in an interview. "We haven't had any word of content discussion since I got [hired] there."[48]

Another compelling reason to take seriously the agency of policy experts comes from the considerable body of academic research showing that think tanks can at times establish a degree of autonomy from their sponsors and political clients. Donald Critchlow's illuminating study of the Brookings Institution's early history, for example, emphasizes the relative freedom with which Brookings fellows carried out their work in the 1940s, even as they adhered to a stridently promarket position. As Critchlow writes,

It would be easy to conclude after looking at the financial records of the [Brookings] institution and the policies pursued that those who paid the piper selected the tune. But such was not the case. Staff members of the Brookings Institution who had been trained at the nation's leading universities would have resented any such imputation concerning their objectivity. Furthermore, the founders of the Brookings realized from the outset that the institution's prestige rested on its objectivity and absence of party spirit.[49]

Critchlow argues that while Brookings researchers tended to act in a manner consistent with the interests of their sponsors, they were actually operating relatively free of outside constraints.

To dispel the charge that I have ignored the agency of policy experts, I could emphasize again that policy experts are engaged in a tactical balancing act that requires intelligence, savvy, and careful maneuvering. However, this is precisely where a critic might raise the second objection to my argument. By emphasizing the highly instrumental nature of their actions, the critic might say, I have unfairly portrayed policy experts as Machiavellian figures, both scheming and manipulative. Put differently, if my point is that think tanks deliberately signal one message to a general audience and a different message to another audience (of donors, policy makers, and the media), then isn't this tantamount to saying that policy experts are involved in an elaborate deception or hoax?

These are the two questions that the discussion must now address: first, how to account for the close alignment that normally develops between the policy recommendations made by think tanks and the interests of their clients without denying that policy experts possess a certain agency of their own? Second, is it possible to describe the tactical dimension of policy research without reverting to the image of the Machiavellian strategist? As some readers will recognize, these questions correspond directly to two of the most enduring theoretical problems in the social sciences. The first is the problem of how to conceptualize human interest, and the second is the classic structure-agency dilemma, or the problem of how to capture both the objective determinations and the subjective springs of social action without creating an analytic rupture.

In keeping with the theoretical framework outlined in the earlier chapters of this book, I will argue that resolving these problems requires establishing a break with the false oppositions on which they are based. With respect to the first problem, the relevant point is that social action is rarely motivated either by purely utilitarian self-interest or by selfless disinterest alone. We therefore need a more nuanced way of describing human motivation. With respect to the second problem, we should recognize that the distinction between pure freedom and constraint is of little use when describing most forms of social action, including intellectual production. After all, the search for the totally unencumbered intellectual is a futile one, since all intellectuals—from the college professor who must "publish or perish" to the technocrat who cannot challenge the basic premises of her research assignment—face certain necessities and constraints in their work. On the other hand, the language of pure determination is troublesome as well, since even if intellectuals are always constrained in some way, they are inevitably motivated by certain positive ambitions, drives, and desires.

The challenge, then, is to integrate all of these points into a single framework. This is precisely where Bourdieu's concepts of *field, illusio*, and *habitus* become useful. For example, the concept *illusio* is meant as a substitute for a simple or universalistic conception of human interest. Instead it refers to an interested but largely preconscious acceptance of the "rules" of a specific social game and the value of its stakes. Together with the concept of field, illusio pluralizes the idea of interest. Every field, we can say, implies its own set of interests, first, because the field's inhabitants have a stake in accumulating whatever form of capital is produced in that field, and second, because they have a common stake in increasing the value of that capital outside of the field. By describing policy research as the expression of a particular illusio, I am suggesting that a think tank's balancing act depends, not on purely strategic calculation, nor on a form of disinterested action, but on a preconscious acceptance of the historically specific rules of the space of think tanks.

The notion of habitus, meanwhile, is useful for resolving the second theoretical dilemma—the false choice between structure and agency. Broadly speaking, it refers to a socialized subjectivity, or a set of layered mental and bodily schemas acquired through previous socialization experiences.[50] In the theory of action contained here, social agents are neither overdetermined "cultural dopes" who blindly activate social structures, nor are they entirely free agents unencumbered by the constraints of their settings. Instead, they are carriers of perceptual and motivational structures that reflect the objective conditions of their acquisition. In this sense, agency itself is a product of social determination. However, as Bourdieu emphasizes, a habitus is also a *structuring* structure in that the perceptions, evaluations, and dispositions to which it gives rise have a patterning effect on social action. Put differently, a habitus is both generated by and generative of social structures. We can observe the effects of a habitus by taking account of how social agents cognitively carve up the world, how they assign positive and negative valences to their mental categories, and how they act spontaneously and habitually.

To sum up, then, I will address the two possible objections raised above by describing policy research as the expression of a particular illusio, or a historically specific form of *interest*, which, in order to find expression in social life, requires thinking, perceiving agents endowed with the proper habitus. Using this approach, there is no need to describe policy experts as either entirely free agents or as servile dupes. On the contrary, they are actors engaged in a mode of intellectual practice hedged about with certain objective necessities and constraints but also fortified by its own positive ethic. The most successful policy experts, in short, are those who, having internalized the objective necessities and constraints of the field most thoroughly, tend to obey its rules spontaneously or without conscious reflection. Willing agents of "policy research," they become living embodiments of the space of think tanks. Policy research thus functions most smoothly when structure and agency reinforce each other rather than collide — or when the structure of the field operates *through*, rather than against, the will of the policy expert. There is no need in this framework, then, to depict policy research either as a form of purely self-interested action or as a mode of saintly disinterest. On the contrary, my argument is that success in the game of policy research requires both a strategic orientation to the field and a sincere belief in its legitimacy.

Ambivalent Autonomy: On the Motivational Springs of Policy Research

We come, then, to a new set of questions. How do think tank–affiliated policy experts understand their own roles and duties? What does it mean for them to succeed or fail in the "game" of policy research? With respect to these questions, my central finding is that think tank–affiliated policy experts face the difficult task of constructing an "occupational psyche" that combines several disparate elements, including the ability to generate convincing arguments backed by reason and evidence, the ability to "read" the political field strategically and anticipate its dynamics, and the capacity to publicize their ideas widely and raise money. However, lacking a conventional definition of what it means to be a "policy expert," they generally improvise one using a mixture of ready-made cultural materials supplied by the more established fields to which they are linked in their practice. More specifically, policy experts draw on four cultural idioms: those of the *scholar*, the *policy aide*, the *entrepreneur*, and the *media specialist*. While each metaphor underscores an important aspect of their role, it is in the never-ending task of juggling and reconciling these functions that we can find the core of the policy expert's habitus. Let me run through these idioms as a first step in describing the illusio of policy research.

Four Idioms of Duty and Difference

When asked to name the specific attributes needed to excel in the world of think tanks, policy experts often begin by speaking in terms of intellectual proficiency. On this view, the "best" policy experts are those who possess sharp minds, keen analytical abilities, advanced academic training, and highly developed technical skills. In many cases, they use the idiom of academic production to make this point, or a description that underscores the similarities between themselves and academic scholars. For example, many say that a good policy expert is someone who generates cumulative knowledge based on rigorously gathered data and empirical evidence. To the question, "What are the major considerations discussed in a board meeting?" a vice president at one think tank says, "Our board wants to know if we're publishing good quality scholarship and if it contributes to making America a better place."[51] The director of another think tank uses an academic metaphor to describe a rival organization: "Brookings has a very—it's like a university. The range of views there, the range of opinions. The one thing that is consistent is that the people they have there are of the highest caliber. They have all the badges they need to accumulate to be viewed as an expert."[52]

However, the metaphor of academic production is only the first on which policy experts draw to describe their role. A second language of occupational duty builds on the idiom of the *policy aide*. In this trope, a good policy expert should be well versed in the day-to-day rhythms of the policy-making process, its procedural details, and its distinctive norms. On this view, the most important duties of a policy expert include the ability to anticipate "hot" policy issues before they arise and the capacity to churn out useful reports quickly to coincide with these developments. Like a congressional aide, a policy expert should develop specifically political knowledge and skills, including detailed familiarity with the workings of legislative and executive agencies and the ability to brief members of Congress, testify on Capitol Hill, and write "policy briefs." Prior political experience is a valuable asset, and the measure of a good policy report is not so much its scholarly rigor, but its functionality in the policy-making process. Being "too scholarly," in fact, is a fatal flaw.

As the president of one think tank puts it, "You have to be in tune to [policy] developments and take advantage of opportunities to use those developments and respond to them by writing articles, getting that in the press, getting testimony up on the Hill. . . . You have to understand the issues and the players in the policy areas that you're dealing with."[53] The executive director of another think tank explains, "You have to . . . know how to move [an idea] through the policy labyrinth that is this legislative body and administrative body":

INTERVIEWER: And what are the considerations that are taken into account?
RESPONDENT: Well, it's various things. Who sits on what [congressional] committee? Who has seniority? Who sets the policy agenda for that committee? What other stakeholders can be aligned with the proposal that you have that would make it more acceptable to the powers that be on the relevant committees that have to deal with this?
INTERVIEWER: Coalition-building?
RESPONDENT: Yeah, coalition building. Vote-counting, in a way. At the end of the day, on a particular subcommittee, are you going to get out of there with a favorable vote or not? You'll not always, but often, have to think, "Will it sell on the Hill?"[54]

In the words of another policy expert, "Having former government service helps a lot. I think there's a certain aura that comes with, 'He is the former ambassador to the Soviet Union,' or, 'He is the former Undersecretary of State.' You know, the fact that it was twenty years ago and you're kind of pontificating on a subject that you did absolutely nothing on at that point in your life, that doesn't matter. It's just, 'The former this.' You know, people need a title, and that helps."[55]

A third language of occupational duty circulating in the world of think tanks imagines the policy expert, not as a scholar or a policy aide, but as a kind of entrepreneur in a "marketplace of ideas." The metaphors of salesmanship and commercial transaction thus appear repeatedly in the self-accounts of policy experts. Asked to list the attributes needed to excel in policy research, for example, the president of one think tank responds,

> You gotta be a salesman. You have to present your ideas crisply, convincingly, interestingly, and you have to have enormous energy. You have to have what the salesmen call "closing ability." Not only do you make the presentation, but you have to ask for the order. And the order may be a donation or the order may be a bill or a policy idea that you're trying to sell. But you have to be able to ask for the order and get it.[56]

Edwin Feulner, the president of the Heritage Foundation, reflects on the secrets of a successful think tank in similar terms: "The key ingredient is the person who heads it . . . must be entrepreneurial enough to see the unique need [and] salesman enough to convince others (donors, professors to write the papers, and policy makers and journalists) to listen to him and his people."[57] Feulner used the same metaphor in a public speech in 1985: "It takes an institution to help propagandize an idea—to market an idea. . . . Proctor and Gamble does not sell Crest toothpaste by taking out one newspaper ad or running one television commercial. They sell and re-sell it every day, by keeping the product fresh in the consumer's mind. [Think tanks] sell ideas in much the same manner."[58]

The salesmanship metaphor is not new, having crystallized in the widely used term *policy entrepreneur* in the early 1980s.[59] A notable use of the expression appeared in a 1987 *New York Times* profile of policy expert Pat Choate called "The Idea Merchant":

> Choate is known in Washington as a "policy entrepreneur," part of a small community of academics and writers whose articles and speeches and fat Rolodex files help to set the national political agenda. Says William A. Galston of the Roosevelt Center for American Policy Studies, a liberal think tank: "A policy entrepreneur is analogous to the entrepreneur in the private sector. He is the person who creates the venture, who invents the concept of the product and then goes out and markets it." The difference, Galston adds, is that "Pat Choate's working with political capital, not cash."[60]

In this metaphor, policy experts market their intellectual wares to three kinds of consumers: legislators, who "buy" ideas by incorporating them into policy; financial donors, whose purchase is more literal because it involves giving money to the think tank; and journalists, who figuratively buy a think tank's studies when they cite or quote them. The attributes of a successful marketer are therefore valuable among policy experts. These include good "people skills," a taste for self-promotion, and a knack for marketing, including the ability to repackage old ideas skillfully.

Policy experts sometimes invoke the entrepreneurship metaphor as a way of contrasting think tanks and universities, as indicated in the following interview exchange:

INTERVIEWER: Can you tell me something about the set of skills that you need in order to be a successful think tanker, for lack of a better term?
RESPONDENT: Well, there is sort of a public policy entrepreneur personality . . . which basically involves being a good schmoozer. That's really all there is to it.
INTERVIEWER: Schmoozer with journalists? With political figures?
RESPONDENT: With whomever. I mean, a lot of academics are very inarticulate, more so in the hard sciences than in the short sciences [sic]. You know, they write essays and they're shy and stuff. [In] think tanks, you're better off being somewhat gregarious and not being that shy about selling yourself.[61]

Another policy expert uses a similar language to distinguish between a good policy expert and someone who is merely a good thinker: "There are people who are wonderful thinkers, wonderful writers, but they feel very uncomfortable promoting themselves. And what you need [in a think tank] is self-promoters. I think that some of the best people in this game have been shameless self-promoters."[62]

The importance of self-promotion gives rise to a fourth language of occupational duty among policy experts. In this metaphor, a good policy expert should resemble a media or communications specialist in his or her ability to disseminate knowledge that is both accessible and compelling to the wider public. The policy expert should display a knack for writing and speaking in plain language and a willingness to compose short, compact studies in a form similar to press releases or newspaper articles. As the president of one think tank puts it, "Public relations, media relations—or media savvy—is a very important aspect of the business."[63] In some cases, journalists supply the imaginary model for the policy expert. Says one think tank fellow who is also a seasoned journalist: "It's true in journalism and it's true in think tanks: to be a successful think tank person, you need to be able to write in a way that is understandable to non-specialists. . . . It's a matter of making complicated matters understandable in colloquial terms."[64] For other policy experts, the forms of media proficiency that matter the most have more to do with comfort and eloquence on television than with advanced writing skills. As a CEI fellow explains, "With doing broadcast interviews, well specifically TV, your body language is so important—as important, if not more important, than actually the words that you use. [CEI president] Fred [Smith Jr.] is very good at it. He's got

the energy and the quips, and the producers love him, so he's on TV a lot.
And of course he does radio well, too. But his energy—he really does TV.
That's his forte."[65] According to the director of another think tank, policy
experts should always "have a sense of what's going to be newsworthy"
and be "able to consolidate their technical, complex ideas into something
that is really very understandable—that is, a sound bite, if you will."[66]

Perhaps the clearest evidence of the importance of media savvy among
policy experts is the refined set of mental categories with which many perceive and evaluate the news media universe. For example, when asked to
name the most desirable places to be quoted or cited, or to publish their
work, few policy experts find themselves at a loss for words, and many
invoke highly nuanced distinctions:

> [In the] print media, the place to be is the *New York Times*. The *Wall Street
> Journal*, if you're an economist. The *Washington Post* for local Washington ex-
> posure, including the Congress and the government, but the *Washington Post*
> doesn't have the national reach that the *Times* and the *Journal* do.[67]

*   *   *

> The *Wall Street Journal* or the *Financial Times*—on trade or budget [issues],
> those are the papers that you want to reach for. The *New Republic* or the *Weekly
> Standard* are more niche-oriented weeklies, one being more liberal, one being
> more conservative, but we have friends in both.[68]

*   *   *

> If you want to get your article talked about, it had better be in the *Post*, the
> *Times*, or the *Journal*. In magazines, the *New Republic*, the *Atlantic Monthly*. I
> think to a lesser extent the *Weekly Standard* and *National Review*. . . . *Harpers*,
> I think, has become kind of ridiculous. And the *Atlantic Monthly* . . . has just
> soared beyond *Harpers*.[69]

*   *   *

RESPONDENT: Andy Kohut, who's my boss at Pew, places incredibly great store
    in the [PBS Jim] Lehrer show. It's true, they'll give you five to seven minutes
    or whatever as opposed to forty-five seconds. It's true that thoughtful people
    watch it. . . .
INTERVIEWER: You're on [NPR's] *Marketplace*.

RESPONDENT: Yeah, I'm on *Marketplace*. But that's not nearly as good as being on *All Things Considered*. You know, just a bigger audience and you get more time and, again, a thoughtful audience. [It's] useful in part because I'm amazed at the number of people who listen to NPR commuting. You know, serious people.[70]

The overarching point is that policy experts are rarely content to choose just one of the idioms listed above. Instead, the ethic of policy research is built on the goals of mastering and juggling all four. In this sense, policy experts are like the democracy and human rights promoters whom Nicolas Guilhot describes as "double agents," a term he quickly amends by speaking of " 'triple agents' or even multiple agents."[71] In similar fashion, think tank–affiliated policy experts succeed through the multiplicity of their resources and affiliations. For instance, one Brookings fellow describes how the organization recruits new staff members in the following terms:

INTERVIEWER: If you're hiring a new scholar here at Brookings, what are the marks of a good policy researcher? Who are you looking for?
RESPONDENT: Good track record in writing stuff, usually.
INTERVIEWER: Writing, like, op-ed pieces, or writing in academic journals?
RESPONDENT: Writing both. Brookings would look for somebody who had written a really good book on something or a series of not-too-academic journal articles. But if there had been some op-eds and things, that would be a plus. If this was a person who was a good speaker and presenter, that would be a plus.[72]

The president of another think tank makes a similar point: "We really want you to try and always have one foot in the analytic camp and one foot in the advocacy camp."[73]

I have suggested that we can summarize this balancing act as a game of assembling academic, political, economic, and media capital. However, it is worth considering the special status of academic capital in this project, not least because many policy experts exhibit an acute ambivalence toward academia. For example, some praise their own institutions in a manner that implies a positive valuation of academic autonomy: "Like a good academic institution, there is a real protection of academic freedom here," says one AEI fellow.[74] Nevertheless, stated affinities with academic scholars often give way to sharp critiques of "ivory tower" scholasticism. Says one think tank veteran: "There are countless [academic] disciplines that are very inward looking. I would say inward looking, incestuous, and not very interesting. And that don't add much, don't have much wisdom to contribute to anybody outside of their discipline."[75] Typically, the brunt of policy experts' critiques are aimed at the academic social sciences, the disciplines most proximate to policy research itself. On this count, the most conspicuous charge is that the social sciences have become marred by empty or ritualistic displays of methodological and theoretical proficiency. For example, policy experts trained as economists and political scientists sometimes argue that the statistical modeling techniques favored by their academic counterparts contribute nothing to actual policy-making discussions. In the words of one policy expert, "These economists like to build their models that have nothing to do with the real world and that's one of the reasons I think the think tanks have risen. [Think tanks] are more interested in talking about what the real world is."[76] Another policy expert with a PhD in economics makes a similar point: "In economics, they put a lot of stock in economic modeling and I have to say, I just find that such a waste of time because I could show you anything you want in an economic model. The question is, is it really saying anything about the world? . . . To me [academic publishing] is just absolutely pointless. It is a ritual that gets people tenure."[77]

The common companion to this critique, especially among conservative policy experts, is that the discursive turn in the humanities and social sciences after the 1960s encouraged overly abstract and relativistic thinking in the academy. For example, one Heritage fellow suggests an indirect link between his organization's success and the rise of postmodernist and poststructuralist theory in the academy: "I think what had happened [when Heritage began] is that professors had become increasingly more and more arcane in their studies, had turned inward, affected by the various trends which were going on at that time, whether it was Foucault or Derrida and all the rest of those guys. You know, 'Nothing is real. It's all relative.' Well, that's not exactly what a politician wants. He's looking for some answers to a particular problem, not, 'Well, there is no answer.'" By turning inward, the respondent says, academic scholars "opt[ed] themselves out of being able to be in play in the world of politics and public policy."[78]

Ambivalence toward academia often finds its clearest expression among policy experts who were once scholars themselves. Looking back on their careers in the academy, some express a distaste for the academic sensibility that seems all the more vehement because traces of it endure within themselves. Of course, the same policy experts are also aware of the inevitable counter-accusation: that they are "failed academics" and that their negativity toward scholarship springs more from defensiveness than from an honest appraisal of academic work. They are mindful, for example, that some scholars perceive the work of policy experts as lacking in rigor or seriousness. In response, many policy experts point to the special skills needed to excel in the world of think tanks. For example, one former political science professor at AEI reflects on the considerable level of mastery needed to compose an op-ed piece for the newspaper: "This is an acquired skill and something that is difficult for most academics to do. If you are used to writing journal articles or writing books, there is no discipline that comes to bear in the sense that you have got to limit this to a small space." Compared to academic writing, he says, drafting articles for the newspaper "is harder to do. It takes more internal discipline. . . . You don't have the luxury of meandering around. You've got to focus and pinpoint."[79]

Although the assumption that most policy experts are failed academics might be intuitively attractive to many professors, I believe this formulation is too simplistic to withstand close empirical scrutiny. As Erving Goffman once noted, "There are few positions in life that do not throw together some persons who are there by virtue of failure and other persons who are there by virtue of success."[80] To illustrate the point, Goffman suggested the example of dentistry, an occupation performed by "some who have failed to become physicians and others who have succeeded at not becoming pharmacists or optometrists."[81] The difference between the two types of dentists is rarely obvious, however (even among dentists themselves). "In this sense," Goffman wrote, "the dead are sorted but not segregated, and continue to walk among the living."[82] A similar point can be made about think tank–affiliated policy experts, among whom the "dead" are likewise sorted but not obviously segregated.

However, while the point applies well to policy experts in certain respects, there is an added twist or complexity to it. Whereas a relatively stable status hierarchy orders the relations among physicians, dentists, pharmacists, and optometrists, there is no fixed or agreed upon hierarchy among the role-sets on which policy experts draw. It is possible, then, to adapt Goffman's insight in opposing ways. The first formulation is more likely to resonate among intellectuals for whom the goal of cognitive autonomy is important: whereas some policy experts arrive at a think tank having failed to become scholars, others have succeeded at not becoming lobbyists or politicos. Yet other observers would insist on the opposite formulation: some policy experts work at think tanks because they have failed to become politicos or party officials, while others have succeeded in avoiding the "ivory tower." I have sought to account for this complexity by arguing that the hierarchy of role-sets and forms of value associated with them are important *stakes* of competition in the space of think tanks. Even as policy experts try to influence public policy outcomes, I suggested, they also implicitly assert the superiority of their own combinations of resources, skills, and credentials. A policy expert who is an ex-scholar, for example, has an interest in upholding the value of academic skills and credentials in the space of think tanks. Apart from their struggles to influence policy outcomes, then, policy experts inhabit a "meta-space" of competition over the relative values of the forms of authority used in this struggle.

Policy Research through the Lens of Field Theory

The field theory approach is useful for making sense of the ambivalence many policy experts express toward academia, and of the balancing act central to policy research. "In the manner of a prism," Wacquant writes, a field "refracts external forces according to its internal structure."[83] In much the same way, I would argue, the space of think tanks refracts the force of academic capital by altering, and in some cases inverting, conventional academic hierarchies. Put differently, while academic capital has a certain value within the space of think tanks, the forms of academic capital that garner the most legitimacy tend to be those with the lowest value in the university, and vice versa. Perhaps the clearest illustration of this point is the fact that peer-reviewed publications, the main guarantor of legitimacy within academic disciplines, bring only minor (indeed, almost zero) prestige in the world of think tanks. In fact, few policy experts report reading the major journals in their fields, much less devoting time or energy to publishing in them. At the same time, forms of academic capital that have only secondary importance in the academic field carry great value in the space of think tanks. For example, many think tanks insist on making symbolic displays of kinship with universities—such as by referring to their expert staff members as "scholars" or "fellows," irrespective of their actual academic degrees or titles. Other think tanks establish endowed chair positions reminiscent of university professorships. To list a few examples: the Heritage Foundation has the Chung Ju-Yung Fellow for Policy Studies, Brookings has the Bruce and Virginia MacLaury Chair in Economic Studies, and AEI has the Joseph J. and Violet Jacobs Scholar in Social

Welfare Studies. Other think tanks describe their work using an academic idiom. In 1997, for example, the Cato Institute launched a division called the "Cato University" that offered educational seminars for aspiring libertarians.[84] Finally, a few think tanks, including the Brookings Institution, have World Wide Web addresses with the suffix ".edu."[85]

The central point is that the need to reconcile the pursuit of academic respectability with political, economic, and media judgments leads many think tanks to valorize the most "disposable," least substantive forms of academic capital. Academic capital thus has a double valence in the world of think tanks that mirrors the opposition between "purity and danger," a la Mary Douglas.[86] At one level, think tanks use academic capital to perform a kind of ritual of self-purification. Tarnished by their associations with the government, the market, the media, and the world of lobbying, they must "consecrate" themselves by establishing a connection with the quasi-sacred world of intellectual production and the priestly authority figure of the intellectual. However, because an overabundance of academic capital also threatens to marginalize a think tank in the competition for funding, political access, and visibility, academic capital also has a profaning effect. (As Durkheim notes in *The Elementary Forms of Religious Life*, "Every profanation implies a consecration, but one that is dreadful to whoever is consecrated."[87])

An analogous point can be made about the other forms of capital circulating in the world of think tanks. For example, the most efficient guarantor of political access for a think tank, hypothetically speaking, would be to establish a formal partnership with an official government agency or a political party. However, as we have already seen, such partnerships carry built-in dangers because they always threaten to undermine a think tank's effort to appear independent. Consequently, the most prized forms of political capital are the embodied forms carried by politically savvy policy experts. A similar point can be made about economic capital, since in principle, a think tank could make money by engaging in its own revenue-generating practices, such as by charging conference and membership fees or by selling its own books and periodicals. Yet even after taking into account the limited market for such goods (i.e., the fact that there are few products a think tank can sell that others are not willing to give away for free), there is a *strategic* danger in the act of selling one's products. After all, the more commercialized a think tank's products become, the less plausible are its claims to autonomy from the market. It is not surprising, then, that self-generated revenue constitutes a relatively small share of the income gathered by most think tanks (see figure 4.2).

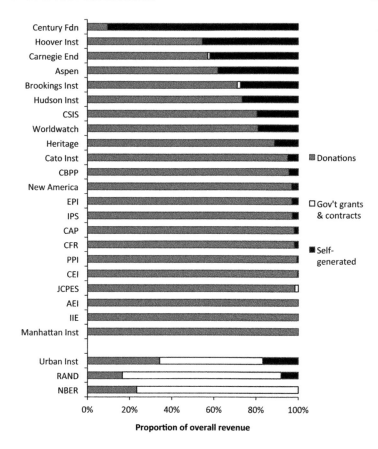

FIGURE 4.2 Revenue sources of major think tanks, 2008. Sources: 2008 IRS 990 tax forms. Note: Self-generated revenue includes investment income (securities, interest on savings, etc.), conference and membership fees, rental income, and publication sale proceeds. Since the Hoover Institution does not file its own federal income tax return, figures come from its annual report.

Instead, most think tanks rely on a patchwork of donations from foundations, individuals, and corporations.

Of course, not all donations are equal in their symbolic effects, as think tank representatives sometimes point out. One think tank director distinguishes between "clean" and "dirty" money in these terms: "When you're getting money from the tobacco industry [or] you're getting money from different industry groups, they're giving it to you for a very specific purpose. The foundations, I'm not going to hold them up as models of benevolence, but they don't have that sort of narrow interest at stake. For the most part I'd say that money is cleaner, even if not 100 percent clean."[88] The best economic asset for a think tank is therefore neither a direct profit-making capacity per se, nor a close partnership with a single moneyed sponsor; instead, it is a staff of highly "entrepreneurial" policy experts, or those who possess the styles, skills, and sensibilities needed to raise money and angle their work to the market for donations.

The same framework helps explain why only certain kinds of media capital are particularly valuable among policy experts. As we would expect from the preceding discussion, many think tanks take the means of publicity into their own hands by publishing their own periodicals and books, sending out electronic newsletters, and maintaining sophisticated websites and blogs. However, like the other forms of capital, too much self-generated publicity always threatens to make a think tank appear like a mere messaging machine or "PR firm in disguise." Transparently self-generated publicity, in other words, has less value in the space of think tanks than publicity bestowed by outside media institutions. Accordingly, the best strategy for earning publicity is to win the attentions of journalists, which itself requires a staff of policy experts who possess embodied media capital, or the styles and judgments of a journalist or media specialist. In the topological model I have suggested, the main point is that the best way for a think tank to maintain its political alliances, its funding, its media visibility, and its intellectual credibility is to hire policy experts who exist near the center of the space of think tanks, or in between its parent fields.

The multisided role implied by this structural location is doubly difficult to master, not only because each of its elements requires extensive social learning, but also because they are generally at loggerheads with one another. As the president of one think tank laments, "Mostly all those skills don't come together in one person, and so . . . almost everyone we hire, I believe, is stronger in one side or the other."[89] A think tank vice president makes a similar observation: "It really is difficult to find somebody who is very smart and knowledgeable [and] who also is able to write effectively and clearly for people who aren't experts and can talk to the media to provide sound bites." Whereas academic scholars are likely "to be very narrow in their focus," former political specialists "are more likely to have the skills to be able to communicate and talk in sound bites. The flip side of that, though, is the heft. They typically don't have PhDs, by and large. They haven't developed an expertise beyond the 'faster turnaround' kind of stuff."[90] To compensate for these shortcomings, think tanks often hire policy experts with career backgrounds in multiple occupational set-

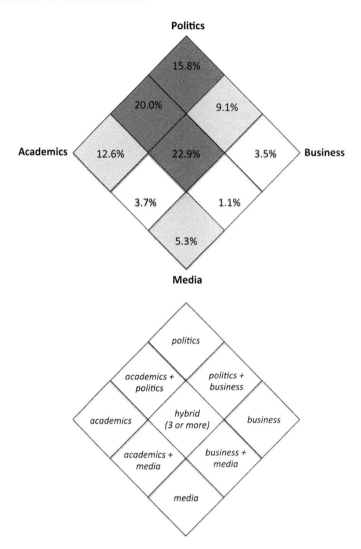

FIGURE 4.3 Distribution of policy experts within the space of think tanks by career background.

tings. Figure 4.3 illustrates the wide range of possible career trajectories into the space of think tanks.

To construct this figure, I coded the self-reported employment backgrounds of all the policy experts at 21 major think tanks for whom such data were available (n=898). As the bottom portion of the diagram indicates,

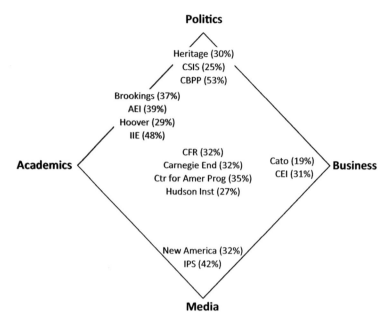

FIGURE 4.4 Selected think tanks by modal career background of policy experts.

the data are divided into nine structural origin categories, plus an additional "other" category.[91] Although policy experts follow multiple career paths into the think tank, one conclusion we can draw from this figure is that it is common for policy experts to acquire a mixture of career skills before working in a think tank. Fully 56.8 percent of the expert staff members included in this figure report job experience in two or more of the think tank's four anchoring fields—and if we expand our notion of "career hybridity" to include those who have worked previously in one of these sectors plus the nonprofit sector, then the figure jumps to 71.6 percent. Strikingly, 22.9 percent of the policy experts report work experience in three or all four of the main anchoring fields.

Figure 4.4 aggregates the same data at the level of the organization and locates several think tanks analytically within the space of think tanks. Once again, we get a sense of the field's interior structure. At the Brookings Institution, AEI, Hoover, and IIE, for example, the largest share of policy experts report mixed job experiences in the academic and political fields. By contrast, at more overtly "ideological" think tanks, such as the Heritage Foundation, the Center for Strategic and International Studies, and the Center on Budget and Policy Priorities, a plurality of policy experts report career backgrounds in politics only. Meanwhile, two think tanks are positioned nearest the field's economic pole: the Cato Institute and the Competitive Enterprise Institute. Moving around the field's perimeter, we also find two think tanks (IPS, New America) that employ substantial numbers of policy experts with backgrounds in the media, especially ex-journalists. Finally, at the Council on Foreign Relations, the Carnegie Endowment for International Peace, the Center for American Progress, and the Hudson Institute, "hybrid" career backgrounds predominate. These are think tanks at which a plurality of policy experts report mixed job experiences before their employment at the think tank. It is worth noting also that at no think tank in my database is an exclusively academic career background the most common kind. In other words, even the organizations with the most scholarly reputations, such as Brookings and Hoover, tend to hire ex-academic scholars who have also established some experience in politics, business, or the media.

Toward a Social Topology of the Space of Think Tanks

We are now in a better position to understand the differences among think tanks. The main takeaway point of this discussion is that these differences are an emergent property of the field, or the system of competitive and collaborative relations among think tanks. Rather than divide think tanks into "types," then, we can represent the differences among them in terms of their strategic orientations to the field's anchoring poles. Typologies miss the forest for the trees by obscuring the social relations in which think tanks are embedded. While think tanks run the full gamut from organizations inserted deeply in the academic field to those visibly harnessed to business corporations, political parties, activist networks, social movements, and media organs, more important than the properties of any single organization is the fact that collectively think tanks make up a structured social universe with its own "rules" and hierarchies. Let me now elaborate on the topography of this space.

The starting point for this discussion is the observation that the identities of specific think tanks can be described largely in terms of the combination of their relationships to the more established fields surrounding them. I can illustrate this point by looking at a think tank situated nearest the field's economic pole: the Competitive Enterprise Institute. Like all think tanks, CEI leads a kind of double life. On the one side, CEI is a nonprofit organization that employs a roster of affiliated staff members who issue policy recommendations built on certain claims to expertise. And yet it would be nearly impossible to overlook the fact that CEI has also established a clear reputation as an advocate of probusiness policies. Fred Smith Jr., CEI's founder and president, describes his organization's mission in these terms: "We have to illustrate that business needs allies in the war for survival. . . . We're sort of a 'battered business bureau.' Businessmen who get in real trouble may well then decide they need allies, and they'll reach out and say, 'Is there anyone out there we can help whose work parallels our interests?' "[92] While CEI's directors would not likely embrace the label *corporate think tank*, neither do they make any secret of their ultimate aims or sources of financial support. ("I probably have as much business funding as any group out there," Smith says.[93])

Of course, CEI's officers would likely point out that if big business can look to their organization as an ally in the "war for survival," then capital's perennial adversaries—namely, organized labor—can also depend on certain think tanks for intellectual support. As I have already discussed, an example of a prolabor think tank is the Economic Policy Institute, which was formed in 1986 by a collection of liberal economists, including soon-to-be Secretary of Labor Robert Reich. Over its 25-year history, EPI has established a clear reputation as an organization that speaks on behalf of the labor movement. And while EPI has often disputed the label "labor-backed think tank"—a point I explored above—in years past it has accepted up to 40 percent of its funding from unions. The image of a field is thus useful for capturing both the similarities and the differences between CEI and EPI. For example, their proximity in the field's economic pole (or the region of the space of think tanks linked to the market) is reflected in the fact that both organizations have focused their attentions squarely on economic and trade policies, such as the North American Free Trade Agreement. At the same time, the fact that CEI and EPI generally take divergent intellectual stances on these issues can be explained by their opposing relationships to capital and labor. Even in the rare instances when the two organizations align on a particular issue, they typically do so for different reasons. For example, both CEI and EPI have been critical of NAFTA, albeit for different reasons: CEI has argued that the treaty's side deals inhibited free trade by adding new environmental and labor regulations, whereas EPI has argued that it deprives American workers of jobs.[94]

Of course, not all think tanks derive their main identities from their relationships to the economic field. Others are tied more closely to the bureaucratic field. Perhaps the best example of a quasi-bureaucratic think tank is the RAND Corporation, which derives most of its resources directly from the US Department of Defense. RAND's defense-oriented cousins (e.g., MITRE, CNA, Hudson) can also be described in these terms, as can another think tank often cited as RAND's domestic policy counterpart, the Urban Institute, founded in 1968 at the behest of the Johnson White House to carry out research on the implementation and evaluation of social policies for the Great Society programs. Since its inception, Urban has received most of its funding from cabinet departments such as Housing and Urban Development; Health, Education, and Welfare (later Health and Human Services); and Labor.

Other think tanks overlap the political field, or the system of struggles among parties, politicians, political specialists (e.g., pollsters, campaign advisers), and activists over the powers of delegation and political representation. A clear example of a think tank that derives its main identity from its ties to the political field is the Progressive Policy Institute, created in 1989 as the research arm of the Democratic Leadership Council, the organizational base of the "New Democrat" movement.[95] Two lesser-known think tanks that also sit in this region of the field are linked to legislative coalitions in Congress: the Northeast-Midwest Institute and the California Institute. Both organizations were formed by regional congressional groups seeking to ensure bipartisan unity on issues affecting their geographic regions. We can also identify various think tanks that rely on activist networks for the majority of their resources, political access, and legitimacy. For example, each of the major progressive movements of the past half-century has at least one think tank tied visibly to its cause. The Worldwatch Institute, for example, describes itself as playing a "pivotal role in the global environmental movement," while the Joint Center for Political and Economic Studies has dedicated itself to the struggle for civil rights. Likewise, the Institute for Women's Policy Research, a think tank run by sociologist Heidi Hartmann, is often described as the main think tank of the women's movement.

As I have noted, the activist network with the most extensive representation in the space of think tanks is the conservative movement. Precisely for this reason, there is advanced differentiation among the think tanks of the right, which vary considerably in terms of issue orientation and scope. For example, whereas Heritage, AEI, Manhattan, and the National

Center for Policy Analysis have all fashioned themselves as all-purpose conservative torchbearers, other think tanks are tied to specific subgroups on the right. The Cato Institute, for example, has long operated as a beacon of libertarianism. ("We're crusaders," a Cato policy expert told the *Washington Post* in 1999. "We all work here because we want to change the world."[96]) Also worth mentioning in this context is the Project for the New American Century, a think tank that existed from 1997 to 2006 as an organizational base of the neoconservative foreign policy movement. Many of PNAC's founding members (among them Richard Perle, Paul Wolfowitz, and Donald Rumsfeld) went on to play key roles in the George W. Bush administration.[97] Finally, one finds several think tanks associated with prominent conservative politicians and activists, such as the Free Congress Foundation, the Liberty Institute, and the Progress and Freedom Foundation.

Still other think tanks overlap the major culture-producing institutions of American society, including universities and the media. In the former category, two of the most notable cases are the Hoover Institution and the National Bureau of Economic Research. Hoover boasts a roster of experts that includes many university professors, most of whom are affiliated with Hoover's parent institution, Stanford University. NBER likewise trades on its scholarly reputation and counts among its "family members" hundreds of full-time university professors, the vast majority of whom are economists. Finally, a small number of think tanks are known for their direct ties to the media and journalistic fields. On this count, the best example is the New America Foundation, a think tank formed in 1999 by Ted Halstead, Michael Lind, and Sherle Schwenninger. In keeping with its journalistic pedigree (Lind was an editor of the *National Interest* and Schwenninger was a founding editor of *World Policy Journal*) New America has excelled in the competition for media attention on a relatively modest budget. Its main strategy has been to create symbiotic partnerships with prominent media organs. In 2002, for example, New America forged an agreement with the *Atlantic Monthly* to co-produce an annual "State of the Union" issue featuring essays by New America experts. New America's founders have also used their social ties to the journalistic field to hire ex- and part-time journalists as policy experts, such as Pulitzer Prize-winners Katherine Boo and Steve Coll (NAF's current president) and *New Yorker* staff writer Margaret Talbott. At the time of its founding, New America's use of journalists as policy experts was a relatively novel approach among think tanks, albeit one that was anticipated by other media-oriented think tanks, such as the Heritage Foundation.

The objective differences among think tanks give rise to certain predictable clashes of intellectual style among them that shape the field's interior dynamic. On this point, consider the following story told by a Brookings Institution fellow about the experience of venturing into the foreign territory known as the Heritage Foundation:

> Some years ago, I was invited to engage in a debate at the Heritage Foundation.... I did my thing, and the audience—there was cheering and booing! Now, you'd never have that at Brookings. And afterwards there was a kind of wine and cheese thing and nobody talked to me. It was kind of amazing. Brookings is a very polite place. We don't generally stage debates, but we have a spectrum of opinion on the panel and everybody is always very polite to each other. We can't imagine a Brookings audience cheering or booing or having anything like that. It was very clear that I had ventured into the camp of the enemy. One or two people that I know on the Hill came over and said hello, but it was really a rather awkward moment.[98]

The story contains all of the familiar elements of culture shock, in the anthropological sense of the term, including confusion and anxiety about once taken-for-granted norms, mutual suspicion, and a sense of longing for the home culture. What is striking, of course, is that the story takes place entirely inside of the space of think tanks.

The oppositional dynamic described here corresponds to a wider culture clash in Washington politics between "hacks" and "wonks." As journalist Bruce Reed explains:

> Strip away the job titles and party labels, and you will find two kinds of people in Washington: political hacks and policy wonks. . . . Some journalists are wonks, but most are hacks. Some columnists are hacks, but most are wonks. All members of Congress pass themselves off as wonks, but many got elected as hacks. Lobbyists are hacks who make money pretending to be wonks. The *Washington Monthly*, the *New Republic*, and the entire political blogosphere consist largely of wonks pretending to be hacks. "The Hotline" is for hacks; *National Journal* is for wonks. "The West Wing" is for wonks; "K Street" was for hacks. After two decades in Washington as a wonk working among hacks, I have come to the conclusion that the gap between Republicans and Democrats is as nothing compared to the one between these two tribes.[99]

Projecting these categories into the space of think tanks, the point is that the most "wonkish" policy experts are those who bring technical skills and credentials to the practice of policy research, whereas "hacks" enter the field with fewer academic credentials but tend to be better equipped with political know-how. Based on the self-descriptions of policy experts, we can further subdivide the "hack" category by speaking of "policy entrepreneurs," who trade on their salesmanship and fundraising abilities, and "quotemeisters," who regard eloquence and media punditry as their main stock-in-trade.

The main point, however, is that the distinction between hacks and wonks mirrors a key structural opposition in the space of think tanks that crosscuts and sometimes eclipses political ideology in the minds of policy experts. An AEI fellow, for example, sees a greater affinity between his organization and Brookings (a think tank normally counted as AEI's ideological rival) than between AEI and its conservative ally, Heritage. Asked how he cognitively carves up the think tank world, he replies, "There is a real distinction between think tanks like AEI and Brookings and the Urban Institute, say, places that are in some respects rough copies of 'universities without students' . . . and places like Heritage and some of the others, that are called think tanks, that have a few scholars but are more lobbying organizations who try to affect more directly policy decisions, often on a day-to-day basis."[100] Broadly speaking, the gap between hacks and wonks corresponds to the bipolar opposition between universalistic and temporal forms of authority.

Nevertheless, I would also insist that we remain attentive to the four-sidedness of the space of think tanks, since economic, political, and media capital can also operate in tension with one another. On this point, consider the little known case of the Roosevelt Center for American Policy Studies, a short-lived think tank established in 1982 by Richard Dennis, a Chicago commodities trader who had amassed a personal fortune in excess of $200 million by the age of 31. Hoping to promote the ideals of civic engagement and bipartisanship in Washington, Dennis committed $5 million of his personal funds to start the new think tank, which opened its doors on Capitol Hill with a staff of about 25.[101] By all outward appearances, the Roosevelt Center was well situated to become a major player among Washington think tanks. Dennis had stocked the organization with a sizeable collection of talent, including Douglas Bennet, a former Democratic legislative aide and foreign aid official whom the *Washington Post* called the "the consummate Washington 'public policy entrepreneur.' "[102]

However, tension soon developed between Dennis and the organization's managers, some of whom believed that the founder's agenda was out of step with the political environment. In 1983, the conflict reached a boiling point, and Dennis carried out what one of the organization's original vice presidents called a "major purge" of the organization.[103] As the *Washington Post* reported, "Dennis flew into Washington . . . , walked into the office of Douglas J. Bennet, the president, and asked him to resign."[104]

Bennet's replacement was Roger Molander, a former National Security Council staff member and public-interest lobbyist who was more sympathetic to Dennis's vision. Four years later, however, Dennis incurred $20 million in personal losses in the October 1987 stock market crash, roughly the same amount of money he had invested in his think tank up to that point. He was also slapped with a costly class action lawsuit filed by investors, who charged him with mismanaging two futures funds worth $100 million. Faced with these new challenges, Dennis abruptly decided to end his pricey experiment in policy research. Even this setback, however, need not have spelled the end for the Roosevelt Center. From an optimistic point of view, Dennis' withdrawal from the organization might have seemed like a blessing. After all, the center's directors were now free to chart their own course rather than take orders from a "meddling" outsider. However, what might have seemed like an opportunity for growth proved to be the Roosevelt Center's death knell. The center limped through the next year in search of new funding before finally closing its doors in June 1989.[105]

What caused the Roosevelt Center's demise? I would argue that the main process leading to its collapse was a struggle internal to the organization between holders of economic and political capital. On the one side was the founder, Richard Dennis, who bankrolled the organization with clear expectations that he could therefore shape its intellectual agenda. On the other side were the center's directors, a seasoned group of political specialists whose strategies were shaped by their accumulated political capital. From their standpoint, Dennis had underestimated the importance of political competence in the practice of policy research. (Soon after his firing, for example, Bennet, the deposed president, offered the following self-defense to the *Washington Post*: "I do understand Washington and how it works. What I do must look as arcane to Dennis as what he does looks to me."[106]) But when exigent circumstances caused Dennis to pull the plug on his funding, the staff could not save the organization, all of their political capital notwithstanding. Even after the founder's departure, the Roosevelt Center could not shake the image that it was just the vanity project of a lone sponsor.

As a former Roosevelt Center fellow puts it, "Look, it was, and is, tough to get funding for genuinely nonpartisan exercises. Most people who want to give money to inside-the-beltway organizations have an agenda of one sort or another. So Roosevelt Center survived as long as its principal funder was willing to keep it going. And when he decided, after a number of years, that it was time for the Center to go out on its own and meet a market test, it didn't last very long."[107]

Conclusion: Think Tanks as Blurring Organizations

I have characterized think tanks as inhabitants of a peculiar social universe in which achieving centrality means positioning oneself as a relevant, albeit marginal, player in each of four highly institutionalized fields (those of academics, politics, business, and the media), whereas marginality attaches to organizations that partake most meaningfully of any of these same four worlds. Doubtless the most appropriate question at this point is why any organization would voluntarily undertake this strenuous balancing act. Why bother, in other words, to heed principles of academic, political, economic, and media judgment all at once, excelling in none of these areas, but neither failing altogether in any of them? One possibility, of course, is that the strategy itself is a misguided one and that think tanks are at bottom organizations divided against themselves. Indeed, rather than simply dismiss this possibility out of hand, let me point out that a conventional use of the field theory approach I have recommended might arrive at the very same conclusion. After all, in the logic normally associated with fields, the power at stake in a field is rooted in a principle of distinction: the field's inhabitants accumulate their own form of authority to the degree that they manage to separate themselves collectively from other fields by monopolizing the evaluation of their own products. In the case of think tanks, however, we can see that this description does not quite work. Even though think tanks seek to establish a curious form of independence, their strategy for doing so involves signaling their *dependence* on academic, political, market, and media institutions.

A conventional application of field theory therefore seems to put us at an impasse by portraying think tanks as members of a "lesser" field, and the goal of separation itself as futile. At the same time, think tanks cannot become major players in any of their parent fields, since their "quadruple bind" demands that they remain always at the margins of each one. For example, the main strategy available to a think tank for separating itself from expressly political organizations is to adhere to the norms of (or at least to display the outward trappings of) scholarly proficiency. Likewise, the main strategy available to a think tank for distinguishing itself from academia is to subordinate its production to the rules of the political, economic, and media fields.

If the problem I am pointing to seems obscure when posed in these theoretical terms, let me illustrate it with a specific example. Consider again the Heritage Foundation, by all accounts one of the most successful think tanks of the past four decades. How would we describe the nature of Heritage's "power" or influence? The puzzle is that by almost any conventional measure of power—political, economic, or cultural—we would find it to be lacking. For example, despite its considerable funding, Heritage is not truly an economic powerhouse, its financial assets being overshadowed by those of many other political organizations (e.g., lobbying firms and large advocacy groups), to say nothing of business corporations. (If Heritage were a private corporation, for instance, it would not rank among the 1,000 largest firms in the United States.) Nor of course does Heritage have any formal political authority. Like all think tanks, it must compete for the attentions of politicians and bureaucrats. It would also be incorrect to say that Heritage has ever possessed much cultural authority, especially outside of specifically conservative circles. In this sense, its claims to expertise are tenuous. As Paul Weyrich himself noted in an interview, "At the time that we started Heritage . . . we had no real experts. We had a bunch of eager young people who in time became expert. But at the time that I had them, nobody knew who they were."[108] To this day, in fact, Heritage employs relatively few PhD holders, and its policy staff members rarely publish their work in scientific journals. Finally, despite the organization's considerable media savvy, Heritage does not actually control the means of publicity. Instead, it must depend on journalists and media specialists to get its message out.

Most puzzling of all, perhaps, is the fact that each element of Heritage's strategy seems to undermine all of the others. For example, to the degree that Heritage cultivates "insider" ties to Republicans, it risks becoming an arm of the party, thus canceling out any attempt it might make to generate intellectual credibility in any universalistic sense. One possibility, as I noted, is that Heritage is simply an organization divided against itself.

However, I believe that to jump to this conclusion is to think about its power and influence in the wrong terms. Concretely, what has Heritage accomplished? Remember that the organization's cofounders drew on multiple resources, including their social ties to Capitol Hill Republicans, insider knowledge of legislative and executive procedures, and personal connections to wealthy businessmen (most notably, beer magnate Joseph Coors). Recognizing the importance of media relations, they also hired ex-journalists and public relations specialists to serve in key managerial roles. To all of this, the Heritage founders have added a small but visible dose of academic capital. Remember, also, that this combination of resources allowed Heritage to create novel, hybrid products that were useful to politicians, activists, and the media. (In particular, Heritage became known for its brief policy reports and its presidential transition document, *Mandate for Leadership*.)

To capture the significance of this contribution in sociological terms, we have to establish a break with the language of "distinction" and speak instead in terms of *indistinction*. In other words, I would argue that the main source of Heritage's power has not been its capacity to occupy a specific field per se, but rather its ability to *blur the boundaries* among fields. The same point holds true for think tanks in general. Their chief power lies in their ability to claim for themselves a kind of mediating role in the social structure. The plausibility of this claim rests in turn on their capacity to establish a mixture of resources captured from other fields. Throughout this book, I have described the significance of this power from a macro-structural point of view. From this perspective, the rise of think tanks in the United States was the result of a historical reconfiguration of the American field of power that began in the nineteenth century with the emergence of the academic and social scientific fields and continued with the expansion of the bureaucratic field (and, more broadly, with the growth of legal-rational authority as a legitimating principle). A major consequence of this reconfiguration was that holders of political and economic power increasingly had to incorporate appeals to scientific and technical authority into their practices.

At one level, then, the rise of think tanks must be understood as part and parcel of the growing influence of science and technical expertise on the political and economic spheres. The limit in this formulation, however, is that in the very same moment that think tanks put forward claims to expertise, they also pose acutely certain basic questions about the meaning of the term "expertise" itself and its value in modern societies.

Who counts as an "expert," and which experts (and forms of expertise) have the most influence? What is the current hierarchy among cultural authorities vying to influence policy making and public debate? The central point of my analysis in this chapter is that the formation of the space of think tanks—a system of knowledge production inhabited by experts whose success depends on a strategy of self-subordination to political, bureaucratic, economic, and media demand (a self-subordination that is nearly invisible because it is carried out willingly by the most advanced policy experts)—is symptomatic of the *de-autonomization* of the scientific field. For all of the variation in their orientation to the ethos of scientific production, and for all of the fuzziness surrounding them, think tanks must therefore be examined in the context of growing threats to the autonomy of science itself.[109]

The point becomes clearest when we consider the utility of think tanks from the standpoint of a politician. While American politicians cannot always dismiss scientific claims entirely, the presence of a large, stable, and internally differentiated think tank universe allows them to "shop" for policy expertise to support their pre-held views and thus to pit multiple forms of expertise against one another. Thus, when autonomously produced social scientific knowledge does not suit their purposes, politicians can always count on the assistance of policy experts willing to lend the stamp of scientific or technical credibility to their views. My argument, then, is that the "power" of think tanks is the greatest precisely when such organizations have no independent policy influence whatsoever—which is to say, when they are most deeply involved in the business of endorsing policy prescriptions determined strictly by political and economic interests.

But how is this a form of *power*? By way of analogy, I would point out that it is a power akin to that of an expert witness called to testify in a courtroom, not primarily to persuade the judge or jury, but to undermine the authority of an expert on the other side. Even without inducing the audience to adopt his or her view, the second expert may establish *doubt* or uncertainty (or in any case, the need for a third expert to adjudicate between the first two). In a similar fashion, think tanks may exercise influence even through the production of highly degraded forms of social scientific knowledge—by which I mean knowledge that few autonomous social scientists would recognize as social science. Put differently, even when their prescriptions are persuasive to no one apart from those previously committed to the same views as their own, think tanks may still produce a nullifying effect on the value of expertise itself.[110]

In the next chapter, I will put this theory into action by examining the role played by think tanks and other organs of expertise in the debates surrounding poverty and welfare policy from the late 1950s until the passage of the 1996 welfare reform legislation. The story will not be a tale of simple cause-and-effect, since much of what was at stake in this process was the efficacy of social scientific knowledge in the policymaking process itself and its relationship to other forms of cultural authority.

CHAPTER FIVE

From Deprivation to Dependency

*Expert Discourse and the
American Welfare Debate*

Were mental technicians and experts, their distant cousins, to pre-empt the field that intellectuals now occupy, modern culture would likely perish through ossification. — Lewis Coser, 1965

This chapter examines the political and intellectual debates surrounding poverty and welfare policy during the period from the late 1950s, just prior to the Economic Opportunity Act of 1964, to the passage of the 1996 Personal Responsibility and Work Opportunity Reconciliation Act (PRWORA). Before I can summarize my argument, let me address both the choice of empirical topic and my general analytic approach in this chapter. First, why add further to a scholarly discussion on which so much has already been written? Apart from the topic's inherent importance, the main reason is to establish a kind of "crucial test" for my theory of think tanks. In other words, if the theory put forward in this book can add something new to our knowledge about one of the most heavily traveled of all policy topics, then it is also likely to prove useful when applied to other policy areas. It is worth noting, furthermore, that since the production and consumption of expert knowledge are themselves aspects of the phenomenon I wish to investigate, the abundance of writing on welfare policy supplies rich empirical material for this discussion. Put differently, I will approach other writings on poverty and welfare, less as rival explanations per se than as part of the social universe under investigation.

The basic premise of this chapter is that understanding the passage of the 1996 welfare reform legislation demands close attention to the social relations of knowledge production and consumption in the United States, including the history of struggles over expertise and authoritative knowledge. As I have argued throughout this book, think tanks have positioned themselves at the center of these struggles in the United States over the past four decades. In this chapter, I will argue that the crystallization of the space of think tanks from the late 1960s to the early 1980s was one of the main processes leading to the discursive shift from a problematic of *deprivation* to one of *dependency*, the main cognitive frameworks within which policy makers worked to achieve policy solutions during the latter half of the twentieth century. Underpinning this argument is the premise that in order to understand the passage of the 1996 legislation, we must first grasp the shift in the *problematic* of welfare knowledge itself, by which I mean the underlying perception of the social malady that needed to be addressed through political means. A good place to begin this discussion is with the body of writing that emerged in the wake of the 1996 welfare reform to critique the role of experts in the debate. Generally speaking, this writing focused on their lack of reflexivity, or their failure to scrutinize the received categories and assumptions that shaped the welfare reform discussion in the 1990s. I will refer to this body of writing as the "reflexive critique."[1]

At the core of the reflexive critique is the observation that analytically prior to the identification of a solution to the "problem of welfare" was the process of defining the problem itself. Every definition of the problem, in other words, implied already both a culprit and a remedy, not to mention an attendant marker of policy success. Accordingly, the reflexive critics held, the definitional process sat not at the background of the policy debate but at its center. For example, to the degree that fraud, dependency, and fiscal costs were taken as the main problems with the welfare system, the culprit was likely to be understood as "personal irresponsibility" in all of its forms—including dishonesty, out-of-wedlock births, and simple laziness—and the solution was to encourage "self-sufficiency" by forcibly reducing the welfare rolls. On the other hand, if the problem of welfare was defined in terms of economic precariousness affecting millions of Americans, then merely reducing the welfare rolls not only would not address the issue, it would likely exacerbate the problem. Thus, the basic premise of the reflexive critique of welfare experts was that in order to understand the passage of the 1996 legislation, we must first grasp a historical shift in the problematic of welfare itself; this shift shaped dominant understandings about which forms of knowledge and expertise would be considered relevant to the search for a policy solution.

The reflexive critics held, in other words, that behind the seemingly peripheral act of defining the "problem of welfare" lurked a whole process of meaning making that largely outlined a whole orientation to the issue.[2] In particular, the reflexive critique charged policy experts with lending the stamp of scientific authority to regressive welfare policies, and thereby aiding in their development by accepting wholesale the boundaries and categories of public debate as established by political decision-makers. The most impassioned versions of the critique, in fact, suggested an insidious collusion between political elites and social scientists in which the latter, operating under the guise of objectivity, buried from view the ideological underpinnings of their research in exchange for political recognition.[3] More specifically, the reflexive critique highlighted a multitude of theoretical "sins" thought to harness experts to the interests of political professionals and economic elites, including:

methodological individualism, or the tendency to neglect social structures in favor of individual-level attributes and behaviors, especially the behavioral defects of the poor;[4]

empiricism, or the refusal to resituate narrow empirical findings within a broader theoretical context;[5]

provincialism, or an arbitrarily narrow focus on the United States, especially given the fact that related social policy changes were taking place in other countries;

elitism, or the propensity to see the welfare issue from the standpoint of political and economic decision-makers rather than from the standpoint of ordinary citizens, to say nothing of the American subproletariat; and,

ahistoricism, or the failure to trace the development of the welfare problematic to its historical roots.[6]

Given the last of these charges, it is not surprising that historians were at the leading edge of the reflexive critique, which also insisted that welfare reform be understood as a multistaged process encompassing, first, the creation of the welfare problematic that identified dependence as the major defect of the earlier system, and second, the brief subsequent period in which the range of viable policy alternatives, once narrowed, was legitimated by available expert knowledge.

As I noted, the reflexive critique offers a useful starting point for explaining my argument in this chapter. However, I would insist that the critique cannot by itself supply the basis for a sound theory of the role of experts in the welfare reform process for several reasons. First, some (but by no means all) reflexive accounts slip into the dubious claim that social science is, *eo ipso*, a futile, conservative, or counterproductive endeavor. Some of the reflexive critics, in other words, veer toward a kind of antiscience postmodernism in their approach by moving subtly from the sensible claim that scientific knowledge is always shaped by the conditions of its own production to the far more ambitious argument that reliable social scientific knowledge itself is therefore impossible or inherently harmful.[7] As this discussion will make clear, I do not share this view. A second and related limitation of some reflexive studies lies in their failure to account for important differences among intellectuals, even those who hold sharply contrasting views on the topic. Schram, for example, portrays such dissimilar figures as Charles Murray and William Julius Wilson as essentially similar parts of the same phenomenon.[8] This is not to say that there cannot be notable points of convergence between thinkers like Murray and Wilson, only that a more exacting theory would be capable of differentiating between them.

The third limitation of the reflexive critique is the most important. This is its tendency to "sample on the dependent variable" by overlooking the existence of expert knowledge that does not fit the pattern it identifies. Put differently, the reflexive thesis that social science has by itself "failed the poor" (to paraphrase the title of one account) can be sustained only by overlooking the existence of a strong tradition of independent social scientific research about poverty that was marginalized or excluded from American public debate. By itself, then, a reflexive critique cannot provide a thorough accounting of the role of expertise in welfare reform. What is needed in addition is an analysis of the institutional processes by which certain knowledge was produced, consumed, and/or marginalized by policy makers. Of course, there are already a large number of institutionalist studies of welfare reform. The problem is that only rarely do they highlight the central importance of experts and expertise in this process. A purely objectivist approach, furthermore, by which I mean an analysis focused only on the generative and constraining effects of institutions, is bound to overlook the cognitive content of the welfare reform debate.

To summarize my view, then, an authoritative theory of the role of expert knowledge in the welfare reform process must avoid two opposing pitfalls. First, it must dodge the error of pure structuralism that involves ignoring the cognitive or mental parameters within which policy debates unfolded. Second, it must avoid the opposite, intellectualist error of considering only the content of the debate and neglecting the wide array of institutional forces that shaped the selection and use of certain ideas by political actors while systematically relegating others to the dustbin of history. To put the point succinctly, understanding the passage of the 1996 welfare reform legislation requires performing a reflexive analysis of the role of ideas and experts and then reinserting this analysis into a structuralist framework. What is needed, in other words, is a study of the "political economy of ideas," or the social relations guiding the production and consumption of expert knowledge, including the processes through which policy makers and other actors in policy debate endowed certain forms of expertise with political relevance and marginalized or ignored other forms.[9]

This chapter will trace the broad outlines of such a theory by describing the process leading to welfare reform. I can summarize this process briefly in terms of three historical stages:

STAGE ONE: THE DEVELOPMENT OF THE "DISCOURSE OF DEPRIVATION" (1958–64). Starting in the late 1950s, a jointly produced social scientific/journalistic "discourse of deprivation" became the basis for a new public debate about poverty and welfare provision in the United States. This discourse problematized mass poverty by documenting its prevalence, scope, and structural underpinnings. Its main premise was that the problem of poverty could be remedied through a carefully designed federal government intervention. This discourse of deprivation, it is worth noting, never became hegemonic inasmuch as its opponents always remained a considerable force in public debate. However, lacking the distance from politics that gave social scientists and journalists their authority, the opponents of welfare were forced to adopt a more defensive public stance and their views more often took on a nakedly self-interested appearance. Consequently—and despite longstanding public suspicion toward the poor in the United States—the discourse of deprivation enjoyed a brief moment of public legitimacy during the late 1950s and early 1960s. Concretely, the discourse influenced the Kennedy and Johnson administrative initiatives to eradicate poverty, culminating in the Economic Opportunity Act of 1964. To some observers, the legislation was a sign of the growing political role of experts, including social scientists, in American life.

STAGE TWO: THE EXPANSION OF TECHNOCRATIC MACHINERY AND THE GROWTH OF AN EXPERT "DISCOURSE OF DEPENDENCY" (1964–80). The subsequent period saw two key changes in the institutional conditions surrounding the production, consumption, dissemination, and use of expert knowledge about welfare policy in the United States. The first, a direct result of the 1964 legislation, was the growth of what Alice O'Connor calls the "poverty knowledge industry." By this term, O'Connor means a large machinery of technocratic production anchored in a network of government-funded and privately funded organizations, including some organizations that are now classified as think tanks. Two new research centers, the Urban Institute and the Institute for Research on Poverty at the University of Wisconsin, quickly emerged as the leading suppliers of technocratic knowledge about poverty and welfare. Among existing organizations, the RAND Corporation, having already established itself as the headquarters of defense-oriented systems analysis, also became important as both an organizational model and a direct source of personnel for the new organs of technocratic production. The rapid expansion of the poverty knowledge industry in the years immediately after the 1964 legislation paralleled the growth of technoscientific machinery as described in chapter 2.

Second, the 1964 legislation gave rise to a sharp backlash among conservative activist-experts, who gradually formulated their own challenger discourse about poverty and welfare. I will refer to this system of thought as the "discourse of dependency." The conservative anti-welfare discourse drew on a longstanding cultural tradition that defined poverty as an individual-level phenomenon and regarded the poor as responsible for their own deprivation. Notable among the articulators of this discourse were the neoconservatives, a loosely connected band of intellectuals whose careers spanned the academic, political, and journalistic fields. Promoted with the material support of American business, their critiques of the welfare system were built on an extended defense of capitalism, a faith in the self-correcting tendencies of the market, and a moralistic attitude toward the poor.

Two parallels with the preceding argument of the book are worth noting here. First, in line with my earlier account, the leading promoters of the discourse of dependency were members of the conservative activist-expert group described in chapter 3. Recall the central point about the activist-experts of the 1960s and 1970s from that chapter: facing a problem of excessive openness in the field of expertise, they undertook an aggressive closure strategy, or an attempt to "certify" their knowledge through the creation of new research centers. This strategy in turn became critical to the formation of the space of think tanks. The second parallel with my previous argument is that the conservative discourse of dependency gained public momentum during the 1970s and 1980s through the formation of the space of think tanks. Think tanks, in fact, would eventually become the main organs of its dissemination. By the start of the 1980s, leading conservative think tanks such as the American Enterprise Institute, the Heritage Foundation, the Cato Institute, and the Manhattan Institute—all major beneficiaries of conservative philanthropy—were actively engaged in the promotion of antiwelfare policy framed according to the discourse of dependency.

STAGE THREE: THE ASCENDANCE OF THE DISCOURSE OF DEPENDENCY (1981–96). Although welfare policy developments during the Reagan administration were minor in comparison with what would come later, the administration nonetheless played a critical role in transforming both the institutional structure and the intellectual content of welfare policy research. Its key contribution was to reorder the space of technocratic production by soliciting studies and recommendations about welfare that were framed according to the discourse of dependency while cutting off federal funding for research oriented to the problematic of deprivation. Accordingly, the discourse of deprivation became increasingly marginalized on the terrain of policy debate. The growth of the space of think tanks played an integral role in this process as the incubator of "policy experts," whose success depended on their willingness to orient their work to the reigning categories of policy debate. When the challenger discourse of dependency began to permeate the new machinery of technocratic production, the eclipse of the short-lived discourse of deprivation was complete. As think tanks proliferated, non-think tank affiliated experts who wished to take part in the policy debate—including academic social scientists and journalists—faced increasing pressures to frame their knowledge according to the conservative welfare problematic.

My argument, then, is that a broad change in the institutional conditions surrounding the production and consumption of knowledge about poverty and welfare led to the passage of the 1996 welfare reform legislation. In the first phase of this process, academic social scientists and journalists enjoyed relatively unmediated access to a highly permeable political field. By the 1980s, the same social scientists faced an abundance of competitors whose most important characteristic was their willingness to tailor their work directly to the demands of politicians and journalists. Crucially, the presence of activist think tanks ensured that holders of economic capital could insert their voices into the public debate by proxy rather than directly, which enabled them to present their arguments, not as self-interested claims, but as a series of technical and moral assertions. Put simply, the opponents of welfare developed their own form of expertise. Gradually, then, the discourse of dependency acquired hegemonic status in the debate over welfare policy. By the start of the 1990s, intellectuals who subscribed to the problematic of deprivation and wished to participate in this debate faced three changes as compared to the early 1960s: first, a reconfigured field of expertise dominated by technocratic producers, who now played the leading role as suppliers of knowledge deemed politically relevant to welfare policy; second, a more crowded space of public debate in which the attentions of journalists were more often diverted by a growing breed of policy experts, whose intellectual products were tailored specifically for their use; and third, a less permeable political field that required more specialized forms of expertise for entry. As a result of these structural shifts, the problematic of deprivation was overwhelmed in the public debate by the problematic of dependency.

The Revival and Transformation of Poverty Research, 1958–64

After two decades in which the topic had largely fallen by the wayside in both academic and journalistic discourse, interest in poverty was suddenly revived in American public debate during the early 1960s. During the previous decade, much of the writing on the national economy had centered on the enormous creation of wealth since World War II, a development that led many commentators to assume that aggregate growth and welfare-related benefits had rendered poverty a thing of the past, or at least an exceptional phenomenon.[10] As the 1960s began, poverty did not register among the main issues on the national agenda. In 1960, for example, Dwight Eisenhower formed the President's Commission on National Goals to "identify the great issues of our generation and describe our objectives in these various areas."[11] The subsequent commission report, issued in November of that year, made no mention of poverty.[12] Two years earlier, John Kenneth Galbraith's *The Affluent Society* had noted poverty's persistence in America but downplayed it as "no longer . . . a universal or massive affliction [but] more nearly an afterthought."[13]

Because authoritative data on the topic was lacking, an effort to measure poverty's prevalence gradually gained a foothold in the academy.[14] In 1962, an interdisciplinary team of researchers at the University of Michigan Survey Research Center conducted a path-breaking study of poverty based on the new Survey of Consumer Finances, a poll administered jointly by the Federal Reserve and the Treasury Department.[15] Led by James N. Morgan, the Michigan researchers found poverty to be more widespread than previously thought and estimated its prevalence at 20 to 30 percent of the US population. Not surprisingly, the Michigan researchers found that the disabled, elderly, less educated, and non-whites were overrepresented among the poor, as were those with fathers of low occupational standing. The Morgan study was also groundbreaking in its identification of educational attainment as a crucial link in the intergenerational transmission of poverty. Finally, the researchers found, less than a quarter (23 percent) of poor families had received any public benefits in 1959, and a single public assistance program, Aid to Dependent Children (ADC), carried the brunt of government welfare expenditures.[16]

Spurred partly by the Michigan research, other social scientists increased their study of poverty, welfare, and related topics, such as the effects of public housing on the poor and the social characteristics of welfare recipients.[17] In addition to studying poverty's prevalence and scope, scholars began to question the common historical assumption that wealth and income inequality had been substantially mitigated by welfare programs during the 1940s and 1950s. In his influential 1962 study of American wealth distribution, for example, economist Robert J. Lampman found that the richest 1 percent of Americans still held 26.0 percent of the nation's total personal wealth in 1953 (and 76.0 percent of corporate stock), as compared to 31.6 percent in 1922 (and 61.5 percent of corporate stock), a moment long assumed to be the apogee of American economic inequality.[18] The same year, historian Gabriel Kolko argued that nothing resembling substantial income redistribution had occurred in the United States since the dawn of the New Deal.[19]

As the study of poverty and inequality gained momentum in the academy, journalists increasingly picked up on the topic. Although periodicals of the left such as *Dissent* and *The Nation* had thematized poverty for years, their commentary had produced few ramifications in the wider public debate.[20] Now the topic garnered more mainstream attention. The 1962 publication of Michael Harrington's *The Other America: Poverty in the United States* became the watershed moment in this shift. Harrington, a journalist, former Catholic Charities worker, and labor activist, summarized the state of American poverty in dramatic terms by arguing that more than 40 million Americans lived in conditions of material hardship.

His book also focused on the political marginalization, social isolation, and public invisibility of the American poor and argued provocatively that the embryonic American welfare state gave the fewest benefits to the most needy. While the United States offered generous assistance to the middle class in the form of Social Security and unemployment assistance, Harrington argued, the poorest Americans had only meager sources of public support at their disposal.

Harrington's book was released to modest sales expectations, but unexpected support from other journalists, including Dwight MacDonald's forty-page *New Yorker* essay, thrust the book into the national spotlight.[21] The next three years saw a groundswell of public discussion about material deprivation in America. A 1962 report issued by the Conference on Economic Progress, a nonprofit research organization founded by economist Leon Keyserling, garnered considerable attention as a statistically oriented companion to Harrington's qualitative account.[22] Gunnar Myrdal's 1964 *Challenge to Affluence* was the next major salvo in the debate.[23] Two years later, economist Alice Rivlin began her review of a pair of books called *Poverty in America* by noting, "So many books on poverty have appeared in the last couple of years that the publishers have run out of titles."[24] In 1965, sociologist Lewis Coser summarized the state of public discussion by writing that Harrington's book and others had "suddenly helped to picture deprivation as the central domestic issue in the United States and led to the emergence of a new social definition of poverty."[25] Writing in the inaugural issue of the *Public Interest* in 1965, sociologist Nathan Glazer similarly noted, "Presidents, socialists, reformers and academicians have set the prevailing contemporary tone in discussing poverty in America—shock and outrage that it should exist, followed by a direct and earnest passion that we should do everything necessary to wipe it out."[26]

The new expert discourse of deprivation helped to focus the Kennedy administration's attention on poverty. Kennedy himself had been moved by the spectacle of rural poverty while campaigning in West Virginia in 1960. By 1963, several of his closest advisers—including Walter W. Heller, chairman of the Council of Economic Advisers (CEA), Robert J. Lampman, a staff member for the CEA, and Theodore C. Sorensen, a top aide—were urging the president to make the eradication of poverty a top domestic goal.[27] According to some, it was Sorensen who, having read MacDonald's review of *The Other America*, pressed the issue most energetically.[28] Later reflection by Kennedy advisers corroborates the importance of Harrington's text and other journalistic and scholarly writings in steering the Kennedy administration's focus toward poverty. (For example, White House adviser Arthur M. Schlesinger Jr. wrote in his memoir, "I believe that *The Other America* helped crystallize [Kennedy's] determination in 1963 to accompany the tax cut by a poverty program."[29]) R. Sargent Shriver, soon to be the first director of the Office of Economic Opportunity, likewise maintained that Kennedy became interested in poverty in 1963 because "a large number of books and articles happened to appear in that year."[30]

Kennedy's first significant action on the matter was to ask the Council of Economic Advisers and the Department of Labor to examine the poverty problem further in 1963. The same year, Wisconsin economist Robert Lampman prepared an influential Census Bureau report that estimated the national poverty rate at about 20 percent and argued that, after a long period of wartime prosperity, the rate was no longer in decline.[31] By November, a decision had been made within the Kennedy administration to pursue, in Schlesinger's words, "a national assault on the causes of poverty, a comprehensive program, across the board."[32] Kennedy's assassination that month did little to derail the antipoverty agenda in the White House. In a move that amounted to a continuation of Kennedy's plan, Lyndon Johnson declared "war on poverty" in his January 1964 State of the Union address.

As sociologist Lee Rainwater summarized in 1964, "Increasingly insistent promptings by government officials, social scientists, and journalists over the past three years have now brought forth from President Johnson a clear statement that poverty is to be regarded as a state of the union."[33] Social scientific and journalistic analyses had helped to bring the issue to the forefront of public view, although their ability to influence the political course of action that followed was far more limited. Instead, strategic decisions within the Kennedy and Johnson administrations were instrumental in reducing Johnson's campaign to what sociologist and critic Herbert Gans later called a "Skirmish on Poverty."[34] Chief among these was the decision to define poverty in terms of absolute rather than relative deprivation, which ultimately precluded any talk of radical income or wealth redistribution. For example, in an internal CEA memorandum to chairman Walter Heller, Lampman wrote, "Probably a politically acceptable program must avoid completely any use of the term 'inequality' or of the term 'redistribution of income or wealth.' "[35] Pressure from the political right, along with the dominance of Keynesian thought in economics, led to a focus on aggregate growth and employment as the only legitimate solutions to the poverty problem. Johnson administration rhetoric and policy thus emphasized "self-help" over "handouts" as the chief modality of the antipoverty initiative. Thus, while journalists and academic social scientists had helped to focus the debate on poverty, any discussion of aggressive redistribution proved too radical.[36]

Institutional Transformations in the Field of Knowledge Production, 1964–80

The creation of a joint social scientific/journalistic discourse about poverty prompted the development of the 1964 Economic Opportunity Act. Almost immediately, however, the legislation reshaped the institutional structure of knowledge production and consumption, with profound consequences. On this count, the legislation's main effect was to trigger the growth of what historian Alice O'Connor calls a "poverty research industry" anchored in a network of government agencies, university-based research centers, public policy schools, and research-oriented nonprofit groups.[37] The backbone of this technocratic system lay in two federal agencies: the research division of the Office of Economic Opportunity (OEO), an office created by the 1964 legislation, and the office of the Assistant Secretary for Planning and Evaluation in the Department of Health, Education, and Welfare (HEW). Among already-existing research centers, the RAND Corporation became especially influential as the source of a direct transfer of analytical technique and personnel to the OEO and HEW.

With respect to the first form of influence, RAND's main contribution originated in its development of systems analysis years earlier (see chapter 2 for a general discussion). First used exclusively within the defense industry, systems analysis had recently been adapted by Secretary of Defense Robert McNamara from a specialized military procedure into a more general administrative technique that could be used in various aspects of bureaucratic decision-making, including budgeting and planning. McNamara employed the technique to great effect in his reorganization of the Pentagon, and in 1965 the Johnson administration began using a variant of it in its revamped budgetary process. As the OEO grew, a spontaneous effort to extend systems analysis to poverty and welfare research began. A series of personnel ties further reinforced the connection between RAND and the OEO, including Joseph A. Kershaw, a former research director at RAND who became head of OEO's research division. Robert

Levine and Thomas K. Glennan, both former RAND analysts, also became key figures at OEO.[38] The RAND Corporation also became a model for the newly created Institute for Research on Poverty, a center based at the University of Wisconsin. Formed in 1966, the institute was a joint project of the Office of Economic Opportunity and the university, whose economics department was already home to several prominent poverty researchers, including Robert Lampman. The institute's mixed pedigree reflected its double goal of developing both basic and applied knowledge about poverty and welfare. As a "think tank that thinks for the poor," a 1968 *Business Week* magazine article reported, IRP was staffed largely by economists, although sociologists, anthropologists, and psychologists could also be found in its ranks.[39] The organization's first major project was the New Jersey Income Maintenance Experiment, a prominent early case of social scientific experimentation applied to social policy.[40]

RAND also became the primary model for the creation of a domestic-policy counterpart called the Urban Institute. The main figure in Urban's founding was Joseph A. Califano, a special assistant to President Johnson and former deputy secretary of the Department of Defense under Robert McNamara. At the Defense Department, Califano had seen the symbiotic relationship between his agency and RAND. In staffing Urban, he drew liberally from the defense industry establishment. RAND veteran William C. Gorham, for example, served as Urban's first director. As if to demonstrate its kinship with RAND, Urban developed a new analytic technique for poverty research known as *applied microsimulation modeling*, a highly formalized method of cost-benefit assessment based directly on systems analysis. The Urban Institute grew steadily in its first decade, with initial support from three cabinet departments: HUD, Labor, and HEW. Like its defense industry counterpart, the Urban Institute became a model of technocratic production, its research having been "built up around the compartmentalized categories and political priorities of the policy world it was set up to serve."[41]

The Rise of the Discourse of Dependency

Just as antipoverty measures gained momentum in response to a public discourse created by journalists and social scientists about widespread deprivation in America—and as a machinery of technocratic production grew up to support it—an alternative discourse pinpointing dependence on the government as the core problem of the welfare system began to grow. To be sure, this line of thinking was rooted in a longstanding cultural tradition that cast poverty in terms of individual and cultural pathologies as opposed to macrostructural conditions.[42] However, the post-1960s version of this discourse of dependency had two novel features: first, its use of the language of science and rationality for its authority; second, its explicit, negative orientation to the newer discourse of deprivation and the liberal social scientists who had become its primary spokespeople.

Initially, the leading promoters of the discourse of dependency were the neoconservative intellectuals, including Daniel P. Moynihan, whose 1965 Department of Labor report, *The Negro Family: The Case for National Action* invoked the notion of cultural pathology in attributing black poverty to a matriarchal culture that condoned illegitimacy.[43] In later years, Moynihan's attack on the public welfare system became even more direct. In 1968, for example, he wrote in the *Public Interest* of "mounting crises in the American welfare system" and called for a "thorough reassessment" of it.[44] The country was now enjoying steady economic growth, Moynihan argued, and yet "with each year of growing affluence the number of persons dependent on public charity also grows."[45] According to Moynihan, the problem was mostly localized to a single program: Aid to Families with Dependent Children. Not only was AFDC unique in its increasing number of recipients, but it had become the most expensive welfare program.

As Moynihan sounded the distress signal, other members of the neoconservative intellectual circle became increasingly alarmed about the growth of the welfare system. A survey of articles from the *Public Interest*, the leading neoconservative journal of the era, is illuminating on this count. Upon its founding in 1965, the journal initially took a positive view of the 1964 legislation. Yet its tone shifted noticeably around 1968 when MIT economist Edwin Kuh noted, "Welfare payments have recently been rising at 25 percent a year with disturbing indications that the system has gotten out of control. Chaos, with more to come, makes major change essential."[46] The next year, political scientist Edward Banfield sought to answer two questions on the *Public Interest*'s pages: "First, why has dependency been increasing during a time of full employment, and at a rate unprecedented since the Great Depression? Second, what if anything should be done to reduce dependency?"[47] In the same issue, Nathan Glazer gave extensive consideration to the possibility that welfare receipt "destroys the incentive to work and thereby get off welfare."[48] By the end of the 1960s, welfare dependency occupied a central place on the list of domestic problems in the neoconservative mind.

During the 1970s, competition intensified between the two expert discourses, now the two main poles in the debate on welfare policy. On one side stood the view, articulated largely by academic social scientists and mainstream journalists, that poverty and inequality remained core social problems, and that the existing welfare system, while undoubtedly flawed, provided an essential shield against material deprivation for millions of Americans. Sociologists Frances Fox Piven and Richard Cloward exemplified this view in their 1971 book *Regulating the Poor*, which developed a critical theory of welfare as an instrument for maintaining social order. Piven and Cloward posited that welfare expansion and contraction were driven primarily by economic cycles and public disorder. Historically, they argued, welfare expanded to mitigate social unrest, especially during times of economic turmoil, and contracted to push people back onto the low-wage labor market. Their theory challenged the prevalent social scientific view that welfare states followed an ineluctable logic of progress as the prosperity of nation-states increased.[49] Despite its broadly negative stance toward the welfare system, Piven and Cloward's theory extended the problematic of deprivation with its picture of welfare recipients as trapped in a wage labor relation that failed to meet their basic material needs.

On the other side of the debate was the argument that dependence on the state had become a problem that superseded the simple fact of poverty in its effects. Crucially, this discourse also drew on social scientific language and forms of argumentation for its authority. In 1974, for example, Irving Kristol argued that the present welfare system failed to heed one "crucial sociological fact": namely, that "dependency, for those who are not by nature and necessity dependent, can have demoralizing consequences."[50] Leaving no room for doubt as to the nature of these consequences, Kristol maintained that "the welfare system encourages various social pathologies—broken families, illegitimacy, drug addiction—which easily overwhelm the single statistical fact of 'the abolition of poverty.'"[51] The antiwelfare complaint was part of a broader attack waged by neoconservatives on the Great Society programs for their supposed fiscal irresponsibility, bureaucratic unwieldiness, and support of moral corruption. In the growth of the welfare system the neoconservatives also saw a creeping form of socialism driven by a "New Class" composed of technocrats, professionals, and intellectuals.

As I argued in chapter 3, the 1970s was the crucial decade for the crystallization of the space of think tanks, a process centered on a battle and eventual convergence among various expert groups, including technocrats and conservative activist-experts. By the end of the decade, conservative think tanks became the main intellectual machinery for a reinvigorated attack on the welfare system. A 1978 Heritage Foundation study by Charles Hobbs, for example, argued that welfare had become an enormous fiscal strain on the federal government. Listing 44 federal programs under its rubric, Hobbs defined welfare inclusively as all federal means-tested programs, including Medicaid and various job training and college aid programs.[52] Likewise, in 1979 Heritage castigated the "$2 billion a year" poverty research industry and suggested that liberal technocrats were the main beneficiaries of its expansion.[53] Funded by conservative philanthropists and business corporations, conservative think tanks now occupied the leading edge of a movement to generate expert knowledge critical of welfare provision and government dependency.

The Triumph of the New Welfare Problematic, 1980–96

The next stage in the making of a new welfare problematic was caused by further transformations on the terrain of technocratic production. Ronald Reagan's election to the presidency in 1980 had dramatic effects for the producers of technocratic knowledge, who were increasingly compelled to orient their work to the problematic of dependency. This shift culminated in the proclamation of a "new consensus" on welfare policy during the late 1980s. While the topic of welfare dependency had motivated significant research as early as the mid-1970s, the topic was given unprecedented priority by the Reagan administration through its control of federal funding for poverty research.[54] From the outset, the Reagan White House instituted a series of guidelines requiring that federally funded welfare research focus on dependency as opposed to deprivation. The administration began in August 1981 by severing ties with the University of Wisconsin's Institute for Research on Poverty, which had received funding from the OEO and its successors for the previous fifteen years. The Urban Institute faced a similar situation as the Reagan administration slashed its budget by 75 percent over three years during the early 1980s. The new guidelines also shifted the emphasis of poverty research in the Office of the Assistant Secretary for Planning and Evaluation, now a subdivision of the Department of Health and Human Services.[55]

There was no clearer expression of the administration's new approach to welfare research than Reagan's well known declaration in the 1986 State of the Union address that, "The success of welfare should be judged by how many of its recipients become independent of welfare." Given this new metric, government-funded experts who relied on federal support for their research now faced a clear choice: either reconfigure their studies according to the problematic of dependency or seek funding from alternative sources. In practice, most organizations affected by the shift pursued a combination of the two approaches. The Urban Institute, for example, increasingly sought funding from philanthropic foundations more sympathetic to its earlier approach. At the same time, Urban also adjusted the premises and categories of its research to fit the Reagan administration directives. A 1992 Urban Institute study on federal housing policy, for example, summarized the change as follows: "Policy debate on housing assistance is moving from a focus on how best to alleviate poverty . . . to how best to reduce economic dependency more broadly."[56] The report then dutifully promised to "inform policymakers charged with reorienting housing assistance" by "examining the fundamental issues that must be confronted in reconceptualizing housing policy as a tool for economic independence." In the same vein, Urban Institute scholars also testified before Congress to recommend ways to limit and prevent fraud in the collection of Supplemental Security Income (SSI) by immigrants.[57]

Think tanks not directly under bureaucratic controls were similarly affected by the Reagan administration policy. As members of a technocratic network that overlapped the official research agencies created by the 1964 legislation, they depended on the recognition of politicians and the media for their success, and in turn for their funding. Ostensibly nonbureaucratic think tanks thus faced comparable pressures to reorient their work to the prevailing terms of policy debate. Thus, organizations as ideologically various as the Brookings Institution, the Hudson Institute, and the Ethics and Public Policy Center began to add their voices to the growing body of research on welfare's "disincentive effects."[58]

In sum, now that research on welfare had become a largely technocratic affair, the Reagan administration's shift in funding priorities meant that conservative presuppositions increasingly underpinned the studies deemed relevant to welfare policy. The primary concerns of this new work were the causes and extent of welfare receipt and the social characteristics of welfare recipients, especially as it pertained to issues of family structure (especially the prevalence of teenage pregnancy).[59] The size and characteristics of the so-called "underclass" also became major areas of concern. All of these themes congealed neatly in Charles Murray's 1984 book *Losing Ground*, which argued that the availability of AFDC benefits had created a durable culture of dependency that encouraged illegitimate childbearing, criminal activity, drug abuse, and labor market avoidance. Building on the premise that social transfers inevitably reinforced the behavior that qualified the recipient for the transfer, Murray advocated automatic welfare ineligibility for teenage and out-of-wedlock mothers.[60] As I noted earlier, Murray's book had been funded by two conservative think tanks: the Heritage Foundation, which underwrote the pilot study on which it was based, and the Manhattan Institute, which supported Murray's writing and poured considerable resources into the book's promotion.[61] Although most scholars roundly criticized *Losing Ground* for its methodological, logical, and empirical shortcomings, journalists and politicians found Murray's arguments too appealing to resist. Writing in the *New Republic*, Charles Lane called it the "most important work on poverty and social policy since Michael Harrington's *The Other America.*"[62] *Losing Ground*'s attraction lay less in its scientific cachet than in its journalistic style, its provocative, ready-made policy recommendations, and its savvy marketing.

Having shifted the terms of the debate by the late 1980s, welfare opponents now proclaimed a "new consensus" on the issue. Nowhere was the role of think tanks in this process plainer than in the research group called the Working Seminar. Cosponsored by the Reagan White House and the American Enterprise Institute and funded by the conservative Bradley and Olin Foundations, the group was chaired by AEI's Michael Novak and Douglas Besharov. The Working Seminar brought together twenty prominent social policy commentators to offer their recommendations on welfare policy. Joining Novak and Besharov were Alice Rivlin (Brookings Institution), Robert Reischauer (Brookings, and later president of the Urban Institute), John Cogan (Hoover Institution, and a former RAND economist), Charles Murray (Manhattan Institute), and S. Anna Kondratas (Heritage Foundation), among others. The Working Seminar also included several business leaders who had served in prominent political positions (Barbara Blum, Franklin Raines) and a pair of conservative academic scholars (Larry Mead, Glenn Loury). Out of this convocation came a major policy statement, the 1987 AEI-published study *The New Consensus on Family and Welfare: A Community of Self-Reliance.*[63]

The Working Seminar report notably downplayed the role of race as a factor in generating economic inequality in America. In its place, the authors developed a questionable distinction between the "involuntarily" poor of respectable two-parent families and the "behaviorally dependent" poor, whose poverty was said to emerge from their irresponsibility. In line with Moynihan's and Murray's earlier arguments, the Working Seminar report also suggested that family structure (by which the authors meant the prevalence of female-headed households) was the most important factor in generating inequality. Finally, *The New Consensus* authors endorsed the conservative priority on mandatory work requirements for welfare recipients. As Ron Haskins wrote in his 2006 account of welfare reform, the report "uncannily anticipated several major provisions of the 1996 reform legislation."[64]

It is worth pausing to consider the rhetorical strategy of the Working Seminar report. On its face, the so-called new consensus of its title referred to the unanimity that had supposedly developed among policy experts around the position that welfare dependency and its attendant pathologies constituted major social ills that could be addressed through legislation promoting self-reliance and personal responsibility. However, an alternative interpretation is that any reference to consensus was both a misnomer and a *strategic move* in a social struggle among groups with different claims to expertise. On this view, the term indicated not an actual re-alignment of ideas around welfare reform, but rather a tautological redefinition of the *boundary* of the debate itself so that any thinkers who did not already hold a pro-retrenchment position on welfare were already excluded from the debate. In other words, "consensus" could be said to exist on welfare policy only because intellectuals who wished to preserve or strengthen the welfare state, or retain a focus on deprivation as the core social problem related to welfare, had now been effectively marginalized from the public discussion. Through a complex institutional process, a new discursive boundary had been drawn to encompass conservative and centrist commentators and exclude their progressive counterparts.

Indeed, a significant body of social scientific and journalistic writing retained its focus on the problem of deprivation in the mid-1980s and 1990s. One thinks, for example, of books published in the early 1990s by sociologists such as Herbert Gans, Christopher Jencks, William Julius Wilson, and Elliot Liebow, all of which remained oriented to the problematic of deprivation. Journalists and independent writers such as Barbara Ehrenreich and Jonathan Kozol also wrote significant treatises on the subject that extended the discourse of deprivation.[65] Perhaps the best illustration of the discourse of dependency's hegemony, however, was its ability to co-opt and recast empirical findings drawn from studies framed according to the problematic of deprivation in order to bolster an anti-welfare view. To name but one example, in 1991 sociologist Kathryn Edin deconstructed the notion of welfare dependence by demonstrating the elaborate lengths to which welfare recipients had to go in order to "survive the welfare system," given its meager benefits.[66] Against the image of welfare recipients as lazy or passive "takers," Edin painted an empirically rich picture of energetic and, indeed, enterprising mothers trying to scrape together a passable existence on the low-wage labor market. In the context of showing that neither welfare benefits nor low-wage work alone paid enough to support their families, Edin noted that all of her respondents supplemented their welfare benefits with casual, off-the-books wages. Contrary to the main thrust of her analysis, however, Edin's finding that welfare mothers often took unreported income was cited repeatedly by conservative critics as evidence that welfare receipt itself produced detrimental effects on the "values" of recipients by encouraging dishonesty and fraud.[67]

By the time of the Family Support Act's passage in 1988, the boundaries of public debate had been narrowed considerably. In the years between 1988 and 1996, the expertise deemed relevant to the debate became focused in three areas: first, the effects of welfare receipt on an individual's propensity enter or stay in the labor market; second, welfare's effects on the structure of poor families; and third, the effectiveness of job training and personal rehabilitation programs designed to prepare people for the labor market. Researchers working within the problematic of dependency tested welfare's so-called disincentive effects, such as whether the availability of benefits encouraged out-of-wedlock childbearing. Among the other key questions guiding this literature were the following: What explained the recent rise in AFDC caseloads? How long did welfare families receive AFDC benefits? Was AFDC receipt mostly a transitional phenomenon that occurred after the breakup of a family, or did families tend to stay on the welfare rolls for a long time? Were out-of-wedlock births increasing or decreasing?[68] Beneath its technical surface, the literature's unifying theme was its moralism, or its preoccupation with the presumed degeneracies of welfare recipients and their contribution to the problems of illegitimacy, drug abuse, and labor market avoidance.[69] Indeed, welfare receipt was increasingly seen as a kind of degeneracy in and of itself.

A series of factors, including a sudden increase in AFDC caseloads and an increase in out-of-wedlock births, quickly placed the issue of welfare reform back at the forefront of the national agenda after the 1988 legislation.[70] By the start of the 1990s, however, all of the politically viable reform proposals, even the most liberal, shared a focus on government dependency as the central problem, and nearly all of them included mandatory work requirements as a condition for continued welfare receipt.[71] As Kent Weaver explains in his account of the debate preceding the 1996 reform,

> To be serious contenders, reform proposals would have to offer plausible answers to questions like, Which policy choices will most effectively reduce teenage pregnancy? Which policies will be most effective at moving AFDC mothers into the labor force and keeping them there? How can fathers be made to pay an increased share of the costs of raising their children? How can this reform be enacted without the perverse incentive of luring persons who are not currently receiving welfare onto the rolls?[72]

According to Weaver, one fact was clear: "the current welfare system was left virtually without intellectual defenders on the political right, center, or left."[73]

The purpose of this section has been to suggest that a change in the institutional forces governing the production and consumption of welfare-related knowledge was a major factor driving a change in the boundaries of permissible political discussion on the issue. Furthermore, I have suggested that it is impossible to understand this process without taking into account the formation of a semidistinct space of think tanks that straddled, and helped to define, the boundary between politics and research. By the early 1990s, think tanks had established themselves as the boldest, most prolific, and most media-savvy suppliers of welfare-related expertise. The following brief survey of the work carried out by think tanks in the years immediately prior to PRWORA's passage illustrates the convergence of this research around the problematic of dependency and the virtual absence of the problematic of deprivation.

The Narrow Confines of Policy Choice, 1988–96

Leading the conservative flank in the competition to produce relevant expertise on welfare policy were three think tanks: the Heritage Foundation, the Cato Institute, and the Dallas, Texas-based National Center for Policy Analysis. Together they generated an ambitious and highly audible critique of the welfare system comprising hundreds of policy reports, books, briefings, and press releases on the topic. Each think tank portrayed welfare receipt as both the root of major social ills and a case of fiscal irresponsibility. Heritage, for example, possessing resources virtually unrivaled among think tanks, published studies lamenting America's "growing dependence on the welfare state" as the central factor in the country's "social and economic decline."[74] Heritage also argued that existing welfare programs promoted long-term criminality, dooming the children of recipients to lifetimes of economic precariousness. In 1995, for example, Heritage's Robert Rector approvingly cited a Congressional Budget Office study arguing that "increasing the length of time a child spends on welfare may reduce the child's IQ by as much as 20 percent."[75] Another report by Rector took President Clinton to task for not following up on his campaign promise to reduce the welfare rolls: "Little has been done to discourage dependency and promote responsible behavior," Rector wrote, and Clinton "has not acted to remove the incentives for illegitimacy posed by the AFDC program."[76] Elsewhere, Rector called Clinton's 1994 reform plan a "public relations facade intended to forestall real criticism and change" and calculated that only 7 percent of AFDC recipients would be required to work by the end of the century.[77] Rector also attacked a National Governors Association welfare proposal for its insufficient focus on the problem of dependency and evaluated a series of reform proposals currently under consideration "based on their ability to reduce the welfare system."[78]

The centerpiece of Heritage's attack on the existing system was a 1995 report co-authored by Rector and William F. Lauber that sought to provide a comprehensive historical analysis of the size, scope, and social impact of welfare, as well as viable strategies for reform. The authors' recommendations focused on the goals of achieving fiscal restraint, reducing illegitimacy, and "demand[ing] that welfare recipients return something to society."[79] The same year, Heritage also released a major budget plan for the new Republican Congress meant to strengthen what it called "the core functions of national government"—especially defense—while "closing down obsolete and wasteful programs."[80] The proposal called for $152 billion in tax cuts, a $138 billion increase in defense spending, "the elimination of nine cabinet departments, the end of most entitlement programs, and the privatization of commercial government activity." Finally, Heritage endorsed a $200 million block grant plan to fund teen abstinence programs in order to address the nation's "soaring illegitimacy rates" and an overhaul of federal adoption programs to ensure that children born out of wedlock would end up in two-parent homes.[81] Heritage also took the lead in helping like-minded state-level think tanks produce similar studies aimed at their own localities. After the 1994 elections, which gave

Republicans majorities in both houses of Congress, Heritage published a compendium of reference guides produced by state and local think tanks to "roll back government."[82] The guide brought together reports from think tanks in Ohio (Buckeye Center for Public Policy), Colorado (Independence Institute), North Carolina (John Locke Foundation), South Carolina (South Carolina Policy Council), and Washington (Evergreen Freedom Foundation).

Like Heritage, the libertarian Cato Institute argued that welfare programs functioned as a system of disincentives that, in the words of Cato fellow Michael Tanner, "shield[ed] people from the natural consequences of their actions" and trapped them in a life of poverty and "destructive behavior."[83] Despite its libertarian orientation, Cato aligned itself with the traditionalist wing of the conservative movement by focusing on the supposed moral degeneracies that accompanied welfare receipt. Cato studies endorsed the notion that "the key issue in welfare reform is to avoid bringing more people into a circle of welfare, illegitimacy, and fatherlessness" and recommended a paradigm shift in social policy: America should abandon altogether the idea that government can provide the answer to poverty and instead create a "vigorous network of private, localized, nonbureaucratic charities" rooted in civil society.[84] The same year, Cato recommended drastic cuts and a partial privatization of the Supplemental Security Income (SSI) program.[85]

Cato pursued several innovative strategies in its critique of the welfare system. In 1995, with a new Republican majority in Congress, the organization published its first *Handbook for Congress*, a 39-chapter legislative guide featuring specific recommendations for reducing the size of the federal government, including welfare reform.[86] Cato also took the goal of quantifying welfare's negative effects to a new level. A 1996 Cato study, for example, sought to estimate the effects of a hypothetical increase in Aid to Families with Dependent Children benefits on various "social pathologies," namely "dependency, poverty, out-of-wedlock births, nonemployment, abortion, and violent crime." The study's model predicted increases in each behavior for every incremental rise in welfare spending.[87] To prove that welfare functioned as a disincentive to work, another Cato study argued that welfare benefits exceeded the post-tax take-home income of minimum wage earners, and, in some states, the average entry-level salaries for teachers and secretaries.[88]

The most prominent of Cato's interventions in the welfare debate was Michael Tanner's 1996 book *The End of Welfare*.[89] Effectively seeking to de-legitimate government-provided welfare benefits altogether, Tanner wrote, "Individuals who are able to work but cannot support themselves through the job market should be forced to fall back on the resources of family, church, community, or private charity."[90] Tanner endorsed "eliminat[ing] the entire social welfare system for individuals who are able to work."[91] He further characterized American welfare policy as having had a "corrosive effect" on taxpayers, the "mediating institutions of community, church and family," and the poor themselves, who are "trapped" in the system. *The End of Welfare* indicted the existing system for destroying both economic opportunity and, even worse, "hope." Tanner's use of the $5.4 trillion welfare price tag first developed by the Heritage Foundation illustrated the considerable degree of complementarity between the two think tanks.

Among state-level think tanks, none was more active in the discussion of welfare reform than the Dallas-based National Center for Policy Analysis. NCPA reports reiterated the conservative position that by "reward[ing] people for not working," welfare programs contributed to the problems of "urban decay, crime, drug addiction, . . . illegitimacy," and the "collapse of work and family."[92] The organization also praised the idea of block grants to allow states to implement their own welfare reforms.[93] Some of NCPA's reports contained novel suggestions for implementing these ideas. For example, a 1995 NCPA study recommended placing private charities in competition for welfare tax dollars by allowing taxpayers to "give up to 40 percent of their personal income taxes to any qualified charity, public or private."[94] The think tank also reported approvingly on a Singapore law that instituted compulsory tax-exempt savings accounts for health, education, and retirement expenses.[95] To head off any potential discussion that poverty remained a national problem, NCPA measured durable goods consumption and argued that "even those on welfare have extraordinary access to conveniences, labor-saving devices, and even luxury goods."[96] Finally, in a report titled, "How Not To Be Poor," NCPA advised Americans to "(1) finish high school, (2) stay married, (3) get a full-time job and (4) if a woman, don't have children before age 20."[97]

Centrist Policy Knowledge

Among centrist think tanks, the Urban Institute, the Progressive Policy Institute, and the Brookings Institution became the leading contributors to the welfare debate in the years immediately prior to the 1996 reform.

The Urban Institute carried on its role as a provider of technocratic analy-ses by focusing much of its effort on the evaluation of state-level welfare programs. The organization's goal, in its words, was to find out "what works, what doesn't, and why."[98] For example, a study of a Washington state program designed to increase participation in education, training, and employment found that the initiative actually "had little or no impact on education and training . . . [and] increased welfare participation sub-stantially."[99] In 1995, Urban offered its most substantial contribution to the debate, an edited volume called *The Work Alternative: Welfare Reform and the Realities of the Job Market* with contributions by Nathan Glazer, Robert H. Haveman, and Rebecca M. Blank, among others. Embracing the "make work pay" slogan, the book endorsed supplements for low-wage jobs, increased education and job training commitments from the federal government, and better job placement mechanisms.[100]

The Progressive Policy Institute, then the research arm of the Demo-cratic Leadership Committee (DLC), sought to capitalize on its ties to the Clinton administration to influence the welfare debate. With the stated aim of overcoming the traditional "left versus right" antinomy, the or-ganization adopted a stance that was largely consistent with the reigning conservative orthodoxy. For example, PPI endorsed welfare time limits, amplified the alarm over out-of-wedlock parenting, and released studies emphasizing personal "stakeholding" and entrepreneurialism as avenues to successful welfare reform.[101] In 1990, the think tank formulated a plan for the creation of tax-free "Individual Development Accounts" for low-income families that could be used to pay for postsecondary education, home ownership, self-employment, or retirement accounts.[102] The next year, PPI advocated a plan for "nurtur[ing] entrepreneurialism in Amer-ica's inner cities" through small loans and business advice.[103] In 1994, PPI president, Will Marshall, released a proposal that combined conservative and centrist priorities by calling for an expansion of "workfare" programs, but also emphasizing the need to "make work pay," universalize access to health care, and increase child support provisions.[104] Another 1994 report approvingly referred to two-year welfare receipt limits as the "lynchpin of [Clinton's] plan" and decried Democratic Rep. Robert Matsui's more liberal reform proposal for "forc[ing] the welfare debate back to the left-right standoff that President Clinton's proposal had cleared."[105]

Reiterating the idea that "the key to genuine welfare reform remains work," a 1995 PPI report laid out a plan for Job Placement Vouchers to provide a new mechanism for moving welfare recipients into the labor force.[106] The same year, PPI released a reform plan called Work First that proposed converting the entire welfare system into a series of employment programs that made use of the Job Placement Vouchers outlined in its other reports.[107] PPI also recommended "reviv[ing] an old institution—the maternity home" with federal seed money to create a network of community-support organizations for unwed teenage mothers.[108] Finally, PPI criticized the existing Job Opportunity and Basic Skills (JOBS) training program for being insufficiently market oriented and recommended replacing it with a voucher program that emphasized immediate work placement.[109]

The Brookings Institution weighed in prominently on the welfare debate with an approach to reform broadly similar to that of Urban and PPI. Like the Urban Institute, Brookings gravitated toward technocratic evaluation, as in its 1993 joint study with the Century Foundation to assess the success of five "welfare-to-work" programs created by the 1988 Family Support Act.[110] In other respects, however, Brookings situated itself closer to the progressive side of the debate. Policy reports from 1994 and 1995, for example, warned that Clinton's welfare initiative carried major risks for poor children and predicted that, if enacted, the Republican plan to devolve social welfare programs to the state level through block grants would result in a "race to the bottom" in which states would reduce benefits to avoid becoming "welfare magnets."[111] In 1995, Brookings issued a cautionary report called *Looking Before We Leap* that predicted the negative consequences of repealing AFDC and imposing time limits, strict work requirements, and exclusions for teen mothers.[112]

The editors of the Brookings report, Kent Weaver and William Dickens, also decried the growing marginalization of social scientific knowledge from the welfare debate. Social science, they wrote, "can provide important insights regarding the promise, limitations, and risks" associated with welfare reform proposals. However, even this moderate claim proved controversial within the organization. A decade after *Looking Before We Leap*, Brookings fellow Ron Haskins reflected negatively on the report and its seemingly innocuous endorsement of social scientific knowledge as a buttress for sound policy making. Haskins wrote, "There is nothing in the Constitution or the rules of the House or the Senate that stipulates any role for research or other evidence. Rather, policy is based on tradition, values, political philosophy, opinion, party loyalty, and bargaining—along with, at times, evidence from social science."[113] That a policy expert at the Brookings Institution, an organization often identified among the most scholarly of American think tanks, should take such a lukewarm stance toward the political relevance of social scientific knowledge speaks plainly to its advanced marginalization in the welfare debate. Indeed, by this time social's science's authority in the welfare debate had been reduced to a level approaching zero.

Progressive Policy Knowledge

Among think tanks that staked out progressive positions in the welfare debate, the two most prominent were the Economic Policy Institute and the Center on Budget and Policy Priorities. EPI was founded in 1986 by a small group of liberal economists that included Robert Kuttner and Robert Reich. CBPP was established in 1981 by Robert Greenstein, a former Department of Agriculture official who ran the Food Stamp program. However, neither organization was as large or well funded as its conservative adversaries in the debate. EPI sought to reintroduce the issue of deprivation by pointing out weaknesses in the low-wage labor market and tracing their effects on low-income Americans.[114] In 1995, for example, Bernstein and Mishel tracked wage and employment trends for less educated Americans and argued that the "segment of the labor market that is most accessible to former welfare recipients is presently characterized by low and falling wages and high and rising unemployment."[115] EPI also released a series of biennial assessments known as *The State of Working America* that attempted to reinsert the discussion of poverty into public debate by tracking rising poverty rates and declining median family income.[116] Like EPI, CBPP predicted that eliminating welfare entitlements would cause wages to decline for the most precariously situated American workers. Ironically, though, the organization might have unwittingly played a role in streamlining PRWORA's passage. In his insider account of the process, Haskins credits two CBPP reports with convincing Republican leaders that the Medicaid reform act with which the welfare bill had originally been linked was a political "loser" and should be strategically decoupled from welfare reform.[117] In general, though, the two progressive think tanks were scarcely audible over the din of their conservative competitors.

Conclusion: Policy Knowledge and Social Science

By the closing stages of the welfare reform process, a clear separation had opened between technocratic and social scientific knowledge about

welfare. One manifestation of the divide appeared in 1994 when Sheldon
Danziger, a professor of public policy at the University of Michigan, attempted to mobilize social scientific authority against Charles Murray's
argument that welfare caused illegitimacy and in turn led to an array of
societal pathologies. A few months after Murray's October 1993 *Wall
Street Journal* op-ed on the topic had garnered enormous public attention,
Danziger coauthored a rebuttal with Bob Greenstein of the Center on
Budget and Policy Priorities. The two authors gathered signatures from
76 prominent social scientists for a press release stating that Murray's arguments were at loggerheads with existing social scientific knowledge.[118]
The publicity effort backfired, however, with Robert Rector of the Heritage Foundation coming to Murray's defense and calling the signers of the
statement "intellectually fatigued liberals engaging in a last-ditch defense
of the welfare system."[119] More importantly, the social scientists did not
get nearly the same level of public attention as Murray had in his earlier
intervention. As Ron Haskins concludes, "Despite the best efforts of the
social scientists, there was only modest media coverage of the entire episode."[120] Moreover, Haskins argues, "Murray's already considerable noto-
riety was greatly enhanced by this attack."[121]

While it might be tempting to summarize this story in terms of a battle
between two sets of intellectuals identified and separated by their institutional affiliations—namely, think tank–affiliated actors on the one side
versus academic social scientists on the other—I believe this formulation
would be too simplistic to capture the main features of the process. To
be sure, it is true that think tanks and their affiliated actors had come to
play an increasingly prominent role in policy discussions, including those
surrounding welfare reform, and arguably at the expense of academic
scholars. As Weaver notes in his detailed account of the process, "conservative think tanks and social conservative organizations" quickly came to
outnumber academic scholars on the witness lists of the House Ways and
Means and Senate Finance committees (the two congressional committees
with jurisdiction over AFDC) after the Republican takeover of Congress
in 1995 (see table 5.1).[122]

Nevertheless, any simple tale of "think tanks versus universities" begins to break down once we recognize that academic scholars were by
no means excluded from the welfare reform discussion. In fact, several
prominent academic social scientists—including sociologist William Julius Wilson and economist David Ellwood, both of Harvard—became
advisers to Clinton in the period leading up to welfare reform's passage.
Yet I would argue that the role played by these social scientists better

TABLE 5.1 **Testimony by expert witnesses during congressional welfare reform hearings, 1993–96. Adapted from Weaver 2000, 142. On Weaver's count, expert witnesses constitute about 19% of total witnesses. Others include federal officials, advocacy group representatives, professionals, union delegates, and "everyday citizens."**

	Witnesses			
	103rd Congress		104th Congress	
	House	Senate	House	Senate
Affiliation	No. (%)	No. (%)	No. (%)	No. (%)
University	15 (37.5)	0 (0)	18 (35.3)	7 (33.3)
Think tank	18 (45.0)	2 (66.7)	26 (51.0)	12 (57.1)
Conservative	5 (12.5)	0 (0)	14 (27.5)	8 (38.1)
Centrist	5 (12.5)	1 (33.3)	4 (7.8)	3 (14.3)
Liberal	8 (20.0)	1 (33.3)	8 (15.7)	1 (4.8)
Other expert groups	7 (17.5)	1 (33.3)	7 (13.7)	2 (9.5)
Total expert witnesses	40 (100.0)	3 (100.0)	51 (100.0)	21 (100.0)

illustrates the profound influence of think tanks and the *limits* of social scientific knowledge as a force in the welfare reform discussion. In the first place, the proposals put forward by Wilson, Ellwood, and other social scientists were strategically adapted to (and counted as "relevant" to the debate *only because* they) fit within its already-narrowed confines. In an effort to inch the debate closer to the political center, Wilson and Ellwood advocated for an expansion of universalistic social programs from which the poor would derive disproportionate benefits (such as childcare and parental leave protections, health insurance, stricter enforcement of child support laws, tax credits, and job training).[123] The strategic rationale behind their recommendations lay in the understanding that it was now impossible to neutralize the stigma attached to means-tested welfare initiatives. Serving as cochair of Clinton's welfare reform task force, for example, Ellwood adopted a "mix and match" approach to reform that endorsed work requirements along with a minimum wage increase, an expansion of the Earned Income Tax Credit, universal health insurance, and increased child support mechanisms.[124]

Thus, while pushing the debate toward the center, Ellwood's proposals also "helped legitimize the idea of putting time limits on cash welfare benefits," according to Weaver.[125] (Likewise, in a study with collaborator Mary Jo Bane, Ellwood gave added credibility to the conservative alarm over welfare dependency by showing that a greater-than-expected number of recipients remained on the rolls for long periods of time.[126]) As Weaver argues, by the mid-1990s "a broad-based attack on poverty with a special focus on inner cities [was] simply not palatable to politicians in an era of chastened and budget-constrained government."[127] I would amend this point by arguing that a targeted antipoverty program was not feasible in an era of conservative political ascendancy in which welfare receipt had come to be defined, *eo ipso*, as a form of moral degeneracy that led to other forms of "bad behavior."

Thus, I would contend that the suppliers of intellectual discourse who had the greatest impact on the welfare reform process were those who shaped the terms of the debate itself during the three decades preceding Clinton's presidency. To understand the centrality of think tanks in this process, we must make two fundamental breaks with the scholastic commonsense view of the issue. First, the importance of think tanks cannot be captured by a simple "billiard ball" model of causality whereby a particular think tank–generated policy proposal (or set of proposals) was adopted wholesale by policymakers. Instead, the role of think tanks must be grasped in terms of their reconfiguring effects on the social structure—not just on the formal institutions of politics, but also on the market, the media, and the space of knowledge production. Second, I would argue that this role should be described less in terms of what think tanks produced than in terms of what they *precluded*, especially with respect to the potential relevance of more autonomous intellectuals.

Combining the two points, the main argument of this chapter is that think tanks *reordered the institutional space of knowledge production and consumption in the United States in a way that prevented the most autonomous social scientists from constituting themselves as effective participants in policy debate.* In the early 1960s, academic social scientists and journalists had collaborated in the production of a "discourse of deprivation" that quickly placed the issue of poverty at the forefront of the national agenda. This was no "golden age" of public intellectuals, however, for three reasons. First, as other scholars have ably shown, the resulting "War on Poverty" was ambivalent in its aims, limited in its effects, and weak in its design. Second, the 1964 legislation led immediately to the growth of a technocratic machinery of "poverty knowledge" that undermined the subsequent influence of autonomously produced social scientific knowledge. As O'Connor argues, by developing their own methods, criteria of judgment, terminology, credentials, and "distinctive subculture," technocratic specialists "effectively colonized poverty knowledge."[128] In particular, the growth of technocratic research centers ensured that the research deemed most relevant to welfare policy discussion remained focused on categories and assumptions driven by political rather than scientific considerations. Third, the 1964 legislation led immediately to a sharp backlash among economic elites, who funded a network of activist-expert organizations during the 1970s and 1980s that resuscitated, and wrapped in social scientific clothing, a rival "discourse of dependency."

As this book has shown, the rise of think tanks was central to both of the latter two processes. Consequently, I would argue, it was the main factor in establishing a "buyer's market" in expertise that effectively nullified any independent role for social scientific knowledge in policy debate. By the 1990s, then, any politician engaged in the welfare reform battle could select freely from a never-ending stream of arguments, statistics, and talking points to support whichever policy position he or she held. This argument accords with Bane's observation that the welfare research of the 1990s "was well suited to be used as ammunition by all sides, a process that was at least acquiesced in if not actively encouraged by policy researchers seeking to be relevant."[129] More broadly, my argument coincides with the conclusion of Carol Weiss, who, in an interview study of congressional staff members, finds that "by all accounts, the most common form of legislative use [of policy analysis] is support for preexisting positions."[130] To support the claim that policy actors rarely use knowledge or expertise to reconceptualize problems, Weiss quotes an informant who declares, "Information is used to make a case rather than to help people make up their minds." By contrast, Weiss's interview respondents could easily cite "cases in which a committee or a chairman requested information specifically to bolster a position that she wished to promote."[131]

Doubtless the most contentious point in this argument is the implied counterfactual: namely, that in the absence of a highly developed space of think tanks in the United States, autonomously produced social scientific knowledge likely would have played a greater role in shaping the terms and conditions of policy debate after the 1960s. One could plausibly disagree with this claim and argue that even without heteronomous competitors to undermine their relevance, autonomous social scientists would have remained marginal to political life. In a country known for its "anti-intellectualism," this argument might go, social scientific knowledge would not have altered the political orthodoxy in any way. However, of the two possibilities, I find the first to be far more compelling. In a setting free of think tanks, the existing cultural authorities would have been fewer and the competition to intervene in public debate less intense. America's "exceptionalism" notwithstanding, the nation had followed a trajectory broadly similar to that of other advanced countries in granting scientific and technical argumentation a central role in political debate.[132] My view, then, is that for autonomous social scientists to have remained marginal to political life after the 1960s, even in the absence of competition from heteronomous counterparts (of which think tanks are now the exemplars), the United States would have had to become an extreme outlier among nations by expunging scientific and technical argumentation from politics altogether.

Conclusion: Anti-intellectualism, Public Intellectualism, and Public Sociology Revisited

[Scientists] are in a position to help you . . . gain *clarity*. . . . As far as this is the case, we can make clear to you the following: . . . If you take such and such a stand, then, according to scientific experience, you have to use such and such a *means* in order to carry out your conviction practically. Now, these means are perhaps such that you believe you must reject them. Then you simply must choose between the end and the inevitable means. Does the end "justify" the means? Or does it not? The teacher can confront you with the necessity of this choice. He cannot do more, so long as he wishes to remain a teacher and not to become a demagogue. — Max Weber

If we want to avoid . . . an attitude of accepting the world "as it is," we must . . . keep our future conceptually open for some measure of progress. In this regard scholarship is an inherently affirmative activism that is sustained by its own rationalist ethos of intellectual mastery of the world, although it takes place at a great remove from instrumental action in the political and economic spheres. — Guenther Roth, on Weber's theory of rationalism

In this book, I have sought to sketch the broad outlines for a sociological theory of think tanks. In doing so, the initial challenge was an analytical one: How can I conceptualize think tanks without allowing the study to become trapped in the largely tacit (yet by no means unimportant) struggle over the boundary of the object itself? To solve this riddle, I argued that it was necessary to establish a break with everyday folk representations of the think tank and sketch instead the history of the social relations of force and meaning through which the category itself became institutionalized in American life. On this count, I argued that we must shift the study's focus to the formation of the *space of think tanks*, a hybrid institutional arena situated at the nexus of the political, academic, economic, and media fields. The field concept was useful, in fact, not only for locating think tanks within the social structure, but also for historicizing the empirical object itself. Adopting a historical approach allowed us steer a middle course between a purely "externalist" analysis, which would have reduced think tanks to a series of macrostructural forces, and a purely "internalist" account, which would have overstated their autonomy. Instead, we could trace the formation of a relatively bounded subspace of knowledge production in the United States that grew more distinct as its inhabitants succeeded in establishing their own norms, conventions, intellectual products, and forms of prestige.

Constitutively dependent on the more established domains of academics, politics, business, and the media, I argued, think tanks could also be examined as a hybrid "space between fields." To consider think tanks in these term is to count them as the offspring of more established institutions, the "parental" ties being at once material and symbolic: *material* because the surrounding institutions confer financial support and personnel to think tanks, *symbolic* because the figures of the policymaker, the scholar, the entrepreneur, and the media specialist supply the imaginary models from which policy experts fashion their hybrid self-understandings. This double-sided approach also allowed me to examine "policy research" as a project to balance openness and closure, and heteronomy and autonomy, in the American field of expertise. By deploying novel tactics and mobilizing new combinations of resources—including political know-how, the language of social science, media access, journalistic writing, and the techniques of activism, public relations, and marketing—think tanks locate themselves in a privileged central position in the field of expertise.

In broad terms, I argued that the formation of a semidistinct space of think tanks in the United States must be understood as part of a large-scale reconfiguration of the space of knowledge production. In the scholarly literature on intellectuals, one often finds the argument that "in the post–World War II period, the most conspicuous intellectuals in the United States have been university professors."[1] Doubtless this remained true through the 1960s. However, my argument has been that the claim is in need of revision, and that the period since the 1960s has been marked by the rise of a new public figure in American intellectual discourse called the "policy expert."

Existing scholarship has often judged the effects of think tanks exclusively from the standpoint of the political field, by reducing their role to a series of policy-level effects. Insofar as scholars have considered the role of think tanks as intermediaries between the worlds of science and politics, they have too readily accepted the notion—often reinforced by think tanks themselves—of think tanks as intellectual bridging mechanisms. (The original mission statement of the Brookings Institution, for instance, read, "Brookings serves as a bridge between scholarship and policymaking, bringing new knowledge to the attention of decisionmakers and affording scholars greater insight into public policy issues.") In *The Coming of Post-Industrial Society*, Daniel Bell predicted that as academic knowledge became more specialized, bridging institutions would emerge to make this knowledge accessible to policymakers. My argument, however, was that in the act of spanning the divide between academic and political institutions, think tanks have more often served to reinforce a separation between scientific knowledge and politics than to promote an interchange between the two. This argument sprang directly from the empirical description of the think tank itself. At the outset of the book, I argued that we could not neglect the structural blurriness of the think tank if we were to arrive at an adequate description of the object. Later, I took this point a step further by arguing that to artificially cleanse the think tank of its blurriness would also be to obscure its effects as a *blurring* institution with respect to the boundary between intellectuals and nonintellectuals. As Jerome Karabel writes, "the presence of sharp boundaries separating intellectuals from non-intellectuals" is one of the main conditions leading to the development of collective identity and action among intellectuals.[2] In keeping with this point, I would argue that the more distinct the space of think tanks has become, the more it has blurred the separation between intellectuals and nonintellectuals in America by serving as a conduit for the imposition of political, market, and media forces upon the intellectual field.

Rather than simply offer a recap of the main argument of the book, however, I would like, by way of conclusion, to engage briefly with three ongoing debates about the role of intellectuals in American politics and the public sphere. Each of these debates gives us an opportunity to contextualize this study further and reframe its central contribution. The first of the three debates is the two-century-old discussion about *anti-intellectualism* in American life. Almost since the nation's birth, observers of American culture have noted that one of its distinctive features is its anti-intellectual spirit, or a pattern of suspicion directed toward "the life of the mind" and the corresponding valorization of practical know-how and "common sense." The second discussion is a more recent debate about the status of so-called public intellectuals in the United States. Since the 1987 publication of Russell Jacoby's *The Last Intellectuals*, a lively debate has focused on whether the quality of public intellectual life in America has declined as a result of increased specialization and insularity among scholars. The third discussion is the ongoing debate within academic sociology over the discipline's proper orientation and mission, and more specifically the possibility of a socially beneficial "public sociology." The study of think tanks, I would argue, allows us to recast and extend each of these debates.

Three Problems in the Study of Intellectuals

The Concept of Anti-intellectualism and Its Critics

The notion of anti-intellectualism has a long pedigree in American commentary and scholarship. Ever since Alexis de Tocqueville identified suspicion toward ideas as a common strain in American thinking, the notion has been invoked repeatedly in diagnoses of the national psyche.[3] In 1883, for example, Ralph Waldo Emerson observed that Americans regarded ideas as "subversive of social order and comfort"; three-quarters of a century later, journalist Max Lerner wrote of the American "fear of ideas, ranging from the good-natured epithet of 'egghead' to the unremitting hatred which some congressmen and newspapers express for any liberal intellectuals."[4] By the mid-twentieth century, a substantial body of historical research and writing sought to identify the main sources and expressions of the anti-intellectual spirit.[5] Among its roots, historians posited, were the rugged pragmatism needed for westward expansion, the entrepreneurial creed that elevated action over reflection and gave rise to widespread suspicion toward all those who "meddled" in economic affairs, and the populist tradition that led politicians to portray themselves as "self-made men" and denounce their opponents as elites. Other writers pointed to the evangelical tradition of the first and second Great Awakenings, which opposed faith to learning, decried the hubris involved in attempts at scholarly understanding, and endorsed direct, personal access to God as opposed to access mediated by the clergy.[6] Even in the history of American education, scholars have detected anti-intellectualism in the instrumentalist views of progressive educators, who elevated "life-adjustment" and vocational training as central principles of curriculum design.[7] Across all of these domains, the common theme was the value of utilitarianism as a guiding principle.[8]

Despite its enduring appeal, however, the idea of anti-intellectualism has proven awkward and difficult as a conceptual tool. The ambivalence among historians toward the idea is captured well in the body of criticism directed at the most sustained investigation of American anti-intellectualism, Richard Hofstadter's *Anti-Intellectualism in American Life*. Despite earning a Pulitzer Prize and an enduring place in the canon of great historical texts, Hofstadter's book has garnered a series of harsh reactions from historians and journalists, both at the time of its publication in 1963 and more recently. When the book was first published, the main criticism directed at Hofstadter was that the concept anti-intellectualism itself was too nebulous an idea, impossible to pin down either empirically or theoretically, and thus not an appropriate tool for scholarly investigation. Writing in the *American Historical Review*, for example, Arthur Bestor noted that the "difficulty (which, for me, persisted through several rereadings) is to define exactly what it is a history of."[9] In Bestor's view,

> sometimes intellectuals as a class are pictured as under attack by other classes in society, such as businessmen. . . . At still other times, antiintellectualism is viewed as a clash of ideas rather than a clash of interested social groups. . . . What, then, is the essential subject matter of this study? Is it a history of the changing status and repute of the intellectual class in America? Or the history of a body of ideas? Or the history of a psychological state, compounded of suspicion and hostility?[10]

Historian Philip Gleason similarly charged Hofstadter with reifying the book's central concept. Anti-intellectualism, he wrote, "is treated as a *thing* which has objective reality, rather than being consistently handled as a conceptual instrument."[11] Finally, Rush Welter noted, "What Hofstadter examines [is] not a national commitment so much as a cluster of expressions and activities that may or may not have held the same meaning for all the men who engaged in them. In other words, anti-intellectualism may prove to be as protean a concept as Manifest Destiny—and as difficult to employ wisely in historical analysis."[12]

Equally troubling to Hofstadter's critics was the author's peculiar suggestion that anti-intellectualism's main purveyors were themselves "men of ideas."[13] In the book's preamble, Hofstadter characterized anti-intellectualism as a style, an attitude, or a system of expressions whose common characteristic was "a resentment and suspicion of the life of the mind and of those who are considered to represent it."[14] Nevertheless,

In so far as anti-intellectualism becomes articulate enough to be traced historically or widespread enough to make itself felt in contemporary controversy,
it has to have spokesmen who are at least to some degree competent. These
spokesmen are in the main neither the uneducated nor the intellectual, but
rather the marginal intellectuals, would-be intellectuals, unfrocked or embit-
tered intellectuals, the literate leaders of the semi-literate.[15]

To Hofstadter's critics, of course, this was the height of circular reasoning,
especially in light of the suggestion that "real" intellectuals were subordi-
nated to their "unfrocked" counterparts. In the views of critics, American
intellectuals could be described as dominated only through a kind of conceptual sleight of hand in which the concept *intellectual* itself was tacitly
predefined in terms of self-marginalizing quirkiness, defiance of the mainstream, or an "outsider" sensibility.

Writing in the *American Sociological Review*, for example, David Riesman noted that Hofstadter "does not give sufficient recognition to the
ways in which today . . . men with some claim to being intellectuals are
linked to power, opportunity, and privilege."[16] Howard Mumford Jones
similarly took issue with the selection of writers and literary thinkers
whom Hofstadter cited as intellectuals, and noted that a "list made up,
say, of Vannevar Bush, Jerome Bruner . . . Sidney Hook . . . the staff members of the Astrophysical Observatory of the Smithsonian Institution, and
the staff members of the Brookings Institute [sic], all, I suggest, influential
members of the 'clerisy,' would scarcely exhibit 'alienation' or suggest it in
the same way."[17] To these writers, intellectuals in the United States did not
clearly occupy subordinate positions in society. Moreover, the conceptual
difficulties attached to this point suggested that the whole idea of anti-
intellectualism was hopeless.

Before I address this dispute between Hofstadter and his critics, let me
note a second, related critique of *Anti-Intellectualism in American Life*
that has been raised more recently in light of more than four decades of
hindsight. In 2006, David Brown's biography of Hofstadter prompted a series of essays that re-examined the historian's legacy, including his famous
study of anti-intellectualism. It was in the context of this discussion that a
new critique emerged. According to the new generation of critics, it is well
known that Hofstadter's ultimate purpose in writing the book was to issue
a warning about the dangers of anti-intellectualism in his own day.[18] And
yet, the critique goes, history has shown that the late 1950s and early 1960s
were actually the *pinnacle* of intellectuals' influence in American society

and politics. In light of this point, it appears that Hofstadter lacked sufficient historical perspective on his own era. In 2006, for example, journalist
Sam Tanenhaus suggested that "disingenuous, and faintly ludicrous, is the
spectacle of a much-honored public eminence warning against the dangers of American philistinism at the height of the Kennedy years, when
a conveyor belt ran from Harvard Yard to the White House, and a major
historian, Arthur Schlesinger Jr., served as a presidential adviser."[19] Jon
Wiener similarly noted that in hindsight, "the book seems mistaken about
the period in which it was published." After all,

> Anti-intellectualism was hardly a major problem in the United States in 1964.
> American intellectuals in the early '60s had never had it so good: Universi-
> ties were growing as never before, Congress provided lavish funding for elite
> institutions and professors like Hofstadter were highly paid and won big book
> contracts. Popular magazines followed the hot debates among intellectuals—
> Daniel Bell on the "end of ideology," David Riesman on "the lonely crowd,"
> C. Wright Mills on "the power elite," Irving Howe on "the age of conformity,"
> C. Vann Woodward on "the strange career of Jim Crow," Michael Harrington
> on "the other America." As Russell Jacoby argued in *The Last Intellectuals*, the
> 1950s were the golden age for liberal thinkers like Hofstadter.[20]

On this view, the late 1950s and early 1960s were not a period of anti-
intellectualism at all, but one in which American intellectuals were emerging as a major force in public life. How, the critics asked, could Hofstadter
have been so nearsighted about his own day?

This discussion points to the three main challenges facing anyone who
would wish to reconstruct an analytic concept of anti-intellectualism today: First, is it possible to define the concept coherently, nontautologically,
and in such a way that renders it analytically useful? Second, what should
we make of Hofstadter's claim that anti-intellectualism's main purveyors
are themselves intellectuals of a sort, albeit "marginal," "would-be," or
"unfrocked" intellectuals? The third challenge is the historical puzzle:
Why would the charge of anti-intellectualism receive its clearest and most
forceful expression precisely at the moment in American history when
intellectuals seemed to be enjoying their greatest authority and influence?
More broadly, how should we account for the seeming distinctiveness
of the 1950s and 1960, when a kind of nascent "public intellectualism"
seemed to flicker in America, only to be snuffed out in later years? This
last question moves us seamlessly to the second ongoing debate with which

I would like to engage in this chapter: the debate on the supposed demise of the "public intellectual."[21]

The Death of Public Intellectualism?

In 1987, the publication of Russell Jacoby's book *The Last Intellectuals* sparked a spirited debate among scholars, critics, journalists, and others about the status and fate of the so-called public intellectual in the United States. Whereas most writers who have weighed in on the topic have generally concurred with the main thesis of Jacoby's book—namely that after a period in which public discourse was enriched by intellectuals, American thinkers have increasingly been lured into the cocoon of the academy—others have argued that public intellectuals are not in decline at all, and even that their numbers are growing.[22] On the surface, the "public intellectuals" debate might seem to like a useful backdrop for any study that seeks to assess the significance of think tanks. After all, in the standard narrative associated with Jacoby, the putative demise of the public intellectual takes place concurrently with the rise of think tanks. Perhaps there is a causal connection between the two processes. At another level, however, I would argue that the debate on public intellectuals only promises to impede our understanding of think tanks. Having become predictably mired in confusion over the meaning of the central concept, the debate on public intellectuals has generated more heat than light.

I am wary of the concept *public intellectual* for two reasons. The first, as I discussed in the prologue, stems from the danger of being drawn into what Eyal and Buchholz call the "problematic of allegiance," or a mode of analyzing intellectuals that becomes centered on questions about their ultimate loyalties and commitments.[23] In general, the problem with this analytic approach is that it tends to draw scholars into futile and arbitrary debates over who the "true" intellectuals are. In the case of "public intellectuals," for example, we would be forced to decide "on paper," and without solid justification, which thinkers count as public intellectuals and which do not prior to any assessment of their rise or fall.

A second, related reason to be wary of the public intellectual concept becomes apparent when we place the concept into a wider historical perspective. What a long historical view makes clear is that that the exact *prototype* of the "public intellectual" tends to change over time—and not at random, but in response to the dynamic structural conditions under which intellectuals can intervene effectively in public debate. Thus we might agree, for example, that Walter Lippmann was the quintessential public intellectual of the 1950s, or that Paul Krugman fits the dominant model of the public intellectual today. However, their markedly different forms of expertise, credentials, career trajectories, and modes of expression suggest that, regardless of whether public intellectuals have multiplied or disappeared, there have been important shifts in the institutional conditions under which public intellectualism itself is understood and enacted in the United States. At this point, our interest begins to shift away from questions about the presence or absence of intellectuals in public debate and toward questions about the totality of relations shaping the production and consumption of intellectual discourse in the United States. Once we begin to think in these terms, it becomes clear that we can dispense with the use of ideal-types such as "public intellectual," and its implied counterparts, as bases for the discussion. (Indeed, wherever one finds mention of the public intellectual, two other ideal-types are never far behind. The first is the so-called "ivory tower" figure, while the second is the "mercenary" figure, or the intellectual wolf-in-sheep's-clothing who looks very much like a "true" intellectual at first glance, but actually performs cognitive work on behalf of self-interested clients. The differences among these three ideal-types can be captured in a simple formulation: whereas the ivory tower figure fails to be *public*, the mercenary fails to be an *intellectual*.) In Jacoby's argument, for example, it was the public intellectuals of the past who became the ivory tower intellectuals of the present—or the self-absorbed specialists whose narrow competence and privileged isolation suggested a betrayal of their duties as intellectuals.

The central point of the relational approach I have outlined—which is sketched most fully in chapter 3—is that these ideal-types refer only to the unstable corner locations in a field of expertise organized, first, by the opposition between autonomy and heteronomy, and second, by the opposition between open and closed social relations. In the final section of this chapter, I will use this approach to situate my discussion of think tanks in relation to the "public intellectuals" debate. First, however, let me introduce the third discussion to which this study speaks.

The Prospects for a Public Sociology

In 2004, Michael Burawoy initiated a fierce debate within sociology by proposing the revitalization of "public sociology."[24] His recommendations generated sharp (and sometimes highly defensive) reactions from other sociologists who found in his program a divisive agenda that threatened the health of the discipline itself. Yet with so much focus on the relations among sociologists, and between sociologists and their publics, I believe this debate has largely overlooked what is actually the main obstacle to the development of a viable civic sociological tradition: namely, the growing presence of intellectual competitors in the public and political spheres since the 1960s. In fact, I would argue that the very categories on which Burawoy's framework is built—"professional," "policy," "public," and "critical" forms of sociological knowledge—refer to divisions that have been exacerbated within the sociological field by the rise of heteronomous knowledge producers. This process threatens to destabilize the discipline by luring its practitioners in separate directions—for example, by drawing some sociologists toward a technocratic model of production (i.e., the "policy sociology" of Burawoy's scheme), others toward purely self-referential modes of inquiry ("professional sociology"), others toward forms of sociological practice meant to uphold the standpoints of designated publics ("public sociology"), and others toward a mode of sociological production that collapses ideological and analytic categories ("critical sociology"). However, it is impossible to grasp this process without situating sociology analytically within the wider system of relations among intellectuals.

American Intellectualism: Grounded, Historicized, and Localized

The analytic framework I have deployed in this book, which builds on the contributions of many sociologists (especially Weber, Durkheim, Bourdieu, Eyal, and Wacquant), points the way toward a solution to these problems. For example, the first puzzle I mentioned concerned the ambiguity and seemingly tautological quality of the term *anti-intellectualism*. In keeping with the relational mode of analysis that has guided this study, let me first suggest that the charge of anti-intellectualism is best understood as a strategic *move* (or what Bourdieu would call a "position-taking") in a space of struggles among producers of intellectual discourse. The strategy I am referring to is that of the relatively autonomous intellectual who (like Hofstadter himself) aims to discredit his or her less autonomous counterparts, often by pointing to their lack of insulation from the market and politics. We can use this observation to make sense of Hofstadter's otherwise puzzling insistence that the main purveyors of anti-intellectualism in

America are themselves intellectuals. What Hofstadter is describing—and taking part in—in other words, is a struggle within the field of expertise.

This approach also helps explain why the charge of anti-intellectualism would receive its clearest expression at precisely the moment it did. The 1960s was a brief period in which a small flame of "public intellectualism" had begun to flicker in the United States—but also an era of what Eyal calls "intensified struggle over the prototype of intellectual work" as a new breed of heteronomous cultural producers quickly began to encroach upon the territory of their more autonomous counterparts. As we saw in chapter 5, it had now become possible for a small network of social scientists, historians, philosophers, and journalists who had wrested a considerable degree of control over their own products and expertise to begin reinvesting their authority in the public sphere. But as Lewis Coser warned in 1965, "Were mental technicians and experts, their distant cousins, to pre-empt the field that intellectuals now occupy, modern culture would likely perish through ossification."[25] Whether we now live in an age of political or cultural ossification is a matter for the reader to decide, but I take it as a matter of fact that technicians and experts—having merged with the activist-experts of the 1960s—have collectively preempted the field that "intellectuals" briefly occupied.

In my view, then, Hofstadter's critics were correct to point out that his argument was not simply a neutral observation—free of strategy or detached from its social moorings. However, I believe the same critics also failed to give Hofstadter his due when they concluded that the whole idea of anti-intellectualism was therefore hopeless. Instead, I would suggest that the idea of anti-intellectualism remains useful in the context of a study of the struggles among producers of intellectual discourse, for referring to a relational stance adopted by certain intellectuals. Hofstadter himself already suggested as much when he referred to anti-intellectualism as a "complex of historical *relations*," although it was a point he never developed fully (and one he later contradicted by referring to anti-intellectualism as a style or an attitude).[26] To extend Hofstadter's insight, I would argue that the charge of anti-intellectualism is most likely to find expression in situations when autonomous intellectuals are threatened with a loss of their clientele by more heteronomous counterparts. This is precisely what was taking place in the mid-1960s.

At first glance, these points might seem to put me in agreement with those who argue for the demise of the public intellectual. However, I would disagree with this notion on three counts. First of all, following

Eyal and Buchholz, I would argue that terms such as *public intellectual* are best understood as referring, not to flesh-and-blood actors, or even to ideal-types per se, but rather to *locations* in a space of struggles among intellectual groups. Second, while it is arguably true that some kind of embryonic public intellectual project was indeed incubating among scholars and journalists during the 1950s and early 1960s, it is imperative that we avoid romanticizing this brief period as a "golden age" of public intellectualism. To paraphrase Mark Twain, reports of the public intellectual's life were greatly exaggerated, since it was only a small network of academic social scientists and journalists who managed to intervene in civic affairs from a standpoint of greater autonomy and openness—and even then only briefly and to limited political effect. In chapter 3, I described this project as a challenge to the growing role of technocrats in political affairs. However, my larger point in that chapter was that this public intellectual project was not the most important such challenge to technocracy developing at the time. This point leads me to my third disagreement with the "death of public intellectuals" thesis, which sets out from its simplistic focus on the retreat of scholars into the academy as the main causal factor in the decline of public intellectualism. In doing so, it overlooks the more important threat to the marriage of autonomy and civic engagement since the 1960s: namely, the influx of new competitors into the space of knowledge production. One of the purposes of this book, in fact, has been to nominate the rise of think tanks as the focal point of this process.

If academic social scientists did not simply retreat opportunistically into the academy, then how should we describe their recent trajectories? On this question, my central claim is that, unlike the structural *convergence* between technocrats and activist-experts that made possible the space of think tanks (and the emergence of the policy expert), the chief modality among academic scholars has been one of *divergence*. Using the field of expertise as an analytic backdrop, in fact, we can discern at least three basic strategies and trajectories among American social scientists since the 1960s. First, as other scholars have noted, there has been a movement toward greater professionalization (or even "hyper-professionalization," in the phrase of Steve Shapin) among social scientists.[27] In other words, many social scientists became more inward looking and focused on increasingly narrow disciplinary debates, as Jacoby suggests. However, a second tendency among scholars has been to engage in policy debate by imitating the style of intellectual production institutionalized in the space of think tanks. Many scholars, in short, have become "policy researchers" in the model established by think tanks. As I have argued (especially in chapter 4), given the current state of relations marking the American field of power, to become a policy researcher is to subordinate one's production to the rules of the political, market, and media fields.

A third strategy observable among American social scientists since the 1960s involves neither retreating into the "ivory tower" nor following the technocrat's lead by tailoring one's products to the demands of powerful clients. Instead, it is worth noting that many social scientists have succumbed to neither pressure, but have persevered in their civic-intellectual missions and have sought to remain both cognitively independent and engaged in civic affairs. The problem with this strategy, however, is that those who adopt it now face a *double marginalization* not encountered by their 1960s counterparts. First, there is marginalization from the mainstream of their disciplines, which are less likely to reward those who dedicate their work to the goal of enlightening public debate. This point helps to explain why this third strategy is viable mainly to scholars with a profusion of academic capital already in their symbolic bank accounts. While social scientists with little left to prove in the academy can afford to reinvest their academic capital in public debate—and often do—rank-and-file scholars have little incentive to follow this route. More important than the first form of marginalization, however, is the second: namely, marginalization from a public debate increasingly dominated by policy experts operating in symbiotic partnership with politicians, political professionals, and media specialists who can select from a wide range of intellectual products to bolster their pre-held views.

Thus, the main conclusion of this study is that the growth of think tanks over the past forty years has played a pivotal role in undermining the relevance of autonomously produced social scientific knowledge in the United States by fortifying a system of social relations that relegates its producers to the margins of public debate. To the degree that think tanks arrogate for themselves a central role in the policy-making process, they effectively limit the range of options available to more autonomous intellectuals, or those less willing to tailor their work to the demands of moneyed sponsors and politicians. Earlier in the book, I referred to the space of think tanks as a *terra obscura*, a term that was meant to convey the image of an organizational network that, while hybrid in its form and function, nonetheless exhibits certain field-like properties of its own. But if we are to take this term seriously (the second part of which derives from the Latin verb *obscurare*, meaning "to render indistinct" or "to cause to be forgotten"), then we must ask what is being forgotten by virtue of the rise of think tanks. The answer, I would argue, is the value of self-directed knowledge in public life. The rise of think tanks must therefore be set analytically against the backdrop of a series of processes that have contributed to the growing subordination of knowledge to political and economic demand—including the reassertion of control over the economy by holders of economic capital, the development of specialized forms of political expertise, the growth of the mass media as a conduit for the imposition of market forces into politics, the corporatization of the university, and the withdrawal of the state from the financing of public education. The question posed acutely by the rise of think tanks in America concerns the social value of social scientific knowledge itself: Put simply, should money and political power direct ideas, or should ideas direct themselves?

Appendix A: Note on Data Sources

This study is based on a multimethod research procedure with five empirical components:

(1) I examined archival records from fourteen manuscript collections (both organizational and personal) at various historical archives, including those of the Library of Congress, the Brookings Institution, the Carnegie Endowment for International Peace, the American Enterprise Institute, the Columbia University Rare Book and Manuscript Collection, the Wisconsin Historical Society, and the Bancroft Library of the University of California, Berkeley. Records include the self-accounts of key figures in the field, organizational histories, personal letters and memoirs, mission statements, biographical accounts, and archival materials on the founding and decision-making processes of think tanks.

I selected these archives because each one contains a sizable repository of data related to think tanks, donor foundations, or individuals who had a hand in founding or managing key think tanks. For example, the Wisconsin Historical Society contains the complete archives of the Institute for Policy Studies, a left-wing think tank. Most of these archives were recommended to me by knowledgeable think tank staff members.

(2) I conducted 44 formal interviews with individuals variously situated in the American think tank world and proximate institutions, including the political news media, federal government agencies, and the philanthropic sector. The think tank interview subjects ranged from founders and upper managers to rank-and-file researchers and staff members. I also interviewed political actors who deal routinely with the work of think tanks, such as Congressional staff members, newspaper and magazine reporters, and administrators at philanthropic foundations.

(3) I compiled a database of the educational and career backgrounds of the policy experts at 22 major think tanks. The data include previous employment and affiliations and educational degrees. The central purpose of constructing this database was to facilitate an analytical mapping or *social topology* of the think tank universe through a series of internal comparisons between individuals and organizations, based on the structural origins and trajectories of their research staff. For example, I examined personnel movement between think tanks to determine whether certain organizations cluster together, and I compared organizations on the basis of the proportion of their research staff who had earned certain educational degrees. These data also allowed for broad and unprecedented empirical generalizations about the internal composition of the think tank universe. I supplement this career trajectory data with detailed biographical and organizational vignettes on certain key figures in the world of think tanks. In presenting these data, I ask how these pioneering figures subverted some of the most basic "rules of the game" structuring policy research through their pursuit of innovative, and previously unthinkable, strategies for contributing expertise to national politics. What predisposed these actors and organizations to be pioneers in the think tank arena? What trajectories did they follow through social space? What practical dispositions did they bring to the field and how were they deployed? What were their goals and self-understandings, and what did they stand to gain, either materially or symbolically, from the effort?

(4) I counted the "output" of think tanks in two areas: news media pickup and Congressional testimony. First, using the Lexis-Nexis database, I counted news media citations of 30 think tanks in two ways: a historical count of citations in the *New York Times* and *Washington Post*, the two most highly respected national news media publications among political actors, ranging from the years 1970 to 2002, and a count of citations of the same 30 think tanks in more than 25 print and electronic news media outlets over a recent five-year period. Second, using the Congressional Universe database, I counted Congressional testimony appearances by representatives from think tanks and major research universities in the period 1950 to 2000. The purpose of these data is to compare the relative contributions of policy knowledge from different organizations over time.

(5) Finally, I carried out segmented firsthand observation in various think tank settings. Over the course of a year and a half, I attended dozens of think tank events, including conferences, debates, book releases, and parties. At these events, I spoke with people on a casual basis, witnessed speeches and panel

discussions, overheard private conversations, and got an "on-the-ground" view of the day-to-day operations of political think tanks. In addition, I took every opportunity to "hang around" at think tanks before and after my interviews and archival research. During the course of my research, I visited some 25 policy research organizations in three American states and the District of Columbia.

Interviews

23. Henry Aaron, Brookings Institution   November 19, 2003
24. Greg Anrig, The Century Foundation   November 21, 2003
25. Eric Alterman, *The Nation*, Center for American   November 21, 2003
    Progress
26. John Judis, *The New Republic*, Carnegie Endow-   November 24, 2003
    ment
27. David Boaz, Cato Institute   November 24, 2003
28. Charles Kolb, Committee for Economic Develop-   November 26, 2003
    ment
29. James Smith, Georgetown University   December 2, 2003
30. Fred Smith Jr., Competitive Enterprise Institute   December 16, 2003
31. Jody Manley Clarke, Competitive   December 16, 2003
    Enterprise Institute
32. David Keene, American Conservative Union   December 17, 2003
33. Alice Rivlin, Brookings Institution   February 10, 2003
34. Adam Meyerson, Philanthropy Roundtable   March 16, 2004
35. William Galston, University of Maryland   June 1, 2004
36. Charles Murray, American Enterprise Institute   June 14, 2004
37. Norman Ornstein, American Enterprise Institute   June 15, 2004
38. Jacob Hacker, New America Foundation and Yale   June 22, 2004
39. Paul Weyrich, Free Congress Foundation   June 29, 2004
40. Al From, Democratic Leadership Council   June 30, 2004
41. Perry Quick, Charles River Associates (Roosevelt   July 2, 2004
    Center)
42. Mark Agrast, Center for American Progress   July 27, 2004
43. Grover Norquist, Americans for Tax   August 2, 2004
    Reform
44. Lawrence Mishel, Economic Policy Institute   April 10, 2008

Archival Sources

LIBRARY OR INSTITUTION	COLLECTION
Library of Congress	The Papers of Clare Boothe Luce
Archival Manuscript Room	The Papers of Vannevar Bush
	The Papers of W. Averell Harriman
	The Papers of William A. Rusher
	The Papers of Robert H. Bork
	The Papers of William J. Baroody
	The Papers of Paul H. Nitze
Rare Book & Manuscript Library	Carnegie Corporation of New York papers
Butler Library, Columbia University	Carnegie Endowment for International Peace papers
Bancroft Library	Sara Diamond Collection
University of California, Berkeley	
Brookings Institution	Organizational archives
Carnegie Endowment for International Peace	Organizational archives
American Enterprise Institute	Organizational archives
Wisconsin Historical Society	Institute for Policy Studies papers

Educational and Career Background Database

The database includes all personnel identified as "scholars," "fellows," "researchers," "research associates," "policy analysts," or equivalent descriptors by 22 think tanks. Nonresident scholars and other loosely affiliated experts (e.g., "partners") are not included in these counts, but visiting scholars-in-residence are included. The data were gathered in 2004.

Educational Data

I gathered the following educational background data:

Highest educational degree
Institution of highest degree
Discipline of study
Year of highest degree

Honorary degrees are excluded from these data, as are degrees in progress.

Occupational Data

I coded all previous and concurrent occupational affiliations according to the following three-tier system:

Sector	Field	Industry
(1) For-profit		
	(A) For-profit journalism	
		(i) Magazine
		(ii) Newspaper
		(iii) TV/radio
		(iv) Internet
	(B) Business	
		(v) Research/consulting
		(vi) Banking/finance
		(vii) Energy
		(viii) Pharmaceutical
		(ix) High tech
		(x) Automotive
		(xi) Defense contracting
		(xii) Insurance
		(xiii) Engineering
		(xiv) Marketing
		(xv) Aviation/aerospace
		(xvi) Other
	(C) Professions	
		(xvii) Law
		(xviii) Medicine
(2) Nonprofit		
	(D) Academic	
		(xix) Professor
		(xx) Research fellow
		(xxi) Journal/publishing
		(xxii) Administrator/trustee
	(E) Think tank	
		(xxiii) [Organization]
	(F) Research/advocacy	
		(xxiv) Labor
		(xxv) Business
		(xxvi) Other
	(G) Religious clergy	

(3) State
    (H) Federal
        (xxvii) Full-time staff
        (xxviii) Advisory/consulting
        (xxix) Elected official
        (xxx) Law/judicial
        (xxxi) Military
    (I) International
        (xxxii) Full-time staff
        (xxxiii) Advisory/consulting
    (J) State/local
        (xxxiv) Full-time staff
        (xxxv) Elected official
        (xxxvi) Advisory/consulting

Notes: In this coding scheme, semiactive positions such as organizational board memberships are noted as "advisory" roles. The category "Academic—research fellow" includes postdoctoral research fellows, directors/staff members of academic research institutes, etc. The category "Government—international" refers to service in foreign governments or within international governing bodies such as the United Nations (though US representatives to the United Nations General Assembly are considered officials of the US federal government). The category "Research/advocacy" includes NGOs, charities, public interest groups, activist and social movement organizations, advocacy groups, political campaigns, and other nonprofit organizations not classified as think tanks. The category "Journalism" refers to policy experts previously or concurrently employed by magazines, newspapers, TV or radio shows, journals, or other news media agencies. Many think tank scholars list news media citations, op-ed pieces, and personal appearances in their biographies and resumes, but in this analysis such experiences do not count as journalism credentials. Finally, this database does not include positions within the think tank itself.

Appendix B: Supplementary Figures and Tables

TABLE B.1 **Characteristics of 25 major American think tanks. Source: 2008 IRS 990 forms (available at http://www.guidestar.org/). Figures in column one are taken from line 18 ("total expenses for current year"); column two figures reflect "net assets or fund balances at end of year" as reported on line 22. Figures for the Century Foundations are from 2008 IRS 990PF (lines 24a and 27c).**

	FY 2008 expenditures (in millions)	FY 2008 assets (in millions)	Expert staff (2010)	Year founded
RAND Corporation	250.3	172.1	283	1948
Brookings Institution	87.9	296.0	269	1916
Urban Institute	64.7	84.4	67	1968
Heritage Foundation	64.6	133.2	76	1973
Aspen Institute	63.5	141.3	49	1950
Council on Foreign Relations	48.3	300.4	65	1921
National Bureau of Economic Research	35.1	73.2	*	1920
Hoover Institution†	34.1	36.7	167	1919
Center for Strategic and Int'l Studies	28.6	46.7	149	1962
American Enterprise Institute	29.9	104.4	87	1943
Center for American Progress	26.3	25.7	104	2003
Carnegie Endowment for Int'l Peace	23.9	206	65	1910
Cato Institute	23.2	25.7	55	1977
Center on Budget and Policy Priorities	19.3	61.1	35	1981
Manhattan Institute	13.4	12.6	41	1978
New America Foundation	12.3	13.1	66	1999
Hudson Institute	11.9	14.7	62	1961
Institute for International Economics	10.4	58.6	37	1981
Joint Ctr for Political & Economic Studies	7.1	4.4	10	1970
Economic Policy Institute	6.5	4.4	25	1986

TABLE B.1 (*continued*)

	FY 2008 expenditures (in millions)	FY 2008 assets (in millions)	Expert staff (2010)	Year founded
Competitive Enterprise Institute	4.7	2.0	21	1984
Century Foundation	4.5	2.2	17	1919
Institute for Policy Studies	3.6	1.8	24	1963
Worldwatch Institute	3.2	0.4	17	1974
Progressive Policy Institute‡	2.1	0.5	9	1989

Notes: *NBER does not employ full-time policy experts.
†Hoover Institution figures are 2007 fiscal year data reported in "2008 Report: Financial Review" (http://www
.hoover.org/about/report/2008/financial-review; retrieved on August 5, 2011).
‡PPI data are from Third Way Foundation, Inc. tax returns.

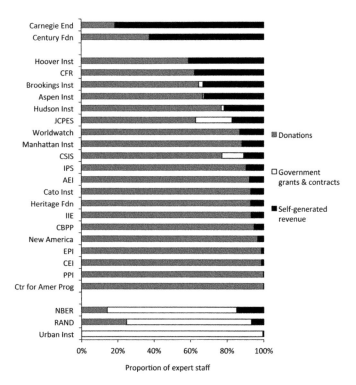

FIGURE B.1   Revenue sources of major think tanks, 2003. Sources: 2003 IRS 990 tax forms. Note: Self-generated revenue includes income from investments (securities, interest on savings, etc.), conference and membership fees, rental income, and proceeds from the sale of publications. Since the Hoover Institution does not file its own federal income tax return, figures for the organization come from Hoover's annual report.

TABLE B.2 **Policy experts reporting past or present employment in nonprofit, state, and for-profit sectors.**

Nonprofit	Percent	State	Percent	For-profit	Percent
Any nonprofit	**78.0**	**Any state**	**62.5**	**Any profit sector**	**43.9**
Academic	52.3	Federal or int'l gov't	48.9	Business (nonprofessional)	22.5
Professor	42.7	Advisory/consulting	21.3	Journalism	21.2
Advocacy/research	40.5	State or local gov't	7.7	Research/consulting	11.8
Other think tank	28.3	Military	7.2	For-profit law	6.8

Note: "Academic" refers to policy experts who report past or present employment as college or university professors, administrators, trustees, or graduate research fellows, and a small number who report employment in the fields of academic journal and book publishing. "Federal or international government" refers to policy experts who report past or present employment as staff or elected officials in the US federal government, other national governments, or international governing bodies such as the United Nations. "Business (various)" refers to all for-profit employment excluding journalism, law, and medicine.

TABLE B.3 **Academic disciplines studied by policy experts.**

Field of study	Percent
Public policy*	30.7
Economics	20.6
Law/legal studies	14.4
Political science	9.9
Natural sciences & medicine	6.4
History/area studies	6.1
Business	4.0
Other art & humanities†	3.5
Other social science‡	3.5
Journalism	0.9
Total	100.0

Notes: Data include all policy experts (n=700) who report the field of their highest degree.
*Includes public affairs, international relations, and comparative politics.
†Philosophy, literature, and theology are the best represented disciplines within this category.
‡Includes sociology, anthropology, and ethnic studies.

TABLE B.4 **Total media citations by think tank, 1997–2005.**

Rank	Think Tank	Political Orientation*	Citations
1	Brookings Institution	Neutral/centrist	2,180
2	Institute for International Economics	Neutral/centrist	1,621
3	American Enterprise Institute	Conservative	1,351
4	Cato Institute	Conservative	873
5	Hoover Institution	Conservative	658
6	Economic Policy Institute	Liberal	634
7	Urban Institute	Liberal	577
8	Heritage Foundation	Conservative	548

TABLE B.4 *(continued)*

Rank	Think Tank	Political Orientation*	Citations
9	Center on Budget and Policy Priorities	Liberal	421
10	Carnegie Endowment for Int'l Peace	Neutral/centrist	355
11	Progressive Policy Institute	Undefined	346
12	Hudson Institute	Conservative	328
13	Milken Institute	Undefined	275
14	Center for Strategic and Int'l Studies	Neutral/centrist	265
15	Council on Foreign Relations	Liberal	259
16	National Center for Policy Analysis	Undefined	220
17	Economic Strategy Institute	Liberal	184

Source: Susanne Trimbath. 2005. "Think Tanks: Who's Hot?" *The International Economy.* Summer: 10–15, 39–47.
*The source study takes these labels from Tim Groseclose and Jeffrey Milyo. "A Measure of Media Bias." *Quarterly Journal of Economics* 120, no. 4: 1191–237.

TABLE B.5 **Most cited think tank economists, 1997–2005. Source: Susanne Trimbath. 2005. "Think Tanks: Who's Hot?"** *The International Economy.* **Summer: 10–15, 39–47.**

Rank	Economist	Think Tank Affiliation(s)	Citations
1	C. Fred Bergsten	Institute for Int'l Economics	461
2	Robert D. Reischauer	Urban Institute and Brookings Institution	383
3	Robert E. Litan	Brookings Institution	335
4	Marshall Wittmann	Progressive Policy Institute, Heritage Foundation, and Hudson Institute	330
5	Gary C. Hufbauer	Council on Foreign Relations & Institute for Int'l Economics	294
6	Nicholas R. Lardy	Brookings Institution and Institute for Int'l Economics	292
7	Jared Bernstein	Economic Policy Institute	291
8	James K. Glassman	American Enterprise Institute	255
9	William G. Gale	Brookings Institution	217
10	Kevin A. Hassett	American Enterprise Institute	215
11	Will Marshall III	Progressive Policy Institute	185
12	Stephen Moore	Cato Institute	179
13	Morris Goldstein	Institute for Int'l Economics	174
14	Peter R. Orszag	Brookings Institution	170
15	Robert Greenstein	Center on Budget and Policy Priorities	163
16	John H. Makin	American Enterprise Institute	155
17	Bruce Bartlett	National Center for Policy Analysis	154
18	Clyde V. Prestowitz Jr.	Economic Strategy Institute	152
19	William H. Frey	Milken Institute and Brookings Institution	143
20	Nicholas Eberstadt	American Enterprise Institute	123
21	Bruce Katz	Brookings Institution	113
22	Henry J. Aaron	Brookings Institution	111
23	Ross C. DeVol	Milken Institute	110
24	Michael D. Tanner	Cato Institute	109
25	Marilyn Moon	Urban Institute	107

Notes

Prologue

1. Mone 2002.

2. Charles Murray, author interview, American Enterprise Institute, June 14, 2004. Unless otherwise noted, all Murray quotations are from this interview.

3. See, for example, Lane 1985, Blumenthal 1986, and Stefanic and Delgado 1996.

4. Quoted in Blumenthal 1986c, 295.

5. Ibid.

6. Samuelson 1984, 60.

7. Raspberry 1984; see also Kuttner 1984.

8. Lemann 1986a; Lemann 1986b. For critiques of this concept, see Gans 1991; Wacquant 1996; Wacquant 2008.

9. Summarizing the history of *Losing Ground*'s success, Lawrence Mone emphasizes the importance of courting journalists:

> Prior to Charles' book, others had said that antipoverty programs hurt the poor. But no one had drawn together, critically, all the data . . . in a way that could capture the strategic audience. In this case, that audience was journalists, who could reframe the terms of the debate. Charles targeted this audience, and his book hit the bull's eye. . . . Slowly, but surely, over the course of the next ten years, it totally flipped the conventional wisdom on welfare. And that flip led ultimately to the welfare reform bill of 1996.

Mone 2002.

10. Ellwood and Bane 1986.

11. For these critiques, see Ellwood and Summers 1985; Allen 1984. See also Boskoff 1985; Fuchs 1985; Muzzio 1985; *New York Times* 1985; Hall 1986; Hutchens 1987.

12. Miller 1985, 687. Nevertheless, Miller closed his review with a pair of questions: "In the case of *Losing Ground*, will the strong critiques limit Murray to the

242   NOTES TO PROLOGUE

fifteen minutes of celebrity that Andy Warhol predicts will be the common fate? Or will doubts and criticisms be ignored or undervalued because Murray's basic arguments fit the temper of the times, the outlook of the old class, and the intellectual politics of the rich?"

13. This characterization of Murray's argument is not an exaggeration. For example, in one of the book's most often cited passages, Murray suggests, as a "thought experiment," "scrapping the entire Federal welfare and income-support structure for working-aged persons, including A.F.D.C., Medicaid, food stamps, unemployment insurance, worker's compensation, subsidized housing, disability insurance and the rest." Murray 1984, 227.

14. Wilson 1987, 160.

15. Herrnstein and Murray 1994. For discussion of Murray's departure from the Manhattan Institute, see Elvin 1990; Deparle 1990.

16. Murray 1993a.

17. Murray 1993b.

18. Quoted in Mone 2000.

19. Quote is from Goldman 1997. See also Besharov 1996; Scott 1997; and *Economist* 2006, which notes that "it would be foolish to underestimate Mr. Murray's ability not just to stir debate but to steer policy: 12 years after *Losing Ground* was dismissed as the work of a wild-eyed fanatic, Congress had passed the welfare reform act."

20. On the role of think tanks in the Iraq War, see Abelson 2006. On the promotion of "broken windows" and zero-tolerance policing, see Wacquant 2009. On intelligent design, see Pennock 2001; Pennock 2003; Forrest and Gross 2004. On climate change, see McCright and Dunlap 2000; McCright and Dunlap 2003; McCright and Dunlap 2010; Dunlap and McCright 2010.

21. McCombs 1983.

22. Debray 2006.

23. Bush 2006.

24. As half a dozen CNAS policy experts migrated to top administrative positions, the *Wall Street Journal* called the organization the "top farm team for the incoming Obama administration." Dreazen 2008.

25. McGann and Weaver 2000, 3.

26. For Mills' central thesis on the role of elites in the United States, see Mills 1956. For Millsian studies of think tanks, see Shoup and Minter 1977; Dye 1978; Silk and Silk 1980; Saloma 1984; Domhoff and Dye 1987; Peschek 1987; Domhoff 1990; Domhoff 1999; Burris 2008; Domhoff 2010.

27. Domhoff 2010, 115.

28. Dye 2000.

29. Ellis 2001, 11516–20.

30. On this point, see Abelson 2002, 13.

31. Lukes 2004.

32. Polsby 1983; emphasis added.

33. Eyal and Buchholz 2010.

34. Eyal and Buchholz 2010, 122n2.

35. Gieryn 1983; Gieryn 1999.

36. Eyal and Buchholz 2010, 120.

37. Abelson 2002, 36.

38. Ibid., 15.

39. See, for example, Teichler 2007.

40. Jacobs and Townsley 2011.

41. I take the term *business-activists* from Phillips-Fein 2009.

42. Haas 1992, 3.

43. Wacquant 2004, 7.

44. Eyal 2003, 200.

45. DeMuth 2009. The full award citation reads: "To Charles Murray / Exemplary social scientist / Whose measurements are means to moral understanding / Engaged Aristotelian / Who teaches of human heritage and pursuit." Alterman 2003, 10, 53.

46. Charles Murray, author interview, American Enterprise Institute, June 14, 2004.

47. Wacquant 2011, 439.

Chapter One

1. James 1998, 409–10.

2. I take this phrase from Stone and Denham, who devote several pages to it while noting that "virtually all of our contributors point to this dilemma." Stone and Denham 2004, 2.

3. Eyal 2006; Eyal (forthcoming).

4. The phrase "antagonistic cooperation" comes from Sumner 1906. However, I take the idea from Wacquant 1998.

5. *New York Times* 1898, 17.

6. *Washington Post* 1895, 6. The term *balance wheel* refers to the timekeeping mechanism in a clock.

7. "Think-tank, *n.*" *Oxford English Dictionary.*

8. The center was established in 1954 with support from the Ford Foundation. The first *New York Times* reference to an organization as a "think tank" was to CASBS in *New York Times* 1958, 66.

9. "Think-tank, *n.*" *Oxford English Dictionary.*

10. Evans and Novak 1964, E7.

11. A notable exception is a 1963 *New York Times* piece about the Santa Barbara–based Center for the Study of Democratic Institutions. The article is also notable for its assertion that "there were 54 such white-collar 'think tanks' at last count." It is not clear what definition the author employed to arrive at this number. Curtis 1963, 16.

12. *Los Angeles Times* 1962, B4.

13. Seidenbaum 1963, C2.

14. Dickson 1971.

15. NIRA's internet based directory may be accessed at http://www.nira.go.jp/ice/nwdtt/. Retrieved on May 3, 2006. See also Hellebust 1996; Innis and Johnson 2002.

16. United Nations Development Program 2003.

17. For example, the Carnegie Endowment for International Peace and the Century Foundation typically file IRS Form 990-PF, "Return of Private Foundations."

18. *Economist* 2006.

19. National Public Radio 2005; for a similar depiction, see *Harvard Law Review* 2002.

20. Thus, Dye footnoted his 1977 presidential address to the Southern Political Science Association, which took think tanks as its theme, with an apology "to those eminent political scientists who told me that the activities of private policymakers was not 'political science.'" Dye 1978, 309n. Peschek makes the very same point. Peschek 1987, 7.

21. Domhoff 1967.

22. Ibid., 65, 71.

23. More fine-grained changes in the terms of Domhoff's analysis can be traced in the books he published in the years between the first and second editions of *Who Rules America?* In his 1970 book, *The Higher Circles*, for example, Domhoff writes of "policy-planning groups" and "think factories." See especially pp. 123–26. In the 1978 follow-up, *The Powers that Be*, Domhoff refers to "think tanks," but they seem to be distinct from "policy-planning groups," of which the Council on Foreign Relations and the Committee for Economic Development are examples. "Think tanks," in this iteration, are more likely to be university- or government-affiliated research centers. Domhoff identifies the RAND Corporation, the National Bureau of Economic Research, Resources for the Future, and the MIT Center for International Studies as the most important think tanks. See especially pp. 75–78.

24. Domhoff 1983, 84. The distinction between a "policy group" and a "think tank," however, remains unclear.

25. Domhoff 1998; Domhoff 2002; Domhoff 2006.

26. Domhoff 2006, 87.

27. Stone 2001, 15668–71; emphasis added.

28. Rich 2004; emphasis added. Similar definitions abound. For example, Hames and Feasey define a think tank as a "non-profit public policy research institution with *substantial organizational autonomy*." Hames and Feasey 1994, 216; emphasis added.

29. McGann and Weaver 2002, 4; emphasis added.

30. Stone 1996, 17; emphasis added.

31. See, for example, Rich 2004.

32. For illustration, see the various contributions in Stone and Denham 2004.

33. Dror 1980; Stone 1996, 13; emphasis added.

34. Stone 1996, 17.

35. Rich 2004, 11.

36. McGann 1995, 9. Quoted in Abelson 2002, 8.

37. Hellebust 1996; Smith 1991b, 214; Rich 2004, 738; McGann 2005; McGann 2007a.

38. Thus Rich notes "the eager efforts of some interest groups to win the label 'think tank,' for whatever added credibility and stature it might bring their efforts." Rich 2004, 13. It is also possible to identify certain organizations that, having once embraced or tolerated the label, now actively distance themselves from it. For example, the organization cited above as the "original" think tank—the Center for Advanced Study in the Behavioral Sciences—now disavows the label. Personal communication, Robert Scott, associate director, CASBS, September 6, 2010.

39. Gallie 1956.

40. Bourdieu [1989] 1996.

41. Here I am paraphrasing Bourdieu, writing on the French journalistic field: "To understand a product like *L'Express* or *Le Nouvel Observateur*, there is little point in studying the target readership. The essential part of what is presented in *L'Express* and *Le Nouvel Observateur* is determined by the relationship between *L'Express* and *Le Nouvel Observateur*." Bourdieu 2005, 45.

42. At the time of this writing, the Brookings Office of Communications was advertising a position for a director of communication with the following notice under "Education/experience requirements":

> Bachelor's degree required. Also required: 8–10 years professional experience creating overall communications strategies, working with media in a fast-paced, policy-oriented environment, knowledge of and experience in using electronic/direct communications and publication/production. Strong experience in politics, public policy advocacy, issue campaigns (or issue-driven communications) highly preferred. Experience in couching communications for fundraising preferred.

Brookings Institution website, http://www.brookings.edu/about/employment/metroweb 15908.aspx. Retrieved on January 22, 2009.

43. Author interview, Henry Aaron, Brookings Institution, November 19, 2003.

44. Among them, R. Kent Weaver is a fellow at the Brookings Institution; James McGann is president of the Foreign Policy Research Institute and has written reports for the Tokyo-based National Institute for Research Advancement; Diane Stone has done consulting work for various policy research organizations such as the Asian Development Bank Institute and the World Bank Institute; James Smith wrote commissioned histories for Brookings and the Center for Strategic and International Studies; and Andrew Rich was president and CEO of the Roosevelt Institute from 2009 to 2011.

45. Goodman 2005.

46. My emphasis. Goodman also suggests that think tanks should learn how to exploit the "enormous untapped potential in the academic and scholarly world," by contracting with scholars whose salaries are paid by a university.

47. My emphasis.

48. My emphasis. Goodman's suggestion that the NCPA "introduced all of these techniques" into the world of think tanks is highly dubious.

49. Says Goodman: "We invest in new programs and judge our success by the return on those investments."

Chapter Two

1. Smith 1991b; Linden 1987.

2. McGann 1992, 773; Abelson 2002.

3. Armstrong 1927, 7, emphasis added.

4. Wilson 1930, 128.

5. McGann 1992. Andrew Rich offers a characteristic expression of this view in his study of think tanks:

> Scholars quarrel over whether policy research is most helpful in offering specific prescriptions for public problems or, as is more commonly suggested, as general enlightenment on public issues. But by most all appraisals, more experts are good for policy making. For much of the twentieth century, this judgment was accurate; experts fulfilled these mandates. Even if their work was sometimes used by others for quite political purposes, experts remained ostensibly neutral and detached. Experts offered ideas and policy prescriptions that were rigorously crafted, rational, and, in the long run, helpful to the work of decision makers.

In Rich's analysis, this discussion is the point of departure for the claim that, over the past four decades, the role of think tanks "has become one focused more on providing skewed commentary than neutral analysis." Rich 2004, 3, 204.

6. It is to the credit of the elite theorists that their approach avoids any anachronistic historical claims about think tanks. This is because the theory turns ultimately on the evolution of a "policy-planning network," not the existence of a distinctive category of organizations called "think tanks."

7. On the history of the progressive movement, see Wiebe 1967; Leary Link 1969; Gould 1974; Chambers 1980; Sklar 1992; Keller 1994; Clemens 1997; McGerr 2003.

8. Link 1967, 81. Lukacs dates the birth and recognition of an American intelligentsia to the first decade of the twentieth century. He notes that the word "intelligentsia" was taken from Russian and first used by Russian and Jewish immigrants in the 1880s. By the 1910s, Lukacs writes, "It was no longer possible to exclude the influence of the American intelligentsia from the main currents of American thought." Lukacs 2004, 304.

9. Yates 1987.

10. Towne 1886.

11. Longo 2011.

12. Haskell [1977] 2000 is a key source. See also Calhoun 2007; Bernard and Bernard 1943.

13. Calhoun argues that Herbert Spencer's application of evolutionary principles to the study of society was influential among early American sociologists, including Lester Frank Ward and William Graham Sumner, and that "most American sociologists shared the pervasive individualism of their national context." Calhoun 2007, 5.

14. *New York Times* 1900b, 7.

15. Ibid. The speaker was lawyer and businessman Franklin H. Head.

16. *New York Times* 1900a, 9.

17. *New York Times* 1901b, 2.

18. *New York Times* 1901a, 1.

19. *Washington Post* 1907, 13.

20. Ibid.

21. Glenn, Brandt, and Andrews 1947; Greenwald and Anderson 1996. Key sources on the history and political role of philanthropy in the United States include Bremner 1988; Powell and Clemens 1998; Friedman and McGarvie 2004; Zunz 2011.

22. On the origins and early history of the organization, see Hopkins 1912.

23. *New York Times* 1907, 8. The *Chicago Daily Tribune* made a similar distinction in stating that the New York bureau's "aim is not merely the stopping of 'graft' but the correcting of methods and, above all else, the providing the taxpayer with adequate information of just how his money is being spent." *Chicago Daily Tribune* 1908, 10.

24. *New York Times* 1910, 10.

25. Ibid.

26. *Chicago Daily Tribune* 1908, 10.

27. Schachter 2002.

28. Clements 1998, 327.

29. Smith 1991.

30. Ibid.

31. Ibid.

32. Quoted in *Washington Post* 1911a, 4.

33. *Chicago Daily Tribune* 1911, 5.

34. *Washington Post* 1911b, 6.

35. This quote is from Carnegie's 1910 deed of gift to the organization. See, for example, http://carnegieendowment.org/about/index.cfm?fa=history. Retrieved on January 16, 2012.

36. *Washington Post* 1911b, 6.

37. *Washington Post* 1914, 6.

38. *New York Times* 1914, 3.

39. Slany 1996.

40. Wilson brought many of the Inquiry members to the Paris Peace Conference in 1919 and incorporated their ideas into his Fourteen Points speech and his League of Nations endorsement.

41. On the history of the Council of Foreign Relations, see Grose 1996; Schulzinger 1984; Shepardson 1960; Wala 1994. The other major foreign policy research organization established during this era included the Foreign Policy Association (founded in 1918) and the Institute of Pacific Relations (1925). For case studies of the two organizations, see Raucher 1978.

42. Grose 1996, 8.

43. Ibid.

44. Grose 1996, 27. See also Domhoff 1967; Domhoff 1970, especially chap. 5, "How the Power Elite Make Foreign Policy"; Domhoff 1978.

45. Grose 1996, 16.

46. *Foreign Affairs* also became known for its book review section edited by the historian, and student of Coolidge, William L. Langer. In 1925, the journal published a series of five articles on race relations by the African American sociologist W. E. B. Du Bois.

47. Grose 1996.

48. Ibid.

49. For case studies of the Foreign Policy Association and the Institute of Pacific Relations, see Raucher 1978.

50. *New York Times* 1928, 53.

51. *New York Times* 1927, 8.

52. The organization most often identified as the model for IPR at the time of its founding was the Williamstown, Massachusetts–based Institute of Politics, which facilitated debate on American relations with Europe. On the history of IPR, see Raucher 1978; Hooper 1994 and 1995; Yamaoka 1999; Akami 2002.

53. *Los Angeles Times* 1925a, 1.

54. Ibid.

55. Brier 1936, 11.

56. *Los Angeles Times* 1925b, 2.

57. Hunt 1929, A4.

58. For example, the same article noted that a recent IPR study of the characteristics of Asian immigrants had succeeded in injecting actual "facts and figures" into an argument once driven by "prejudice and misinformation." *New York Times* 1929, E4.

59. *Los Angeles Times* 1925a, 1.

60. Brier 1936, 11.

61. See, for example, Griffith 1987, 77; Newman 1992, 253.

62. Holland 1985, 91.

63. As Arthur Link notes, the corporate growth and consolidation that had begun in the late nineteenth century continued and became especially pronounced in banking. New York Stock Exchange trading nearly doubled from 1923 to 1926, from 236 million to 451 million shares. Financial institutions more than doubled their share of the national income, from 2.2 to 4.6 percent. By 1929, 1 percent of the nation's banks controlled 46 percent of its total resources. Link 1967, 266–70.

64. Kennedy 1999, 25.

65. *Los Angeles Times* 1922, 122.

66. Critchlow 1985, *Brookings Institution*, 40.

67. Smith 1991a, 17.

68. *New York Times* 1927b, 14.

69. Quoted in McGann 1992, 734.

70. Smith 1991b, 84.

71. Later, others such as William O. Douglas, a Yale Law School professor, and Felix Frankfurter of Harvard Law School, would come to be associated with this group.

72. Kennedy 1999, 124.

73. Bockman and Eyal 2002; Kelley 1997.

74. Because the first attempt is often seen as a false start, most accounts list 1943 as the official year of AEI's founding.

75. These studies on the structure of the federal state were the forerunner to AEI's series, Vital Statistics on Congress.

76. Phillips-Fein 2009.

77. Hoplin and Robinson 2008; Hartwell 1995; Mirowski and Plehwe 2009; Starbuck 2001.

78. On the history of the Committee for Economic Development, see McCabe 1950; Schriftgiesser 1960; Schriftgiesser 1967.

79. Schriftgiesser 1960, 19.

80. Ibid., 23–24.

81. I have found no source that indicates exactly how these two groups became aware of one another or when they initially established contact.

82. CED's original research directors included Theodore O. Yntema, a conservative University of Chicago economist and a director of the National Bureau of Economic Research, and Gardiner Means, a former economic advisor to National Recovery Administration and the National Resources Planning Board.

83. Schriftgiesser 1960, 30–31. This number refers to the aggregate value of the corporations represented by the CED trustees. Schriftgiesser estimates that in 1959 that value—counting industrial corporations alone and excluding banks, utility systems, and the like—was $59.9 billion.

84. Ibid., 28.

85. Ibid.

86. Ibid., 50–51.

87. Ibid. For more on the CED's elaborate structure, see ibid., 38–39.

88. Patterson 1996, 99. Among them were a considerable number of Central European scientists and intellectuals who had come to the United States as refugees.

89. On the history of the RAND Corporation, see RAND Corporation 1963; Smith 1966; Digby 1967; Dickson 1971, especially chap. 5; Kraft 1960; Miller 1989.

90. Dickson 1971, 55.

91. Ibid., 82.

92. RAND's engineering research also led to the identification of titanium as a material for aerospace construction and to the development of various satellites and weather balloons.

93. Quoted in Dickson 1971, 77.

94. Quoted in *Chicago Daily Tribune* 1916, 7. See also *New York Times* 1916, 6, which describes the aims of these organizations as "scrutiniz[ing] from a non-partisan and businesslike point of view the processes of government and mak[ing] constructive suggestions for their improvement."

95. The main figures in this group included John Foster Dulles, a lawyer and later Secretary of State under Dwight Eisenhower; Henry L. Stimson, who later served as Secretary of War and later Secretary of State; Robert A. Lovett, an investment banker and Secretary of Defense under Truman; W. Averell Harriman, a railroad baron and Democratic politician who served as an ambassador and as Secretary of Commerce under Truman, and later as governor of New York; and Dean Acheson, a lawyer and Secretary of State under Truman. See Isaacson and Thomas 1986; Patterson 1996.

96. See, for example, Dye 1978; Peschek 1987; Domhoff 1999.

97. For example, in 1951 RAND entertained a government request to select locations for new Air Force bases. To the surprise of its military sponsors, RAND returned a study that advised against building any such bases because of their excessive cost and vulnerability as targets. The episode has sometimes been credited with prompting a general shift away from "first-strike capacity" as the sole focus of American Cold War strategy. However, we should be cautious not to overstate RAND's propensity to question the underlying premises of its research assignments. After all, it is telling that at least *five* profiles of the organization rely on this specific example to illustrate the point that RAND researchers were occasionally "rebellious." See *Business Week* 1963; Kraft 1960; Dickson 1971; Meyer 1982; Smith 1991b. Additional illustrations of RAND's rebelliousness are more difficult to come by. Furthermore, as Dickson properly notes, "RAND was able to sell this conclusion to the military because it was logical and helped beef up American defenses. One wonders, if only rhetorically, how the military would have greeted suggestions for a winding down of the arms race." Dickson 1971, 62.

98. For a comparative analysis of the development of the economics profession in the United States, Britain, and France, see Fourcade 2009. On the role of experts, technocrats, and intellectuals in policy making more broadly, see Aikin 1977; Aaron 1978; Fischer 1990; Brint 1994; Rueschemeyer and Skocpol 1996; Babb 2001; Dezelay and Garth 2002; Charle, Schriewer, and Wagner 2004; Wagner 2006; Babb 2009.

99. The definitive source on the proliferation of credentials and the corresponding process of "credential inflation" is Collins 1979. See also Collins 2002.

100. Ross 1991, xiii.

101. See Bernard and Bernard 1943; Deegan 1988; Lengermann and Niebrugge-Brantley 1998; Lengermann and Niebrugge-Brantley 2002; Lengermann and

Niebrugge-Brantley 2007. For a broader analysis of the social organization of the American intelligentsia, see Kadushin [1974] 2009.

102. Smith 1991a, 19.

103. Letter from Harold G. Moulton (president, Brookings Institution) to Dr. Vannevar Bush (Carnegie Institution of Washington and Brookings Trustee), May 18, 1942, Papers of Vannevar Bush, Library of Congress Archival Manuscript Collection, Box 15, Folder 352.

104. Ibid. Subsequent correspondence between Moulton and Bush was taken up with the question of how Brookings should best allocate and invest its finances in the long term.

105. Smith 1991a, 25.

106. Schriftgiesser 1960, 23–24.

107. Ibid.

108. There is a vast literature on the characteristics of American political parties, much of it written from a historical-comparative perspective. Among many sources, see Epstein 1967; Janda and Harmel 1978; Ladd and Hadley 1978; Brady et al. 1979; Burnham 1981; Shafer 1983; Epstein 1986; Mayhew 1986; McGerr 1986; Rae 1989; Milkis 1993; Shefter 1994; Aldrich 1995; Ware 1996; Mair 1998; Dalton and Wattenberg 2000; Sartori and Mair [1976] 2005; Green and Coffey 2006; Rae 2007.

109. Grose 1996.

110. Beard 1947. See also Martin 1982.

111. Mitchell 1991; Mitchell 1999.

Chapter Three

1. Quoted in Wacquant 1993, 20.

2. See, in particular, Eyal 2002, 2006, forthcoming.

3. Bourdieu 1991b, 661.

4. For example, Gulliver observes of the Laputans: "Their houses are very ill built … and this defect arises from the contempt they bear to practical geometry, which they despise as vulgar and mechanic; those instructions they give being too refined for the intellects of their workmen."

5. Merton 1968.

6. Etzioni 2006.

7. Eyal 2006, 30.

8. Herzog 1963, 16.

9. Arthur Link writes that "the hope of reform and redemption under Roosevelt's leadership stirred intellectuals as they had not been roused since 1917." Link 1967, 446.

10. Woodlock 1944, 6.

11. Students for a Democratic Society 1962.

12. Himmelstein 1990.

13. On this point, see Brennan 1995.

14. The Republican nomination of Barry Goldwater for president in 1964 has increasingly been identified as the watershed moment of conservative influence within the party. See, for example, Brennan 1995; Goldberg 1995; Perlstein 2001. The scholarly literature on New Class theory is vast; key contemporary sources include Bruce-Briggs 1979; Gouldner 1979; Konrad and Szelenyi 1979; Brint 1984; Szelenyi and Martin 1988; Eyal 2003; King and Szelenyi 2004.

15. Raskin 1968. The memorandum is for a proposed seminar called "Being and Doing," the same title Raskin gave to his 1971 book.

16. Quoted in Blumenthal 1986b, D1.

17. "The Institute for Policy Studies," c1963. Quoted in Heritage Foundation 1977.

18. Ibid.

19. Raskin 1968.

20. These included the Stern Family Fund, the Daniel J. Bernstein Foundation, the Samuel Rubin Foundation, the Field Foundation, and the Janss Foundation. Administrative materials, Institute for Policy Studies archival manuscript collection, Wisconsin Historical Society; Reid 1977, A4.

21. The organization's original trustees included Harvard professors Christopher Jencks and David Riesman; James Dixon, the president of Antioch College; and Gerard Piel, the publisher of *Scientific American*.

22. Raskin 1968.

23. Raskin 1971b, B6.

24. Reid 1977, A4.

25. See http://www.jointcenter.org/index.php/about_the_joint_center/history. Retrieved on May 15, 2011.

26. Author interview, Bruce Stokes, *National Journal*, June 30, 2003.

27. Laird served as Secretary of Defense under President Richard M. Nixon from 1969 to 1973.

28. Weyrich's boss, Senator Allott, had been invited to the strategy session because of his involvement in breaking the southern filibuster of the 1957 Civil Rights Act and Weyrich attended in his place.

29. Author interview, Paul Weyrich, Free Congress Foundation, June 29, 2004. Unless otherwise noted, all subsequent Weyrich quotes are from this interview.

30. The outbreak of World War II put the project on hold until 1943, when it was moved from New York City to Washington, DC. Because this first attempt is often seen as a false start, most accounts list 1943 as the official year of AEI's founding. Brown died in 1951, sending AEA into a period of hibernation. The organization was granted a second life in 1954 when Chamber of Commerce official Allen D. Marshall spearheaded an effort to revive it. Marshall became AEA's second president and brought in William J. Baroody, also from the Chamber of Commerce, to serve as executive director of the Washington office. AEA's administrators began a major

retooling effort and closed its New York office in 1956. In 1962, the trustees installed Baroody as the third president and renamed the organization the American Enterprise Institute for Public Policy Research. By 1969, the organization was beginning to show signs of growth. According to Edwards, in 1974 "AEI listed a staff of fifty, twenty-four adjunct scholars, a 'Talent Bank' of six thousand scholars and experts, [and] the publication of sixty-four books and studies" the previous year. Edwards 1997, 2. The above description is based on archival materials from the American Enterprise Institute, as well as an unpublished internal history of the organization prepared by Karlyn Bowman.

31. Barry Goldwater's 1964 presidential campaign had taken several advisers and speechwriters from the institute, including Baroody and project director Karl Hess. See, for example, Klaidman 1977, F3.

32. Author interview, Paul Weyrich, Free Congress Foundation, June 29, 2004. The story has become part of Heritage Foundation lore for what it reveals about the organization's philosophy. Versions of it are included in Edwards 1997 and Smith 1991b.

33. Heritage fellow Lee Edwards reflects that AEI "had become more interested in debating the issues, not having a point of view. They had also gotten into the habit of doing big long studies, fat studies and volumes, and so forth. Being a little too, in their writing, perhaps a little too scientific." Author interview, Lee Edwards, Heritage Foundation, July 8, 2003.

34. Weyrich 2003.

35. There is a seeming discrepancy in Edwards's account of the timing of these events. Edwards quotes Feulner as saying, "It was at that moment [in the spring of 1971, following the AEI-supersonic transfer incident] that Paul [Weyrich] and I decided that conservatives needed an independent research institute designed to influence the policy debate as it was occurring in Congress." Edwards 1997, 4. But elsewhere in his account, Edwards describes Feulner and Weyrich as fully engaged in the search for organizational funding in 1969. (See, for example, p. 7.) It seems to me most likely that the AEI report did not really inspire the idea for the Heritage Foundation, as Feulner reports, but that the incident may nevertheless have focused Feulner's and Weyrich's strategic approach.

36. Author interview, Paul Weyrich, Free Congress Foundation, June 29, 2004.

37. Ibid.

38. Vogel 1989.

39. Among the culprits listed in the memo, Powell ranked academic scholars as the largest threat. He wrote of the anticapitalist sentiment that "there is reason to believe that the campus is the single most dynamic source." The full text of the "Powell memorandum" is available from many sources on the Internet. All quotes are from this memo.

40. Simon 1978. See also Asen 2009.

41. See, for example, Diggins [1975] 1994; Steinfels 1979; Blumenthal 1986c; Ehrman 1995; Himmelstein 1990.

42. Quoted in Goodman 1981, 90. The first quote is from Kristol 1973, 10.

43. For accounts of Olin's philosophy and giving patterns, see Miller 2006 and Phillips-Fein 2009. The most comprehensive analyses of conservative giving to think tanks are Covington 1997; Callahan 1999; Krehely et al. 2004.

44. Klaidman 1977, F3.

45. Burns, a former chairman of both the Federal Reserve Bank and the Council of Economic Advisers, was, according to John Kenneth Galbraith, "the most respected voice on fiscal and monetary matters in all the land." Galbraith 1981, A25.

46. Blumenthal 1986d, A16.

47. Author interview, Norman Ornstein, American Enterprise Institute, June 15, 2004.

48. Morgan 1981, A1.

49. Ibid.

50. Author interview, Stephen Hess, Brookings Institution, July 16, 2003. Economist Alice Rivlin similarly remembers that "there seemed to be adequate funds for whatever most people wanted to do." Author interview, Alice Rivlin, Brookings Institution, February 10, 2003.

51. Report of the Committee on Staff Participation in Outside Public Affairs Activities, January 7, 1972. Brookings Institution archives. Unmarked box.

52. Author interview, Alice Rivlin, Brookings Institution, February 10, 2003.

53. Author interview, Stephen Hess, Brookings Institution, July 16, 2003.

54. Pine 1980, K1.

55. Author interview, Henry Aaron, Brookings Institution, November 19, 2003.

56. Maxa 1977, 4.

57. Rothmyer 1981, C1.

58. McCombs 1983, B1.

59. Author interview, Paul Weyrich, Free Congress Foundation, June 29, 2004. In a 2006 Internet column, Meese similarly recalled, "At that time, Reagan and all of us who worked with him looked to The Heritage Foundation for guidance and they came through with one of the most important books ever published: *Mandate for Leadership*. Reagan insisted that all of his cabinet secretaries read this book—he did himself—and use it as the road map to steer America back toward the City on a Hill that she is destined to be." Meese 2006. As of this writing, Meese is the Ronald Reagan Distinguished Fellow in Public Policy and chairman of the Center for Legal and Judicial Studies at the Heritage Foundation.

60. Executive Summary of the December 1981 Report, *A Review of Development Planning and Programs, The Brookings Institution*," Barnes & Roche, Inc., February 1982. Brookings Institution archives. Unmarked box. The following quotations are all taken from this report.

61. Ibid.

62. Toner 1985.

63. Ibid. Hess was quoted to the same effect in Tolchin 1983, A30.

64. Farrell 1979.

65. Ibid.

66. Tolchin 1983, A30. MacLaury explained the shift to the *New York Times*: "We are looking to where we can make the greatest contribution. At the moment, arms control, international issues and the debt issues are the areas in which our society is threatened." Toner 1985, A20.

67. Ibid.

68. McCombs 1983, B1.

69. Library of Congress Archival Manuscript Collection 1986b. The same year, Feulner summarized Heritage's successes to his trustees: "1986 was the most productive year in our history whether measured by numbers of studies published, inches (or perhaps miles) of news stories generated, the impact of Heritage ideas on Washington policymakers, or our total income raised." Library of Congress Archival Manuscript Collection 1987.

70. Library of Congress Archival Manuscript Collection 1986a. The money allowed Heritage to establish an operating reserve, a building fund, and an endowment for the organization's new Asian Studies Center.

71. Weaver 1989.

72. Toner 1985, A20.

73. Rich 2004, 204.

74. Council on Foreign Relations 1988, 10.

75. Ibid.

76. Ibid., 12-13.

77. Council on Foreign Relations 1989, 101,

78. Ibid., 102. Central to this strategy was the creation of *Critical Issues*, a periodical consisting of "brief, easily readable articles by Senior or Visiting Fellows" designed to cover "fast-unfolding events or interesting sidelights." Ibid., 57. CFR also noted, "We have begun experimenting with television." Council on Foreign Relations 1988, 10.

79. Author interview, Paul Weyrich, Free Congress Foundation, June 29, 2004.

80. McCombs 1983, B1.

81. Farnsworth 1982, B6. The same article quoted Brookings Institution President Bruce MacLaury as saying, "Public policy research is a proliferating industry. . . . If we believe in competition in the real world, then we'd better believe it for ideas as well." Of course, this comment disregards all relevant questions concerning the "rules" of this "competition": Do think tanks compete to determine which is the most scientific? Or which can garner the most funding, public visibility, or political access, irrespective of their capacity for scientific judgment? Or do they compete to achieve the most even mixture of these forms of authority?

82. State Policy Network website, http://www.spn.org/about/spn-purpose. Retrieved on December 11, 2008.

83. http://www.spn.org/directory/organizations.asp. Retrieved on June 28, 2011.

84. The conference, which I attended, was held on May 18, 2004, at the Hyatt Regency Capitol Hill in Washington, DC. The ten sponsoring organizations, eight of which are think tanks, were: Brookings Institution, Cato Institute, Center on Budget and Policy Priorities, Committee for Economic Development, Committee for a Responsible Federal Budget, Concord Coalition, Heritage Foundation, New America Foundation, Progressive Policy Institute, and the Urban Institute. The conference's featured events were speeches by Senators John McCain (R-AZ) and Joseph Lieberman (D-CT).

85. Author interview, Charles Kolb, Committee for Economic Development, November 26, 2003.

86. For the sake of exposition, this figure omits certain high-profile Washington think tanks, such as the New America Foundation, that would tend to muddy the picture. However, I should note that in many cases, the geographic placement of these organizations would actually uphold, rather than undercut, the pattern I have identified insofar as these organizations reside physically *in between* the clusters.

87. Weaver 1989.

88. Author interview, Lee Edwards, Heritage Foundation, July 8, 2003.

89. Author interview, Paul Weyrich, Free Congress Foundation, June 29, 2004.

90. In 1980, Meese served as Reagan's campaign chief of staff; following the election, he headed the president-elect's transition team. When Reagan took office, Meese became a member of the National Security Council, a cabinet-level post; he later became US Attorney General.

91. Yet writing a transition manual also poses a major risk for a think tank, because if an organization's favorite candidate does not win, then the allocation of resources may be for naught. Shortly before the 2004 presidential election, for example, Center for American Progress fellow Mark Agrast explained, "We are working on a [John Kerry] transition document. I don't know that it will be quite as grandiose as [*Mandate for Leadership*]. But certainly we're going to lay out what we consider to be progressive priorities for the administration . . . but, obviously, the opportunity presents itself only if there is a change in government." Author interview, Mark Agrast, Center for American Progress, July 27, 2004.

92. Richburg 1984, A25. See also Berke 1988, B10, which contains the following claim: "Heritage, in fact, is largely responsible for turning the Presidential transition into a cottage industry for think tanks." And see Lawrence 1988, F25, which notes, "Transition fever started with the Heritage Foundation, a conservative think tank whose 1980 "Mandate for Leadership" was a road map to much of the conservative agenda in Reagan's first term." Cato's 1984 transition manual was called *Beyond the Status Quo: Policy Proposals for America.*

93. Richburg 1984, A25.

94. Lawrence 1988, F25.

95. Ibid.

96. Author interview, William Galston, University of Maryland, June 3, 2004.

97. Struyk 2003.

98. Reed 2000.

99. The contributing organizations were the Asia Society, AEI, Brookings, CEIP, Cato, the Center for American Progress, CSIS, CFR, Heritage, the Hudson Institute, the Manhattan Institute, the New America Foundation, and the RAND Corporation.

100. PRM Consulting 2004.

101. McGann 2007b, 2008, 2009, 2010, 2011.

102. My count. The data come from two sources: (1) Library of Congress Archival Manuscript Collection 1985; (2) Library of Congress Archival Manuscript Collection 1986a. Out of the remaining fifteen large contributions, thirteen were anonymous and two were from non-profit organizations.

103. Kaiser and Chinoy 1999, A1; Chinoy and Kaiser 1999, A25.

104. Rothmyer 1981, C1.

105. Ibid.

106. Miller 2003. See also Borsuk 2003.

107. Wayne 1994.

108. With holdings in the petroleum, chemical, paper, ranching, and financial services industries, and annual sales exceeding $60 billion, Koch Industries became the largest privately held company in the United States in 2005. Sorkin 2005. On the Koch brothers' philanthropy, see also Mayer 2010.

109. Remnick 1985. According to Krehely et al., by 2004 Charles Koch had given Cato more than $12 million.

110. Institute for Policy Studies 1973a

111. Institute for Policy Studies 1972b.

112. Memorandum, "Institute for Policy Studies, Projected Income, Fiscal Year, 1977–1978." Institute for Policy Studies archival manuscript collection, Wisconsin Historical Society, Box 3, "Trustees Meeting—Oct. 21 & 22, 1977" folder. Rubin was born in Russia in 1901. At the age of five, he immigrated with his parents to the United States. He grew up in Brooklyn, and, with an elementary school education, helped his parents run their general store. Rubin trained as a concert violinist until the age of seventeen, but ultimately abandoned his training to run a trading company from 1925 until 1937. Soon after, he founded Faberge, a cosmetic and perfume company, which he sold in 1963 for $25 million. Known for his parsimonious lifestyle, Rubin established the Samuel Rubin Foundation in the late 1940s. Hall 1978, B4.

113. Author interview, Paul Weyrich, Free Congress Foundation, June 29, 2004.

114. An FBI field memo acquired later by IPS through the Freedom of Information Act referred to the Bureau's interest in both the "vast scope of IPS activities" and "a more personal detailed look at a few IPS personnel." Institute for Policy Studies 1973b.

115. For example, the minutes of a 1973 administrative meeting asked all IPS employees "to write up as specifically as possible their experiences with taps, questioning, harassment, investigation, etc., by police and federal agencies." Institute for Policy Studies 1973c.

116. Throughout the proceedings, IPS lawyers alleged that the FBI had wire-tapped its phones, a charge the Bureau consistently denied (even while court exhibits showed that the Bureau had set up a "listening post" across the street from IPS and that Raskin and Barnet had been "overheard" in other wiretapped calls). In pursuing these charges, the IPS also filed a civil action against the Chesapeake and Potomac (C&P) Telephone Company alleging complicity in the surveillance, but the case was dismissed in June 1978.

117. Robinson 1979, C8.

118. Institute for Policy Studies 1972. The specific charges against IPS were complex. In its report, the IRS accused several IPS fellows, including Barnet, Raskin, Jencks, and Riesman, of "private inurement of funds" from books they had published in their capacity as IPS fellows. Because the books were written partially at the think tank's expense, royalties should count among the organization's net earnings. Tax law prohibited nonprofit employees from benefiting personally from the organization's earnings. The second charge was more indistinct. It was that private rather than public interests were being served by IPS activities, since "the books promote the individual views of the author rather than presenting a full and fair exposition of the pertinent facts to permit an individual or the public to form an independent opinion or conclusion." In other words, since the organization's fellows published their individual views, IPS activities were "not educational within the meaning of the statute."

119. Institute for Policy Studies 1973d.

120. Suplee 1981, C1. See also Kelley 1976; Kincaid 1983.

121. Muravchik 1981.

122. In the novel, a left-wing Washington think tank named the Institute for Progressive Reform with a satellite office in Amsterdam called the Multinational Institute engaged in covert Soviet operations. See Suplee 1981.

123. Sica and Turner 2005, xii.

Chapter Four

1. Author interview, Fred Smith Jr., Competitive Enterprise Institute, December 16, 2003.

2. Wacquant 2004, 8.

3. Bourdieu 1991a.

4. Weaver 1989.

5. Sherk 2009. The headline is from http://blog.heritage.org/2009/06/18/big-labor-admits-emmployer-violations-rare-in-elections/. Retrieved on June 30, 2011; Warren 2011.

6. See http://www.epi.org/content.cfm/newsroom_describing_epi. Retrieved on November 20, 2008. EPI also points out that its main rivals—Heritage, Brookings, Cato, and AEI—"are generally not labeled according to their funding sources."

7. http://www.gpn.org/statement-purpose.html.

8. Mishel and Walters 2003; DiNardo 2009.

9. Rich 2004, 11.

10. Author interview, Fred Smith Jr., Competitive Enterprise Institute, December 16, 2003.

11. Author interview, Adam Meyerson, Philanthropy Roundtable, March 16, 2004. Meyerson was editor-in-chief of Heritage's *Policy Review* from 1983 to 1998 and vice president for educational affairs from 1993 to 2001.

12. Brookings Institution "Policy Statement on Nonpartisan, Independent Research," http://www.brookings.edu/index/aboutresearch.htm. Retrieved on May 24, 2007.

13. Century Foundation website, http://www.tcf.org/about.asp. Retrieved on May 24, 2007. See also the Council on Foreign Relations website, which characterizes the organization as "an independent . . . nonpartisan center for scholars dedicated to producing and disseminating ideas." Council on Foreign Relations website, http://www.cfr.org/about/cfr_mission.html. Or the Institute for International Economics website, which touts the organization's "objective analysis." IIE website, http://www.iie.com/institute/aboutiie.cfm. Retrieved on February 5, 2012.

14. Urban Institute website, http://www.urban.org/about/index.cfm. Retrieved on May 24, 2007. The statement adds that the Urban Institute was founded to provide "independent nonpartisan analysis of the problems facing America's cities." RAND Corporation website, http://www.rand.org/about/history/. Retrieved on May 24, 2007. Interviews with policy experts and think tank administrators yield similar assertions. For example, the president of the Committee for Economic Development says that "one of the things that I think has characterized CED throughout its history is that we have a pretty high degree of integrity and objectivity. . . . I think people understand with CED we really come at these issues as objectively as we can, without any sort of upfront ideological or partisan bias." Author interview, Charles Kolb, Committee for Economic Development, November 26, 2003. Finally, speaking on the topic of partisanship, the executive vice president of the Cato Institute says that "we think that is a bad thing in a think tank, and so we are proud to be non-partisan. We have a philosophical vision, but we're non-partisan." Author interview, David Boaz, Cato Institute, November 24, 2003.

15. American Enterprise Institute website, http://www.aei.org/about/filter.all/default.asp. Retrieved on May 24, 2007.

16. Economic Policy Institute website, http://www.epi.org/content.cfm/about. Retrieved on May 24, 2007. In addition, the Institute for Policy Studies says that "in order to give our scholars and projects the widest freedom to explore and express their own views, IPS as an institution does not take positions on issues." Institute for Policy Studies website, http://www.ips-dc.org/overview.htm. Retrieved on May 24, 2007.

17. Author interview, James Weidman, Heritage Foundation, June 26, 2003.

18. Author interview, Paul Weyrich, Free Congress Foundation, June 29, 2004.

19. Author interview, James Weidman, Heritage Foundation, June 26, 2003.

20. See http://www.brookings.edu/execed/corporateprograms.aspx. Retrieved on June 30, 2011.

21. See http://www.cfr.org/about/corporate/corporate_about.html. Retrieved on June 30, 2011.

22. See http://www.cfr.org/about/corporate/corporate_benefits.html. Retrieved on June 30, 2011. The following quotes are all taken from this site.

23. See http://www.cfr.org/about/corporate/roster.html. Retrieved on June 30, 2011.

24. Morin and Deane 2003b, A31. The report's author worked for the United Kingdom Commission on Intellectual Property Rights.

25. Author interview, Charles Kolb, Committee for Economic Development, November 26, 2003.

26. Author interview, Henry Aaron, Brookings Institution, November 19, 2003.

27. Author interview, Richard Munson, Northeast-Midwest Institute, July 10, 2003.

28. Clemons 2003. Since the journal is published online, there are no page numbers. Clemons presented a longer version of this essay, titled "The Corruption of Think Tanks: The Unintended Consequence of Regulating American Lobbyists" at a conference called "Lobbying and Foreign Policy," French Institute for International Relations (IFRI) and the German Marshall Fund, Paris, November 14–16, 2002. All quotes are from the published version.

29. Morin and Deane 2002d, A23.

30. Blumenthal 1986a, D1.

31. Ibid.

32. Ibid.

33. I take this phrase from Easterbrook 1986.

34. "Christopher DeMuth to Resign as AEI President in 2008." AEI press release, October 11, 2007. <http://www.aei.org/press/26945>. Retrieved on June 30, 2011.

35. Center for American Progress, "Progress Report," July 7, 2005.

36. A striking symbol of this shift came in the 1990s, when the Brookings Institution, an organization once averse to news media attention, built an $800,000 television studio on its own premises. Author interviews: Stephen Hess, Brookings Institution, July 16, 2003; Ed Berkey, Brookings Institution, March 28, 2006.

37. Author interview, Mark Agrast, Center for American Progress, July 27, 2004.

38. Author interview, Joshua Micah Marshall, July 14, 2003.

39. Ibid.

40. Author interview, Alice Rivlin, Brookings Institution, February 11, 2004.

41. Author interview, John Cavanagh, Institute for Policy Studies, August 26, 2003.

42. Author interview, Bruce Stokes, *National Journal*, June 30, 2003. Another sign of the importance of media visibility is the regularly updated ranking of think tank media citations published by the organization Fairness and Accuracy in Reporting, a

progressive watchdog group. See Dolny 1996, 1997, 1998, 2000, 2001, 2002, 2003, 2004, 2005, 2006, 2007, 2009.

43. Author interview, William Galston, University of Maryland, June 3, 2004. Antitax activist Grover Norquist highlights the difference between academic and political temporalities in similar terms:

INTERVIEWER: What are the marks of a good policy report?
GN: Timeliness. Legislation moves at certain times. A study of the impact of the French Revolution done at a university is interesting this year. It will be interesting in five years. A study on why a particular piece of legislation would be good or bad for the economy is only of interest in the context of the fact that the legislation is going to be discussed and voted on.

Author interview, Grover Norquist, Americans for Tax Reform, August 2, 2004.

44. Author interview, Tim Ransdell, California Institute, July 21, 2003.

45. Author interview, Lee Edwards, Heritage Foundation, July 8, 2003.

46. Manhattan Institute website, http://www.manhattaninstitute.org/html/about_mi.htm. Retrieved on May 24, 2007.

47. Carnegie Endowment for International Peace 1979, 7.

48. Author interview, Eric Alterman, Center for American Progress, November 21, 2003.

49. Critchlow 1985. Critchlow goes on to cite the Brookings bylaw stating that "the primary function of the trustees is not to express their views on scientific investigations conducted by the institute, but only to make it possible for such scientific work to be done under the most favorable auspices."

50. See Wacquant 2005.

51. Author interview, David Boaz, Cato Institute, November 24, 2003.

52. Author interview, Greg Anrig, The Century Foundation, November 21, 2003.

53. Author interview, Clyde Prestowitz, Economic Strategy Institute, July 28, 2003.

54. Author interview, Richard Munson, Northeast-Midwest Institute, July 10, 2003.

55. Author interview, Bruce Stokes, *National Journal* and Council on Foreign Relations, June 30, 2003.

56. Author interview, Clyde Prestowitz, Economic Strategy Institute, July 28, 2003.

57. *Washington Post* online chat, http://www.washingtonpost.com/. Retrieved on September 11, 2004. Feulner went on to explain the meteoric rise of his organization in these terms: "If an entrepreneur markets what people want, he will be successful. That's what it's all about."

58. Feulner 1985, 22.

59. The earliest use of this term in a major newspaper appears to have been in Hall 1983, B1.

60. Rothenberg 1987, 36.

61. Author interview, Eric Alterman, Center for American Progress, November 21, 2003.

62. Author interview, Bruce Stokes, *National Journal* and Council on Foreign Relations, June 30, 2003.

63. Author interview, Clyde Prestowitz, Economic Strategy Institute, July 28, 2003.

64. Author interview, Eric Alterman, Center for American Progress, November 21, 2003.

65. Author interview, Jody Clarke, Competitive Enterprise Institute, December 16, 2003.

66. Author interview, Richard Munson, Northeast-Midwest Institute, July 10, 2003.

67. Author interview, Alice Rivlin, Brookings Institution, February 11, 2004.

68. Author interview, Charles Kolb, Committee for Economic Development, November 26, 2003.

69. Author interview, David Boaz, Cato Institute, November 24, 2003.

70. Author interview, Bruce Stokes, *National Journal* and Council on Foreign Relations, June 30, 2003.

71. Guilhot 2005, 12. For example, Guilhot writes, "The actors who contributed the most to constructing and expanding the field of promoting democracy are those who were able to play on different levels, to occupy pivotal positions at the junction of academe, national and international institutions, activist movements, and to mobilize the diversified resources of all these fields" (p. 11). In similar ways, think tank–affiliated policy experts are also comparable to the emerging category of "public engagement experts" whose role in the recent "democracy reform" movement is likewise based on ambiguous claims to expertise. See Lee 2011; Lee (forthcoming).

72. Author interview, Alice Rivlin, Brookings Institution, February 10, 2003.

73. Author interview, Fred Smith Jr., Competitive Enterprise Institute, December 16, 2003. Smith has no relation to Frederick W. Smith, the founder and CEO of FedEx.

74. Author interview, Norm Ornstein, American Enterprise Institute, June 15, 2004.

75. Author interview, Adam Meyerson, Philanthropy Roundtable, March 16, 2004.

76. Author interview, David Boaz, Cato Institute, November 24, 2003.

77. Author interview, Dean Baker, Center for Economic and Policy Research, June 11, 2003.

78. Author interview, Lee Edwards, Heritage Foundation, July 8, 2003.

79. Author interview, Norm Ornstein, American Enterprise Institute, June 15, 2004.

80. Goffman 1952, 463.

81. Ibid.

82. Ibid.

83. Wacquant 1992, 17.

84. See http://www.cato-university.org/. Retrieved on June 15, 2006.

85. The Frederick S. Pardee RAND Graduate School awards degrees in policy analysis, which the organization describes as "a multidisciplinary, applied field that tries to use research to unlock difficult policy problems." See http://www.prgs.edu/curriculum. Retrieved on July 31, 2006.

86. Douglas 1966.

87. Durkheim [1912] 1995, 238.

88. Author interview, Dean Baker, Center for Economic and Policy Research, June 11, 2003. It was apparent to me that Baker was speaking in hypothetical terms rather than suggesting that his organization takes money from the tobacco industry. On money's symbolic dimensions, see the work of Viviana Zelizer, especially Zelizer 1997.

89. Author interview, John Cavanagh, Institute for Policy Studies, August 26, 2003. Likewise, Anrig says, journalists "haven't had an opportunity to develop a focused expertise in a particular realm."

90. Author interview, Greg Anrig, The Century Foundation, November 21, 2003.

91. The categories are "academics," "academic + politics," "politics," "politics + business," "business," "business + media," "media," "media + academic," "hybrid," and "other." Not included in this figure are policy experts with backgrounds that combine two structurally opposing locations—academic + business (2.9 percent) or politics + media (3.3 percent)—as well as policy experts in the "other" category (6.0 percent). "Other" refers to individuals with career backgrounds exclusively in other sectors, which typically means in the fields of nonprofit research and advocacy. A policy expert who reported no prior job experience would also fall into this category. The figures presented here refer to proportions of the total population of experts in the database.

92. Author interview, Fred Smith Jr., Competitive Enterprise Institute, December 16, 2003.

93. Ibid.

94. See, for example, Hoffman and Sheehan 1993; Sheehan 1993; Scott 1996; Scott 1999; and Scott et al. 2006.

95. William Galston, a former PPI fellow who became a domestic policy adviser to Bill Clinton, reflects on the organization's role: "Not only did [PPI] give Bill Clinton a national platform and the ability to travel around the country without having to declare a presidential campaign, which was very beneficial to him, but also, PPI, between late 1988 and late 1992, created the governing agenda for a new Democratic Party [and] put it between hard covers." Author interview, William Galston, University of Maryland, June 3, 2004. Galston continues, "Now, I don't mean to suggest that PPI created Bill Clinton, or painted on a blank canvas. It was a meeting of the

minds . . . but, at the very least, we fleshed out some of [his] intuitions, published
policy papers that got them widely discussed inside the Beltway, [and] helped to vali-
date that new way of thinking about progressive politics to provide a platform for
Clinton."

96. Segal 1999, E1.

97. Altheide and Grimes 2005; Abelson 2006; Ryan 2010.

98. Author interview, Alice Rivlin, Brookings Institution, February 10, 2003.

99. The *Washington Monthly, New Republic,* and *National Journal* are all political
magazines; "The Hotline" is the *National Journal's* "blogometer," a daily compendium of political web blogs (see http://blogometer.nationaljournal.com/. Retrieved
on July 31, 2006); *The West Wing* was a television series that aired on NBC from 1999
to 2006; *K Street* was a short-lived HBO television series that aired in 2003.

100. Author interview, Norm Ornstein, American Enterprise Institute, June 15,
2004.

101. Etzioni 1985, C1.

102. Hall 1983, B1.

103. Author interview, Perry Quick, Charles River Associates, July 2, 2004. Prior
to joining the Roosevelt Center, Quick served as chief economic adviser to Colorado
Senator and Democratic presidential candidate Gary Hart.

104. Hall 1983, B1.

105. Balz 1989, A21.

106. Hall 1983, B1.

107. Author interview, William Galston, University of Maryland, June 1, 2004.

108. Author interview, Paul Weyrich, Free Congress Foundation, June 29, 2004.

109. On this topic, see Bourdieu 2004.

110. An emerging research literature traces the production of "doubt" as a political strategy. See, for example, Michaels 2008; Dunlap and McCright 2010; McGarity
and Wagner 2010; Oreskes and Conway 2010.

Chapter Five

1. This literature is vast. See, for example, Handler 1995; Katz 1995; Schram 1995;
Epstein 1997; Wacquant 1997; O'Connor 2001; Schram and Soss 2001. Growing out
of the reflexive critique, some studies have sought to assess welfare reform according
to alternative criteria that emphasize the life conditions of former recipients. See, for
example, Hollar 2003.

2. An important general formulation of this argument may be found in Stone
1989.

3. Epstein, for example, argues that the worst consequence of poverty research has
been to lend credence to the dubious notion that the United States has ever tried welfare to begin with. Rather, he argues, American redistributive and direct assistance
programs have been so meager as to preclude testing their effects properly, especially

their supposed work disincentive effects, while also ruling out interference from other factors. Epstein 1997.

4. See in particular Schram 1995.

5. See in particular Katz 1995.

6. With their emphasis on historical continuity rather than change, reflexive critics have pointed out that the image of the "unworthy poor" has been a fixture of the debate on poverty and that, throughout American history, public discussion has often centered on the paternalistic goal of "improving poor people" rather than on eradicating poverty itself. See, for example, Katz 1995.

7. I am not alone in this interpretation. See also Katznelson 1998; and Kelly 2002, who critiques O'Connor for suggesting that "efforts to understand social systems that seek scientific objectivity and that go uninformed by political analysis and action quickly become the ideological tools for elites."

8. Katznelson describes Katz as more judicious than Schram because he takes seriously the "best" policy analysis and isn't so quick to implicate it in reproducing the status quo. Katznelson 1998.

9. Wacquant 2011.

10. In 1965, Jack Roach noted in the *American Journal of Sociology* that "the subject of poverty in contemporary America received slight attention prior to 1960." Roach 1965.

11. Kenworthy 1960, 44; quoted in Jeffries 1978, 458.

12. President's Commission on National Goals for Americans 1960.

13. Galbraith 1958, 323. For example, Robert C. Davis credits Galbraith's book with having "effectively reopened the discussion of poverty in the midst of abundance." Davis 1963, 338.

14. Galbraith's book led Davis to conclude that "much of the current discussion of the economic state of American society has been based on shaky premises and inadequate data." Davis 1963, 342.

15. Morgan et al. 1962.

16. Ibid.

17. Schorr 1963; Burgess and Price 1963. The latter book was based on interviews with 5,500 ADC-receiving families in 43 states.

18. Lampman 1962.

19. Kolko 1962.

20. See, for example, Brand 1960.

21. MacDonald 1963. Harrington himself concurred on the significance of Mac-Donald's review. Writing in the *New York Review of Books*, Harrington said of Mac-Donald: "His *New Yorker* review of *The Other America* helped transform the fate of that book, the issue which it raised, and its author. For that I have been, and still am, grateful." See Harrington 1969.

22. Conference on Economic Progress 1962.

23. Myrdal 1964.

24. Rivlin 1966, 1357–58.

25. Coser 1965, 143.

26. Glazer 1965, 71.

27. White 1961.

28. See, for example, Lander 1971. Lander places enormous stock in Harrington's significance, arguing that "the significant role in helping the President see the larger dimensions of poverty and resulting in its becoming a political issue rests with one individual book—that by Michael Harrington" (p. 516).

29. Schlesinger 1965. Quoted in Lander 1971, 519.

30. United States Senate, Committee on Labor and Public Welfare 1964, 58. Quoted in Lander, 1971, 519–20.

31. United States Bureau of the Census 1963.

32. Schlesinger 1965, 1012; quoted in Lander 1971, 524.

33. Rainwater 1964, 127–28.

34. Gans 1995.

35. O'Connor 2001, 154.

36. In addition to its best-known features, the Economic Opportunity Act of 1964 instituted such benefits as preschool training, neighborhood health centers, and immigrant aid. The US Department of Health, Education, and Welfare produced a major summary statement at the time of the legislation's passage. Cohen and Sullivan 1964.

37. O'Connor 2001.

38. Ibid., 175–92.

39. Quoted in O'Connor 2001, 217.

40. Kershaw and Fair 1976; Watts and Rees 1977a; Watts and Rees 1977b.

41. O'Connor 2001, 229.

42. See, for example, Somers and Block 2005; Steensland 2006.

43. Moynihan 1965. The Moynihan report generated enormous public debate. See, for example, Jencks 1965; Rainwater and Yancey 1967.

44. Moynihan 1968, 4.

45. Ibid.

46. Kuh 1969, 112.

47. Banfield 1969, 89.

48. Glazer 1969, 103.

49. Five years later, Piven and Cloward followed up their first book with *Poor People's Movements*, a study of the successes and failures of lower-class protest movements that challenged conventional wisdom about interest group organizing and electoral participation. Here Piven and Cloward argued that institutionalized channels of political participation were so heavily stacked against the poorest and most socially marginalized groups that their best political bets lay in the occasional capacity to extract concessions from elites through social disruption. The book included a study of the welfare rights movement of the 1960s and '70s. Other voices from the academy were equally focused on deprivation and at least implicitly endorsed some form of redistribution. In 1972, for example, Christopher Jencks and his colleagues

argued in favor of redistributive mechanisms such as income insurance. Jencks et al. 1972.

50. Kristol 1974, 24.

51. Ibid.

52. Hobbs 1978. Quoted in Weaver 2000, 105.

53. Lambro 1979.

54. See, for example, Pechman and Timpane 1975; Lyon 1976.

55. On this point, see O'Connor 2001, 251.

56. Newman and Schnare 1992.

57. Fix, Passel, and Zimmermann 1996.

58. Prominent sources from think tanks include Nightingale and Burbridge 1984; Hopkins 1987; Munnell 1987; Ruggles 1988; Mehuron 1991; Shuptrine, Grant, and McKenzie 1994. Two key reviews of the "disincentive effects" literature are Danziger, Haveman, and Plotnick 1981; Moffitt 1992.

59. On the debates surrounding teenage pregnancy, see Luker 1996.

60. Murray 1984. See also Murray 1993, A14.

61. Author interview, Charles Murray, American Enterprise Institute, June 14, 2004.

62. Lane 1985, 14–15. Quoted in O'Connor 2001, 250.

63. Novak et al. 1987.

64. Haskins 2006, 13.

65. Among many examples, see Wilson 1987; Newman 1988; Ehrenreich 1990; Gans 1990; Katz 1990; Jones 1992; Kozol 1992; Liebow 1993; Silver 1993; Jencks 1994a; Jencks 1994b; Jennings 1994; Rainwater 1994; Rank 1994; Bourgeois 1995.

66. Edin 1991.

67. See, for example, Tanner, Moore, and Hartman 1995, which cites Edin and Christopher Jencks to support the point that "there is substantial welfare fraud by recipients who are in the workforce and receiving unreported income. . . . In such cases, welfare serves as an illegal supplement to earned income." See also *Washington Times* 1997; Glastris et al. 1997, 30; Vobejda and Havemann 1997, A1. Finally, see Shea and Mercer 1997, which notes that "liberals say [Edin's research] shows the inadequacy of the welfare safety net; conservatives cry 'Welfare fraud!'"

68. The latter three questions are taken directly from Weaver 2000, 136.

69. Wacquant writes that scholars of the ghetto have "devoted an inordinate amount of attention to the assumed 'pathologies' of ghetto residents, namely, to those behaviors that so-called middle-class society considers abnormal, offensive or unduly costly, from violent crime, school 'dropouts,' teenage pregnancy and labor market 'shiftlessness,' to the proliferation of 'female-headed households,' drug consumption and trading, and 'welfare dependency.'" Wacquant 1997, 348.

70. The most important statistic motivating the renewed focus on welfare was a nearly 30 percent increase in AFDC caseloads from 1988 to 1994 after about fifteen years of little change. The program's combined federal and state costs had returned

to their 1970s peak levels as well. Also contributing to this alarm was an increase in out-of-wedlock births. However, the increase was accounted for by declining teenage *marriage* rates, not by rising teenage birthrates, in which the long-term trend was one of decline followed by a small uptick in the late 1980s. Finally, Weaver notes that Clinton made welfare reform a centerpiece of his 1992 campaign because, owing to his experience on the National Governors' Association welfare reform task force, the issue "allowed him to highlight the most prominent of his thin credentials in national policymaking." See Weaver 2000, especially chap. 5. Quote is from page 127.

71. Weaver identifies six politically viable reform proposals—by which he means proposals supported by "highly developed intellectual critiques and strong political backers"—in the years leading up to PRWORA's passage. Weaver 2000, 107.

72. Ibid., 106.

73. Ibid., 124.

74. Unz 1994.

75. Rector 1995b.

76. Rector 1994b.

77. Rector 1994a.

78. Rector 1996; Rector 1995a.

79. Rector and Lauber 1995. As in the earlier Heritage Foundation studies, Rector and Lauber defined welfare broadly as all federal mean-tested programs, including Medicaid and various job training and college aid programs to arrive at a $5.4 trillion price tag over thirty years. For a similar observation see Weaver 2000, 105.

80. Hodge 1995.

81. Piccione and Scholle 1995; Fagan 1995.

82. Davis 1995.

83. Tanner 1994.

84. Ibid.

85. Wright 1995.

86. Cato Institute 1995.

87. Niskanen 1996.

88. Tanner, Moore, and Hartman 1995.

89. Tanner 1996.

90. Tanner 1994.

91. Ibid.

92. Ferrara 1995.

93. Carleson 1995.

94. Goodman, Reed, and Ferrara 1995.

95. Asher 1995.

96. Bartlett 1995.

97. National Center for Policy Analysis 1995. A few other conservative think tanks also became prominent voices in the welfare reform debate. For example, the Hudson Institute sponsored a 1995 symposium on the subject, a major theme of which was

that welfare should be left entirely up to the individual states. For a summary report, see Hudson Institute 1995.

98. Smith-Nightingale et al. 1991; Pavetti and Duke 1995. It is worth noting that the RAND Corporation, too, generated a comprehensive database of federal and state policies related to job training and education, including welfare-to-work programs. McDonnell and Zellman 1993.

99. Long, Smith-Nightingale, and Wissoker 1994.

100. Smith-Nightingale and Haveman 1995.

101. Sylvester 1994. The report called for a "national partnership of families, communities, schools, churches, and the media" to address the problem.

102. Sherraden 1990.

103. Solomon 1991.

104. Marshall 1994.

105. Hogan 1994.

106. Kilgore and Hogan 1995.

107. Marshall, Kilgore, and Hogan 1995.

108. Sylvester 1995.

109. Hogan 1995.

110. Nathan 1993. A lower-profile think tank, the Century Foundation, also released a report "designed to substitute facts for myth" by reviewing the welfare issue and placing it into historical context. Century Foundation 1995.

111. Weaver 1994; Peterson 1995.

112. Weaver and Dickens 1995.

113. Haskins 2006, 296–97.

114. Mishel and Schmitt 1995.

115. Bernstein and Mishel 1995.

116. Mishel and Bernstein 1996.

117. Haskins 2006, especially chap. 13.

118. Danziger 1994.

119. Quoted in Haskins 2006, 146.

120. Ibid., 147.

121. Ibid., 146.

122. Weaver 2000, 143.

123. Weaver 2000 calls this the "targeting within universalism" perspective. Prominent examples include Skocpol 1991; Garfinkel 1992; Skocpol and Wilson 1994, A21; Garfinkel 1996; Wilson 1996.

124. Weaver 2000, 125. See, for example, Ellwood 1988.

125. Weaver 2000, 125–26; see also p. 133.

126. Bane and Ellwood 1994.

127. Weaver 2000, 151.

128. O'Connor 2001, 214.

129. Bane 2001, 193.

130. Weiss 1989, 425.

131. Weiss 1989, 425. Weiss also notes that "over all, with a few notable exceptions, the *substantive* influence of formal analysis seems limited" (p. 429).

132. See, for example, Bell 1973; Habermas 1984.

Chapter Six

1. Lemert 1991, 177.

2. Karabel 1996, 213.

3. Tocqueville [1835] 2001.

4. Emerson 1883, 253. Quoted in Curti 1955, 259. Lerner 1957. Quoted in Peck 1963, 386.

5. For early scholarly discussions of American anti-intellectualism, see Spargo 1911; Russell 1935; Havelock 1950; Bestor 1953; Hofstadter 1953; Levenstein 1953; Riesman 1953; Curti 1955.

6. Sources on anti-intellectualism that date to the intervening years between Curti's AHA address and Hofstadter's book include Barber 1955; Rudin 1958; Hage 1959; Greeley 1962; White 1962; Peck 1963; Wolff 1963.

7. These examples draw on Hofstadter 1963.

8. Curti 1955, 263–64.

9. Bestor 1965, 1119.

10. Ibid. Bestor opened his review as follows: "It is obviously possible to write a history of antislavery or of the Anti-Saloon League. Is it possible, in the same fashion, to write a history of anti-intellectualism?" (p. 1118).

11. Gleason 1966, 241.

12. Welter 1964, 482.

13. Coser 1965.

14. Hofstadter 1963, 7. My emphasis.

15. Ibid., 21.

16. Riesman 1963, 1039.

17. According to Jones, the former group "has considerable influence and . . . the members of it do not exhibit the self-pity characteristic of literary sensibility." Jones 1963, 598. It is of course noteworthy that Jones should select a number of individuals who were affiliated with think tanks as exemplars of public influence—on which more appears below.

18. Hofstadter was taken aback not only by McCarthyism but also by the scorn heaped upon Adlai Stevenson for being an "egghead," which contributed to his subsequent defeat in the presidential elections of 1952 and 1956.

19. Tanenhaus 2006.

20. Wiener 2006, 36–40. These observations come from the benefit of several decades of hindsight. Among Hofstadter's contemporaries, only Cushing Strout noted

that the author "surprisingly ignores the important emergence of the scientific intellectuals, as dramatized in the Oppenheimer case." Strout 1963, 545.

21. For more recent work on American anti-intellectualism, see Hodges 1966; Wolff 1971; Allen 1977; Shaffer 1977; Isaacson 1982; Howley 1987; Rigney 1991; Howley, Howley, and Pendarvis 1995; Claussen 2004; Fuller 2004; Gore 2008; Jacoby 2008.

22. For arguments in favor of the decline of the "public intellectual," see Bawer 1998; Boynton 1995; Epstein 2000; Posner 2001; and two contributors (Carter, Elshtain) to the *Nation's* forum on "The Future of the Public Intellectual." Donatich et al. 2001. For arguments against, see Young's contribution in Todorov et al. 1997; Romano 1999; Etzioni 2006.

23. Eyal and Buchholz 2010.

24. Prominent entries in this debate include Brady 2004; Burawoy et al. 2004; Stacey 2004; Tittle 2004; Burawoy 2005a; Burawoy 2005b; Calhoun 2005; Kalleberg 2005; Light 2005; Turner 2005; Vaughan 2006; Agger 2007; Clawson et al. 2007; Nichols 2007; Hale 2008; Jeffries 2009; Nyden et al. 2011.

25. Coser 1965, xviii.

26. Hofstadter 1963, 7. My emphasis.

27. Shapin 2005.

References

Aaron, Henry. 1978. *Politics and the Professors: The Great Society in Perspective.* Washington, DC: Brookings Institution Press.

Abelson, Donald E. 1995. "From Policy Research to Political Advocacy: The Changing Role of Think Tanks in American Politics." *Canadian Review of American Studies* 25, no. 1: 93–126.

———. 1996. *American Think Tanks and Their Role in US Foreign Policy.* London: Macmillan.

———. 1998. "Think Tanks in the United States." In *Think Tanks across Nations: A Comparative Approach,* edited by Diane Stone, Andrew Denham, and Mark Garnett. Manchester: Manchester University Press.

———. 2002. *Do Think Tanks Matter? Assessing the Impact of Public Policy Institutes.* Montreal: McGill-Queen's University Press.

———. 2006. *A Capitol Idea: Think Tanks & US Foreign Policy.* Montreal: McGill-Queen's University.

Agger, Ben. 2007. *Public Sociology: From Social Facts to Literary Acts.* Lanham, MD: Rowman & Littlefield.

Aikin, William E. 1977. *Technocracy and the American Dream: The Technocracy Movement 1900–1941.* Berkeley, CA: University of California Press.

Akami, Tomoko. 2002. *Internationalization of the Pacific: The United States, Japan, and the Institute of Pacific Relations in War and Peace, 1919–45.* London: Routledge.

Aldrich, John. 1995. *Why Parties? The Origin and Transformation of Party Politics in America.* Chicago: University of Chicago Press.

Allen, Francis A. 1977. "The New Anti-intellectualism in American Legal Education." *Mercer Law Review* 28, no. 2: 447–62.

Allen, Jodie T. 1984. "That Charles Murray Book: How Good Is It?" *Washington Post,* November 2, A23.

Alter, Jonathan. 1982. "Think-Tanks, Politick!" *New York Times,* December 27, A19.

Alterman, Eric. 2003. *What Liberal Media? The Truth about Bias and the News.* New York: Basic Books.

Altheide, David L., and Jennifer N. Grimes. 2005. "War Programming: The Propaganda Project and the Iraq War." *Sociological Quarterly* 46, no. 4: 617–43.

Amenta, Edwin. 1998. *Bold Relief: Institutional Politics and the Origins of Modern American Social Policy.* Princeton, NJ: Princeton University Press.

American Enterprise Institute. 2002, 2004. *Annual Report.* Washington, DC: American Enterprise Institute.

Asen, Robert. 2009. "Ideology, Materiality, and Counterpublicity: William E. Simon and the Rise of a Conservative Counterintelligentsia." *Quarterly Journal of Speech* 95, no. 3: 263–88.

Asher, Mukul G. 1995. *Compulsory Savings in Singapore: An Alternative to the Welfare State.* Dallas, TX: National Center for Policy Analysis.

Aspen Institute. 2004. *Annual Report.* Washington, DC: Aspen Institute.

Associated Press. 2003. "Heir to Coors Brewing Fortune Dies at Age 85." March 17.

Babb, Sarah L. 2001. *Managing Mexico: Economists from Nationalism to Neoliberalism.* Princeton, NJ: Princeton University Press.

———. 2009. *Behind the Development Banks: Washington Politics, World Poverty, and the Wealth of Nations.* Chicago: University of Chicago Press.

Bailey, Ronald, ed. 2002. *Global Warming and Other Eco-myths: How the Environmental Movement Uses False Science to Scare Us to Death.* Roseville, CA: Prima Publishing.

Balz, Dan. 1989. "Moderate, Conservative Democrats Buck 'Constraints,' Form Think Tank." *Washington Post,* June 30, A21.

Bane, Mary Jo. 2001. "Presidential Address: Expertise, Advocacy, and Deliberation; Lessons from Welfare Reform." *Journal of Policy Analysis and Management* 20, no. 2: 191–97.

Bane, Mary Jo and David T. Ellwood. 1986. "Slipping into and out of Poverty: The Dynamics of Spells." *Journal of Human Resources* 21: 1–23.

———. 1994. *Welfare Realities: From Rhetoric to Reform.* Cambridge, MA: Harvard University Press.

Banfield, Edward. 1969. "Welfare: A Crisis without 'Solutions.'" *Public Interest* 16: 89–101.

Barber, Bernard. 1955. "Sociological Aspects of Anti-intellectualism." *Journal of Social Issues* 11: 25–30.

Bartlett, Bruce. 1995. "How Poor Are the Poor?" *Brief Analysis,* no. 185. Dallas, TX: National Center for Policy Analysis.

Battiata, Mary. 1980. "Think-Tank Tribute." *Washington Post,* December 12, E1.

Bawer, Bruce. 1998. "Public Intellectuals: An Endangered Species?" *Chronicle of Higher Education* 44: A72.

Beard, Charles A. 1947. "Who's to Write the History of the War?" *Saturday Evening Post,* October 4, 172.

Bell, Daniel. 1973. *The Coming of Post-industrial Society: A Venture in Social Fore-casting*. New York: Basic Books.

Benda, Julien. [1927] 1969. *The Treason of the Intellectuals (La Trahison des Clercs)*. Translated by Richard Aldington. New York: Norton.

Bennett, William J. 1994. "The Best Welfare Reform: End It." *Wall Street Journal*, March 30, A19.

Berke, Richard L. 1988. "Think Tanks: Bush and Aides Getting Advice from All Over." *New York Times,* November 21, B10.

Bernard, Luther L., and Jessie Bernard. 1943. *The Origins of American Sociology: The Social Science Movement in the United States*. New York: Thomas Y. Crowell Co.

Bernstein, Jared, and Lawrence Mishel. 1995. *Trends in the Low-Wage Labor Market and Welfare Reform: The Constraints on Making Work Pay*. Washington, DC: Economic Policy Institute.

Besharov, Douglas J. 1996. "At Issue: Shaping the Debate on Welfare." *Washington Post,* August 11, 5.

Bestor, Arthur E. 1953. *Educational Wastelands: The Retreat from Learning in Our Public Schools*. Urbana: University of Illinois Press.

———. 1965. Review of *Anti-intellectualism in American Life,* by Richard Hofstadter. *American Historical Review* 70, no. 4: 1118–20.

Bjerre-Poulsen, Niels. 1991. "The Heritage Foundation: A Second Generation Think Tank." *Journal of Policy History* 3: 152–72.

Blumenthal, Sidney. 1985. "Heritage Led by a True Believer." *Washington Post,* September 24, A10.

———. 1986a. "Hard Times at the Think Tank for American Enterprise Institute." *Washington Post,* June 26, D1.

———. 1986b. "The Left Stuff: IPS & the Long Road Back." *Washington Post,* July 30, D1.

———. 1986c. *The Rise of the Counter-Establishment: From Conservative Ideology to Political Power*. New York: Times Books.

———. 1986d. "A Well-Connected Conservative." *Washington Post,* June 22, A16.

Bockman, Johanna, and Gil Eyal. 2002. "Eastern Europe as a Laboratory for Economic Knowledge: The Transnational Roots of Neoliberalism." *American Journal of Sociology* 108: 310–52.

Boffey, Philip M. 1985. "Heritage Foundation: Success in Obscurity." *New York Times,* November 17.

Borsuk, Alan J. 2003. "Funding's New Heavy-Hitter." *Milwaukee Journal Sentinel*, February 9, 1A.

Boskoff, Alvin. 1985. Review of *Losing Ground: American Social Policy, 1950–1980*, by Charles Murray. *Annals of the American Academy of Political and Social Science* 481: 194–95.

Bourdieu, Pierre. 1964. "The Attitude of the Algerian Peasant toward Time." In *Mediterranean Countrymen*, edited by Jesse Pitt-Rivers, 55–72. Paris: Mouton.

———. [1980] 1990. *The Logic of Practice.* Stanford, CA: Stanford University Press.

———. 1983. "The Field of Cultural Production, or the Economic World Reversed." *Poetics* 12: 311–56.

———. 1984. *Distinction: A Social Critique of the Judgment of Taste.* Translated by Richard Nice. Cambridge, MA: Harvard University Press.

———. 1985. "The Genesis of the Concepts of *Habitus* and *Field.*" *Sociocriticism* 2, no. 2: 11–24.

———. [1986] 1990. "The Intellectual Field: A World Apart." In *In Other Words: Essays toward a Reflexive Sociology,* 140–49. Stanford, CA: Stanford University Press.

———. 1988. *Homo Academicus.* Translated by Peter Collier. Stanford, CA: Stanford University Press.

———. [1989] 1996. *The State Nobility: Elite Schools in the Field of Power.* Stanford, CA: Stanford University Press.

———. 1991a. "Political Representation: Elements for a Theory of the Political Field." In *Language and Symbolic Power,* edited by John B. Thompson, 171–202. Cambridge, MA: Harvard University Press.

———. 1991b. "Universal Corporatism: The Role of Intellectuals in the Modern World." *Poetics Today* 12, no. 4: 655–69.

———. 1993. *The Field of Cultural Production: Essays on Art and Literature.* Edited by Randal Johnson. New York: Columbia University Press.

———. [1997] 2000. "Bodily Knowledge." In *Pascalian Meditations,* 12863. Cambridge: Polity.

———. 2004. *Science of Science and Reflexivity.* Translated by Richard Nice. Chicago: University of Chicago Press.

———. 2005. "The Political Field, the Social Science Field, and the Journalistic Field." In *Bourdieu and the Journalistic Field,* edited by Rodney Benson and Erik Neveu, 29–47. Cambridge: Polity Press.

Bourdieu, Pierre, and Loïc Wacquant. 1992. *An Invitation to Reflexive Sociology.* Chicago: University of Chicago Press.

Bourgeois, Philippe. 1995. *In Search of Respect: Selling Crack in El Barrio.* New York: Cambridge University Press.

Boynton, Robert S. 1995. "The New Intellectuals." *Atlantic Monthly* 275, no. 3: 53–71.

Brady, David. 2004. "Why Public Sociology May Fail." *Social Forces* 82, no. 4: 1629–38.

Brady, David W., Joseph Cooper, and Patricia A. Hurley. 1979. "The Decline of Party in the House of Representatives." *Legislative Studies Quarterly* 4: 381–407.

Brand, Horst. 1960. "Poverty in the United States." *Dissent* 7, no. 4: 334, 338–39.

Bremner, Robert H. 1963. Review of *The Other America: Poverty in the United States,* by Michael Harrington. *Industrial and Labor Relations Review* 16, no. 2: 315–16.

———. 1988. *American Philanthropy*. Chicago: University of Chicago Press.

Brennan, Mary C. 1995. *Turning Right in the Sixties: The Conservative Capture of the GOP*. Chapel Hill: University of North Carolina Press.

Brier, Royce. 1936. "Pacific 'Peace or War' Problem Puzzles Meet." *Los Angeles Times*, August 30, 11.

Brint, Steven. 1984. " 'New-Class' and Cumulative Trend Explanations of the Liberal Political Attitudes of Professionals." *American Journal of Sociology* 90, no. 1: 30–71.

———. 1994. *In an Age of Experts: The Changing Role of Professionals in Politics and Public Life*. Princeton, NJ: Princeton University Press.

Broder, David S. 1990. "The Right Discovers the Poor." *Washington Post,* April 8, B7.

Brookings Institution. 1956. *Institute for Government Research: An Account of Research Achievements*. Washington, DC: Brookings Institution.

———. 1960–1985, 2002, 2004, 2005. *Annual Report*. Washington, DC: Brookings Institution.

———. 2007. *Brookings Institution Press Spring 2007 Catalogue*. Washington, DC: Brookings Institution.

Brown, David S. 2006. *Richard Hofstadter: An Intellectual Biography*. Chicago: University of Chicago Press.

Bruce-Briggs, B., ed. 1979. *The New Class?* New Brunswick, NJ: Transaction Publishers.

Burawoy, Michael. 2005a. "For Public Sociology." *American Sociological Review* 70, no. 1: 4–28.

———. 2005b. "The Return of the Repressed: Recovering the Public Face of US Sociology, One Hundred Years On." *Annals of the American Academy of Political and Social Science* 600: 68–85.

Burawoy, Michael, William Gamson, Charlotte Ryan, et al. 2004. "Public Sociologies: A Symposium from Boston College." *Social Problems* 51, no. 1: 103–30.

Burchinal, Lee G., and Hilda Siff. 1964. "Rural Poverty." *Journal of Marriage and the Family* 26(4): 399–405.

Burgess, M. Elaine, and Daniel O. Price. 1963. *An American Dependency Challenge*. Chicago: American Public Welfare Association.

Burnham, Walter Dean. 1981. *The Current Crisis in American Politics*. New York: Oxford University Press.

Burris, Val. 2008. "The Interlock Structure of the Policy-Planning Network and the Right Turn in US State Policy." *Research in Political Sociology* 17: 3–42.

Bush, George W. 2006. Interview with Bob Schieffer. *Face the Nation*. CBS. Washington, DC: January 29.

Business Week. 1963. "Planners for the Pentagon." July 13, 2–14.

Calhoun, Craig. 1991. "The Ideology of Intellectuals and the Chinese Student Protest Movement of 1989." In *Intellectuals and Politics: Social Theory in a Changing World*, edited by Charles Lemert, 113–40. Newbury Park: Sage.

———. 2005. "The Promise of Public Sociology." *British Journal of Sociology* 56, no. 3: 355–63.

———. 2007. "Sociology in America: An Introduction." In *Sociology in America*, 1–38. Chicago: University of Chicago Press.

Callahan, David. 1999. "$1 Billion for Conservative Ideas." *Nation*. April 26.

———. 1999. *$1 Billion for Ideas: Conservative Think Tanks in the 1990s*. Washington, DC: National Committee for Responsive Philanthropy.

Carleson, Robert. 1995. *Welfare Reform: Should There Be Strings Attached?* Dallas, TX: National Center for Policy Analysis.

Carlisle, Rodney. 1994. "Washington Think Tanks and the Chaos of Policy Making," *Reviews in American History* 22, no. 1: 163–67.

Carnegie Endowment for International Peace. 1979. *Carnegie Endowment for International Peace in the 1970s*. Washington, DC: Carnegie Endowment for International Peace.

Cataldi, E. F., E. M. Bradburn, and M. Fahimi. 2005. *2004 National Study of Postsecondary Faculty (NSOPF:04): Background Characteristics, Work Activities, and Compensation of Instructional Faculty and Staff: Fall 2003*. US Department of Education. Washington, DC: National Center for Education Statistics. Retrieved July 31, 2006, from http://nces.ed.gov/pubsearch.

Cato Institute. 1984. *Beyond the Status Quo: Policy Proposals for America*. Washington, DC: Cato Institute.

———. 1995. *The Cato Handbook for Congress: 104th Congress*. Washington, DC: Cato Institute.

———. 2004. *Annual Report*. Washington, DC: Cato Institute.

Cauthen, Nancy K., and Edwin Amenta. 1996. "Not for Widows Only: Institutional Politics and the Formative Years of Aid to Dependent Children." *American Sociological Review* 61, no. 3: 427–48.

Center for Strategic and International Studies. 2004. *Annual Report*. Washington, DC: Center for Strategic and International Studies.

Century Foundation. 1995. *Welfare Reform: A Twentieth-Century Fund Guide to the Issues*. New York: Century Foundation.

Chambers, John Whiteclay. 1980. *The Tyranny of Change: America in the Progressive Era, 1890–1920*. New York: St. Martin's Press.

Charle, Christophe, Jürgen Schriewer, and Peter Wagner, eds. 2004. *Transnational Intellectual Networks: Forms of Academic Knowledge and the Search for Cultural Identities*. Frankfurt: Campus Verlag.

Chicago Daily Tribune. 1908. "Research and Social Betterment." April 20, 10.

———. 1911. "Carnegie Peace Endowment Chooses Root President." March 10, 5.

———. 1916. "Bureau to Make Wide Inquiry on US Government." July 23, 7.

Chilman, Catherine, and Marvin B. Sussman. 1964. "Poverty in the United States in the Mid-sixties." *Journal of Marriage and the Family* 26, no. 4: 391–98.

Chinoy, Ira, and Robert G. Kaiser. 1999. "Decades of Contributions to Conservatism." *Washington Post,* May 2, A25.

Claussen, Dane S. 2004. *Anti-intellectualism in American Media: Magazines and Higher Education.* New York: Peter Lang.

Clawson, Dan, Robert Zussman, Joya Misra, et al., eds. 2007. *Public Sociology: Fifteen Eminent Sociologists Debate Politics and the Profession of the Twenty-First Century.* Berkeley: University of California Press.

Clemens, Elisabeth. 1997. *The People's Lobby: Organizational Innovation and the Rise of Interest Group Politics in the United States, 1890–1925.* Chicago: University of Chicago Press.

Clements, Kendrick A. 1998. "Woodrow Wilson and Administrative Reform." *Presidential Studies Quarterly* 28, no. 2: 320–36.

Clemons, Steven C. 2003. "The Corruption of Think Tanks." *JPRI Critique* 10, no. 2.

Cohen, Wilbur J., and Eugenia Sullivan. 1964. "Poverty in the United States." *Health, Education, and Welfare Indicators.* US Department of Health, Education, and Welfare. Washington, DC: US Government Printing Office.

Collins, Randall. 1979. *The Credential Society: An Historical Sociology of Education and Stratification.* New York: Academic Press.

———. 1998. *The Sociology of Philosophies: A Global Theory of Intellectual Change.* Cambridge, MA: Harvard University Press.

———. 2002. "Credential Inflation and the Future of Universities." In *The Future of the City of Intellect: The Changing American University*, edited by Steven Brint, 23–46. Stanford, CA: Stanford University Press.

Conference on Economic Progress. 1962. *Poverty and Deprivation in the United States.* Washington, DC: Conference on Economic Progress.

Coser, Lewis A. 1965a. *Men of Ideas: A Sociologist's View.* New York: Free Press.

———. 1965b. "The Sociology of Poverty: To the Memory of Georg Simmel." *Social Problems* 13, no. 2: 140–48.

Council on Foreign Relations. 1988, 1989, 2004. *Annual Report.* New York: Council on Foreign Relations.

Covington, Sally. 1997. *Moving a Public Policy Agenda: The Strategic Philanthropy of Conservative Foundations.* Washington, DC: National Committee for Responsive Philanthropy.

Crandall, Robert W., Christopher DeMuth, Robert W. Hahn, Robert E. Litan, Pietro S. Nivola, and Paul R. Portney. 1997. "An Agenda for Federal Regulatory Reform." Washington, DC: American Enterprise Institute and the Brookings Institution Books and Monographs.

Critchlow, Donald T. 1985. *The Brookings Institution, 1916–1952: Expertise and the Public Interest in a Democratic Society.* DeKalb: Northern Illinois University Press.

Crotty, Paul, and Gary C. Jacobson. 1980. *American Parties in Decline.* Boston: Little, Brown.

Curti, Merle. 1955. "Intellectuals and Other People." *The American Historical Review* 60, no. 2: 259–82.

Curtis, Charlotte. 1963. "Santa Barbara Is Adjusting to an Influx of Intellectuals." *New York Times*, October 25, 16.

Dalton, Russell J., and Martin P. Wattenberg. 2000. *Parties without Partisans: Political Change in Advanced Industrial Democracies.* New York: Oxford University Press.

Danziger, Sheldon. 1994. "Researchers Dispute Contention that Welfare Is Major Cause of Out-of-Wedlock Births." Press release. June 23.

Danziger, Sheldon, Robert Haveman, and Robert Plotnick. 1981. "How Income Transfers Affect Work, Savings, and the Income Distribution: A Critical Review." *Journal of Economic Literature* 19: 975–1028.

Davidann, Jon Thares. 2001. "'Colossal Illusions': US-Japanese Relations in the Institute of Pacific Relations, 1919–1938." *Journal of World History* 12, no. 1: 155–82.

Davis, Julie. 1995. *Policy Guides to Roll Back Government.* Washington, DC: Heritage Foundation.

Davis, Robert C. 1963. "Poverty in the Affluent Society: A Review Article." *Sociological Quarterly* 4, no. 4: 335–43.

Debray, Elizabeth H. 2006. "The Demise of the Clinton Administration's Proposal." In *Politics, Ideology & Education: Federal Policy during the Clinton and Bush Administrations*, 41–62. New York: Teachers College Press.

Deegan, Mary Jo. 1988. *Jane Addams and the Men of the Chicago School, 1892–1913.* New Brunswick, NJ: Transaction Publishers.

DeMuth, Christopher. 2009. "Irving Kristol Award and Lecture for 2009." Speech presented at American Enterprise Institute. Retrieved on February 18, 2011, from http://www.aei.org/speech/100096.

Deparle, Jason. 1990. "Washington at Work: An Architect of the Reagan Vision Plunges into Inquiry on Race and IQ." *New York Times,* November 30, A22.

Dezelay, Yves, and Bryant Garth. 2002. *The Internationalization of Palace Wars: Lawyers, Economists, and the Contest to Transform Latin American States.* Chicago: University of Chicago Press.

Dickenson, James R., and David S. Broder. 1982. "Think Tanks, Sharp Elbows." *Washington Post,* March 14, A6.

Dickson, Paul. 1971. *Think Tanks.* New York: Atheneum.

Digby, James. 1967. *Operations Research and Systems Analysis at RAND, 1948–1967.* Santa Monica: RAND Corporation.

Diggins, John P. [1975] 1994. *Up from Communism.* New York: Columbia University Press.

DiNardo, John. 2009. "Still Open for Business: Unionization Has No Causal Effect on Firm Closures." EPI Briefing Paper no. 230. Washington, DC: Economic Policy Institute.

Dolny, Michael. 1996. "The Think Tank Spectrum: For the Media, Some Thinkers Are More Equal than Others." *Fairness and Accuracy in Reporting*. Retrieved August 9, 2007, from http://www.fair.org/index.php?page=12.

———. 1997. "New Survey on Think Tanks: Media Favored Conservative Institutions in 1996." *Fairness and Accuracy in Reporting*. Retrieved August 9, 2007, from http://www.fair.org/index.php?page=12.

———. 1998. "What's in a Label? Right-Wing Think Tanks Are Often Quoted, Rarely Labeled." *Fairness and Accuracy in Reporting*. Retrieved August 9, 2007, from http://www.fair.org/index.php?page=12.

———. 2000. "Think Tanks: The Rich Get Richer." *Fairness and Accuracy in Reporting*. Retrieved August 9, 2007, from http://www.fair.org/index.php?page=12.

———. 2001. "Think Tanks Y2K: Progressive Groups Gain, but Right Still Cited Twice as Often." *Fairness and Accuracy in Reporting*. Retrieved August 9, 2007, from http://www.fair.org/index.php?page=12.

———. 2002. "Think Tanks in a Time of Crisis: FAIR's 2001 Survey of the Media's Institutional Experts." *Fairness and Accuracy in Reporting*. Retrieved August 9, 2007, from http://www.fair.org/index.php?page=12.

———. 2003. "Spectrum Narrows Further in 2002: Progressive, Domestic Think Tanks See Drop." *Fairness and Accuracy in Reporting*. Retrieved August 9, 2007, from http://www.fair.org/index.php?page=12.

———. 2004. "Special Report: Think Tank Coverage." *Fairness and Accuracy in Reporting*. Retrieved August 9, 2007, from http://www.fair.org/index .php?page=12.

———. 2005. "Right, Center Think Tanks Still Most Quoted." *Fairness and Accuracy in Reporting*. Retrieved August 9, 2007, from http://www.fair.org/ index .php?page=12.

———. 2006. "Study Finds First Drop in Think Tank Cites." *Fairness and Accuracy in Reporting*. Retrieved August 9, 2007, from http://www.fair.org/ index .php?page=12.

———. 2007. "Think Tank Sources Fall, but Left Gains Slightly." *Fairness and Accuracy in Reporting*. Retrieved August 9, 2007, from http://www.fair.org/ index .php?page=12.

———. 2009. "Right Ebbs, Left Gains as Media 'Experts': Think Tank Balance Still Skews Right." *Fairness and Accuracy in Reporting*. Retrieved January 26, 2012, from http://www.fair.org/index.php?page=3857.

Domhoff, G. William. 1967. *Who Rules America?* Englewood Cliffs, NJ: Prentice-Hall, Inc.

———. 1970. *The Higher Circles*. New York: Vintage Books.

———. 1978. *The Powers That Be: Processes of Ruling-Class Domination in America*. New York: Random House.

———. 1983. *Who Rules America Now? A View for the '80s*. 2nd ed. Englewood Cliffs, NJ: Prentice-Hall.

———. 1990. *The Power Elite and the State: How Policy Is Made in America.* Hawthorne, NY: Aldine de Gruyter.

———. 1998. *Who Rules America Now? Power and Politics in the Year 2000.* 3rd ed. Mountain View, CA: Mayfield Publishing Company.

———. 1999. *Who Rules America 2000.* New York: Simon & Schuster.

———. 2002. *Who Rules America? Power and Politics.* 4th ed. Boston: McGraw-Hill.

———. 2006. *Who Rules America? Power, Politics, & Social Change.* 5th ed. Boston: McGraw-Hill.

———. 2010. *Who Rules America? Challenges to Corporate and Class Dominance.* 6th ed. New York: McGraw-Hill.

Domhoff, G. William, and Thomas R. Dye, eds. 1987. *Power Elites and Organizations.* London: Sage Publications.

Donatich, John, Russell Jacoby, Jean Bethke Elshtain, et al. 2001. "The Future of the Public Intellectual: A Forum." *Nation* 272, no. 6: 25–35.

Douglas, Mary. 1966. *Purity and Danger: An Analysis of the Concept of Pollution and Taboo.* New York: Routledge.

Dreazen, Yochi J. 2008. "Obama Dips into Think Tank for Talent." *Wall Street Journal*, November 16.

Dror, Yehezkel. 1980. "Think Tanks: A New Invention in Government." In *Making Bureaucracies Work*, edited by Carol H. Weiss and A. H. Barton, 139–52. Beverly Hills: Sage.

Dunlap, Riley E., and Aaron M. McCright. 2010. "Climate Change Denial: Sources, Actors, and Strategies." In *Routledge Handbook of Climate Change and Society*, edited by Constance Lever-Tracy, 240–59. London: Routledge.

Dunlavy, Colleen A. 1993. *Political Structure and Industrial Change: Early Railroads in the United States and Prussia.* Princeton, NJ: Princeton University Press.

Durkheim, Émile. [1912] 1995. *The Elementary Forms of Religious Life.* Edited and translated by Karen Fields. New York: Free Press.

Dye, Thomas R. 1978. "Oligarchic Tendencies in National Policy-Making: The Role of the Private Policy-Planning Organizations." *Journal of Politics* 40, no. 2: 309–31.

———. 2000. *Top Down Policymaking.* New York: Chatham House Publishers.

Easterbrook, Gregg. 1986. "Ideas Move Nations." *Atlantic Monthly* 257, no. 1: 66–80.

Economic Policy Institute. 2002. *Annual Report.* Washington, DC: Economic Policy Institute.

Economist. 1979. "Brookings, Flattered by Rivals." March 3, 43.

———. 2006. "The Battle of Ideas." May 23.

Edin, Kathryn. 1991. "Surviving the Welfare System: How AFDC Recipients Make Ends Meet in Chicago." *Social Problems* 38, no. 4: 462–74.

Edwards, Lee. 1997. *The Power of Ideas: The Heritage Foundation at 25 Years.* Ottawa, IL: Jameson Books, Inc.

Ehrenreich, Barbara. 1987. "The New Right Attack on Social Welfare," in Frances Fox Piven, Richard A. Cloward, Barbara Ehrenreich, and Fred Block, eds. *The Mean Season: The Attack on the Welfare State.* New York: Pantheon.

———. 1990. *Fear of Falling: The Inner Life of the Middle Class.* New York: HarperCollins.

Ehrman, John. 1995. *The Rise of Neoconservatism: Intellectuals and Foreign Affairs, 1945–1994.* New Haven, CT: Yale University Press.

Ellis, R. J. 2001. "Pluralism." In *International Encyclopedia of the Social & Behavioral Sciences,* edited by Neil J. Smelser and Paul B. Baltes, 11516–20. Oxford: Pergamon.

Ellwood, David T. 1988. *Poor Support: Poverty in the American Family.* New York: Basic Books.

Ellwood, David T., and Mary Jo Bane. 1985. "The Impact of AFDC on Family Structure and Living Arrangements." *Research in Labor Economics* 7: 137–207.

Ellwood, David T., and Lawrence Summers. 1985. "Poverty in America: Is Welfare the Answer or the Problem?" NBER Working Paper Series, vol. w1711.

Elvin, John. 1990. "Touchy Subject." *Washington Times,* July 25, A6.

Emerson, Ralph Waldo. 1883. *The Complete Works of Ralph Waldo Emerson.* Vol. 4. New York: Sully and Kleinteich.

Epstein, Joseph. 2000. "Intellectuals—Public and Otherwise." *Commentary* 109, no. 5: 46–51.

Epstein, Leon D. 1967. *Political Parties in Western Democracies.* New York: Praeger.

———. 1986. *Political Parties in the American Mold.* Madison: University of Wisconsin Press.

Epstein, William M. 1997. *Welfare in America: How Social Science Fails the Poor.* Madison: University of Wisconsin Press.

Etzioni, Amitai. 1985. "The World-Class University That Our City Has Become." *Washington Post,* April 28, C1.

———. 2006. "Are Public Intellectuals an Endangered Species?" In *Public Intellectuals: An Endangered Species?,* edited by Amitai Etzioni and Alyssa Bowditch, 1–27. Lanham, MD: Rowman & Littlefield.

Evans, Rowland, and Robert Novak. 1964. "Anderson's Hard Choice." *Washington Post,* November 15, E7.

Eyal, Gil. 2002. "Dangerous Liaisons between Military Intelligence and Middle Eastern Studies in Israel." *Theory and Society* 31, no. 5: 653–93.

———. 2003. *The Origins of Postcommunist Elites: From Prague Spring to the Breakup of Czechoslovakia.* Minneapolis: University of Minnesota Press.

———. 2005. "The Making and Breaking of the Czechoslovak Political Field." In *Pierre Bourdieu and Democratic Politics,* edited by Loïc Wacquant, 151–77. Cambridge: Polity Press.

―――. 2006. *The Disenchantment of the Orient: Expertise in Arab Affairs and the Israeli State.* Stanford, CA: Stanford University Press.

―――. Forthcoming. "The Spaces between Fields." In *Bourdieusian Theory and Historical Analysis,* edited by Philip Gorski. Durham, NC: Duke University Press.

Eyal, Gil, and Larissa Buchholz. 2010. "From the Sociology of Intellectuals to the Sociology of Interventions." *Annual Review of Sociology* 36: 117–37.

Fagan, Patrick. 1995. "Why Serious Welfare Reform Must Include Serious Adoption Reform." *Backgrounder,* no. 1027. Washington, DC: Heritage Foundation.

Farnsworth, Clyde H. 1982. "No Recession in Ideas at Capital Think Tanks." *New York Times,* November 10, B6.

Farrell, Jim. 1979. Memorandum to Bruce K. MacLaury, President and Research Program Directors, Re: Secondary Dissemination of Brookings Research Findings through Magazine and Newspaper Articles. Washington, DC: Brookings Institution archives, unmarked box. February 5.

Ferrara, Peter J. 1995. *The Welfare Reform Sections of the Contract with America.* Dallas, TX: National Center for Policy Analysis.

Feulner, Edwin. 1985. "Ideas, Think-Tanks, and Governments." *Quadrant.* November 22–26.

Finegold, Kenneth, and Theda Skocpol. 1995. *State and Party in America's New Deal.* Madison: University of Wisconsin Press.

Fischer, Frank. 1990. *Technocracy and the Politics of Expertise.* Newbury Park, CA: Sage Publications.

―――. 1991. "American Think Tanks: Policy Elites and the Politicization of Expertise." *Governance* 4, no. 3: 332–53.

Fix, Michael, Jeffrey S. Passel, and Wendy Zimmermann. 1996. "The Use of SSI and Other Welfare Programs by Immigrants." Testimony before the US House of Representatives, Ways and Means Committee, May 23. Accessed on April 17, 2007 at http://www.urban.org/url.cfm?ID=900287.

Flacks, Dick. 1991. "Making History and Making Theory: Notes on How Intellectuals Seek Relevance." In *Intellectuals and Politics: Social Theory in a Changing World,* edited by Charles Lemert, 3–18. Newbury Park, CA: Sage.

Flanagan, Maureen A. 2007. *America Reformed: Progressives and Progressivisms, 1890s–1920s.* New York: Oxford University Press.

Fligstein, Neil. 1996. "Markets as Politics: A Political-Cultural Approach to Market Institutions." *American Sociological Review* 61: 656–73.

Forrest, Barbara, and Paul R. Gross. 2004. *Creationism's Trojan Horse: The Wedge of Intelligent Design.* New York: Oxford University Press.

Foucault, Michel. 1977. *Discipline and Punish.* New York: Vintage Books.

Fourcade, Marion. 2009. *Economists and Societies: Discipline and Profession in the United States, Britain, and France, 1890 to 1990s.* Princeton, NJ: Princeton University Press.

Friedman, Lawrence J., and Mark D. McGarvie, eds. 2004. *Charity, Philanthropy, and Civility in American History*. Cambridge: Cambridge University Press.

Fuchs, Victor R. 1985. Review of *Losing Ground: American Social Policy, 1950–1980*, by Charles Murray. *Population and Development Review* 11, no. 14: 768–70.

Fuller, Steve. 2004. "Intellectuals: An Endangered Species in the Twenty-First Century?" *Economy and Society* 33, no. 4: 463–83.

Galbraith, John Kenneth. 1958. *The Affluent Society*. Boston: Houghton Mifflin.

———. 1981. "All Quiet on the Conservative Front." *Washington Post,* April 29, A25.

Gallie, W. B. 1956. "Essentially Contested Concepts." *Proceedings of the Aristotelian Society* 56: 167–98.

Gans, Herbert J. 1990. "Deconstructing the Underclass: The Term's Dangers as a Planning Concept." *Journal of the American Planning Association* 52: 271–77.

———. 1991. "The Dangers of the Underclass: Its Harmfulness as a Planning Concept." In *People, Plans and Policies: Essays on Poverty, Racism, and Other National Urban Problems*, 32843. New York: Columbia University Press.

———. 1995. *The War against the Poor: The Underclass and Antipoverty Policy*. New York: Basic Books.

Garfinkel, Irwin. 1992. *Assuring Child Support: An Extension of Social Security*. New York: Russell Sage.

———. 1996. "Economic Security for Children: From Means Testing and Bifurcation to Universality." In *Social Policies for Children*, edited by Irwin Garfinkel, Jennifer L. Hochschild, and Sara S. McLanahan, 33–82. Washington, DC: Brookings Institution.

Garnett, Mark, and Diane Stone. 1998. *Think Tanks of the World: Global Perspectives on Ideas, Policy, and Governance*. New York: St. Martin's.

Gellner, Winard. 1995. "The Politics of Policy: 'Political Think Tanks' and their Markets in the US Institutional Environment." *Presidential Studies Quarterly* 25: 497–510.

Gieryn, Thomas F. 1983. "Boundary-Work and the Demarcation of Science from Non-science: Strains and Interests in Professional Ideologies of Scientists." *American Sociological Review* 48, no. 6: 781–95.

———. 1999. *Cultural Boundaries of Science: Credibility on the Line*. Chicago: University of Chicago Press.

Gitlin, Todd. 2000. "The Renaissance of Anti-intellectualism." *Chronicle of Higher Education*. December 8.

Glastris, Paul, Elise Ackerman, Dorian Friedman, and Warren Cohen. 1997. "Was Reagan Right?" *US News & World Report*, October 20, 30.

Glazer, Nathan. 1965. "Paradoxes of American Poverty." *Public Interest* 1: 71–81.

———. 1969. "Beyond Income Maintenance—A Note on Welfare in New York City." *Public Interest* 16: 102–22.

Gleason, Philip. 1966. "Anti-intellectualism and Other Reconsiderations." *Review of Politics* 28, no. 2: 238–42.

Glenn, John M., Lilian Brandt, and F. Emerson Andrews. 1947. *Russell Sage Foundation 1907–1946.* New York: Russell Sage Foundation.

Goffman, Erving. 1952. "On Cooling the Mark Out: Some Aspects of Adaptation to Failure." *Psychiatry: Journal of Interpersonal Relations* 15, no. 4: 451–63.

Goldberg, Robert Alan. 1995. *Barry Goldwater.* New Haven, CT: Yale University Press.

Goldman, Henry. 1997. "N.Y. Think Tank Is Making Waves with Conservative Agenda." *Philadelphia Inquirer*, October 13, A3.

Goodman, John C. 2005. "What Is a Think Tank?" National Center for Policy Analysis, Retrieved on July 10, 2008, from http://www.ncpa.org/pub/special/2005/220-sp.html.

Goodman, John, Gerald Reed, and Peter Ferrara. 1995. *Why Not Abolish the Welfare State?* Dallas, TX: National Center for Policy Analysis.

Goodman, Walter. 1981. "Irving Kristol: Patron Saint of the New Right." *New York Times,* December 6, 90.

Gore, Al. 2008. *The Assault on Reason.* New York: Penguin Books.

Gorski, Philip. Forthcoming. "Conclusion: Maps and Methods." *Bourdieusian Theory and Historical Analysis.* Durham, NC: Duke University Press.

Gottlieb, Martin. 1986. "Conservative Policy Unit Takes Aim at New York." *New York Times,* May 5, B4.

Gould, Lewis L., ed. 1974. *The Progressive Era.* Syracuse, NY: Syracuse University Press.

Gouldner, Alvin W. 1979. *The Future of Intellectuals and the Rise of the New Class.* New York: Seabury Press.

Greeley, Andrew M. 1962. "Anti-intellectualism in Catholic Colleges." *American Catholic Sociological Review* 23, no. 4: 350–68.

Green, John Clifford, and Daniel J. Coffey. 2006. *The State of the Parties: The Changing Role of Contemporary American Politics.* New York: Rowman & Littlefield.

Greenwald, Maurine W., and Marge Anderson. 1996. *Pittsburgh Surveyed: Social Science and Social Reform in the Early Twentieth Century.* Pittsburgh, PA: University of Pittsburgh Press.

Griffith, Robert. 1987. *The Politics of Fear: Joseph R. McCarthy and the Senate.* Amherst: University of Massachusetts Press.

Grose, Peter. 1996. *Continuing the Inquiry: The Council on Foreign Relations from 1921 to 1996.* New York: Council on Foreign Relations.

Grove, Lloyd. 1993. "A Liberal Dose of Idealism: Think Tank Fetes 30 Years on the Left." *Washington Post,* October 4, B1.

Guilhot, Nicolas. 2005. *The Democracy Makers: Human Rights and International Order.* New York: Columbia University Press.

Haas, Peter M. 1992. "Introduction: Epistemic Communities and International Policy Coordination." *International Organization* 46, no. 1: 1–35.

Habermas, Jürgen. 1984. *The Theory of Communicative Action.* Translated by Thomas McCarthy. Boston, MA: Beacon Press.

Hage, G. S. 1959. "Anti-intellectualism in Press Comment: 1828 and 1952." *Journalism Quarterly* 36, no. 4: 439–46.

Hale, Charles R. 2008. *Engaging Contradictions: Theory, Politics, and Methods of Activist Scholarship.* Berkeley: University of California Press.

Hall, Carla. 1978. "Perfume Philanthropist: Samuel Rubin's Commitment to the Poor." *Washington Post,* September 23, B4.

———. 1983. "Outsider at the Center: The Contrary Ways of Richard Dennis." *Washington Post,* June 29, B1.

Hall, Robert L. 1986. Review of *Losing Ground: American Social Policy, 1950–1980,* by Charles Murray. *Journal of American History* 73, no. 3: 816–17.

Hames, Tim, and Richard Feasey. 1994. "Anglo-American Think Tanks under Reagan and Thatcher." In *A Conservative Revolution? The Thatcher-Reagan Decade in Perspective,* edited by Andrew Adonis and Tim Hames. Manchester: Manchester University Press.

Handler, Joel F. 1995. *The Poverty of Welfare Reform.* New Haven, CT: Yale University Press.

Harrington, Michael. 1962. *The Other America: Poverty in the United States.* New York: Macmillan.

———. 1969. "A Reply." *New York Review of Books* 11, no. 12.

Hartwell, R. M. 1995. *A History of the Mont Pelerin Society.* Indianapolis, IN: Liberty Fund.

Harvard Law Review. 2002. "The Political Activity of Think Tanks: The Case for Mandatory Contributor Disclosure." 115, no. 5: 1502–24.

Harvey, David. 1990. *The Condition of Postmodernity.* Cambridge: Blackwell.

Haskell, Thomas L. [1977] 2000. *The Emergence of Professional Social Science: The American Social Science Association and the Nineteenth-Century Crisis of Authority.* Baltimore, MD: Johns Hopkins University Press.

Haskins, Ron. 2006. *Work over Welfare: The Inside Story of the 1996 Welfare Reform Law.* Washington, DC: Brookings Institution Press.

Hattam, Victoria C. 1993. *Labor Visions and State Power: The Origins of Business Unionism in the United States.* Princeton, NJ: Princeton University Press.

Havelock, Eric A. 1950. *The Crucifixion of Intellectual Man.* Boston, MA: Beacon Press.

Heclo, Hugh 1978. "Issue Networks and the Executive Establishment." In *The New American Political System,* edited by Anthony King, chap. 3. Washington, DC: American Enterprise Institute.

Hellebust, Lynn, ed. 1996. *Think Tank Directory: A Guide to Nonprofit Public Policy Research Organizations.* Topeka, KS: Government Research Service.

Heritage Foundation. 1977. "Institute for Policy Studies." *Institute Analysis* no. 2. Washington, DC: Heritage Foundation.

———. 1980. *Mandate for Leadership.* Washington, DC: Heritage Foundation.

———. 1984. *Mandate for Leadership II: Continuing the Conservative Revolution.* Washington, DC: Heritage Foundation.

———. 1988. *Mandate for Leadership III: Policy Strategies for the 1990s.* Washington, DC: Heritage Foundation.

———. 2004. *Annual Report.* Washington, DC: Heritage Foundation.

Herrnstein, Richard, and Charles Murray. 1994. *The Bell Curve: Intelligence and Class Structure in American Life.* New York: Simon and Shuster.

Hershey, Robert D., Jr. 1986. "Shifts at Enterprise Institute." *New York Times,* June 27, D1.

Herzog, Arthur. 1963. "Report on a 'Think Factory.'" *New York Times,* November 10, 16.

Hess, Robert D. 1964. "Educability and Rehabilitation: The Future of the Welfare Class." *Journal of Marriage and the Family* 26, no. 4: 422–29.

Higgott, Richard, and Diane Stone. 1994. "The Limits of Influence: Foreign Policy Think Tanks in Britain and the USA." *Review of International Studies* 20, no. 1: 15–34.

Hill, Greg J., Martha S. Duncan, and Sal D. Hoffman. 1988. "Welfare Dependence within and across Generations." *Science,* January 29.

Himmelstein, Jerome L. 1990. *To the Right: The Transformation of American Conservatism.* Berkeley: University of California Press.

Hobbs, Charles D. 1978. *The Welfare Industry.* Washington, DC: Heritage Foundation.

Hodge, Scott. 1995. *Rolling Back Government: A Budget Plan to Rebuild America.* Washington, DC: Heritage Foundation.

Hodges, Donald Clark. 1966. "Anti-intellectualism in a Society of Eggheads." *American Journal of Economics and Sociology* 25, no. 4: 427–37.

Hodgson, Godfrey. 1978. *America in Our Time.* New York: Vintage Books.

Hoffman, Matthew C., and James M. Sheehan. 1993. *The Free Trade Case against NAFTA.* Washington, DC: Competitive Enterprise Institute.

Hofstadter, Richard. 1953. "Democracy and Anti-intellectualism in America." *Michigan Alumnus Quarterly Review* 59.

———. 1963. *Anti-intellectualism in American Life.* New York: Knopf.

Hogan, Lyn A. 1994. *The Matsui Welfare Reform Bill: Status Quo Plus.* Washington, DC: Progressive Policy Institute.

———. 1995. *Jobs Not JOBS: What It Takes to Put Welfare Recipients to Work.* Washington, DC: Progressive Policy Institute.

Holland, William L. 1985. "Source Materials on the Institute of Pacific Relations: Bibliographical Note." *Pacific Affairs* 58, no. 1: 91–97.

Hollar, Danielle. 2003. "A Holistic Theoretical Model for Examining Welfare Reform: Quality of Life." *Public Administration Review* 63, no. 1: 90–104.

Hooper, Paul, ed. 1994. *Rediscovering the IPR: Proceedings of the First International Research Conference on the Institute of Pacific Relations*. Honolulu: University of Hawaii at Manoa.

———. 1995. *Remembering the Institute of Pacific Relations: The Memoirs of William L. Holland*. Tokyo: Ryukei Shyosha.

Hoover Institution. 1980. *The United States in the 1980s*. Stanford, CA: Hoover Institution.

Hopkins, George B. 1912. "The New York Bureau of Municipal Research." *Annals of the American Academy of Political and Social Science* 41: 235–44.

Hopkins, Kevin R. 1987. *Welfare Dependency: Behavior, Culture and Public Policy*. Alexandria, VA: Hudson Institute.

Hoplin, N., and R. Robinson. 2008. *Funding Fathers: The Unsung Heroes of the Conservative Movement*. Washington, DC: Regnery.

Howley, Craig B. 1987. "Anti-intellectualism in Programs for Able Students (Beware of Gifts): An Application." *Social Epistemology* 1, no. 2: 175–81.

Howley, Craig B., Aimee Howley, and Edwina D. Pendarvis. 1995. *Out of Our Minds: Anti-intellectualism and Talent Development in American Schooling*. New York: Teachers College Press.

Hudson Institute. 1995. "Ending Welfare as We Know It." *Briefing Paper*, no. 172. Washington, DC: Hudson Institute.

———. 2002. *Annual Report*. Washington, DC: Hudson Institute.

Hunt, Rockwell D. 1929. "Institute of Pacific Relations." *Los Angeles Times*, November 17, A4.

Hutchens, Robert. 1987. Review of *Losing Ground: American Social Policy, 1950–1980*, by Charles Murray. *Industrial and Labor Relations Review* 40, no. 3: 448–49.

Immergut, Ellen M. 1992. *Health Politics: Interests and Institutions in Western Europe*. Cambridge: Cambridge University Press.

Innis, Matt, and Justin Johnson. 2002. *Directory of Think Tank Publications*. London: Methuen Publishing.

Institute for Policy Studies. 1972a. Letter from IRS agent Ronald R. Payne to IPS. Wisconsin Historical Society. Box 10, "IRS—papers pertaining to 72–73 investigation" folder. October 8.

———. 1972b. Memorandum from Len Rodberg to "IPS." Wisconsin Historical Society. Box 3, Administrative meetings—current" folder. October 31.

———. 1972c. "Preliminary Draft of Budget Committee Recommendations." Wisconsin Historical Society. Box 3, "Administrative meetings—current" folder. November 14.

———. 1973a. Draft of *Report from the Fellow Trustees*. Wisconsin Historical Society. Box 3, "Board of Trustees—Hubbard" folder.

———. 1973b. FBI field memorandum. Wisconsin Historical Society. Box 84, "FBI FOIA" folder. March 15.

———. 1973c. Minutes of Administrative Meeting. Wisconsin Historical Society. Box 3, "Administrative meetings—current" folder. September 17.

———. 1973d. Personal letter from Mitchell Rogovin to Senator Samuel J. Ervin Jr., Chairman of the Senate Select Committee on Presidential Campaign Activities. Wisconsin Historical Society. September 28.

———. 2004. *Annual Report.* Washington, DC: Institute for Policy Studies.

Isaacson, David. 1982. "Anti-intellectualism in American Libraries." *Library Journal* 107, no. 3: 227–32.

Isaacson, Walter, and Evan Thomas. 1986. *The Wise Men: Six Friends and the World They Made.* New York: Simon and Schuster.

Jacobs, Ronald N., and Eleanor Townsley. 2011. *The Space of Opinion: Media Intellectuals and the Public Sphere.* New York: Oxford University Press.

Jacoby, Russell. 1987. *The Last Intellectuals: American Culture in the Age of Academe.* New York: Basic Books.

Jacoby, Susan. 2008. *The Age of American Unreason.* New York: Pantheon Books.

Jaffe, Frederick S. 1964. "Family Planning and Poverty." *Journal of Marriage and the Family* 26, no. 4: 457–66.

James, Simon. 1998. Review of *Capturing the Political Imagination: Think Tanks and the Policy Process,* by Diane Stone. *Public Administration* 76, no. 2: 409–10.

Janda, Kenneth, and Robert Harmel. 1978. *Comparing Political Parties.* Washington, DC: American Political Science Association.

Jeffries, John W. 1978. "The 'Quest for National Purpose' of 1960." *American Quarterly* 30, no. 4: 451–70.

Jeffries, Vincent, ed. 2009. *The Handbook of Public Sociology.* Lanham, MD: Rowman & Littlefield.

Jencks, Christopher. 1965. "The Moynihan Report." *New York Review of Books,* October 14, 216–18.

———, ed. 1992. *Rethinking Social Policy: Race, Poverty, and the Underclass.* Cambridge, MA: Harvard University Press.

———. 1994a. *The Homeless.* Cambridge, MA: Harvard University Press.

———. 1994b. "The Truth about the Homeless." *New York Review of Books,* April 21, 20–27.

Jencks, Christopher, Marshall Smith, Henry Acland, et al. 1972. *Inequality: A Reassessment of the Effect of Family and Schooling in America.* New York: Basic Books.

Jencks, Christopher, and Paul Peterson. 1991. *The Urban Underclass.* Washington, DC: Brookings Institution.

Jennings, James. 1994. *Understanding the Nature of Poverty in Urban America.* New York: Praeger.

Joint Center for Political and Economic Studies. 2002. *Annual Report.* Washington, DC: Joint Center for Political and Economic Studies.

Jones, Howard Mumford. 1963. Review of *Anti-intellectualism in American Life,* by Richard Hofstadter. *Political Science Quarterly* 78, no. 4: 597–99.

Jones, Jacqueline. 1992. *The Dispossessed: America's Underclasses from the Civil War to the Present.* New York: Basic Books.

Judis, John. 2000. *The Paradox of American Democracy.* New York: Pantheon Books.

Kadushin, Charles. [1974] 2009. The *American Intellectual Elite.* New Brunswick, NJ: Transaction Publishers.

Kaiser, Robert G., and Ira Chinoy. 1999. "How Scaife's Money Powered a Movement." *Washington Post,* May 2, A1.

Kalleberg, Ragnvald. 2005. "What Is 'Public Sociology'? Why and How Should It Be Made Stronger?" *British Journal of Sociology* 56, no. 3: 387–93.

Karabel, Jerome. 1996. "Towards a Theory of Intellectuals and Politics." *Theory and Society* 25: 205–33.

Katz, Michael B. 1990. *The Undeserving Poor: From the War on Poverty to the War on Welfare.* New York: Pantheon.

———. 1995. *Improving Poor People: The Welfare State, the "Underclass," and Urban Schools as History.* Princeton, NJ: Princeton University Press.

Katznelson, Ira. 1989. "Was the Great Society a Lost Opportunity?" In *The Rise and Fall of the New Deal Order,* edited by Gary Gerstle and Steve Fraser, 185–211. Princeton, NJ: Princeton University Press.

———. 1998. "The Doleful Dance of Politics and Policy: Can Historical Institutionalism Make a Difference?" *American Political Science Review* 92, no. 1: 191–97.

Keller, Morton. 1994. *Regulating a New Society: Public Policy and Social Change in America, 1900–1933.* Cambridge, MA: Harvard University Press.

Kelley, David. 1976. "For Socialist Alternatives: A Radical Think Tank Is Working within the System." *Barron's,* August 23, 5.

Kelley, John L. 1997. *Bringing the Market Back In: The Political Revitalization of Market Liberalism.* Basingstoke: Macmillan.

Kelly, Robert F. 2002. Review of *Poverty Knowledge: Social Science, Social Policy, and the Poor in Twentieth-Century US History,* by Alice O'Connor. *Contemporary Sociology* 31, no. 4: 401–3.

Kennedy, David M. 1999. *Freedom from Fear: The American People in Depression and War, 1929–1945.* New York: Oxford University Press.

Kenworthy, E. W. 1960. "President Fills His 'Goals' Panel." *New York Times,* February 7, 44.

Kershaw, David, and Jerilyn Fair, eds. 1976. *Operations, Survey, and Administration.* Vol. 1 of *The New Jersey Income-Maintenance Experiment.* New York: Academic Press.

Kilgore, Ed, and Lyn A. Hogan. 1995. *Job Placement Vouchers: A Progressive Alternative to Block Grants.* Washington, DC: Progressive Policy Institute.

Kincaid, Cliff. 1983. "The IPS and the Media: Unholy Alliance." *Human Events*, April 9, 201–35.

King, Lawrence P., and Ivan Szelenyi. 2004. *Theories of the New Class: Intellectuals and Power*. Minneapolis: University of Minnesota Press.

Klaidman, Stephen. 1977. "A Look at Former President Ford's Think Tank Institution." *Washington Post*, February 20, F3.

Klatch, Rebecca E. 1990. Review of *To the Right: The Transformation of American Conservatism*, by Jerome Himmelstein. *American Journal of Sociology* 96, no. 3: 801–3.

Kolko, Gabriel. 1962. *Wealth and Power in America: An Analysis of Social Class and Income Distribution*. New York: Frederick A. Praeger.

Konrad, György, and Ivan Szelenyi. 1979. *The Intellectuals on the Road to Class Power*. Brighton, UK: Harvester Press.

Kozol, Jonathan. 1992. *Savage Inequalities: Children in America's Schools*. New York: Harper Perennial.

Kraft, Joseph. 1960. "RAND: Arsenal for Ideas." *Harper's*. July.

Krehely, Jeff, Meaghan House, and Emily Kernan. 2004. *Axis of Ideology: Conservative Foundations and Public Policy*. Washington, DC: National Committee for Responsive Philanthropy.

Kristol, Irving. 1973. "The Shareholder Constituency." *Wall Street Journal*, August 14, 10.

———. 1974. "Taxes, Poverty, and Equality." *Public Interest* 37: 3–28.

———. 1976. "What Is a Neo-conservative?" *Newsweek*, January 19, 87.

Kuh, Edwin. 1969. "A Basis for Welfare Reform." *Public Interest* 15: 112–17.

Kuttner, Robert. 1984. "Declaring War on the War on Poverty." *Washington Post*, November 25, 4.

Ladd, Everett C., and Charles D. Hadley. 1978. *Transformations of the American Party System: Political Coalitions from the New Deal to the 1970s*. New York: Norton.

Lakoff, George, and Mark Johnson. 1980. *Metaphors We Live By*. Chicago: University of Chicago Press.

Lambro, Donald. 1979. "Doing Well by Doing Good through Consulting." *Heritage Foundation Policy Review* Winter.

Lampman, Robert J. 1962. *The Share of Top Wealth-Holders in National Wealth, 1922–1956*. Princeton, NJ: Princeton University Press.

Lander, Byron G. 1971. "Group Theory and Individuals: The Origin of Poverty as a Political Issue in 1964." *Western Political Quarterly* 24, no. 3: 514–26.

Lane, Charles. 1985. "The Manhattan Project." *New Republic*, March 25, 14–15.

Lardner, James. 1982. "Thick & Think Tank: David Abshire's CSIS Ponder Policy with Kissinger & Fred Flintstone." *Washington Post*, September 21, B1.

Lawrence, B. H. 1988. "Self-Appointed Transition Advisers Push Their Policy Guides." *Washington Post*, November 14, F25.

Leary, William M., Jr., and Arthur S. Link. 1969. *The Progressive Era and the Great War, 1896–1920.* New York: Appleton-Century-Crofts.

Lee, Caroline W. 2011. "Five Assumptions Academics Make about Deliberation, and Why They Deserve Rethinking." *Journal of Public Deliberation* 7, no. 1: 1–48.

———. Forthcoming. *Disciplining Democracy: Public Engagement Experts and the New Participation Economy.* Unpublished book manuscript.

Lee, Jennifer. 2003. "Exxon Backs Groups That Question Global Warming." *New York Times,* May 28, C5.

Lemann, Nicholas. 1980. "The Republicans: A Government Waits in Wings." *Washington Post,* May 27, A1.

———. 1986a. "The Origins of the Underclass (Part 1 of 2)." *Atlantic Monthly* 257, no. 6: 31–55.

———. 1986b. "The Origins of the Underclass (Part 2 of 2)." *Atlantic Monthly* 258, no. 1: 54–68.

Lemert, Charles C. 1991. "The Politics of Theory and the Limits of Academy." In *Intellectuals and Politics: Social Theory in a Changing World,* edited by Charles C. Lemert, 177–87. Newbury Park, CA: Sage Publications.

Lengermann, Patricia, and Jill Niebrugge-Brantley, eds. 1998. *The Women Founders: Sociology and Social Theory, 1830–1930.* Boston: McGraw-Hill.

———. 2002. "Back to the Future: Settlement Sociology, 1885–1930." *American Sociologist* 33: 5–15.

———. 2007. "Thrice Told: Narratives of Sociology's Relation to Social Work. In *Sociology in America,* edited by Craig Calhoun, 63–114. Chicago: University of Chicago Press.

Lerner, Max. 1957. *America as a Civilization.* New York: Simon and Shuster.

Levenstein, Aaron. 1953. "The Demagogue and the Intellectual." *Antioch Review* 12: 259–74.

Lewis, Paul. 1983. "American-Style Think Tanks Minding Europe's Business." *New York Times,* September 25.

Library of Congress Archival Manuscript Collection. 1942. Letter from Harold G. Moulton (President, Brookings Institution) to Dr. Vannevar Bush (Carnegie Institution of Washington and Brookings Trustee). *Papers of Vannevar Bush.* Box 15, folder 352. May 18.

———. 1985. "Minutes of the Heritage Foundation Board of Trustees Meeting, September 18, 1985." *Papers of Clare Boothe Luce.* Box 702, folder 5.

———. 1986a. Banquet program, "Heritage 10: Funding the Conservative Decade." *Papers of Clare Boothe Luce.* Box 720, folder 5.

———. 1986b. Letter from Rep. Jack Kemp to Clare Boothe Luce. *Papers of Clare Boothe Luce.* Box 720, folder 6. June 18.

———. 1987. Letter from Edwin Feulner Jr. to Clare Booth Luce. *Papers of Clare Boothe Luce.* Box 720, folder 6. April 20.

Lieberman, Robert C. 1988. *Shifting the Color Line: Race and the American Welfare State*. Cambridge, MA: Harvard University Press.

Liebow, Elliot. 1993. *Tell Them Who I Am: The Lives of Homeless Women*. New York: Free Press.

Light, Donald W. 2005. "Contributing to Scholarship and Theory through Public Sociology." *Social Forces* 83, no. 4: 1647–53.

Linden, Patricia. 1987. "A Guide to America's Think Tanks: Powerhouses of Policy." *Town & Country*: 99–106, 170, 174–75, 178–79.

Link, Arthur S. 1967. *American Epoch: A History of the United States since the 1890s*. 3rd edition. New York: Alfred A. Knopf.

Lipset, Seymour Martin. 1959. "American Intellectuals: Their Politics and Status." *Daedalus* 88, no. 3: 460–86.

———. [1960] 1981. *Political Man: The Social Bases of Politics*. Baltimore, MD: Johns Hopkins University Press.

Long, Sharon K., Demetra Smith-Nightingale, and Douglas A. Wissoker. 1994. "The Evaluation of the Washington State Family Independence Program." *Urban Institute Report 94–1*. Washington, DC: Urban Institute.

Longo, Bernadette. 2011. *Spurious Coin: A History of Science, Management, and Technical Writing*. New York: SUNY Press.

Los Angeles Times. 1922. "Seek Cause of Unemployment." March 31, I22.

———. 1925a. "Peace Meet in Pacific." May 25, 1.

———. 1925b. "Chinese Crisis Holds Interest." June 25, 2.

———. 1962. "Prophets of the Automation Age." February 1, B4.

Lukacs, John. 2004. *A New Republic: A History of the United States in the Twentieth Century*. New Haven, CT: Yale University Press.

Luker, Kristin. 1996. *Dubious Conceptions: The Politics of Teenage Pregnancy*. Cambridge, MA: Harvard University Press.

Lukes, Steven. 2004. *Power: A Radical View*. 2nd ed. New York: Palgrave MacMillan.

Lynd, Robert S., and Helen Merrell Lynd. 1929. *Middletown: A Study in American Culture*. New York: Harcourt, Brace and Co.

Lyon, David W. 1976. *The Dynamics of Welfare Dependency: A Survey*. Santa Monica: RAND Corporation.

MacDonald, Dwight. 1963. "Our Invisible Poor." *New Yorker*, January 19, 82–132.

Mair, Peter. 1998. *Party System Change: Approaches and Interpretations*. Oxford: Oxford University Press.

Marshall, Will. 1994. *Replacing Welfare with Work*. Washington, DC: Progressive Policy Institute.

Marshall, Will, and Martin Schram, eds. 1993. *Mandate for Change*. New York: Berkley Books.

Marshall, Will, Ed Kilgore, and Lyn A. Hogan. 1995. *Work First: A Proposal to Replace Welfare with an Employment System*. Washington, DC: Progressive Policy Institute.

Martin, James J. 1982. "Charles A. Beard: A Tribute." *Journal of Historical Review* 3, no. 3: 239–58.

Maxa, Rudy. 1977. "Playing Politics for Keeps and Laughs." *Washington Post Magazine*, December 4, 4.

Mayer, Jane. 2010. "Covert Operations: The Billionaire Brothers Who Are Waging a War against Obama." *New Yorker*, August 30.

Mayhew, David. 1986. *Placing Parties in American Politics*. Princeton, NJ: Princeton University Press.

McCabe, Thomas Bayard. 1950. *The Role of CED Today: An Address, at the Semiannual Meeting of the CED Board of Trustees, November 15, 1950*. New York: Committee for Economic Development.

McCombs, Phil. 1983. "Building a Heritage in the War of Ideas." *Washington Post*, October 3, B1.

McCright, Aaron M., and Riley E. Dunlap. 2000. "Challenging Global Warming as a Social Problem: An Analysis of the Conservative Movement's Counter Claims." *Social Problems* 47, no. 4: 499–522.

———. 2003. "Defeating Kyoto: The Conservative Movement's Impact on US Climate Change Policy." *Social Problems* 50, no. 3: 348–73.

———. 2010. "Anti-reflexivity: The American Conservative Movement's Success in Undermining Climate Science and Policy." *Theory, Culture, and Society* 26, nos. 2–3: 100–133.

McDonnell, L. M., and G. L. Zellman. 1993. *Education and Training for Work in the Fifty States: A Compendium of State Policies*. Santa Monica: RAND Corporation.

McFarland, Gerald W. 1975. *Mugwumps, Morals, & Politics, 1884–1920*. Amherst: University of Massachusetts Press.

McGann, James G. 1992. "Academics to Ideologues: A Brief History of the Public Policy Research Industry." *PS: Political Science and Politics* 25, no. 4: 733–40.

———. 1995. *The Competition for Dollars, Scholars, and Influence in the Public Policy Research Industry*. Lanham, MD: University Press of America.

———. 2007a. *Think Tanks and Policy Advice in the United States: Academics, Advisors, and Advocates*. New York: Routledge.

———. 2007b, 2008, 2009, 2010, 2011. *The Global Go-To Think Tanks Report: The Leading Public Policy Research Organizations in the World*. Philadelphia, PA: Foreign Policy Research Institute.

McGann, James G., and R. Kent Weaver, eds. 2000. *Think Tanks and Civil Societies: Catalysts for Ideas and Action*. New Brunswick, NJ: Transaction Publishers.

McGarity, Thomas O., and Wendy E. Wagner. 2010. *Bending Science: How Special Interests Corrupt Public Health Research*. Cambridge, MA: Harvard University Press.

McGerr, Michael E. 1986. *The Decline of Popular Politics: The American North, 1896–1928.* New York: Oxford University Press.

———. 2003. *A Fierce Discontent: The Rise and Fall of the Progressive Movement in America, 1870–1920.* New York: Free Press.

Mead, Lawrence M. 1986. *Beyond Entitlement: The Social Obligations of Citizenship.* New York: Free Press.

Medvetz, Thomas. 2006. "The Strength of Weekly Ties: Relations of Material and Symbolic Exchange in the Conservative Movement." *Politics & Society* 34, no. 3: 343–68.

Meese, Edwin. "Help Get America Right Again." March 7, 2006. Accessed on May 2, 2006, at http://www.townhall.com/opinion/columns/EdwinMeese/2006/03/07/188378.html.

Mehuron, Tamar Ann. 1991. *Points of Light: New Approaches to Ending Welfare Dependency.* Washington, DC, and Lanham, MD: Ethics and Public Policy Center and University Press of America.

Melton, R. H. 1995. "Dole's Tax-Exempt Group Plans to Refund Millions." *Washington Post,* June 21, A1.

Merton, Robert K. 1968. "The Role of the Intellectual in Public Bureaucracy." In *Social Theory and Social Structure,* edited by Robert K. Merton, 261–78. New York: Free Press.

Meyer, Lawrence. 1982. "How a Think Tank Works." *Washington Post Magazine,* October 10, 26.

Michaels, David. 2008. *Doubt Is Their Product: How Industry's Assault on Science Threatens Your Health.* New York: Oxford University Press.

Milkis, Sidney M. 1993. *The President and the Parties: The Transformation of the American Party System since the New Deal.* New York: Oxford University Press.

Miller, John J. 2003. *Strategic Investment in Ideas: How Two Foundations Reshaped America.* Washington, DC: The Philanthropy Roundtable.

———. 2006. *A Gift of Freedom: How the John M. Olin Foundation Changed America.* San Francisco: Encounter Books.

Miller, Louis. 1989. *Operations Research and Policy Analysis at RAND, 1968–1988.* Santa Monica: RAND Corporation.

Miller, S. M. 1985. "Faith, Hope, and Charity—The Public Relations of Poverty." *Contemporary Sociology* 14, no. 6: 684–87.

Mills, C. Wright. 1956. *The Power Elite.* New York: Oxford University Press.

Mirowski, P., and D. Plehwe. 2009. *The Road from Mont Pèlerin: The Making of the Neoliberal Thought Collective.* Cambridge, MA: Harvard University Press.

Mishel, Lawrence, and Jared Bernstein. 1996. *The State of Working America, 1994–95.* Armonk, NY: M. E. Sharpe.

Mishel, Lawrence, and John Schmitt. 1995. "Cutting Wages by Cutting Welfare: The Impact of Reform on the Low-Wage Labor Market." EPI Briefing Paper no. 58. Washington, DC: Economic Policy Institute.

Mishel, Lawrence, and Matthew Walters. 2003. "How Unions Help All Workers." EPI Briefing Paper no. 143. Washington, DC: Economic Policy Institute.

Mitchell, Timothy. 1991. "The Limits of the State: Beyond Statist Approaches and Their Critics." *American Political Science Review* 85, no. 1: 77–96.

———. 1999. "Society, Economy, and the State Effect." In *State/Culture: State-Formation after the Cultural Turn,* edited by George Steinmetz, 76–97. Ithaca, NY: Cornell University Press.

Moffitt, Robert. 1992. "Incentive Effect of the US Welfare System: A Review." *Journal of Economic Literature* 30: 1–61.

Mone, Lawrence J. 2002. "How Think Tanks Achieve Public Policy Breakthrough." Speech presented at Philanthropy Roundtable Forum. May 29. Retrieved August 29, 2006, from http://www.manhattan-institute.org/html/lm_pr_ address .htm.

Morgan, Bob. 1981. "Conservatives: A Well-Financed Network." *Washington Post,* January 4, A1.

Morgan, James N., Martin H. David, Wilbur J. Cohen, and Harvey E. Brazer. 1962. *Income and Welfare in the United States.* New York: McGraw-Hill.

Morin, Richard, and Claudia Deane. 2001. "Media's New Sugar Daddies: Foundations." *Washington Post,* May 15, A15.

———. 2001. "At Tank's Headquarters, the Art of Economics." October 23, A21.

———. 2002a. "The Hot New Americans Get Hotter." *Washington Post,* November 26, A27.

———. 2002b. "Importing a Leader from Outside the Beltway." *Washington Post,* December 17, A31.

———. 2002c. "Japanese See Sunset at Brookings." *Washington Post,* December 10, A27.

———. 2002d. "Lobbyists Seen Lurking behind Tank Funding." *Washington Post,* November 19, A23.

———. 2002e. "Out of Silicon Valley, and Looking Homeward." *Washington Post,* May 14, A19.

———. 2002f. "Ranking the Most Quotable Economists." *Washington Post,* September 24, A19.

———. 2003a. "For CSIS, It's OSI to the Rescue." *Washington Post,* April 15, A23.

———. 2003b. "Irked Drug Industry May Pull Tank Funds." *Washington Post,* April 8, A31.

Moynihan, Daniel P. 1965. *The Negro Family: The Case for National Action.* Washington, DC: US Department of Labor.

———. 1968. "The Crises in Welfare." *Public Interest* 10: 3–29.

Munnell, Alice, ed. 1987. *Lessons from the Income Maintenance Experiments.* Washington, DC: Brookings Institution Press.

Muravchik, Joshua. 1981. "The Think Tank of the Left." *New York Times Magazine,* April 26.

Murray, Charles. 1984. *Losing Ground: American Social Policy, 1950–1980.* New York: Basic Books.

———. 1993a. "The Coming White Underclass." *Wall Street Journal,* October 29, A14.

———. 1993b. Interview with David Brinkley. *This Week.* ABC. Washington, DC: November 28.

Muzzio, Douglas. 1985. Review of *Losing Ground: American Social Policy, 1950–1980,* by Charles Murray. *American Political Science Review* 79, no. 4: 1198–99.

Myrdal, Gunnar. 1964. *Challenge to Affluence.* New York: Pantheon.

Nathan, Richard P. 1993. *Turning Promises into Performance: The Management Challenge of Implementing Workfare.* Washington, DC: Brookings Institution.

National Center for Policy Analysis.1995. "How Not to Be Poor." *Brief Analysis,* no. 187. Dallas, TX: National Center for Policy Analysis.

National Public Radio. 2005. "Under the Influence: Think Tanks and the Money that Fuels Them." *Marketplace.* June 2–3. Retrieved on April 11, 2011, from http://marketplace.publicradio.org/features/under_the_influence/.

New York Times. 1898. "Betrayed by His Snore." December 18, 17.

———. 1900a. "Industrial Conciliation." December 18, 9.

———. 1900b. "National Civic Federation." June 4, 7.

———. 1901a. "Permanent Board to Settle Labor Disputes." December 18, 1.

———. 1901b. "Plan to Prevent Strikes." May 3, 2.

———. 1907. "Municipal Research. May 22, 8.

———. 1910. "The Reformers of Today." November 18, 10.

———. 1914. "Spent $23,000 in Tolls War." March 14, 3.

———. 1916. "For Efficient Government." March 14, 6.

———. 1927a. "Foreign Policy Association Reviews Nine Years of Work." November 27, 8.

———. 1927b. "Social Research." December 24, 14.

———. 1928. "Problems of World Discussed on Radio." May 13, 53.

———. 1929. "Peace through Facts." October 27, E4.

———. 1958. "49 Scholars Hold Man Up to Mirror." September 21, 66.

———. 1985. "Losing More Ground." February 3, E20.

Newman, Katherine. 1988. *Falling from Grace: The Experience of Downward Mobility in the American Middle Class.* New York: Free Press.

Newman, Robert P. 1992. *Owen Lattimore and the "Loss" of China.* Berkeley: University of California Press.

Newman, Sandra J., and Ann B. Schnare. 1992. "Beyond Bricks and Mortar: Reexamining the Purpose and Effects of Housing Assistance." *Urban Institute Report 92–3.* Washington, DC: Urban Institute.

Nichols, Laurence T., ed. 2007. *Public Sociology: The Contemporary Debate.* New Brunswick, NJ: Transaction Publishers.

Niskanen, William. 1996. "Welfare and the Culture of Poverty." *Cato Journal* 16, no. 1.

Norris, Donald F., and Lyke Thompson, eds. 1995. *The Politics of Welfare Reform.* Thousand Oaks, CA: Sage.

Novak, Michael. 1987. *The New Consensus on Family and Welfare: A Community of Self-Reliance.* Washington, DC: American Enterprise Institute.

Nussbaum, Martha. 1999. "The Professor of Parody." *New Republic.* February 22.

Nyden, Philip, Leslie Hossfeld, and Gwendolyn Nyden, eds. 2011. *Public Sociology: Research, Action, and Change.* Thousand Oaks, CA: Pine Forge Press.

O'Connor, Alice. 2001. *Poverty Knowledge: Social Science, Social Policy, and the Poor in Twentieth-Century US History.* Princeton, NJ: Princeton University Press.

Oreskes, Naomi, and Erik Conway. 2010. *Merchants of Doubt: How a Handful of Scientists Obscured the Truth on Issues from Tobacco Smoke to Global Warming.* New York: Bloomsbury Press.

Parmar, Inderjeet. 2004. *Think Tanks and Power in Foreign Policy: A Comparative Study of the Role and Influence of the Council on Foreign Relations and the Royal Institute of International Affairs, 1939–1945.* New York: Palgrave Macmillan.

Patterson, James T. 1996. *Grand Expectations: The United States, 1945–1974.* New York: Oxford University Press.

Pavetti, LaDonna A., and Amy-Ellen Duke. 1995. *State Welfare Reform Efforts.* Washington, DC: Urban Institute.

Pechman, Joseph A., and P. Michael Timpane, eds. 1975. *Work Incentives and Income Guarantees: The New Jersey Negative Income Tax Experiment.* Washington, DC: Brookings Institution Press.

Peck, John S. 1963. "Anti-intellectualism: Psychoanalytic Notes on a Cultural Trait." *American Imago* 20, no. 4: 385–91.

Pennock, Robert T., ed. 2001. *Intelligent Design Creationism and Its Critics: Philosophical, Theological, and Scientific Perspectives.* Cambridge, MA: MIT Press.

———. 2003. "Creationism and Intelligent Design." *Annual Review of Genomics and Human Genetics* 4: 143–63.

Perloff, James. 1988. *The Shadows of Power: The Council on Foreign Relations and the American Decline.* Boston, MA : Western Islands.

Perlstein, Rick. 2001. *Before the Storm: Barry Goldwater and the Unmaking of the American Consensus.* New York: Hill and Wang.

———. 2002. "Thinkers in Need of Publishers." *New York Times,* January 22.

Peschek, Joseph G. 1987. *Policy-Planning Organizations: Elite Agendas and America's Rightward Turn.* Philadelphia, PA: Temple University Press.

Peterson, Iver. 1997. "In a Battle of Newspapers, a Conservative Spends Liberally." *New York Times,* December 8, D1.

Peterson, Paul. 1995. *The Price of Federalism.* Washington, DC: Brookings Institution.

Phillips-Fein, Kim. 2009. *Invisible Hands: The Making of the Conservative Movement from the New Deal to Reagan.* New York: W. W. Norton.

Piccione, Joseph J., and Robert A. Scholle. 1995. *Combatting Illegitimacy and Counseling Teen Abstinence: A Key Component of Welfare Reform.* Washington, DC: Heritage Foundation.

Pierson, Paul. 1994. *Dismantling the Welfare State? Reagan, Thatcher, and the Politics of Retrenchment.* Cambridge: Cambridge University Press.

Pine, Art. 1980a. "Brookings Economics: 'Watch What We Say, Not What We Do.'" *Washington Post,* July 13, K1.

———. 1980b. "Think Tanks Ponder Their Post-electoral Political Future." *Washington Post,* December 8.

Piven, Frances Fox, and Richard A. Cloward. 1971. *Regulating the Poor: The Functions of Social Welfare.* New York: Vantage Books.

———. 1977. *Poor People's Movements: Why They Succeed, How They Fail.* New York: Pantheon Books.

Polsby, Nelson. 1983. "Tanks but no Tanks." *Public Opinion* April/May: 14–16, 58–59.

Posen, Adam S. 2002. "Think Tanks: Who's Hot?" *International Economy* Fall: 8–11, 54–59.

Posner, Richard. 2001. *Public Intellectuals: A Study of Decline.* Cambridge, MA: Harvard University Press.

Powell, Walter W., and Elisabeth S. Clemens, eds. 1998. *Private Action and the Public Good.* New Haven, CT: Yale University Press.

Powell, Walter W., and Paul J. DiMaggio, eds. 1991. *The New Institutionalism in Organizational Analysis.* Chicago: University of Chicago Press.

President's Commission on National Goals for Americans. 1960. *Goals for Americans: Programs for Action in the 60's.* Englewood Cliffs, NJ: Prentice-Hall.

PRM Consulting. 2004. *Research Organizations: 2004 Total Compensation Study.* 4th ed.

Rae, Nicole C. 1989. *The Decline and Fall of the Liberal Republicans: From 1952 to the Present.* New York: Oxford University Press.

———. 2007. "Be Careful What You Wish For: The Rise of Responsible Parties in American National Politics." *Annual Review of Political Science* 10: 169–91.

Rainwater, Lee. 1964. Review of *Slums and Social Insecurity: An Appraisal of the Effectiveness of Housing Policies in Helping Eliminate Poverty in the United States,* by Alvin L. Schorr; and *An American Dependency Challenge,* by M. Elaine Burgess and Daniel O. Price. *American Journal of Sociology* 70, no. 1: 127–28.

———. 1994. "A Primer on American Poverty, 1949–1992." Russell Sage Foundation Working Paper no. 53. New York: Russell Sage Foundation.

Rainwater, Lee, and William L. Yancey. 1967. *The Moynihan Report and the Politics of Controversy.* Cambridge, MA: MIT Press.

RAND Corporation. 1963. *The First Fifteen Years.* Santa Monica: RAND Corporation.

Rank, Mark R. 1994. *Living on the Edge: The Realities of Welfare in America.* New York: Columbia University Press.

Raskin, Marcus. 1968. Memorandum to "Fellows, Students, Staff." Institute for Policy Studies archival manuscript collection, Wisconsin Historical Society, Box 3, "Marcus G. Raskin, 68–69" folder. October 17.

———. 1971a. *Being and Doing.* New York: Random House.

———. 1971b. "Opening Doors of New Thought." *Washington Post,* July 28, B6.

Raspberry, William. 1984. "Welfare and Work." *Washington Post,* September 17, A15.

Raucher, Alan. 1978. "The First Foreign Affairs Think Tanks." *American Quarterly* 30, no. 4: 493–513.

Rector, Robert. 1994a. "How Clinton's Bill Extends Welfare as We Know It." *Issue Bulletin* no. 200. Washington, DC: Heritage Foundation.

———. 1994b. "President Clinton's Commitment to Welfare Reform: The Disturbing Record So Far." *Backgrounder,* no. 967. Washington, DC: Heritage Foundation.

———. 1995a. "The Case for 'Strings-Attached' Welfare Reform." *Heritage Lectures,* no. 524. Washington, DC: Heritage Foundation.

———. 1995b. "Why Congress Must Reform Welfare." *Backgrounder* no. 1063. Washington, DC: Heritage Foundation.

———. 1996. "Welfare Reform Fraud Once Again: Examining the NGA Welfare Plan." *Backgrounder,* no. 1075. Washington, DC: Heritage Foundation.

Rector, Robert, and William F. Lauber. 1995. *America's Failed $5.4 Trillion War on Poverty.* Washington, DC: Heritage Foundation.

Reed, Bruce. 2004. "Bush's War against Wonks." *Washington Monthly.* March.

Reed, Lawrence W. 2000. "Thinking through a Successful Think Tank." *Insider.* Washington, DC: Heritage Foundation.

Reid, T. R. 1977. "Liberal Think Tank Fights a Union." *Washington Post,* January 23, A4.

Remnick, David. 1985. "The Lions of Libertarianism." *Washington Post,* July 30, E1.

Ricci, David M. 1993. *The Transformation of American Politics: The New Washington and the Rise of Think Tanks.* New Haven, CT: Yale University Press.

Rich, Andrew. 2001. "US Think Tanks and the Intersection of Ideology, Advocacy, and Influence." *NIRA Review* Winter: 54–59.

———. 2004. *Think Tanks, Public Policy, and the Politics of Expertise.* Cambridge: Cambridge University Press.

Rich, Andrew Owen, and R. Kent Weaver. 1998. "Advocates and Analysts: Think Tanks and the Politicization of Expertise." In *Interest Group Politics,* 5th ed., edited by Allan J. Cigler and Burdett A. Loomis, 235–54. Washington, DC: CQ Press.

———. 2000. "Think Tanks in the US Media." *Harvard International Journal of Press/Politics* 5, no. 4: 81–103.

Rich, Spencer. 1988. "Think Tank Survives Lean Times: Foundations Help Fund 'Liberal' Urban Institute During Reagan Era." *Washington Post,* May 16, A13.

Richburg, Keith B. 1984. "Washington Awash in Think Tanks." *Washington Post,* December 7, A25.

Rieder, Jonathan. 1989. "The Rise of the 'Silent Majority.'" In *The Rise and Fall of the New Deal Order,* edited by Gary Gerstle and Steve Fraser, 243–68. Princeton, NJ: Princeton University Press.

Riesman, David. 1953. "Some Observations on Intellectual Freedom." *American Scholar* 23: 9–26.

———. 1963. Review of *Anti-intellectualism in American Life,* by Richard Hofstadter. *American Sociological Review* 28, no. 6: 1038–40.

Rigney, Daniel. 1991. "Three Kinds of Anti-intellectualism: Rethinking Hofstadter." *Sociological Inquiry* 61, no. 4: 434–51.

Rivlin, Alice M. 1966. Review of *Poverty in America,* by Louis A. Ferman, Joyce L. Kornbluh, and Alan Haber; and *Poverty in America,* by Margaret S. Gordon. *American Economic Review* 56, no. 5: 1357–1358.

Roach, Jack L. 1965. "Sociological Analysis and Poverty." *American Journal of Sociology* 71, no. 1: 68–75.

Robinson, Timothy S. 1979. "FBI Yields on Think Tank's Lawsuit." *Washington Post,* October 5, C8.

Rogers-Dillon, Robin H., and John D. Skrentny. 1999. "Administering Success: The Legitimacy Imperative and the Implementation of Welfare Reform." *Social Problems* 46, no. 1: 13–29.

Romano, Carlin. 1999. "The Dirty Little Secret about Publicity Intellectuals." *Chronicle of Higher Education,* February 19, B4.

Rosenbaum, David E. 1985. "Moynihan Reassessing Problems of Families." *New York Times,* April 7, 1.

Ross, Dorothy. 1991. *The Origins of American Social Science.* Cambridge: Cambridge University Press.

Rothenberg, Randall. 1987. "The Idea Merchant." *New York Times Magazine,* May 3, 36.

Rothmyer, Karen. 1981. "The New Right's Mystery Angel." *Washington Post,* July 12, C1.

Rudin, Stanley A. 1958. "Academic Anti-intellectualism as a Problem in Student Counseling." *Journal of Counseling Psychology* 5, no. 1: 18–23.

Rueschemeyer, Dietrich, and Theda Skocpol, eds. 1996. *States, Social Knowledge, and the Origins of Modern Social Policies.* Princeton, NJ: Princeton University Press.

Ruggles, Patricia. 1988. *Welfare Dependency and Its Causes: Determinants of the Duration of Welfare Spells.* Washington, DC: Urban Institute.

Russell, Bertrand. 1935. "The Revolt against Reason." *Atlantic Monthly* 155: 223–32.

Ryan, Maria. 2010. *Neoconservatism and the New American Century.* New York: Palgrave Macmillan.

Saloma, John. 1984. *Ominous Politics: The New Conservative Labyrinth.* New York: Hill & Wang.

Samuelson, Robert J. 1984. "Escaping the Poverty Trap." *Newsweek*, September 10, 60.

Sargent, S. Stansfeld, and Theodore Brameld, eds. 1955. "Thematic Issue: Anti-intellectualism in the United States." *Journal of Social Issues* 11, no. 3.

Sartori, Giovanni, and Peter Mair. [1976] 2005. *Parties and Party Systems: A Framework for Analysis.* Colchester, UK: European Consortium for Political Research Press.

Saunders, Charles B. 1966. *The Brookings Institution: A Fifty-Year History.* Washington, DC: Brookings Institution.

Schachter, Hindy Lauer. 2002. "Philadelphia's Progressive-Era Bureau of Municipal Research." *Administrative Theory & Praxis* 24, no. 3: 555–70.

Schlesinger, Arthur M., Jr. 1965. *A Thousand Days: John F. Kennedy in the White House.* Boston: Houghton Mifflin.

Schorr, Alvin L. 1963. *Slums and Social Insecurity: An Appraisal of the Effectiveness of Housing Policies in Helping Eliminate Poverty in the United States.* US Department of Health, Education, and Welfare, Social Security Administration, Division of Research and Statistics, Research Report no. 1. Washington, DC: Government Printing Office.

Schram, Sanford F. 1995. *Words of Welfare: The Poverty of Social Science and the Social Science of Poverty.* Minneapolis: University of Minnesota Press.

Schram, Sanford F., and Joe Soss. 2001. "Success Stories: Welfare Reform, Policy Discourse, and the Politics of Research." *Annals of the American Academy of Political and Social Science* 577: 49–65.

Schriftgiesser, Karl. 1960. *Business Comes of Age: The Story of the Committee for Economic Development and Its Impact upon the Economic Policies of the United States, 1942–1960.* New York: Harper.

———. 1967. *Business and Public Policy: The Role of the Committee for Economic Development: 1942–1967.* Englewood Cliffs, NJ: Prentice-Hall.

Schulzinger, Robert D. 1984. *The Wise Men of Foreign Affairs: The History of the Council on Foreign Relations.* New York: Columbia University Press.

Scott, Janny. 1997. "Turning Intellect into Influence: Promoting Its Ideas, the Manhattan Institute Has Nudged New York Rightward." *New York Times,* May 12, B1.

Scott, Robert E. 1996. "North American Trade after NAFTA: Rising Deficits, Disappearing Jobs." EPI Briefing Paper no. 62. Washington, DC: Economic Policy Institute.

———. 1999. "NAFTA's Pain Deepens: Job Destruction Accelerates in 1999 with Losses in Every State." EPI Briefing Paper no. 88. Washington, DC: Economic Policy Institute.

304   REFERENCES

Scott, Robert E., Carlos Salas, and Bruce Campbell. 2006. "Revisiting NAFTA:
    Still Not Working for North America's Workers." EPI Briefing Paper no. 173.
    Washington, DC: Economic Policy Institute.
Segal, David. 1999. "At the Cato Institute, an Idea Catches On." *Washington Post,*
    January 30, E1.
Seidenbaum, Art. 1963. "Plush Retreat Is Genius Think Tank." *Los Angeles Times,*
    November 7, C2.
Shafer, Byron E. 1983. *Quiet Revolution: The Struggle for the Democratic Party and
    the Shaping of Post-reform Politics.* New York: Russell Sage Foundation.
Shaffer, Leigh S. 1977. "The Golden Fleece: Anti-intellectualism and Social Sci-
    ence." *American Psychologist* 32, no. 10: 814–23.
Shapin, Steven. 2005. "Hyperprofessionalism and the Crisis of Readership in the
    History of Science." *Isis* 96: 238–43.
Shapiro, Margaret. 1985. "Republican Think Tank Faces Funding Problem." *Wash-
    ington Post,* December 28, A6.
Shapiro, Walter, and Daniel Pedersen. 1985. "Fight Over 'Losing Ground.'" *News-
    week,* April 29, 33.
Shea, Christopher, and Joye Mercer. 1997. "Sociology Department at U. of Penn-
    sylvania Lures 2 Prominent Scholars." *Chronicle of Higher Education,* Novem-
    ber 14.
Sheehan, James M. 1993. "Two Years after NAFTA: A Free Market Critique and
    Assessment." Washington, DC: Competitive Enterprise Institute.
Shefter, Martin. 1994. *Political Parties and the State: The American Historical Ex-
    perience.* Princeton, NJ: Princeton University Press.
Shepardson, Whitney H. 1960. *Early History of the Council on Foreign Relations.*
    Stamford, CT: Overbrook Press.
Sherraden, Michael. 1990. *Stakeholding: A New Direction in Social Policy.* Wash-
    ington, DC: Progressive Policy Institute.
Sherk, James. 2009. "Organized Labor Concedes: Employer Violations Rare in
    Secret Ballot Elections." *Backgrounder* no. 2287. Washington, DC: Heritage
    Foundation.
Shoup, Laurence H., and William Minter. 1977. *Imperial Brain Trust: The Coun-
    cil on Foreign Relations and United States Foreign Policy.* New York: Monthly
    Review Press.
Shuptrine, Sarah C., Vicki C. Grant, and Genny G. McKenzie. 1994. *A Study of the
    Relationship of Health Coverage to Welfare Dependency.* Columbia, SC: South-
    ern Institute on Children and Families.
Sica, Alan, and Stephen Turner. 2005. *The Disobedient Generation: Social Theo-
    rists in the Sixties.* Chicago: University of Chicago Press.
Silk, Leonard, and Mark Silk. 1980. *The American Establishment.* New York: Basic
    Books.
Silver, Hilary. 1993. "National Conceptions of the New Urban Poverty." *Interna-
    tional Journal of Urban and Regional Research* 17: 337–54.

Simon, William E. 1978. *A Time for Truth*. New York: Reader's Digest Press.

Sinclair, John F. 1929. "Notable Conclave Opens." *Los Angeles Times*, October 29, 16.

Sklar, Martin J. 1992. *The United States as a Developing Country: Studies in US History in the Progressive Era and the 1920s*. Cambridge: Cambridge University Press.

Skocpol, Theda. 1985. "Bringing the State Back In: Strategies of Analysis in Current Research." In *Bringing the State Back In,* edited by Peter Evens, Dietrich Rueschemeyer, and Theda Skocpol. New York: Cambridge University Press.

———. 1991. "Targeting within Universalism: Politically Viable Policies to Combat Poverty in the United States." In *The Urban Underclass*, edited by Christopher Jencks and Paul E. Peterson. Washington, DC: Brookings Institution.

———. 1992. *Protecting Soldiers and Mothers: The Political Origins of Social Policy in the United States*. Cambridge, MA: Harvard University Press.

———. 1995. *Social Policy in the United States: Future Possibilities in Historical Perspective*. Princeton, NJ: Princeton University Press.

Skocpol, Theda, and William Julius Wilson. 1994. "Welfare as We Need It." *New York Times,* February 9, A21.

Slany, William Z. 1996. *A History of the United States Department of State 1789–1996*. Office of the Historian, Department of State. Available online at http://www.state.gov/www/about_state/history/dephis.html. Retrieved on April 30, 2011.

Smith, Bruce L. R. 1966. *The RAND Corporation: Case Study of a Nonprofit Advisory Corporation*. Cambridge, MA: Harvard University Press.

Smith, Fred L., Jr. 1988. "Two Cheers!" *The World and I*, March, 381–93.

———. 1998. "Traitors in the War of Ideas." *Liberty*, November, 43–46, 68.

Smith, Fred L., Jr., and Alex Castellanos, eds. 2004. *Field Guide for Effective Communication*. Washington, DC: Competitive Enterprise Institute.

Smith, James A. 1991a. Brookings at Seventy-Five. Washington, DC: Brookings Institution.

———. 1991b. *The Idea Brokers: Think Tanks and the Rise of the New Policy Elite*. New York: Free Press.

Smith-Nightingale, Demetra, and Lynn C. Burbridge. 1984. *Measuring the Reduction of Welfare Dependency: The Experience of Job Training Programs*. Washington, DC: Urban Institute.

Smith-Nightingale, Demetra, and Robert H. Haveman. 1995. *The Work Alternative: Welfare Reform and the Realities of the Job Market*. Washington, DC: Urban Institute Press.

Smith-Nightingale, Demetra, Douglas A. Wissoker, Lynn C. Burbridge, D. Lee Bawden, and Neal Jeffries. 1991. "Evaluation of the Massachusetts Employment and Training (ET) Choices Program." *Urban Institute Report 91–1*. Washington, DC: Urban Institute.

Smith Richardson Foundation. 2004. *Annual Report*. Westport, CT: Smith Richardson Foundation.

Snyder, Eleanor M. 1963. Review of *The Other America: Poverty in the United States,* by Michael Harrington. *Journal of Political Economy* 71, no. 1: 86–87.

Solomon, Lewis D. 1991. *Microenterprise: Human Reconstruction in America's Inner Cities.* Washington, DC: Progressive Policy Institute.

Somers, Margaret, and Fred Block. 2005. "From Poverty to Perversity: Ideas, Markets, and Institutions over 200 Years of Welfare Debate." *American Sociological Review* 70, no. 2: 260–87.

Sorauf, Frank J. 1988. *Money in American Elections.* Boston, MA: Scott, Foresman.

Sorkin, Andrew Ross. 2005. "Paper Maker to Be Sold to Koch." *New York Times,* November 14, C1.

Spargo, John. 1911. "Anti-intellectualism in the Socialist Movement: A Historical Survey." In *Sidelights on Contemporary Socialism,* 67–106. New York: B. W. Huebsch.

Stacey, Judith. 2004. "Marital Suitors Court Social Science Spinsters: The Unwittingly Conservative Effects of Public Sociology." *Social Problems* 51, no. 1: 131–45.

Starbuck, Dane. 2001. *The Goodriches: An American Family.* Indianapolis, IN: Liberty Fund.

Steensland, Brian. 2006. "Cultural Categories and the American Welfare State: The Case of Guaranteed Income Policy." *American Journal of Sociology* 111, no. 5: 1273–1326.

Stefanic, Jean, and Richard Delgado. 1996. *No Mercy: How Conservative Think Tanks and Foundations Changed America's Social Agenda.* Philadelphia, PA: Temple University Press.

Steinfels, Peter. 1979. *The Neoconservatives: The Men Who Are Changing America's Politics.* New York: Simon and Schuster.

Steinmo, Sven. 1993. *Taxation and Democracy: Swedish, British, and American Approaches to Financing the Modern State.* New Haven, CT: Yale University Press.

Steinmo, Sven, Kathleen Thelen, and Frank Longstreth, eds. 1992. *Structuring Politics: Historical Institutionalism in Comparative Analysis.* New York: Cambridge University Press.

Stone, Deborah A. 1989. "Causal Stories and the Formation of Policy Agendas." *Political Science Quarterly* 104: 281–300.

Stone, Diane. 1996. *Capturing the Political Imagination: Think Tanks and the Policy Process.* London: Frank Cass.

———. 2000. "Non-governmental Policy Transfer: The Strategies of Independent Policy Institutes," *Governance: An International Journal of Policy and Administration* 13, no. 1: 45–62.

———. 2001. "Think Tanks." In *International Encyclopedia of the Social & Behavioral Sciences,* edited by Neil J. Smelser and Paul B. Baltes, 15668–71. Oxford: Pergamon.

Stone, Diane, and Andrew Denham, eds. 2004. *Think Tank Traditions: Policy Research and the Politics of Ideas.* Manchester: Manchester University Press.

Strout, Cushing. 1963. Review of *Anti-intellectualism in American Life,* by Richard Hofstadter. *Journal of Southern History* 29, no. 4: 544–45.

Struyk, Raymond J. 2003. *Managing Think Tanks: Practical Guidance for Maturing Organizations.* Washington, DC: Urban Institute.

Students for a Democratic Society. 1962. "Port Huron Statement." Retrieved on December 12, 2011, from http://www.h-net.org/~hst306/documents/huron.html.

Sumner, William Graham. 1906. *Folkways.* Boston, MA: Ginn and Company.

Suplee, Curt. 1981. "All in the Name: Changes Made in 'Spike' after Threat of Libel Suit." *Washington Post,* May 23, C1.

Sylvester, Kathleen. 1994. *Preventable Calamity: Rolling Back Teen Pregnancy.* Washington, DC: Progressive Policy Institute.

———. 1995. *Second-Chance Homes: Breaking the Cycle of Teen Pregnancy.* Washington, DC: Progressive Policy Institute.

Szelenyi, Ivan, and Bill Martin. 1988. "Three Waves of New Class Theories." *Theory and Society* 17, no. 5: 645–67.

Tanenhaus, Sam. 2006. "The Education of Richard Hofstadter." *New York Times,* August 6.

Tanner, Michael. 1994. *Ending Welfare as We Know It.* Washington, DC: Cato Institute.

———. 1996. *The End of Welfare: Fighting Poverty in the Civil Society.* Washington, DC: Cato Institute.

Tanner, Michael, Stephen Moore, and David Hartman. 1995. "The Work versus Welfare Trade-Off: An Analysis of the Total Level of Welfare Benefits by State." *Policy Analysis* no. 240. Washington, DC: Cato Institute.

Teichler, Thomas. 2007. "Think Tanks as an Epistemic Community: The Case of European Armaments Cooperation." Paper presented at the annual meeting of the International Studies Association 48th Annual Convention. Chicago, IL.

Thimmesch, Nick. 1980. "Bill Baroody Deserved More Years." *Washington Post,* August 9, A19.

"Think-tank, *n.*" 1989. *Oxford English Dictionary.* 2nd ed. New York: Oxford University Press.

This Week with David Brinkley. Transcript. October 31, 1993. Available through LexisNexis Academic database.

Tittle, Charles R. 2004. "The Arrogance of Public Sociology." *Social Forces* 82, no. 4: 1639–43.

Tocqueville, Alexis de. [1862] 2001. *Democracy in America.* Translated by Henry Reeve. New York: Alfred A. Knopf.

Tolchin, Martin. 1983. "Brookings Thinks about Its Future." *New York Times,* December 14: A30.

Toner, Robin. 1985. "New Day Dawns for Think Tanks." *New York Times*, December 27, A20.

Towne, Henry R. 1886. "The Engineer as an Economist." *Transactions of the American Society of Mechanical Engineers* 7: 428–32.

Tucker, David M. 1998. *Mugwumps: Public Moralists of the Gilded Age.* Columbia: University of Missouri Press.

Turner, Jonathan H. 2005. "Is Public Sociology Such a Good Idea?" *American Sociologist* 36, no. 3–4: 27–45.

Tzvetan, Todorov, Alina Clej, Lawrence D. Kritzman, et al. 1997. "Forum." *PMLA* 112, no. 5: 1121–28.

United Nations Development Program. 2003. *Thinking the Unthinkable: From Thought to Policy.* Bratislava, Slovakia: UNDP Regional Bureau for Europe and the Commonwealth of Independent States.

United States Bureau of the Census. 1963. *Current Population Reports, Consumer Income.* Series P-60, no. 41, October 21. Washington, DC: Government Printing Office.

United States Senate, Committee on Labor and Public Welfare. 1964. *Economic Opportunity Act of 1964, Hearings before the Select Committee on Poverty.* 88th Congress, 2nd Session on S. 2642, June 17–25. Washington, DC: Government Printing Office.

Unz, Ron K. 1994. *Immigration or the Welfare State: Which Is Our Real Enemy?* Washington, DC: Heritage Foundation.

Vaughan, Diane. 2006. "NASA Revisited: Theory, Analogy, and Public Sociology." *American Journal of Sociology* 112, no. 2: 353–393.

Vobejda, Barbara, and Judith Havemann. 1997. "Welfare Clients Already Work, Off the Books; Experts Say Side Income Could Hamper Reforms." *Washington Post,* November 3, A1.

Vogel, David. 1989. *Fluctuating Fortunes: The Political Power of Business in America,* New York: Basic Books.

Wacquant, Loïc J. D. [1989] 1996. "Foreword," in *The State Nobility: Elite Schools in the Field of Power,* ix–xxii. Stanford, CA: Stanford University Press.

———. 1992. "Toward a Social Praxeology: The Structure and Logic of Bourdieu's Sociology." In *An Invitation to Reflexive Sociology,* edited by Pierre Bourdieu and Loïc Wacquant, 1–59. Chicago: University of Chicago Press.

———. 1993. "From Ruling Class to Field of Power: An Interview with Pierre Bourdieu on *La Noblesse d'État.*" *Theory, Culture & Society* 10: 19–44.

———. 1996. "'L'Underclass Urbaine' dans l'Imaginaire Social et Scientifique Américain." In *L'Exclusion: l'État des Savoirs,* edited by Serge Paugam, 248–62. Paris: Editions La découverte.

———. 1997 "Three Pernicious Premises in the Study of the American Ghetto." *International Journal of Urban and Regional Research* 21, no. 2: 341–53.

———. 1998. "A Fleshpeddler at Work: Power, Pain, and Profit in the Prizefighting Economy." *Theory and Society* 27, no. 1: 1–42.

———. 2001. "Deadly Symbiosis: When Ghetto and Prison Meet and Mesh." *Punishment & Society* 3, no. 1: 95–134.

———. 2004. "Pointers on Pierre Bourdieu and Democratic Politics." *Constellations* 11, no. 1: 1–15.

———. 2005. "Habitus." In *International Encyclopedia of Economic Sociology*, edited by Jens Beckert and Milan Zafirovski, 315–19. London: Routledge.

———. 2008. *Urban Outcasts: A Comparative Sociology of Advanced Marginality.* Cambridge: Polity Press.

———. 2009. *Prisons of Poverty.* Minneapolis: University of Minnesota Press.

———. 2011. "From 'Public Criminology' to the Reflexive Sociology of Criminological Production and Consumption: A *Review of Public Criminology?* by Ian Loader and Richard Sparks." *British Journal of Criminology* 51, no. 2: 438–48.

Wagner, Peter. 2006. "Public Policy, Social Science, and the State: An Historical Perspective." In *Handbook of Public Policy Analysis: Theory, Politics, and Methods*, edited by Frank Fischer, Gerald Miller, and Mara S. Sidney, 29–42. Boca Raton, FL: CRC Press.

Wala, Michael. 1994. *The Council on Foreign Relations and American Foreign Policy in the Early Cold War.* Providence, RI: Berghahn Books.

Ware, Alan. 1996. *Political Parties and Party Systems.* Oxford: Oxford University Press.

Warren, Michael. 2011. "Just a Reminder: The Economic Policy Institute Is Dominated by Labor Interests." *Weekly Standard*, February 23. Retrieved on June 30, 2011, from http://www.weeklystandard.com/blogs/economic-policy-institute-dominated-labor-interests_552391.html.

Washington Post. 1895. "Baseball Notes." August 13, 6.

———. 1907. "Mrs. Sage to Direct." March 14, 13.

———. 1911a. "Bill to Aid Carnegie." January 27, 4.

———. 1911b. "Scattering Carnegie's Millions." May 26, 6.

———. 1914. "The Carnegie Lobby Report." May 21, 6.

Washington Times. 1997. "Hard Truths about Welfare." May 4, B2.

Wattenberg, Martin P. 1991. *The Rise of Candidate-Centered Politics: Presidential Elections of the 1980s.* Cambridge, MA: Harvard University Press.

———. 1998. *The Decline of American Political Parties, 1952–1996.* Cambridge, MA: Harvard University Press.

Watts, Harold W., and Albert Rees, eds. 1977a. *Labor-Supply Responses.* Vol. 2 of *The New Jersey Income-Maintenance Experiment.* New York: Academic Press.

———, eds. 1977b. *Expenditures, Health, and Social Behavior; and the Quality of the Evidence.* Vol. 3 of *The New Jersey Income-Maintenance Experiment.* New York: Academic Press.

Wayne, Leslie. 1994. "Pulling the Wraps Off Koch Industries." *New York Times*, November 20, C1.

Weaver, R. Kent. 1989. "The Changing World of Think Tanks." *PS: Political Science and Politics* September: 563–78.

———. 1994. *Welfare Reform: Policymaking for Low-Income Families in the United States.* Washington, DC: Brookings Institution.

———. 2000. *Ending Welfare as We Know It.* Washington, DC: Brookings Institution Press.

Weaver, R. Kent, and William Dickens. 1995. *Looking before We Leap: Social Science and Welfare Reform.* Washington, DC: Brookings Institution.

Weaver, R. Kent, and Paul B. Stares, eds. 2001. *Guidance for Governance: Comparing Alternative Sources of Public Policy Advice.* Tokyo: Japan Center for International Exchange.

Weaver, Warren, Jr. 1987. "Cato Institute Marks 10 Years." *New York Times,* May 19, B6.

Weber, Max. [1919] 1946. "Science as a Vocation" in H. H. Gerth and C. Wright Mills, eds. *From Max Weber: Essays in Sociology.* New York: Oxford University Press.

Weinraub, Bernard. 1980. "Conservatives Aid Transition Plans behind the Scenes." *New York Times,* December 5, B9.

———. 1980. "Hoover Institution Gains Entrée to White House." *New York Times,* December 22, D14.

———. 1983. "Heritage Foundation 10 Years Later." *New York Times,* September 30, A20.

Weir, Margaret. 1992. *Politics and Jobs: The Boundaries of Employment Policy in the United States.* Princeton, NJ: Princeton University Press.

Weir, Margaret, Ann S. Orloff, and Theda Skocpol, eds. 1988. *The Politics of Social Policy in the United States.* Princeton, NJ: Princeton University Press.

Weiss, Carol H. 1989. "Congressional Committees as Users of Analysis." *Journal of Policy Analysis and Management* 8, no. 3: 411–31.

Welter, Rush. 1964. Review of *Anti-intellectualism in American Life,* by Richard Hofstadter. *Journal of American History* 51, no. 3: 482–83.

Westbrook, Robert B. 1983. "Politics as Consumption: Managing the Modern American Election." In *The Culture of Consumption: Critical Essays in American History, 1880–1980,* edited by Richard Wightman Fox and T. J. Jackson Lears, 145–73. New York: Pantheon.

Weyrich, Paul. 2003. "The Most Important Legacy of Joe Coors." Retrieved on October 11, 2008, from http://www.enterstageright.com/archive/articles/0303/0303coors.htm.

White, Morton. 1962. "Reflections on Anti-intellectualism." *Daedalus* 91, no. 3: 457–68.

White, Theodore H. 1961. *Making of a President, 1960.* New York: Pocket Books.

Wiebe, Robert H. 1967. *The Search for Order, 1877–1920.* New York: Hill and Wang.

Wiener, Jon. 2006. "America, through a Glass Darkly." *Nation,* October 23, 36–40.

Wilson, William Julius. 1987. *The Truly Disadvantaged: The Inner City, the Underclass, and Public Policy.* Chicago: University of Chicago Press.

———. 1996. *When Work Disappears: The World of the New Urban Poor.* New York: Alfred A. Knopf.

Winter, Michael. 1998. "Garlic, Vodka, and the Politics of Gender: Anti-intellectualism in American Librarianship." *Progressive Librarian* 14: 5–12.

Wolff, Kurt H. 1963. "The Enemy Within: Anti-intellectualism." *Centennial Review* 7, no. 1: 46–63.

———. 1971. "The Intellectual: Between Culture and Politics." *International Journal of Contemporary Sociology* 8, no. 1: 13–34.

Woodlock, Thomas F. 1944. "Thinking It Over." *Wall Street Journal*, June 4, 6.

Worldwatch Institute. 2004. *Annual Report.* Washington, DC: Worldwatch Institute.

Wright, Christopher M. 1995. *SSI: The Black Hole of the Welfare State.* Washington, DC: Cato Institute.

Yamaoka, Michio, ed. 1999. *The Institute of Pacific Relations: Pioneer International Non-governmental Organization in the Asia-Pacific Region.* Tokyo: Waseda University, Institute of Asia-Pacific Studies.

Yandle, Bruce. 1983. "Bootleggers and Baptists—The Education of a Regulatory Economist." *Regulation* May/June: 12–16.

Yates, Willard Ross. 1987. *Joseph Wharton: Quaker Industrial Pioneer.* Cranbury, NJ: Associated University Presses.

Zelizer, Viviana. 1997. *The Social Meaning of Money.* New York: Basic Books.

Zunz, Olivier. 2011. *Philanthropy in America: A History.* Princeton, NJ: Princeton University Press.

Index

Printed and bound by CPI Group (UK) Ltd, Croydon, CR0 4YY

09/06/2025

14685701-0001